John Colet's Children

To the generations of remarkable Paulines
the author encountered in more than three decades
teaching at the school.

ST PAUL'S SCHOOL and THE OLD PAULINE CLUB
in association with
GRESHAM BOOKS LIMITED

Statue of John Colet teaching two boys, bronze by Sir William Hamo Thornycroft, cast 1901. *David Bussey.*
© *St Paul's School.*

John Colet's Children

The boys of St Paul's School in later life
(1509–2009)

DAVID BUSSEY

Published by Gresham Books,
Summertown, Oxford

in association with

St Paul's School and the Old Pauline Club,
Lonsdale Road, London SW13 9JT

ISBN : 978-0-946095-56-8

Design and typesetting by
John Saunders Design & Production
Printed and bound in the United Kingdom at the
University Press, Cambridge

Contents

1 The Sixteenth Century   3

The flower of learned men in his time – Old Paulines in King Henry VIII's privy chamber – The father of English antiquaries – An early mapmaker – Traders on the money markets – Farming by numbers – A picture of Merry England and a warning – The story of Britannia – Elizabethan court reporter – Puritans and Catholics – Catholic agitator – Brother composers – A merchant traveller – Alchemy and chemistry: purifying wool and purifying the body – The most famous soldier of his day

2 The Seventeenth Century   23

Two comic playwrights – Popular songs – A poacher turned gamekeeper – Disgraced high master – The preacher of the day – The nature of God – Old school-friends – The greatest of Colet's Children – Latin poet, flatterer and turncoat – Witchcraft – Mathematics of the universe – Beetles and glow-worms – 'The Hanging Judge' – Clergyman and pamphleteer – Political corruption – A life of controversy – Judge and murder suspect – Military leader

3 The Eighteenth Century   45

Professor of astronomy – The South Sea bubble – The only Old Pauline prime minister – Architect of the Mansion House – Masters of the King's Musick –Eighteenth-century antiquarians: letters, travels in disguise, coins and a severed head — Three school-friends and the mystery of Junius – An amiable and convivial bookseller – Fine handwriting – Magistrate and man of letters – Duty, suffering and the fires of Hell – Hangings: an arsonist and thief, a chaplain at Newgate and the execution of a spy – Bringing back from the dead – Midwife – The world of the stage – Old Paulines and early Romantic poetry: a song for Coleridge and a friendship with Blake – Admiral in Nelson's fleet

4 The Nineteenth Century   69

Abolishing the slave trade – Attack on high society – Royal tutor, bishop and patron of Constable – Old Paulines and the later Romantics: a fantasist, a friend of Keats and parodist of Wordsworth, a victim of Byron – Gossip and blackmailer – Actors, managers, and playwrights – The Ingoldsby Legends – Publishers – Architects and builders – Gothic revival – 'The Modern Luther' – Two Victorian headmasters – Master of Balliol – Oxford tutor and bishop – Eccentric monk and preacher – A secret mission in China – Searching for Franklin – Three attorneys-general and a serjeant-at-law – Zoologist – Boomerang theory – Comic verse and a novel detective

5 The Twentieth Century, Part One: 1900–1945   101

GKC – Gutter journalism – The hyphen in Rolls-Royce – Aircraft pioneer – Inventor – Survivor of Scott's final Antarctic expedition – Geography, racism and beauty – A passion for plants – Museum director – Sums and talk – Royal Physician – Fighting for rights in South Africa – Missionary in Johannesburg – Religious thinking – Political extremist and sage – A man of many parts – A publishing revolution – Fraudster turned bookseller – The circle of Keynes – Socialist – A devoted husband – Art, Bloomsbury and bohemians – Cricketing records – Tennis champion – School stories – Stories of school – Film actor

Foreword

*by Lord Baker of Dorking CH, president of the
Old Pauline Club, 2007–09*

Dean Colet would be amazed at the extraordinary mix of Old Paulines that has miraculously emerged from his 153 fishes. Through his foresight and generosity scholars were to come from all backgrounds and countries: and come they have from the shores of Cathay, the East and West Indies, the barely discovered America, the deserts of Arabia and from the lands of spices, silks, ivory and pearls. At the school they met the English boys who came predominantly from London, where their fathers were merchants, tradesmen, scholars and public servants.

It was the all-inclusive nature of St Paul's that marked its history. Scholarship was the magnet though even that has changed radically over the centuries. Cloistered in St Paul's Churchyard and at the small school in the City, the pupils would have become fluent in Latin and Greek. In that wonderful Victorian building in Hammersmith, the laboratories for chemistry, physics and biology were the lode-stars. Today on the banks of the Thames, computers, mobile phones and the internet open the doors to a wider and more accessible learning.

Throughout all this there have been some constant themes: the English language, the rigour of study and the passion for sport. All these fashioned a community of young people where commitment, hope and ambition mingle and inspire. Loyalty and love for the old school are at work here.

All the Old Paulines in this fascinating book have made this journey of learning and what a bag. Great writers like Milton, Pepys and Chesterton; great soldiers like Marlborough and Montgomery, alongside scientists, explorers, financiers, lawyers, politicians, doctors, artists, astronomers, engineers and, inevitably, some crooks.

But this Quincentenary is not just a celebration of famous figures; it is also a reminder of the thirty thousand boys who by going to St Paul's over the centuries enriched their own lives and those of their families in a thousand different ways.

Lord Baker during his term as president of the Old Pauline Club. *Ian Bester.* © *Old Pauline Club.*

Detail taken from general view of the proposed new St Paul's School from the Hammersmith Road, architect's drawing by A. Waterhouse, dated 26 Feb. 1880. *By kind permission of the Worshipful Company of Mercers.*

He pointed through the window to our ornamental gates leading into the Hammersmith Road. 'Only go out through those gates and then open your eyes — I care not whether you turn east or west — you'll see only a profiteering jungle in which everyone's idea is to use everyone else as his milch cow. Look at the screaming advertisements on the hoardings, at the glaring, blaring shops, at the bellowing cheats behind their barrows in the street market, at the hideous factories with their chimneys belching smoke and defacing a whole town with their soot — which is a perfect parable, my poor boys.' He spat a little as he shot 'perfect parable' over to us below. 'Everywhere the smoke and grime and hideousness of a heartless, soulless profiteering. Then look at the big boss profiteers strutting about in the glorious robes of chivalry, with their stars upon their breasts — what? Eh, *what*? Or look at the gross, grasping devilries of a gutter press that cares for nothing but to scratch up its halfpennies, either by pandering to the lowest appetites of poor half-educated people or, after some disaster or murder or something, by raking deep in the wounds of people already deeply hurt. Then look at the yellow press lords in their honoured robes. Eh, what of that? God help us. Civilization? No. Social disease, my boys. A universal infectious social plague.'

(*Mr Olim*, by novelist and Old Pauline Ernest Raymond, 1888–1974. Elam, on whom the character is based, taught 'little from the school curriculum, but much of life'.)

Preface

Through the gates

The chapters that follow describe what happened to about 230 Paulines when they finally went through the school gates into the world the Reverend Horace Elam so much distrusted and deplored. He was the famously idiosyncratic sparring partner of Walker in his final years as high master and lives on in *Mr Olim* (1961), Ernest Raymond's recreation of his schooldays at St Paul's.

John Colet's Children is not a roll of honour. Among its pages are leaders of society and stories of noble and distinguished achievement, but there are also some intriguing, eccentric, even notorious figures. The earliest Old Pauline featured left Colet's school a few years after its foundation, the most recent in 2003. Articles vary from a few lines to about twelve hundred words, and in some cases an old pupil is mentioned only in the caption to an illustration. There is a mixture of biography, anecdote and quotation, and rather than write complete lives, the intention is to bring into focus interesting and unusual aspects of Old Pauline careers and experiences.

Entries are arranged in chapters by century, except that the vastly increased numbers in the school during the twentieth century necessitated two separate chapters, 1900–45 and 1945–2000. There is a separate chapter on Old Paulines and war, 1890–1997, and the book ends with a short afterword on rising stars of the twenty-first century. It was extraordinarily difficult deciding who would be included and who left out. The aim was to make chapters as varied and balanced as possible, but it was a personal selection, and almost certainly others would have chosen differently.

The articles within each chapter are not arranged according to a fixed template but so that they read in a smooth sequence. The order should also give some sense of historical context, particularly in the first four chapters, where the entries are very broadly chronological. Individuals have been allocated to centuries according to when they flourished or began to flourish rather than when they were born or attended the school. This is not a straightforward matter, and there is an index of names at the back for tracking down elusive entries.

Equally, it is not straightforward deciding who attended the school before admissions registers were started in 1748. I have usually followed the guidance of Robert Gardiner and Sir Michael McDonnell, who researched the problem in depth, but there remained a few awkward cases to reconsider. St Edmund Campion is allowed in given McDonnell's persuasive argument that before entering Christ's Hospital he attended St Paul's and indeed delivered an address to Queen Mary. So is the composer Maurice Greene: his name appears as Steward of the Feast in 1727, and other biographical circumstances suggest he was a Pauline. On the other hand, I have departed from McDonnell in two cases. William Jaggard, printer of the first folio edition of Shakespeare, is disallowed given the lack of evidence and his notoriously bad Latin, and so is the playwright William Wycherley, whose only Pauline credential is a note, now lost, by the antiquary John Pridden some 150 years later. I have also imposed a one year minimum attendance qualification. This means leaving out the colourful sixteenth-century rogue Peter Carew who after refusing 'to smell a book' at St Paul's survived until the age of sixty-one despite a life of escapades and conspiracy. It also conveniently avoids dealing with the rumour that St Paul's was one of the schools from which Errol Flynn was expelled.

Through the centuries

The chapters of *John Colet's Children* have been left to speak for themselves, but no one can research the lives of Old Paulines over five centuries without finding some interesting patterns, whether or not they are significant. It is striking for example that from the two hundred boys known to have attended St Paul's in the sixteenth century (presumably a small fraction of the total) came the most powerful group of politicians in the school's history and two royal agents in the Netherlands, one of whom founded the Royal Exchange. It might seem that Paulines were receiving the training in courtly behaviour, diplomacy and statecraft prescribed by Italian Renaissance manuals, but of course that was not the case. Colet dedicated his school to the Virgin Mary and boy Jesus; he prayed that his boys would become great scholars. John Leland (1506–52) and William Camden (1551–1623), two of the century's finest antiquaries, were at St Paul's, and George Lily (c.1512–59), son of the first high master, drew the first printed map of the British Isles.

Religion was to dominate the lives of old pupils for much of the sixteenth and seventeenth centuries, but religious division and uncertainty rather than the ordered Christian life Colet hoped to see fostered by the new learning. Many were imprisoned for their faith or went into exile. John Clement (c.1500–72) was tutor to Sir Thomas More's children and for a time president of the College of Physicians, but he was Roman Catholic, refused to recognize Henry VIII as head of the church and was imprisoned in the Tower with More: he retreated abroad during the reigns of Edward VI and Elizabeth I. Religious views were held and expressed fervently. William Fulke (c.1537–89) and Edmund Campion (1540–1581) confronted each other in debate shortly before the latter's execution. John Howson (1556/7–1632) was intolerant of puritans, Catholics and preachers. He became bishop of Durham and, it is said, was excommunicated by the archbishop of York for denying him the right to make a metropolitan visitation.

In the seventeenth century politics and religion were of course inextricable. For John Milton (1608–74), the failure of the Civil War was a cause of deep spiritual anguish; for his fellow poet Payne Fisher (1615/16–93), all principles were sacrificed to a life of largely unsuccessful flattery. At the end of the century Samuel Johnson (1649–1703), pilloried and whipped for his uninhibited tracts against James II, contrasts with John Churchill, first Duke of Marlborough (1650–1722), whose diplomatic skill steered him relatively smoothly through the 1688 Glorious Revolution and beyond.

Old Paulines in the seventeenth century were also making their mark as scientists or in the language of the day natural philosophers. As president of the Royal Society Samuel Pepys (1633–1703) ordered the printing of Newton's *Principia Mathematica,* although the publication of this work owed much more to the determination of another Old Pauline, Edmond Halley (1656–1742). Richard Cumberland (1632–1718), one of the many bishops among the school's alumni, found in experimental science the path to God's natural law. Sir Charles Scarburgh (1615–94) was a distinguished anatomist and royal physician, to whom William Harvey (discoverer of blood circulation) left his gown and silver instruments. Benjamin Allen (1663–1738) discovered the male glow-worm.

The eighteenth century was not a golden age for the school. Although it produced St Paul's only prime minister, he brought no distinction to that office. Edward Gibbon (1666–1736), grandfather of the historian, was heavily fined for his part in the South Sea Bubble, and at the end of the century two old pupils were hanged, William Jobbins (1769–90) for arson and theft, and

Major John André (1750–80) more nobly as a spy after his courageous rendezvous with an enemy traitor during the American War of Independence. Nonetheless, it was a period when Old Paulines flourished as antiquaries and in the creative arts, with two Masters of the King's Musick, the architect of the Mansion House and one of the century's greatest comic actors. The first two chapters end with military leaders, the third with one of Nelson's admirals, Thomas Troubridge (1758–1807).

Nelson knew Troubridge from boyhood days and said that he was his superior, but it was Troubridge who missed much of the big action. His participation in the battle of the Nile was frustrated when in his eagerness to join the action he cut a corner, and his boat hit a shoal, and he was at the East India Station during the battle of Trafalgar. Being on the edge of greatness seemed to be a feature of Old Pauline life, particularly during the Romantic movement. John Hamilton Reynolds (1794–1852) was a very close friend of Keats but only made his name with a light-hearted parody of Wordsworth. One fantasist made dubious claims of knowing well most of the late Romantics, another conversed with Blake; one irritated Byron, another sang for Coleridge; one was a patron of Constable — but rejected a painting he commissioned because the clouds were too stormy.

The nineteenth century was the age of the lawyer: large portraits depicting two of the three alumni to become attorney-general hang in the school library, and the barrister William Ballantine (1812–87) was leading counsel in several of the most famous and exotic criminal cases of his era. Otherwise, as befits an increasingly complex society, it is futile to generalize about a chapter in Old Pauline history that includes a blackmailer, a dynasty of publishers, the architect of Dartmoor Prison, an eccentric monk and an expert on boomerangs.

Working out who to include in the twentieth century, easily the largest part of the book, was an almost overwhelming challenge. It was not so much a question of choosing from figures of towering greatness: the numbers here were small. The difficulty lay with the extraordinary range of figures who just missed the premier league and yet whose achievements were distinctive and of considerable interest. If the war years are set aside for the moment, it is notable how many early twentieth-century alumni were radical thinkers and actively involved in politics and political theory. Sidney Bunting (1873–1936) dedicated his life to defending workers' rights in South Africa, irrespective of colour. In his early years Sri Aurobindo (1872–1950) wrote inflammatory anti-British articles for a revolutionary newspaper in Bengal. There is a large body of socialist writing from Leonard Woolf

(1880–1969) and Douglas Cole (1889–1959) — late in life, Woolf dismissed what he had produced as '200,000 hours of useless work'.

An intriguing link connects four recent Old Paulines: John Weitz (1923–2002) was told by Cubby Broccoli, the film producer, that he was more handsome than James Bond, a woman was once disappointed to discover Peter Murray (1925–) was not Roger Moore, Major-General Roy Urquhart watched himself being acted by Sean Connery when *A Bridge Too Far* was filmed, and Sir Ken Adam (1921–) designed sets for the James Bond films. Many entries from the last sixty years have been prominent in the worlds of television, film and the stage, as actors, designers, writers, directors, presenters and reporters. Sir Jonathan Miller (1934–) has played several of these roles and is one of an outstanding group of cultured and articulate figures — Lord Winston (1940–) and Oliver Sacks (1933–) are two others — whose interests embrace the arts and sciences. In the twentieth century as a whole there are many notable academics, too many for the space available. In his foreword Lord Baker mentions passion for sport as a theme of the school, and it is surprising that Old Pauline international sporting achievements are not stronger, but the school can claim two chess grandmasters, an Olympic silver medal in fencing from Rome and a rowing gold medal from the Sydney games.

The chapter 'Old Paulines and War: 1890–1997' is strong testimony to the enterprise and moral commitment so many pupils demonstrate throughout their lives: courage, optimism and selflessness on the battlefield, thespian talent (in one case taken too far) and ingenuity in attempting escapes, the creativity and deftness of black war propaganda, some powerful painting and poetry, the intellectual weight of code-breaking and military theory, and of course one exceptional military leader. This chapter is not a microcosm of Old Pauline lives, but it would be good to believe that it represents many of the school's lasting qualities. Very probably it does.

The Text

The text follows conventions drawn from the Oxford Dictionary of National Biography, the Modern Humanities Research Association Style Guide and New Hart's Rules. As this is not an academic book, some minor silent changes have been made within the quotations to make them more accessible. Old Paulines are given full names and dates of birth and death (where known) in the headings to their main entries, or in captions to illustrations if they are not the subject of a separate article. Subsidiary references to Old Paulines should be clear from the context. The abbreviation OP is only used of two Dominican priests (Order of Preachers). The index of names at the back gives the school years, as far as they are known, of those who entered St Paul's after admissions registers were established in 1748. Evidence of when earlier Paulines attended is too sparse and unreliable to be worth recording. A list of high masters is included as an appendix. Since the end notes comprise a list of sources, there is no separate bibliography. Explanatory points, and there are very few of these, appear as footnotes.

Text and picture credits

Textual acknowledgements are embedded in the end notes. Picture credits are included in the captions. Photographers' names are also given in the captions where appropriate. Where no picture credit or acknowledgement is given, the image is out of copyright, belongs to St Paul's School or has been supplied by the Old Pauline depicted. Every effort has been made to trace copyright holders. We apologize for any unintentional omission and would be pleased to insert the appropriate acknowledgement in any subsequent edition.

Acknowledgements

It is impossible to thank everyone who helped me to complete this book, often by a passing suggestion or word of encouragement.

It was Martin Stephen, the high master, who first suggested the idea of a quincentennial volume and supported it as it grew into something much larger than either of us originally envisaged. The president of the Old Pauline Club, Lord Baker, was a strong ally throughout: he reviewed the text at an early stage, wrote the preface and provided some excellent illustrations. The help that came from Alistair Summers, Old Pauline secretary, and Amanda Denny, Ian Bester and Maria Ketley of the Old Pauline Club, was also invaluable. Colleagues in the Common Room at St Paul's were generous with advice and ideas: all was considered and much followed.

Thanks go to the many art galleries, libraries, colleges and other bodies who took an interest in the project and helped our budget by waiving or reducing their usual picture fees. Only in a very small number of cases did the disproportionate size of copyright and other charges force a compromise. Old Paulines and their families were again most willing to provide pictures and information, only one or two proving elusive. Jane Ruddell, archivist at Mercers' Hall, and Simon May, school archivist, were both excellent sources of material; Simon also translated some of the Latin.

Among the team of proofreaders, particular thanks go to Colin Niven, who read the whole text at an early stage, and to Steve Whitty for an enormous amount of detailed work, again on the whole text, as deadlines loomed.

More than any of these, *John Colet's Children* owes its existence to my indefatigable assistant, Memphis Barker, who spent several months of his gap year on the project. He willingly undertook a myriad of tasks, some very difficult, contributing computer skills and an understanding of aspects of modern culture beyond my grasp.

Among others who gave essential advice and assistance are:

George Adie, Patrick Allsop, Carolyn Armitage, Alex Aslett, Robin Baird-Smith, Stephen Baldock, Jenifer Ball, Malcolm Bobbitt, Ray Burton, Tim Cunis, John Davie, Christopher Dean, Charles Duckworth, John Dunkin, John Ellis, Alistair Endersby, Michael and Linda Falter, Philip Hall, Henry Hardy, Penny Holmes, Mike Howat, John Hudson, Peter King, Ken Lawson, Paul Leppard, Hugh Mead, Gail Monahan, Francis Neate, Keith Perry, Michael Roe, Peter Sammut, Hugh Spensley and Stephanie Wickes.

(*Following page*) Memorial of St Paul's School, *c.*1909, proof copy of poster published by Seymour and Company, Cheltenham. Reading left to right and from the top, the names are: first row, Leland, William Lily (high master), Denny; second row, Vere, Whitaker, Halley, Pepys; third row, Milton, Churchill; fourth row, Scarborough (Scarburgh), Gouge, Thomas Gale (high master), Strange, Hawes; fifth row, André, Francis, Thicknesse (high master), Walker (high master), Troubridge, Lawrence; sixth row, Truro, Jowett; seventh row, Pollock, Hannen; last row, Clarke, Symes-Thompson, Ollivant, Lee. With the exception of Sir John Strange (master of the rolls), Sir Soulden Lawrence (judge of the king's bench), James Hannen (lord of appeal), the physician Edmund Symes-Thompson and Alfred Ollivant (bishop of Llandaff), every Old Pauline in the poster appears in this book.
Ken Lawson. © *St Paul's School.*

MEMORIAL OF S.T PAUL'S SCHOOL.

A Short History of St Paul's School

THE NEW FOUNDATION of St Paul's School was created by John Colet, dean of St Paul's Cathedral, in 1509. Its ancestor was a grammar school maintained by the cathedral from the thirteenth century or even earlier. Colet was a friend of Erasmus and Sir Thomas More, and his school provided for the free education of 153 children of 'all nations and countries indifferently' in good manners and literature. Its first high master, William Lily, was a distinguished grammarian and one of the earliest Englishmen to be fluent in both Greek and Latin. The number 153 is associated with the miraculous draught of fishes mentioned in St John's Gospel, and for many years foundation scholars wore the emblem of a silver fish. St Paul's was 'elegantly built in stonework and established in the eastern part' of the cathedral churchyard. Colet gave most of his substantial fortune to its endowment. He assigned management of the school and its revenues to the Mercers' Company, which still provides a large part of the school's governing body and administers Colet's trust. Our knowledge of sixteenth-century Paulines is too sparse to draw any conclusions about their backgrounds, but in his history of the school, *A Miraculous Draught of Fishes*, Hugh Mead has analysed the seventeenth-century evidence. He notes that for a time there were a few members of great families 'as well as the usual sons of clergymen, booksellers, mercers, lawyers, drapers and (already a widely resorted-to coverall) gentlemen'.

No drawings are known to exist of the first school, which was in use until destroyed by the great fire of London. The second school opened on the same site in 1671. The first half of the eighteenth century was a low point in St Paul's history: in May 1748, under High Master George Charles, numbers were down to thirty-five. His successor George Thicknesse quickly refilled the school. Admission registers were kept from 1748, and they reveal that the typical Pauline of that era was 'more often than not, the small son of a city tradesman. His average age, on admission, was ten, and he was likely to leave before he was fourteen' (Mead).

In its turn the second school was replaced in 1824 by the third, a larger building on the same site. It was during the nineteenth century that St Paul's assumed the character which has in large measure survived to this day. Rather than tradesmen, the boys' parents were now more usually from the professions — lawyers, doctors, clergy and army officers. Pressure came from the Public Schools Commission of 1861 and later the Charity Commissioners for the school to broaden its predominantly classical curriculum and adapt to changing society. During Herbert Kynaston's thirty-eight years as high master (1838–76), more subjects were taught, a cricket ground was bought, the school became a foundation member of the Rugby Football Union, debating and music societies were established, and numbers began to grow. Nonetheless, it was the arrival of Frederick William Walker from Manchester

John Colet, engraving by G. Vertue from Samuel Knight, *The Life of Dr John Colet*, 1724. Samuel Knight (1677/8–1746) was one of several Old Pauline eighteenth-century antiquaries.
© *St Paul's School.*

Grammar School in 1877 that signalled the most dramatic developments. The first science master was appointed in 1879, and by 1884 he had fifty-four boys to teach. In the same year the move was made to Alfred Waterhouse's imposing new buildings dominating the Hammersmith skyline. Between 1884 and 1888 numbers rose rapidly (from 211 to 573), and so did the school's formidable academic reputation, which continues to this day. St Paul's secured 173 entrance awards to Oxford and Cambridge between 1886 and 1895, twenty-six more than its nearest competitor.

During the Second World War, the school was evacuated to Crowthorne in Berkshire; the Hammersmith buildings became the headquarters of General, later Field-Marshal Montgomery, an Old Pauline himself (see chapter six). By 1961 the view was that Waterhouse's buildings were inadequate for the educational needs of the time. A superb forty-five acre riverside site in Barnes became available, and it was here that the fifth school opened in 1968. These buildings are now nearing the end of their useful lives, and plans are in place to rebuild the school over the next period of time. A bursary fund has been established, with the intention that in due course all pupils will be able to attend irrespective of financial background. In this way St Paul's will be brought closer to Colet's original vision. In the school's 500th year its 'miraculous draught' of 153 had grown to 853 boys aged from thirteen to eighteen. Colet's children from the twenty-first century are regularly achieving some of the best academic results in the country as well as participating in a vast range of other activities, many of which involve the local community.

The Sixteenth Century

🌿 *The flower of learned men in his time*

THOMAS LUPSET (*c.*1495–1530)

Look upon Saint Laurence, lying broiling upon the burning coals, as merry and as quiet as though he lay upon sweet red roses: when the tormentors turned his body upon the fiery gridiron, he bade the cruel tyrant eat of his burned side, while the other part was a-roasting.

(Thomas Lupset, *A Treatise of Dying Well*)[1]

THOMAS LUPSET spent much of his adult life travelling in Europe and was able to take a broader view of Christianity than Old Paulines caught up in religious divisions later in the century. He knew many humanists of the day and as a boy lived for several years with Colet, who bequeathed him 'all such books printed as may be most necessary for his learning'.[2] He assisted Erasmus with his edition of the New Testament and helped prepare the second edition of Sir Thomas More's *Utopia*. When Erasmus's work was attacked, Lupset sprang to his defence and won an international reputation as his intimate friend and champion of the renaissance in learning. In 1520 Cardinal Wolsey appointed him to the readership in rhetoric and humanity he had founded at Corpus Christi College, Oxford, in succession to another Old Pauline, John Clement (*c.*1500–72), later president of the London College of Physicians.

Then, in a burst of activity during the second half of 1529, Lupset produced his three major prose works: *An Exhortation to Young Men, A Treatise of Charity* and *A Compendious Treatise* [...] *of Dying Well*. The first of these is addressed to Edmund Withypoll, one of two boys he was tutoring, and advises him to attend first to his soul, then to his body and lastly to his worldly possessions. Withypoll is given a reading list incorporating pagan authors, something Colet would not have endorsed: in his view, 'Those books in which Christ is not found are but a table of devils.' Lupset's prose has been praised as the best written before 1630, because it is cogent, artistic in its choice of detail and has a much more natural idiom than the work of his contemporaries.[3] Soon after his death he was called 'the flower of learned men in his time'.[4]

The evils of the passions

Likewise to ensue a delight of dainty and sweet feeding, to be taken with pleasure of the body, to be overthrown with sorrow, to perk up with gladness, to hold up the chin too high in prosperity, to hold down the head too low in adversity, to be in bondage under the fierce rules of sensual lusts, whose cruelty over man hath no pity, measure, nor end. These and such other be things, that so trouble and disquieten man's mind, that quiet charity cannot abide them. For look a little upon the unmerciful man, that cannot forgive, see how he boileth in his appetite to be avenged. Look upon the envious stomach, how he without rest freteth, in coveting the sight of his hurt whom he spiteth. Look upon the glutton, how beastly he purveyeth belly cheer. Look upon the lecher, how busy he is in his ungracious thoughts. Look upon the covetous wretch, how without reason he scrapeth and scrapeth for gains. Look upon the ambitious fellow, how he bestireth him to get worship. These men through their corrupt fantasies be no less greedy to satisfy their desires, than the hungry and the thirsty bodies through natural necessity seek to be refreshed. Whereof we may see, that sleeping and waking these men's minds roll without taking rest. Such wrestling fantasies, such inordinate appetites be called passions, the which move and stir the soul contrary to his nature, either by love without reason, or by hate without measure, when we willingly consent to the wind of these sensible things.

(Lupset: *A Treatise of Charity,* 1529, possibly addressed to Princess Mary, later Queen Mary and then aged sixteen)[5]

D. ERASMVS ROT.
Inscribit to Mr Bros's Marriott.

Erasmus, engraving by G. Vertue after Hans Holbein's painting, from Samuel Knight, *The Life of Erasmus*, Cambridge, 1726. This book is dedicated to Old Pauline Sir Spencer Compton, then speaker of the House of Commons. *David Bussey. © St Paul's School.*

SIR ANTHONY DENNY (1501–49)
EDWARD NORTH, FIRST BARON NORTH (1496–1564)
WILLAM PAGET, FIRST BARON PAGET (*c*.1505–63)
THOMAS WRIOTHESLEY, FIRST EARL OF SOUTHAMPTON (1505–50)

Sir Anthony Denny, drawn by H. Crease, engraved C. Picart, after Hans Holbein's painting. © *St Paul's School.*

Lord North, oil. *Courtesy the master and fellows of Peterhouse, Cambridge.*

While at Trinity Hall, Cambridge, William Paget and Thomas Wriothesley acted in Plautus's *Miles gloriosus*, a play familiar today in its reincarnation as *A Funny Thing happened on the Way to the Forum*. Paget played Melophidippa, a deceiving maidservant, and Wriothesley Palestrio, a crafty slave, both displaying qualities that served them well in later life at the centre of the Tudor court. Paget proved to have excellent diplomatic skills. He managed a network of spies for Henry VIII and in 1544 rose to be senior secretary of state. Wriothesley had gained the king's favour for his contribution to the dissolution of the monasteries and probably for carrying out missions related to the annulment of Henry's marriage to Katherine of Aragon. In the 1540s he became very powerful, and it was his appointment as lord chancellor in 1544 that created the vacancy filled by Paget.

Two other Old Paulines were also rising fast in court circles. Anthony Denny began a career in the privy chamber in 1533. In 1542 he became keeper of the privy purse, which gave him control of considerable royal funds, and in 1546 groom of the stool. Despite its lowly origins, this position was prized in Henry VIII's reign because the holders were effectively private secretaries to the king and had unrestricted access to him. Equally significant, in 1545 he was licensed to add the royal stamp to documents emanating from Henry VIII (by this stage the king was unwill-

ing or unable to write his own signature). In 1544 Edward North was appointed chancellor of augmentations, in charge of the enormous revenues created by the dissolution of the monasteries.

All four had gained influence at a time when Henry VIII no longer had a leading minister. They all made substantial personal fortunes out of confiscated monastic property. They also met as four of the sixteen executors of Henry VIII's will in 1547. Denny had warned the king 'to prepare himself to death […] and to call upon God […] for grace and mercy' and was present when the king spoke his last words.[6] He stood at the king's head during the funeral procession. It was reported that Wriothesley announced Henry's death to parliament full of tears.

Paget had become very close to Henry and appears to have been deeply involved in the drawing up of his will: in front of parliament he did 'say and affirm on his honour that he was privy to the beginning, proceeding and ending of the same last will'. He also told the law reporter Edmund Plowden that 'he wrote the will himself or first draft thereof'. This is where the story becomes murky. There is a tradition that the will only received its stamp (for which Denny would have been responsible) 'when the king himself was new dead, or dying and past all remembrance'. Paget wrote in the privy council register that the king, 'being remembered in his deathbed that he had promised great things to divers men […] willed in his testament that whatever should in any wise appear to his Council to have been promised by him, the same should be performed'. This led to the last-minute inclusion of a so-called 'unfulfilled gifts clause', giving executors the right to make gifts which Henry had promised but not yet carried out at the time of his death.[7] Certainly it is true that Paget and Denny did their best to support each other's claims to large bequests. They both received substantial gifts of land. Wriothesley got the healthy sum of £500, and Paget also deposed that the king had intended to create an earldom for him: he became the first Earl of Southampton on 16 February 1547 (his grandson was Shakespeare's patron). Even North did well with a gift of £300.

Lord Paget, drawn by R. Sutchwell, engraved Holl, after anonymous painting. © *St Paul's School.*

that told the truth of dangers before and was not believed, sorry would I live to be such a one.' The letter goes on to warn how difficult it was to pursue campaigns against Scotland and France when the royal coffers were almost empty, and that English loyalty could not be taken for granted:

No, it may be said, yet will every true man in case of need help with all that he hath for defence of the realm. I know no man but true. But yet I think all men though they be true, be not thoroughly wise and able to understand and weigh his duty, and that which seems to one man well, may seem to another evil.[10]

Sure enough, these wars and popular rebellions brought an early end to Somerset's protectorate. A difficult period for Paget followed with Warwick's rise to power. Although he was made Baron Paget of Beaudesert in December 1549, his influence waned. In November 1551 he was in the Tower while Warwick looked for a serious charge against him. Eventually, he was accused of corruption, but Paget again demonstrated his capacity for survival by pleading guilty and getting the fine reduced after a grovelling letter to the king in November 1552:

Nevertheless forasmuch it hath pleased his majesty to call me most unworthy of all men to the degree of a baron, and that this land being delivered from me, I shall not be able neither myself nor mine heirs after me, to live in sort as that place requireth, unless his majesty be my good and my gracious lord.

A month later he had been pardoned and restored to the privy council. With the accession of Queen Mary and her

Denny was to die prematurely in 1549. Wriothesley opposed Somerset, the protector of England during the first part of Edward VI's minority reign (1547–53), and this ensured his fall from grace, but he enjoyed a very brief final return to power when Warwick successfully deposed Somerset and became virtual ruler of England. Wriothesley even attended Edward VI: '[He] is lodged […] next to the king. Every man repaireth to Wriothesley, honoureth Wriothesley, sueth unto Wriothesley […] and all things be done by his advice.'[8] But after a few weeks Warwick felt that Wriothesley was threatening his position and had him put under house arrest. He died six months later.

North too went over to Warwick's side but unlike the latter survived the transition to Queen Mary's reign and took a part in court life. (Warwick was executed on Mary's accession.) Foxe, best known for his *Book of Martyrs*, tells the doubtless apocryphal story of North being stirred by the queen's phantom pregnancy in 1555 and approaching a poor London woman on behalf of the council to buy her new-born son in order to pass him off as the desperately-wanted prince.[9]

Paget lived on to 1563 and was the most skilled at adapting to political circumstances. He backed Somerset, although he felt that the latter took too little notice of him. A letter to the protector dated 2 February 1549 complains, 'Sir […] make me not to be a Cassandra, that is to say, one

Thomas Wriothesley, first Earl of Southampton, oil. *By kind permission of Lord Montagu of Beaulieu.*

marriage to Philip of Spain, who granted Paget a handsome pension of 1,500 crowns, his influence continued to recover, and he was put in charge of England's weak finances, but his own health was deteriorating. In his final years he could do little more than offer advice from his sickbed.

It is not easy to sum up these four powerful figures. Denny appears preoccupied with advancing his own wealth; on the other hand he was a major benefactor of Sedbergh School, rescuing and restoring its lands and buildings, and his humanist education probably led him to save part of Waltham Abbey's library from destruction. Paget is often dismissed as a political adept without depth: one seventeenth-century comment was, 'His address was with state, yet insinuating, his discourse free but weighted, his apprehension quick but staid, his ready and present mind keeping its pauses of thoughts and expression even with the occasion and the emergency.' Nonetheless, a recent assessment sees him as essentially honest and an

important voice of moderation and realism.[11] North simply remains elusive. The historian G. R. Elton called Wriothesley 'manifestly the most successful civil servant of his day', but self-interest was never far away.[12] He enjoyed the trappings of power and the material wealth that came his way: in public he liked to be preceded by his gentlemen and followed by yeomen dressed in velvet and gold chains. Many saw him as a tough careerist. As lord chancellor he believed firmly in the rule of law, but he had no scruples about reducing his own tax liability immediately after Henry VIII died. He was at his harshest in enforcing Henry's conservative religious policies towards the end of his reign and would punish any protestant or Catholic he thought was causing trouble. But he was also described by Roger Ascham, the humanist and scholar, as a great patron of literature and the University of Cambridge. John Leland (see next entry) called him a 'friend to the muses'.

❧ *The father of English antiquaries*

JOHN LELAND (1506–52)

I was totally inflamed with a love to see thoroughly all those parts of this your opulent and ample realm, that I had read of in the aforesaid writers: in so much that all my other occupations intermitted, I have travelled in your dominions both by the sea coasts and the middle parts, sparing neither labour nor costs, by the space of these six years past, that there is almost neither cape, nor bay; haven, creek, or pier, river or confluence of rivers, breeches, washes, lakes, fenny waters, mountains, valleys, moors, heaths, chases, woods, cities, boroughs, castles, principal manor places, monasteries, and colleges, but I have seen them; and noted in so doing a whole world of things very memorable.

(Dedication to Henry VIII from John Leland's *Itinerary*)

John Leland was the earliest of Old Pauline travellers and topographers, and his work had an enormous influence on those who followed, including Camden and Harrison. Four of his near-contemporaries at school (William Paget, Anthony Denny, Thomas Wriothesley and Edward North — see last entry) became leading political figures, and Leland benefited from their patronage.

His initial interests were scholarly and antiquarian: in 1533 he was given a commission from Henry VIII 'to peruse and diligently to search all the libraries and monasteries and colleges of this your noble realm'. He was responsible for bringing some monastic books into the Royal Collection, both before and after the fall of the monasteries, but probably not in any great numbers, and his travels shifted emphasis as he became more interested in the local history and topography that make up his *Itinerary*.[13] As he journeyed he made descriptive notes but also consulted widely local libraries and records. Leland

was intending to use this material to produce a whole series of works on historical, topographical, antiquarian and literary topics, but only one prose work, on King Arthur, was published in his lifetime, and the *Itinerary* was assembled from his notes. In the mid 1540s he appears to have fallen insane, and this was seen as an omen, warning future scholars from the dangers of excessive devotion to their studies.

The *Itinerary* displays Leland's fascination with such details as distances, epitaphs, bequests, genealogy, etymology, and lists of many kinds. His comments can be remarkably dry: for example he has very little to say about Beverley in Yorkshire and does not even mention its minster. His description of York minster is confined to counting up the number of columns. Even so, there are more personal touches, such as his observation that the King's Bath in Bath 'reeks like a seething pot continually, having somewhat a sulphurous and somewhat unpleasant

Petrifying or dropping well on the river Nidd together with the ruins of Knaresborough Castle, engraving from Nathaniel Spencer, *The Complete English Traveller*, 1771. Leland describes this well. *David Bussey.* © *St Paul's School.*

savour', and moments when his imagination is caught — a study in the Duke of Northumberland's home, or his visit, one of the earliest recorded, to the limestone petrifying or dropping well on the banks of the river Nidd.

A room in the Duke of Northumberland's castle at Wressel

One thing I liked exceedingly in one of the towers, that was a study called Paradise, where was a closet in the middle of eight squares latticed about: and at the top of every square was a desk ledged to set books on coffers within them, and these seemed as joined hard to the top of the closet: and yet by pulling one or all would come down, breast height in rabbets, and serve for desks to lay books on.

A petrifying well in Yorkshire

A little above March, but on the further bank of the Nidd, as I came, is a well of a wonderful nature, called dropping well.

For out of the great rocks by it distils water continually into it. This water is so cold, and of such a nature, that what thing so ever falls out of the rocks into this pit, or is cast in, or grows about the rock and is touched of this water, grows into stone: or else some sand, or other fine ground that is about the rocks, comes down with the continual dropping of the springs in the rocks, and cleaves on such things as it takes, and so cleaves about it and gives it by continuance the shape of a stone.

Dover: a piece of etymology

One [parish] is called S. James of Rudby, or more likely Rodeby, *a statione navium.* But this word is not sufficient to prove that Dover should be that place, the which the Romans called *portus Rutupi* or *Rutupinum.* For I can not yet see the contrary but Ratesboro, otherwise called Richebro by Sandwich, both ways corruptly, must needs be *Rutupinum.*[14]

❧ *An early mapmaker*

GEORGE LILY (*c.*1512–59)

George Lily was the first high master's oldest son. Possibly as early as 1529 he entered the service of Reginald Pole, who was to become England's last Roman Catholic archbishop of Canterbury: by the 1540s his links with Pole led to exile for treason. He worked on major contributions to the Italian physician and historian Paolo Giovio's *Descriptio Britanniae, Scotiae, Hyberniae et Orchadum* (pub-

lished in Venice, 1548) and drew the first map of the British Isles ever to be printed. It received papal approval and was published in 1546. Descended from the so-called Gough map of the mid-fourteenth century, it is mainly of historical importance and distinctly economical in the information it gives: only eight places are named in Norfolk (including of course the shrine at Walsingham) and only eight in Sussex.

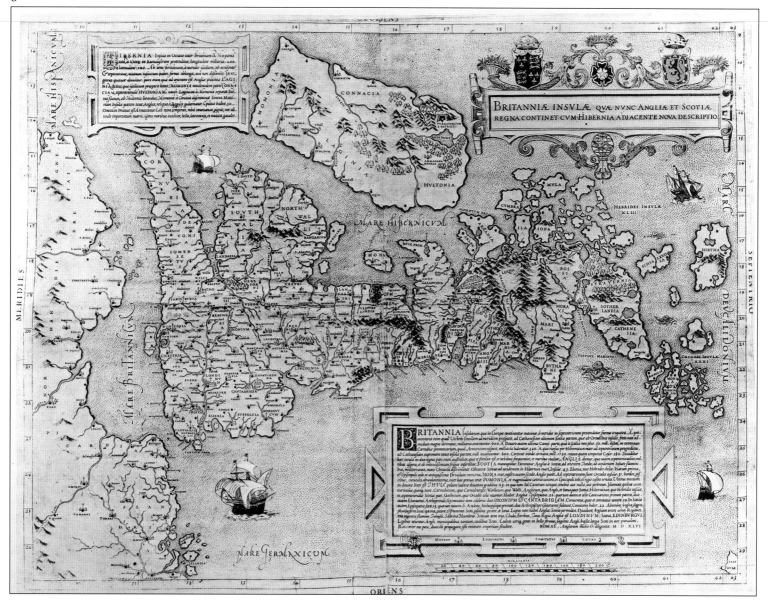

Map of Great Britain, the first to be printed, drawn by George Lily, Rome, 1546. *By permission of Llyfrgell Genedlaethol Cymru/The National Library of Wales.*

His summary of the differences between England and Scotland is brief and judgemental: 'Two contiguous realms: England, with fertile terrain, more densely packed with cities, and more virtuous; and Scotland, rougher and on account of the cold less fertile.'[15]

❧ *Traders on the money markets*

STEPHEN VAUGHAN (*c.*1502–49)
SIR THOMAS GRESHAM (1518–79)

Both Stephen Vaughan and Thomas Gresham were royal agents in the Netherlands, somehow finding their way through the labyrinthine process of raising money on the continent. Vaughan's early negotiations with the Weiser firm of Augsburg were very cautious: 'This house is meet to meddle withal if we find them not too greedy of gain, yet, be they what they will, we mind to taste them as it were a loaf.'[16] A crown loan was secured, albeit at a high rate of interest, but Vaughan was a quick learner and in his two years at the Antwerp bourse (1544–46) made great progress in reducing Henry VIII's debts as well as raising mercenaries for his army. Taking up the post in 1551 after a disastrous few years, Gresham had more spectacular success, with periods of service until 1567, but his financial acumen was complemented by some very helpful market conditions.[17]

There is a more personal side to Vaughan's writing.

young and without discretion to order themselves, and do want a sad, trusty, and womanly matron to look upon th'one and th'other. I am driven into many minds to marry with some honest woman, but not with one […] should bring nothing with her. If such a one come in your way as ye can find in your heart to think meet for me, I pray you keep her in store for your friend. Sharp, foolish, drunken, nor sluttish wives did I never love. An honest mind I regard above all other things in a woman; without which I grant it is a pleasant thing to live, but the consideration of my continual shifting from my house, the lack of well nurturing of my children, the waste and spoil of my things draweth me to marry; which although I consider with myself to be meet for me, yet I do not so stiffly cleave to mine own will but I offer myself to be much trained and ruled by your advice and counsel.[18]

Compensating perhaps for the death of his only son in 1564, Gresham turned his attention in later life to an extraordinarily grandiose project, paying for the building of a Bourse or Exchange for London's merchants, modelled on Antwerp. It is not known how much this cost him, although there was a healthy rental income from the first-floor shops, which became very fashionable following Queen Elizabeth I's visit in 1570 and proclamation that thenceforth it would be called the Royal Exchange.[19] Spending the family fortune in this way did little for his marriage but gave him the immortality he yearned for, as did the founding of Gresham College, which was to come into being after his widow's death in 1596. Vaughan never reached old age. He remarried in 1546 and for the last few years of his life held a modest position as under-treasurer at the Tower of London mint. He 'died inconspicuously, and was soon forgotten'.[20]

After his first wife's death in 1544, he wrote from Antwerp to two influential Old Paulines, William Paget and Thomas Wriothesley (see earlier entry), requesting them (unsuccessfully) to find him a new wife. A long letter to Paget about politics in December 1544 ends:

And now I am a suitor to you in matter of great counsel, which I would bestow upon few besides you. Whiles I am a widower, have a great household and especially children,

Monument to Sir Thomas Offley (c.1505–82) in St Andrew Undershaft, London, watercolour by Thomas Fisher. A prosperous Old Pauline wool exporter, he was lord mayor of London 1556–57 and escorted Philip II of Spain and his queen through the City. Guildhall Library, City of London.

The first Royal Exchange, London, engraving by Wenceslas Hollar. The architect, Hendryck van Paesschen, was a Fleming living in Antwerp and went on to work for William Cecil on Burghley House near Stamford. By kind permission of the Worshipful Company of Mercers.

THOMAS TUSSER (*c.*1524–80)

He was so dead keen to impart his knowledge to his neighbours […] that he rammed his maxims into his metre with a sledge-hammer.

(Rudyard Kipling)[21]

Thomas Tusser's attempts at farming in East Anglia were all unsuccessful, but that did not stop him compiling a verse manual on husbandry, first published in 1557. *A Hundred Good Points of Husbandry* describes the agricultural year in close-packed rhyming couplets. It was later expanded into *Five Hundred Points of Good Husbandry*, a more moralistic work with additional sections in both verse and prose about running a household and rural customs. This became a best-seller during the reign of Elizabeth and beyond: between 1557 and 1638 there were twenty-three editions published. As late as 1723 Lord Molesworth proposed that a school for husbandry should be erected in every county: 'Tusser's old Book of Husbandry should be taught to the boys, to read, to copy and to get by heart.'[22]

Unlike most previous manuals, Tusser aimed his advice at the smaller tenant farmer rather than the large landowner, and its spirit is emphatically one of hard work, efficiency and prudence. He recommends a wary attitude to the neighbours:

> An envious neighbour is easy to find,
> his cumbersome fetches are seldom behind.
> His mouth full of venom, his lips out of frame,
> his tongue a false witness, his friend to defame.
> His breast full of rancour, like canker to fret,
> his heart like a lion, his neighbour to eat.

Bad habits, such as getting up late, can also lead to trouble. Tusser has a lot to say about the housewife, to be selected wisely ('Though love be in choosing, far better than gold,/let love come with somewhat, the better to hold'), and about managing servants:

> Get up in the morning as soon as thou wilt,
> with overlong slugging, good servant is spilt.
> Some slovens from sleeping, no sooner get up,
> but hand is in ambry [pantry], and nose in the cup.
>
> . . . . . .
>
> Beware rascabilia, slothful to work,
> purloiners and filchers, that loveth to lurk.
> Away with such lubbers, so loth to take pain,
> that rolls in expenses, but never no gain.

At harvest time he allows the servants a mirthful celebration, but only after the reaping has been thorough, leaving the poor and then the cattle to clean up:

> Reap well, scatter not, gather clean that is shorn:
> bind fast, shock a-pace, pay the tenth of thy corn.
> Load safe, carry home, lose no time, being fair:
> gotten just, in the barn, it is out of despair.
>
> This done, let the poor over all for to glean:
> and after thy cattle, to eat it up clean.
> Then spare it for pasture, till rowan be past:
> to lengthen thy dairy, no better thou hast.
>
> Then welcome thy harvest folk, servants and all:
> with mirth and good cheer, let them furnish the hall.
> The harvest lord nightly, must give thee a song:
> Tell him then the black bowl, or else he hath wrong.[23]

Sixteenth-century farming scene, woodcut.
E2BN Gallery.

🎍 *A picture of Merry England and a warning*

WILLIAM HARRISON (1535–93)

The situation of our region, lying near unto the north, doth cause the heat of our stomachs to be of somewhat greater force: therefore our bodies do crave a little more ample nourishment, than the inhabitants of the hotter regions are accustomed withal, whose digestive force is not altogether so vehement.

(William Harrison's *Historical Description*)

William Harrison was at St Paul's before going on to Westminster School, where in his own words he was an 'unprofitable grammarian'. His *Historical Description of the Island of Britain* forms the preface to Holinshed's *Chronicles* (1577), the fullest account of British history written up to that time. Harrison gives a lively, varied and generally optimistic picture of British life, geography and history, but his major interest was a much more disturbing project, never published, where he developed a very complex chronological theory about God's purposes for man from the beginning of the world and the conflict between the true church and Satanic paganism.[24] Some of his fear that mankind would fall victim to the evils of excessive consumption and church corruption creeps into his revisions for the second edition of his *Description*, as in the passage below, but for the most part Harrison celebrates Britain and the British, the men's fine constitution, the country's fine diet, colourful attire, spices, precious stones, fairs and markets, antiquities and so on.

Of English apparel and attire

Of how much cost is bestowed nowadays upon our bodies and how little upon our souls, how many suits of apparel hath the one and how little furniture hath the other; how long time is asked in decking up of the first, and how little space left therein to feed the latter: how curious, how nice also are a number of men and women, and how hardly can the tailor please them in making it fit for their bodies: how many times must it be sent back again to him that made it: what chafing, what fretting, what reproachful language doth the poor workman bear away: and many times when he doth nothing to it at all, yet when it is brought home again it is very fit and handsome: then must we put it on, then must the long seams of our hose be set by a plumb-line, then we puff, then we blow, and finally sweat till we drop, that our clothes may stand well upon us. I will say nothing of our heads, which sometimes are polled, sometimes curled, or suffered to grow at length like woman's locks, many times cut off above or under the ears round as by a wooden dish. […] Some lusty courtiers also and gentlemen of courage, do wear either rings of gold, stones, or pearl in their ears, whereby they imagine the workmanship of God not to be a little amended.[25]

🎍 *The story of Britannia*

WILLIAM CAMDEN (1551–1623)

A certain clergyman of this town, being passionately in love with a young woman, and by no means able to move her to comply with his lust, grew stark mad, and in that condition villainously cut off her head. Her head was afterward hung upon an yew tree, where it was reputed holy by the vulgar, till quite rotten; and was often visited in pilgrimage by them; every one plucking off a branch of the tree [as a holy relic.] By this means the tree became at last a mere trunk, but still retained its reputation of sanctity among the people, who even persuaded themselves that those little veins, which are spread out like hair in the rind between the bark and the body of the tree, were indeed the very hair of the Virgin. This occasioned such resort of pilgrims to it, that *Horton*, from a little village grew up soon to a large town, assuming the new name of *Halig-fax* or *Halifax*, which signifies *holy hair*.

(William Camden, *Britannia*)

William Camden is the most famous Old Pauline topographer and historian of the century and in his major work *Britannia* built on the pioneering work of Leland and Harrison (see earlier entries). His antiquarian interests might well have begun at school but certainly grew during his years at Oxford: he met others similarly inclined and specifically refers in *Britannia* to the encouragement he received from Philip Sidney, whose interest in making links between imaginative and historical writing, for example in his *Defense of Poesie*, is also present in Camden's work.[26]

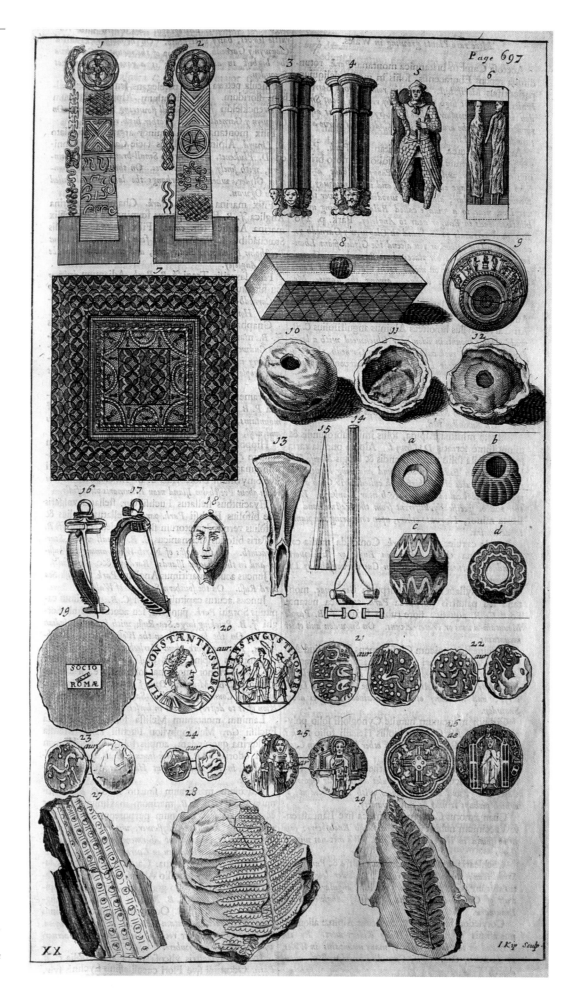

'A Table of Welsh Curiosities', engraving by I. Kip from Camden's *Britannia*, 1695 edition. *Ken Lawson. © St Paul's School.*

Camden spent twenty-two years at Westminster School, first as second master and then as headmaster. During these years he also travelled extensively, produced the first four editions of *Britannia* and managed to compile a Greek grammar. He had a high reputation among European scholars, who would often seek him out in England before *Britannia* first appeared as a small octavo volume in 1586. Over the following twenty years it grew into a substantial folio work with many maps and engravings.

Britannia is remarkable for the massive range of evidence and techniques Camden deploys to explore the country and its history county by county. He looks for himself, reads the landscape, listens to stories, examines coins, pores over records and inscriptions. A passage about a seamy part of the Thames, presumably Bankside, illustrates perfectly his capacity for interweaving scholarship and personal observation, while his account of the etymology of Halifax shows how he cannot resist an interesting myth, however improbable, but still gives it an academic colouring.

Camden's distinctions did not end with his time at Westminster: he went on to be Clarenceux king of arms. He wrote a Latin translation of the gunpowder trial and a significant biography of Elizabeth I.

Southwark

From this along the Thames-side, there runs westward a continued line of houses, in which compass, within the memory of our fathers, there were *Public Stews*, called by the Latin *Lupanaria* (wherein whores prostituted and set to sale their modesty), because they, like rapacious *she-wolves*, hale miserably silly people into their *dens*. But these were prohibited by King Hen.8. at a time when England was at the height of lust and luxury; though in foreign nations they are still continued for gain, under the specious pretence of making allowance to human infirmity. But I do not believe that they called this place in our language *The Stews*, from these bawdy houses, but from the fish-ponds here for the fatting of pikes and tench, and scouring of their muddy fennish taste. Here I have seen the bellies of pikes opened with a knife to show their fatness, and the gaping wounds presently closed by the touch of tenches, and by their glutinous slime perfectly healed up.[27]

❧ *Elizabethan court reporter*

ROBERT LANEHAM (1535–79/80)

A very diverting tract, written by as great a coxcomb as ever blotted paper.

(Sir Walter Scott in *Kenilworth* on Laneham's pamphlet)[28]

Little is known about Robert Laneham or Langham apart from the account he published of an entertainment put on in 1575 for Queen Elizabeth I at Kenilworth Castle, home of the Earl of Leicester, and even there his authorship is not secure, as some critics think it was a parody of Laneham's pompous descriptive style by one William Patten, which would explain why it risks criticism of court behaviour.[29] Sir Walter Scott gave Laneham a cameo role in his period novel *Kenilworth*.

The pamphlet is written in places with a naïve enthusiasm and in places as what seems to be clumsy satire. Laneham clearly relished any opportunity to use quaint imagery and vocabulary or alliteration. Elizabeth stayed at Kenilworth for nineteen days, and we are given descriptions of Italian acrobatics, a tournament, a swimming mermaid eighteen feet long, a marriage, fireworks and a so-called 'Ambrosial Banquet' — 'Her majesty eat smally or nothing: which understood; the courses were not so orderly served and sizely set down, but were by and by as disorderly wasted and coarsely consumed; more courtly me

thought than courteously.' The more directly autobiographical parts include a bizarre account of Laneham's supposed musical talent on the guitar, lute and keyboard: 'Sometime I foot it with dancing: now with my gittern, and else with my cittern, then at the virginals. Ye know nothing comes amiss to me: Then carol I up a song withal; that by and by they come flocking about me like bees to honey: and ever they cry, "Another, good Langham, another!"'

A marriage procession

(Laneham has little time for the 'three pretty puzels' or 'pucelles', who might just be maidens but, given his description of their simpering lips, seem more like ageing slatterns. The poor 'loober woorts', presumably 'leberwurtz' or liver sausage in allusion to his unhealthy complexion, does not come off much better.)

Well, Sir, after these horsemen, a lively morris dance, according to the ancient manner, six dancers, Maid Marion, and the fool. Then three pretty puzels, as bright as a breast of bacon,

Kenilworth: the castle gatehouse, built by the Earl of Leicester between 1563 and 1570, and inhabited until the twentieth century. Henry Taunt, photograph taken 1860–1922. *Reproduced by permission of English Heritage. NMR.*

of a thirty year old apiece, that carried three special spice-cakes, [...] before the bride. Sizely, with set countenance, and lips so demurely simpering, as it had been a mare cropping of a thistle. After these, a lovely loober woorts, frecklefaced, red-headed, clean trussed in his doublet and his hose [...] to bear the bride-cup, formed of a sweet sucket barrel, a fair-turned foot set to it, all seemly besilvered and parcel gilt [....] This gentle cup-bearer yet had his freckled physiognomy some-what unhappily infested as he went, by the busy flies that float about the bride-cup for the sweetness of the sucket that it savoured on; but he, like a tall fellow, withstood their malice stoutly (see what manhood may do), beat them away, killed them by scores, stood to his charge, and marched on in good order.

Then followed the worshipful bride, led (after the country manner) between two ancient parishioners, honest towns-men. But a stale stallion, and a well-spread (hot as the weather was), God wot, and ill-smelling was she: a thirty-five year old, of colour brown-bay, not very beautiful indeed, but ugly, foul ill-favoured; yet marvellous fain of the office, because she heard say she should dance before the Queen, in which feat she thought she would foot it as finely as the best.

(A letter: wherein, part of the entertainment unto the Queen's Majesty, at Kenilworth Castle, in Warwickshire in this summer's progress 1575. is signified: from a friend officer attendant in the court, unto his friend a citizen, and merchant of London)

❧ *Puritans and Catholics*

WILLIAM FULKE (*c.*1537–89)

A violently puritanical divine.
(Sir Michael McDonnell, *Annals of St Paul's School*)[30]

William Fulke's appetite for fierce argument did not take long to emerge. In 1560 he published an attack on astrol-ogy, the *Antiprognosticum,* and in 1563, on becoming a fellow of St John's College, Cambridge, he refused to wear academic dress, which he thought savoured of popery. Most members of the college were encouraged to follow his example, by intimidation if necessary. He became a

notable London preacher who concentrated on demon-strating the faults of Roman Catholic belief, once preach-ing at extreme length at the Tower of London 'in the hearing of such obstinate Papists as then were prisoners there'. He also made a speciality of refuting Roman Catholic publications. So confident was he in his own powers of persuasion that he would print the original text

GVILHELMVS WHITAKERVS THEOL

Whitaker, attacking enemies with mighty blows,
Often triumphs victorious on behalf of Christ his master.

Engraving. Like William Fulke, William Whitaker (1547/48–95) was a fiercely anti-catholic theologian and brought out in 1580 an attack on Edmund Campion for which he was compared to David taking on a 'popish Goliath'. He became master of St John's College and regius professor of divinity at Cambridge. The verse is an elegiac couplet. *Translation by Peter King. © St Paul's School.*

alongside his own reply to it.[31] Fulke took part in the public disputation with Edmund Campion at the Tower of London in 1581 (see next entry). For the final eleven years of his life he was master of Pembroke College, Cambridge.

Papists and church-going

(Fulke revels in his contemptuous punning on Howlet's name. Another refutation of the discourse, bound in with the British Library copy, speaks of 'Howlet's untimely screeching'. Fulke has a strikingly melodramatic style of writing and rejects vehemently Howlet's argument that Roman Catholics could refuse to express outward conformity to the Church of England and attend its services. Howlet was the pseudonym of Jesuit Robert Persons, mentioned in the next entry.)

The first reason why a Papist may not go to church, is the peril of infection: which is as good a reason, as [if] a foul toad may not come into a clear spring, to wash her, and spew out her venom, for fear of infection, not of the well (of which there is greater danger) but of her own body, unto whose poisoned complexion, nothing almost may be added. Or that a man infected with the pestilence, pox, or other contagious disease, may not come near the place where physic and surgery is ministered, lest he should be further infected. So that if a fool or a madman be persuaded that the physician will kill him, by this main reason he must avoid him. For what other force is in this argument, except truth be confessed to be falsehood, and true physic dangerous infection.

(*A Brief Confrontation of a Popish Discourse Lately set forth, and presumptuously dedicated to the Queen's most excellent Majesty: by John Howlet, or some other bird of the night, under that name,* 1581)[32]

❦ *Catholic agitator*

ST EDMUND CAMPION (1540–81)

The people are thus inclined, religious, frank, amorous, ireful, sufferable of pains infinite, very glorious, many sorcerers, excellent horsemen, delighted with wars, great alms givers, passing in hospitality [...] The lewder sort both clerks and lays are sensual and loose to lechery above measure. The same being virtuously bred up or reformed are such mirrors of holiness and austerity that other nations retain but a shadow of devotion in comparison of them.

(Edmund Campion on the disposition of the Irish people)[33]

According to a fellow Jesuit, Robert Persons, Edmund Campion was always a Catholic, despite his taking an oath against papal supremacy in 1564 when he was at Oxford. By 1571, when he wrote his two volume *History of Ireland*, later incorporated into Holinshed's *Chronicles,* his Catholicism appears to have been public knowledge, and he went abroad, entering the Jesuit novitiate in 1573. He was ordained priest in Prague in 1578 and two years later embarked with Persons on a dangerous Jesuit mission to England. Campion assumed the improbable disguise of a travelling jewel salesman from Dublin and proceeded to London, where he wrote his famous *Brag* or *Challenge* to debate religion with protestants, which was soon in circulation, sooner than he intended. He travelled in secret for

St Edmund Campion after his death, engraving, possibly by Jacobus Neeffs or Neefs, early to mid seventeenth century. The caption refers to his being hanged and quartered for his faith. There is a noose round his neck and what appears to be a cleaver near his left arm. © *St Paul's School.*

some months visiting English Catholic families and even issued *Rationes decem,* ten points of the Catholic faith he would defend if protestants took up his *Challenge.* However, the activities of Campion and Persons, who produced his own confession of faith or *Confessio fidei,* were raising government fears about the Catholic threat. Elizabeth I, who had been relatively tolerant of Catholics, was now, according to a privy council letter dated 1 December 1580, minded to 'make some example of [Jesuits] by punishment, to the terror of others'. In July 1581 Campion fell victim to a Catholic informer and was taken to the Tower of London, where over the following three months he was interrogated, sometimes under torture. At the same time, he was allowed a disputation as he had requested in the *Brag:* the odds of course were stacked against him as he faced a panel of protestant divines, including Old Pauline William Fulke (see last entry), who were very well prepared and chose the topics for debate over four public sessions. Even so, the event generated popular ballads ridiculing the protestants' performance and a series of polemical pamphlets on both sides. Philip Howard, Earl of Arundel, was in the audience, and the experience helped convert him to Catholicism. Both Campion and Howard were among the forty English martyrs canonized by Pope Paul VI in 1970.

In November 1581 Campion was tried in Westminster Hall for 'treasonable conspiracy', found guilty against the

evidence and executed the following month. Persons had fled to France and remained in exile until his death in 1610.[34]

From Campion's Brag

(The Brag or Challenge makes nine short points, and for all its claims to be a humble and non-political request, is unmistakably inflammatory in tone: he writes of his 'quarrel' and dismisses protestant theology as 'feeble' compared with his own 'impregnable' evidence.)

To the Right Honourable, the Lords of Her Majesty's Privy Council:

vi. I would be loath to speak anything that might sound of any insolent brag or challenge, especially being now as a dead man to this world and willing to put my head under every man's foot, and to kiss the ground they tread upon. Yet I have such courage in avouching the majesty of Jesus my King, and such affiance in his gracious favour, and such assurance in my quarrel, and my evidence so impregnable, and because I know perfectly that no one protestant, nor all the protestants living, nor any sect of our adversaries (howsoever they face men down in pulpits, and overrule us in their kingdom of grammarians and unlearned ears) can maintain their doctrine in disputation. I am to sue most humbly and instantly for combat with all and every of them, and the most principal that may be found: protesting that in this trial the better furnished they come, the better welcome they shall be.

viii. Moreover I doubt not but you […] will see upon what substantial grounds our Catholic faith is builded, how feeble that side is which by sway of the time prevaileth against us, and so at last for your own souls, and for many thousand souls that depend upon your government, will discountenance error when it is bewrayed [revealed], and hearken to those who would spend the best blood in their bodies for your salvation. Many innocent hands are lifted up to heaven for you daily by those English students, whose posterity shall never die, which beyond seas, gathering virtue and sufficient knowledge for the purpose, are determined never to give you over, but either to win you heaven, or to die upon your pikes. And touching our Society, be it known to you that we have made a league — all the Jesuits in the world, whose succession and multitude must overreach all the practice of England — cheerfully to carry the cross you shall lay upon us, and never to despair your recovery, while we have a man left to enjoy your Tyburn, or to be racked with your torments, or consumed with your prisons. The expense is reckoned, the enterprise is begun; it is of God; it cannot be withstood. So the faith was planted: So it must be restored.[35]

Brother composers

JOHN MUDD (1555–1631)
THOMAS MUDD (*c.*1560–*after* 1619)

Both brothers went up to Gonville and Caius College, Cambridge, after their time at St Paul's. John moved on smoothly to become master of the choristers at Southwell Minster and then organist at Peterborough Cathedral, a post he resigned in favour of his composer son (also called Thomas) shortly before his death in 1631. Thomas's Cambridge career was more colourful: he seems to have been refused a degree at first because of his Catholic leanings. Eventually, he took BA from Peterhouse and MA from Pembroke, but not before he had been sent by the vice-chancellor to the Tolbooth for three days because 'he had censured and too saucily reflected on the mayor of Cambridge' in a comedy he had written, alas now lost: 'saucily' at that time indicated gross insolence rather than simple cheek.[36] Even so, Thomas Mudd held a fellowship and personal lectureship at Pembroke for several years before becoming a Kent clergyman in 1592. Thomas Mudd was described in Francis Meres's *Palladis Tamia* (1598) as one of England's sixteen 'excellent musicians', but since many compositions are attributed to 'Mudd' or 'Mr Mudd', it is often difficult to tell who wrote which piece. The current view is that more works have survived of Thomas Mudd, including anthems and music for keyboard and viols.[37]

Musicians in church, engraving, *c.*1550. *Getty Images.*

A merchant traveller

JOHN SANDERSON (1560–*after* 1602)

Very pleasant is that travel only the heat troubleth, and some fear of thieves which continually rob on that river and alike on the land.

(John Sanderson on the Nile)[38]

Our evidence for John Sanderson's being an Old Pauline is based on disparaging remarks he made about the mean instruction and harsh punishment received from the high master and surmaster, John Cook and Christopher Holden: 'The said Cook with lashes set more than seven scars on my hide which yet remain.'[39] He became a Turkey merchant in the Mediterranean, and his own account of his experiences was given a place in *Purchas, His Pilgrims*, an enormous early seventeenth-century compendium of travel narratives and descriptions of the world's peoples and religions, often remembered as having been read by Samuel Taylor Coleridge, or so he claimed, just before the opium dream that inspired *Kubla Khan*.

Sanderson was adventurous in his travels, and his curiosity was insatiable. On a journey up the Nile he had a crocodile ripped open. In Cairo he was let down into a cave to inspect some mummies, and proceeded to break off limbs to take back to England. This disrespect for other religions carried over into an extraordinary attack on one of Cairo's holy men, dismissed as a 'great fat lubberly beast', and scepticism about another who plucked out his one remaining eye 'because he would see no more sin'. There were lucky escapes when his ship encountered a Spanish warship, and when he entered Jerusalem without surrendering his sword, a solecism atoned for by bribery. His toughest writing is reserved for the cruelty he saw in

Constantinople (where for a short time he was deputy ambassador) and Cairo. In 1595 he reached Constantinople just as Mehmet III had become sultan, signifying his accession by strangling his nineteen brothers: Sanderson saw their bodies carried out for burial. There is a sustained and horrified description of the punishments inflicted on malefactors: perhaps Cook's scars remained in his mind to the end?

Mummies

The mummia, which is some five or six miles beyond, are thousands of embalmed bodies; which were buried thousands of years past in a sandy cave; at which there seemeth to have been some city in times past: we were let down by ropes, as into a well, with wax candles burning in our hands, and so walked upon the bodies of all sorts and sizes, great and small, and some embalmed in little earthen pots, which never had form: these are set at the feet of the greater bodies: which gave no noisome smell at all, but are like pitch, being broken; for I broke off all the parts of the bodies to see how the flesh was turned to drug, and brought home divers heads, hands, arms,

and feet, for a show: we brought also 600 pounds for the Turkey Company in pieces: and brought into England in the *Hercules*: together with a whole body: they are lapped in above an hundred double of cloth, which rotting and peeling off, you may see the skin, flesh, fingers and nails firm, only altered black. One little hand I brought into England, to show; and presented it my brother, who gave the same to a doctor in Oxford.

Turkish punishments

The commonest death for men is gaunshing; which is, to be stripped unto their linen breeches, with their hands and feet bound all four together at their backs, and so drawn up with a rope by a pulley upon the gallows, and let fall upon a great iron hook fastened to a lower cross bar of the gallows, most commonly lighting upon their flank and so through their thigh, there they hang sometimes talking a day or two together, but if they be gaunched through the belly and back, then are they dead in two or three hours. […] But hanging by the neck they use in a favour to any offender who meriteth death, yet sometimes cutting down for dogs to eat. They strangle with a bow-string their brethren, bashaws [pashas]

Hand-coloured map of sixteenth-century Cairo. The sphinx and pyramids are in the lower right-hand corner.

and other great men. But for their religious men false judges, their law is to pash them all to pieces in a stone mortar with wooden mallets. […] And for any found drunk in the time of their Ramadan […] their law is, to melt a ladle full of lead and pour it down their throats.

(Sundry the personal Voyages performed by John Sanderson of London, Merchant, begun in October 1584, ended in October 1600)[40]

ৠ *Alchemy and chemistry: purifying wool and purifying the body*

SIR THOMAS CHALONER (1563/4–1615)

To foredo the rank smell of the armholes, and other the cleansing parts of the body, and folds in the skin: dissolve nitre in warm water, and with a sponge or linen cloth dipped therein, bath and scour away the sweat and rank humours and fumosities expulsed by nature through those loose cleansing parts.

(Sir Thomas Chaloner on the virtues of nitre)

Thomas Chaloner was a friend of the alchemist John Dee and had his own collection of erudite manuscripts. As a man of learning and influence with scientific leanings, he was given some interesting responsibilities: King James made him governor of his eldest son Henry in 1603, a position he took very seriously. Helped by the Prince of Wales, he became involved in a scheme to extract silver from lead.[41] He also investigated the manufacture of water pipes and experimented with improvements in ship-building technique.

Of most historical interest is the alum works Chaloner established on his estate in Guisborough, Yorkshire, and of most scientific interest his *Shorte Discourse of the most rare and excellent virtue of Nitre* (1584). In both cases he was attracted by the quasi-alchemic processes involved in producing the materials. Alum was purified from local shale and used as a dye-fixer for wool, which was much more valuable once dyed. Nitre or saltpetre (potassium nitrate) is an ingredient of gunpowder and was obtained at the time by extracting salts from manure and urine: it had its own alchemic symbol, and its properties were known from ancient times.[42]

Around 1600 Chaloner discovered alum on his estate and made himself guarantor of the Alum Company, which aimed to make England self-sufficient in this substance, instead of depending on unreliable supplies from the Papal States and Middle East. The costs were extreme: he had to compensate customs for the loss of revenue from imported alum, and he shipped fuel from County Durham's coal mines for the purification process. There is a story that he bribed 'some artists well acquainted with the whole mystery' of making alum who were working for the Pope and brought them back to England by taking them clandestinely on board his ship in large casks, for which action they all received an elaborate papal curse.[43]

The company soon went bankrupt, and Chaloner was pensioned off despite (we gather) the heroic gesture of hoarding his own urine to sell to the works at one penny a firkin. The deficit by 1608 was £30,000, a colossal amount in those days, and the whole venture became a public

Sir Thomas Chaloner's tomb in St Nicholas's church, Chiswick. Chaloner and his wife kneel either side of a skull and are flanked by two armed servants holding back curtains. *Courtesy St Nicholas's church.*

scandal, although the banning of foreign imports after 1609 made a great difference. In due course, Charles I confiscated the works for the crown and proceeded to benefit from healthy revenues.[44]

Chaloner's *Shorte Discourse* focused on the myriad medicinal properties of nitre, whether taken inwardly or 'outwardly plasterwise applied'. It was apparently excellent for 'foulness and diseases of the skin: […] as tawny stainings, sunburning, freckles, […] jaundices, yellow, green and black, weals and white whelks […] and to restore the skin and complexion to the native beauty. Also to remove and fordo scurf, dandruff, [...] scabs, pimples, pushes, mange, ringworm, tetters, […] and such effects.' It could be prepared 'in distilled whey, or in distilled goats milk: or else […] with the broth and fatness of figs; or else with the fine meal of the knots of the roots of Aaron called cuckoo pint or the knots of roots of serpentine called dragon or

snakegrasses nine times soaked in rosewater and each time dried by the sun or over a cooking fire'. Nitre dissolved in a warm bath would cure many disorders including 'clamminess, congelation, clinging, cluddering, stopping, stuffing, compression, distension, contraction, cramps or stitches, and slackness or paralysis'.

It did not stop there: mixed with sweet wine it would stop your hair falling out, mixed with white hellebore it cured nits. It was recommended for cleaning teeth (an application still employed in the twenty-first century), nosebleeding, deformed nails, paralysis of the tongue, restoration of 'plumpness and suppleness unto any member decayed and withered by not receiving nutriment', a specific against the biting of a mad dog, henbane or mandragora, to remedy 'suffocation, windiness, heaving, gnawing and torment, of the stomach, underbulk and bowels' and even 'for soldering of gold, silver, or copper'.[45]

❧ *The most famous soldier of his day*

SIR FRANCIS VERE (1560/1–1609)

I chose a good number of lusty and hardy young soldiers, the most of which, I apparelled like the country women of those parts; the rest, like the men: and gave to some, baskets; to others packs, and such burdens as the people usually carry to the market; with pistols, short swords, and daggers under their garments.

(Sir Francis Vere falsely claims credit for a ruse leading to the capture of the city of Zutphen in 1591)

Helped by his own inflated commentaries (published 1657) on how he fought against Spain and a eulogistic Victorian account, Markham's *The Fighting Veres*, Francis Vere became the best-known military (as distinct from naval) commander of his era.

He was destined from birth for a military career and served in the Netherlands from 1581 in the wars against the Spanish. Sir Roger Williams, his first commander, said that Vere wore a 'red mandilion' (a kind of loose coat or cassock) and 'stood always in the head of the armed men at the assaults': as a consequence he suffered frequent injuries.

Vere was knighted for bravery in 1588 and made use of his leave in England to cultivate influential courtiers, so that shortly after his return to the Netherlands early in 1589 he was formally in charge of all the English troops there. There is no doubt that he was a courageous and skilled leader — 'a stout and gallant man, greatly favoured by the States above any other foreigner,' as one Dutch chronicler put it. Apart from a brief interlude in Spain, when participation in the sack of Cadiz brought him booty to the tune of almost £4,000, Vere was in the Netherlands until 1603. He played leading roles in major

actions including the famous victory at Nieuwpoort (1600), but by then power had gone to his head: his report to the council after the battle gave a 'relation […] so partial, as if no man had stroke stroke but the English, and among the English no man almost but Sir Francis Vere'.[46] His manner became increasingly high-handed, both in Elizabeth's court and in his exercise of military power: having fallen out with one west country captain, he prevented all Cornishmen from being promoted. Once James I ascended the throne, however, peace with Spain became a prime objective, Vere's influence waned, and he resigned in 1603.

Vere's arrogance may reflect his insecurity about being a commoner rather than a noble, which meant that he remained a sergeant-major-general rather than assuming the rank of lieutenant-general as had his predecessors commanding English forces in the Netherlands. Even so, his role in the war against Spain was undoubtedly of great importance, and Vere inspired a generation of soldiers who served under him.

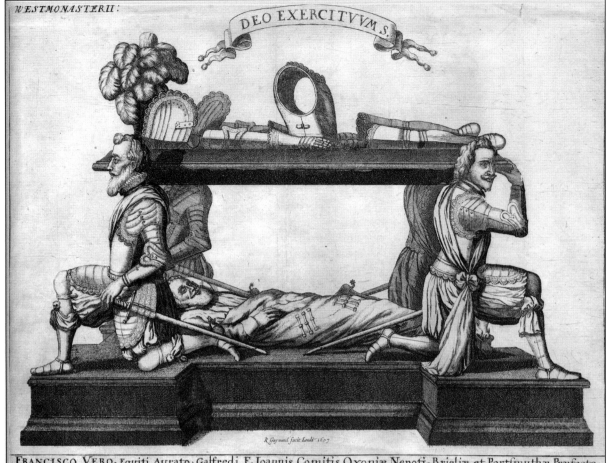

WESTMONASTERII:

DEO EXERCITVVM S.

FRANCISCO VERO, Equiti Aurato, Galfredi F. Ioannis Comitis Oxoniæ Nepoti, Brieliæ et Portſmuthæ Præfecto, Anglicarum copiarum in Belgio Ductori Summo; ELIZABETHA uxor viro Chariſſimo, quocum Conjunctiſſime vixit, hoc Supr.... amoris et fidei conjugalis monumentum mæſtiſſima et cum Lacrymis Gemens Poſuit. Obiit XXVIII Die Auguſti, Anno Salutis MDCVIII et anno Ætatis Suæ LIIII

The grandiose tomb of Sir Francis Vere in Westminster Abbey, engraving by R. Gaywood, 1657. It displays a complete suit of armour as well as the body and was modelled on the tomb of Count Engelbert II at Breda. *Ken Lawson. © St Paul's School.*

Vere describes his part in the battle of Nieuwpoort (1600)

To give our men the more courage, I went into the bottom amongst them, where riding up and down, I was in their eyes both doing the office of a captain and soldier: and with much ado, we entertained the fight, though the enemy encroached and got upon us. At my first coming, I got one shot through my leg, and a quarter of an hour after, another through the same thigh; which I then, neither complained nor bragged of, nor so much as thought of a surgeon: for I knew, if I left the place, my men would instantly quail. I therefore chose, not having been used to have my troops foiled, to try the uttermost, rather than to show them the way to flee. *[Unfortunately, the men still fled, despite Vere's stoic valour.]*

I was forced, seeing them all going, to go for company, with the last; uneasily and unwillingly, God knows! and in the way, my horse fell dead under me and upon me, that I could not stir. *[He is rescued by Sir Robert Drury, who gives him a lift on his horse.]* Thus I rode to the ordnance [...] and willed the cannoneers to discharge upon the enemy that now swarmed upon the sands. *[He also orders his own retreating company to charge the enemy.]* This small number of horse and foot made an exceeding great change on a sudden. For the enemy in hope of victory, followed hard; and being upon the sands, where horse might serve upon them, were soon routed and most of them cut in pieces; the rest saving themselves by flight as they could, in the downs.[47]

St Paul's School, *c.*1670, wash by Hollar? This is probably the earliest picture we have of the second school, built on the site of the first after the great fire of London. *Guildhall Library, City of London.*

The Seventeenth Century

2

❧ *Two comic playwrights*

NATHAN FIELD (*bap*.1587, *d*.1619/20)

NATHAN FIELD began his stage career in 1600 when he was still at St Paul's, taking several parts in the company, the Children of the Chapel Royal, which performed at Blackfriars. Later he joined the King's Men and is listed in the 1623 Shakespeare folio as a principal actor. Shakespeare's eighteenth-century editor Malone believed he 'performed female parts', and Field took leading roles in revivals of Ben Jonson, including Face in *The Alchemist* and Voltore in *Volpone*. He was a very ambitious and well-known actor: even after his death it was assumed that audiences were familiar with his style of performance and how it contrasted with the other giants of the stage at that time, Richard Burbage and Edward Alleyn.[1]

Field also wrote two plays of his own and had a hand in writing at least six others. His comedy, *A Woman is a Weather-Cock*, was performed in 1609. It is a misogynistic piece peppered with such lines as 'an eel by the tail's held surer than a woman', and Field tried to redress the balance in his other independent play, *Amends for Ladies*, written two years later. *A Woman is a Weather-Cock* is scarcely a masterpiece: the characters do not behave consistently, and in the sub-plots in particular the writing has a grossness inspired by the murkiest corners of Jonsonian comedy: one grotesque family comprises Sir Innocent Ninny ('that little, old dried neat's tongue, that eel-skin'), his corpulent alcoholic wife ('methinks, he in his lady, should show like a needle in a bottle of hay') and his impotent son, who is somehow persuaded that he impregnated the less than subtly named Mistress Wagtail and should therefore marry her.

At least the main plot hangs together. The hero finds that the girl he loves is marrying another, but the ceremony is sabotaged by a bogus priest, and after a pseudo-revenge ritual in the final act, harmony is restored in Shakespearian fashion. Field achieves a moment of elo-quence, even depth of emotion, when the hero Scudmore soliloquizes about his unfaithful mistress:

> I never dreamt of lying with my mother,
> Nor wished my father's death, nor hated brother;
> Nor did betray trust, nor loved money better
> Than an accepted friend; no such base thought,
> Nor act unnatural, possessed this breast:
> Why am I thus rewarded? — women! women!
> He's mad by heaven, that thinks you anything
> But sensual monsters, and is never wise
> Nor good, but when he hates you, as I now.
> I'll not come near one; none of your base sex
> Shall know me from this time, for all your virtues
> Are like the buzzes growing in the fields,
> So weakly fastened there by nature's hand,
> That thus much wind blows all away at once.
> Ye fillers of the world with bastardy,
> Worse than diseases you are subject to,
> Know I do hate you all, will write against you,
> And fight against you; I will eat no meat
> Dressed by a woman old or young, nor sleep
> Upon a bed made by their still given hands;
> Yet once more must I see this feminine devil,
> When I will look her dead, speak her to hell.
> I'll watch my time, this day to do't, and then
> I'll be in love with death, and readier still
> His mortal stroke to take, than he to kill!

(*A Woman is a Weather-Cock, A New Comedy. As it was acted before the King in Whitehall. And divers times Privately at the White-Friars, By the Children of her Majesty's Revels*, London, published 1612, ii.1)

'Nathaniel Field A Celebrated Actor in Shakspears Plays', drawn by S. Harding, engraved W. N. Gardiner, after the anonymous portrait in Dulwich Picture Gallery. *By kind permission of the Garrick Club/Art Archive.*

BARTEN HOLYDAY (1593–1661)

The Gnat is the poor man's Revenge: He brings
Small strength; yet makes great noise, and shrewdly stings.
(Barten Holyday, *A Survey of the World*)[2]

Barten Holyday had a respectable career as a clergyman. He held benefices in Oxfordshire and was created chaplain to the king in 1642. It was said that 'had he not acted the vain man' he might have had a bishopric.[3] He was also a writer. *A Survey of the World in Ten Books*, published in the year he died, is a strange collection of epigrammatic heroic couplets, for example, 'Whole pits with Honey in Lithuania flow:/Huge Bears are Chok'd in it: Pleasure's a Foe!' While a student at Oxford he turned his hand to drama with a heavy-handed comedy about university studies, *Technogamia, or, The Marriage of the Arts*. Its début in front of students in 1617 was not a success, but four years later it was revived before James I and guests at Woodstock Castle. In the words of Anthony à Wood, the Oxford antiquary,

It being too grave for the king, and too scholastic for the auditors (or as some have said, that the actors having taken too much wine before they began), his majesty after two acts, offered several times to withdraw. At length, being persuaded by some of those who were near to him to have patience till it was ended, lest the young men should be discouraged, he sat down, though much against his will.[4]

King James I of England and VI of Scotland, oil by John Decritz, 1609. © *Crown copyright: UK Government Art Collection.*

The king's reaction is not in itself significant, as James had a reputation for walking out of plays. Nor is it surprising that this loose and undramatic piece failed to hold his attention, with its laboured puns, Latin quotations, and tedious discussions about emblematic figures such as 'Poeta', 'Logica' and 'Grammaticus'. On the other hand, since James disliked lawyers even more than he did the theatre, he might have enjoyed the scene attacking civil law:

Logicus goes off to consult Causidicus.

Log. Well, I'll to Causidicus, they say his house is here about, and I think this be it: ho, who's within?
Caus. Who's there?
Log. There's an answer indeed; when I ask who's within he asks who's without.

Enter Causidicus in a lawyer's gown, a laced ruff, a black hat, black suit, silk stockings, garters, roses, etc.

Caus. Yes, what would you have Sir?
Log. Have Sir! Nay, I have more already than I would have.
Caus. If you have any business, you may impart it to me.
Log. Business? Then I perceive you are all for business, you have but little entertainment, for a friend, well Sir, are you not a lawyer?
Caus. I may not deny my profession, Sir.
Log. If then you are a lawyer Sir, you are either a civil lawyer, or an uncivil. You must admit a division Sir, for you lawyers are equivocal, and therefore carefully to be distinguished before you be defined.
Caus. Sir, I must confess, I am not a civil lawyer, yet I trust not an uncivil.
Log. Nay, Sir, my division holds; I prove it; either you are a civil lawyer, or you are not a civil lawyer: but you confess you are not a civil lawyer: *ergo*, you are an uncivil lawyer.
Caus. Well then, Sir, if you would have it so, I am an uncivil lawyer.
Log. Marry Sir, I then fear you will scarce plead my cause well: for my complaint is against an uncivil fellow, and therefore I much suspect your uprightness: but yet since I cannot make choice, I must use you.

(*The King's Technogamia*, ii.3)

❧ *Popular songs*

THOMAS RAVENSCROFT (*c*.1592–*c*.1635)

The single most important figure in the preservation of the meagre repertoire of children's dramatic songs that have survived to the present day.

(Linda Phyllis Austern)[5]

Thomas Ravenscroft was a chorister at St Paul's Cathedral in 1598, which is consistent with his being a Pauline, and shortly afterwards became involved with the Children of Paul's, a company of child actors responding to the London audience's growing taste for plays interspersed with specially written songs performed by trained musicians. He wrote some of this music, probably also playing it and acting. By his own account, he took a Cambridge bachelor of music degree at the age of fourteen, which is just possible as it was awarded simply for a completed musical composition and required no systematic instruction or residence at the university. In 1609 he edited *Pammelia*, the earliest printed English collection of rounds and catches. Its anonymous contents range from sacred music to ballads, street cries and songs from plays. 'Hold thy peace, thou knave' from *Twelfth Night* is included, and a song about 'Servants out of service [...] going to the City to look for new' must have a theatrical origin.

Pammelia was intended to reform through art 'what pleasing tunes injurious time and ignorance had deformed'.[6] He published in 1614 the more ambitious *Brief Discourse of the True (but Neglected) Use of Charact'ring the Degrees*, a theoretical work illustrated by some of his own compositions. His high-minded aim was to rescue native music from those common performers who had 'brought it down from a chief liberal science, to the basest almost of mechanic functions', and restore it 'for the honour of our art, of ourselves and our country' to its former 'life, reputation, estimation, and honour'.[7] Much of the book is a confusing discussion of note lengths, but Ravenscroft also praises the ancient Greeks for giving their children a musical education in order to inculcate the virtues of modesty and honesty. He describes the link between music and love, a fashionable Renaissance idea that appealed to Shakespeare:

I have heard it said, that Love teaches a man music, who never before knew what pertained thereto, and the philosophers' three principal causes of music, 1. Dolour, 2. Joy, 3. Enthusiasm or ravishing of the spirit, are all found by him within Love's territory.

Ravenscroft contributed fifty-five settings to his *Whole Book of Psalms* (1621), among the most important psalters of its time, and a wide range of other compositions have survived. Highly regarded at the time, he is seen now as 'a man of great versatility, though of slender talents'.[8]

❧ *A poacher turned gamekeeper*

LIONEL CRANFIELD, FIRST EARL OF MIDDLESEX (1575–1645)

Lionel Cranfield wanted to make money. He left St Paul's at the age of fifteen to be apprenticed to a grocer and merchant who specialized in cloth, spices and silks. In 1601 he was warned, 'That worm covetousness gnaws you, by stretching it to the uttermost as all the world takes notice you do.' Before entering government service in 1613 he was prodigiously successful, quickly multiplying his wealth, but not always scrupulous in his methods. When one of his traders complained about inferior cloth, he advised misleading customers with better 'show' goods: 'My kersies [coarse woollen cloth] are neither of the principal best nor of the worst, but good vendible middle goods and such as will take the market if you take pains to sort them well and make choice of show kersies to my best advantage.' At one stage he gambled on pepper, and it paid off when there was a shortage of imports, although he had to pass off some wet pepper by mixing it with better stuff (as with his cloth) and used bribery to make sure of a profit. Another activity was selling guns so 'faulty in sight that no man will buy but that he will have them better cheap'. He also made substantial profits from money-lending and the purchase of crown land and licences to collect duty (customs farms).[9]

By 1613 Cranfield had amassed a very substantial fortune, estimated at £24,200, but difficult trading conditions now made royal money much more attractive, and he began to advise the crown on how to improve its financial standing, in the process burning his boats as a private trader by giving a frank insider's view of London

Lionel Cranfield, first Earl of Middlesex, engraving after Daniel Mytens's painting. *Archive Photos/Getty Images.*

dramatic contrast to his earlier life, he went on to boast of his own honesty:

I bought my cloth of gold, silver and tissues, my velvets, satins, damasks and taffetas, and my hangings, carpets and all other things of value to the merchants at the first and best hand with ready money and charged His Majesty with no other prices than I paid them. And by that course damned the detestable names of wardrobe prices.[10]

These and other reforms made Cranfield enemies, especially as his wealth grew prodigiously during the period when he pressed for retrenchment: it is reckoned that he doubled his income when he became master of the wardrobe. This did not stop him suggesting to customs farmers and beneficiaries of royal land grants that they should renounce their profits for one year 'by way of thankfulness'. In 1621 he was elevated to the peerage as Baron Cranfield, and the following year he became the first Earl of Middlesex — for a time his campaign against waste served him well, and he was made lord treasurer for two and a half years, during which period the crown's finances probably worsened but Cranfield's own income grew to the astonishing figure of between £25,000 and £28,000 per annum.[11] However, when the climate in 1624 turned in favour of war with Spain, something Cranfield had always opposed, his enemies closed in, and he was impeached on a less than convincing charge of corruption and accepting bribes. There was a substantial fine and other losses, but he did not die in poverty.

mercantile practices. Over the following decade his experience of cheating and shady methods was invaluable. He successfully reduced extravagance in the royal household and the navy, and when in 1618 he became master of the wardrobe, savings again resulted: 'How can it be possible,' he wrote, 'to make a right price for any goods […] when the master of the wardrobe, his deputy and tradesmen agree together and share the overplus of the price.' In

🦎 *Disgraced high master*

ALEXANDER GILL, THE YOUNGER (1596–1642?)

Alexander Gill was violent in word and deed. In 1622 he became under-usher of St Paul's, where his father was high master. He had a talent for Latin verse, which in November 1623 was displayed by a vindictive poem glorifying in the collapse of a secret Catholic chapel in Blackfriars, killing more than ninety worshippers. (William Gouge, Old Pauline and puritan — see next entry — preached a sermon on this event at St Ann, Blackfriars the following week.) He unwisely traded insults with the playwright Ben Jonson, who had criticized his father in *Time Vindicated*. Gill advised him to return to bricklaying.

He also seems to have been in the habit of hurling abuse at royalty. In 1628 Gill was visiting Oxford and drinking with friends in the cellars of Trinity College, when he pronounced Charles I only fit for a Cheapside shop and sug-

gested that both King James I and his recently murdered favourite, the Duke of Buckingham, were in Hell. These remarks reached Gill's godfather William Laud, bishop of London. Not only that: various 'libels and letters' by Gill were found during a search of his friend William Pickering's rooms at Trinity, including some explicit thoughts on the relationship between James and Buckingham. Pupils at St Paul's saw Gill taken away to be interrogated. He went before the Star Chamber and was sentenced to a large fine, the loss of both ears and degrading from his degrees and religious ministry. Partly by 'the tears of the poor old Doctor, his father, and supplication on his knees to his Majesty',[12] a royal pardon was eventually granted, but he probably spent two years in prison and was dismissed from his teaching post (although he seems to have continued teaching unofficially at St Paul's).[13]

Gill set about restoring his standing by sending poems with fulsome dedications to Charles I, Laud and other influential people. He also sent John Milton (see later entry) a copy of an obscene wedding poem he had written. Then, remarkably, he was appointed high master of St Paul's just ten days after his father's death. Of course he was soon in trouble, first with the Court of Assistants governing the school for 'malapert words' and letting out rooms in the schoolhouse, and then more dramatically for accusing a boy, John Bennett, of theft, 'lifting him up by the jaws and other tyrannous using of him and beating of him with a cane and kicking him up and down the school'. During lengthy argument over this occurrence, Gill also stood accused of eighteen days' absence without leave and being discovered by some mercers 'so disguised [by drink] that they held him not fit to teach children'. He was given notice but petitioned the king, claiming that the Mercers were using the 'unjust complaint of a lying thieving boy' as an excuse for dismissing him because he had discovered that a great part of the school revenues were being misapplied. Charles I passed this on to Laud, now archbishop of Canterbury, who tried in vain to convince the Mercers that Gill's bishop would have to endorse any decision to dismiss him. Eventually, Gill agreed to go and was granted a £25 annuity which he lost eighteen months later for using 'wild expressions' against a mercer. It seems that he went on to become headmaster

Archbishop William Laud, oil by Sir Anthony Van Dyck, 1635–7. Laud was godfather of Alexander Gill. *Fitzwilliam Museum, Cambridge.*

of Oakham School in Rutland for a short time before his death.[14]

In his history of St Paul's, Mead sees behind Gill's dismissal a contest for authority over the school between Archbishop Laud and the Mercers.[15] It is certainly true that Gill's resignation in January 1641 followed quickly the Long Parliament's imprisonment of the anti-puritan Laud.

❧ The preacher of the day

WILLIAM GOUGE (1575–1653)

Contrary are the furious, spiteful actions of many unkind husbands whose favours are buffets, blows, strokes, and stripes: wherein they are worse than the venomous viper.

(William Gouge, *Of Domestical Duties*, 1622)[16]

In 1608 William Gouge was appointed to St Ann, Blackfriars, where he preached twice-weekly for thirty-five years, attracting huge crowds. Visitors to the capital 'thought not their business fully ended, unless they had been at Blackfriars Lecture'.[17] Such was his power as a preacher that on Sundays many neighbours adjourned after the service to his house 'where he repeated his sermons after so familiar a manner, that many have professed that they were much more benefited by them in that his repetition, then they were in the first hearing of them'. After a few years the church had to be doubled in size to accommodate swelling congregations.

Gouge had from his days as a scholar and fellow at King's College, Cambridge, the reputation of being an arch-puritan whose life was severely disciplined. He was not afraid of expressing his views and spent some weeks in prison when King James took exception to a work he collaborated on, which concluded that if the Jewish race converted to Christianity it would be given sovereignty over the rest of the world.[18]

Gouge had been obliged to resign his Cambridge fellowship when on the orders of his father he married a seventeen-year-old orphan. He immediately handed over all family affairs to his young wife's management, and by all accounts the marriage was an exemplary one. In 1622 he wrote his most-enduring book, *Of Domestical Duties*. Considering his high religious principles, it is a surprisingly tolerant work, balanced and understanding in its judgments on how members of family and servants should behave.

Of the vices in children:

Pride, when children scorn to give the title of *Father,* or *Mother,* to their parents. This is the mind of many who have gotten more wealth or honour, than ever their parents had. *Loquacity,* and too much importunity, or rather impudence in speech, when children having to do with their parents, can never have done (as we speak) but must needs urge matters to the very uttermost. Many parents are oft much provoked hereby.

Stoutness, when children answer their parents as if they were their equals: giving word for word. It doth as ill become children to *answer again,* as servants.

Indiscretion, when children have no respect to any time, business, or temper, of their parents in speaking to them, and so, much provoke them. It is laid down as a caveat to parents that they *provoke not their children to wrath.* How much more must children observe that caveat?

Stubbornness, when children pout, lour, swell, and give no answer at all to their parents. This is too common a fault in children, and many parents are much offended and grieved thereat.

(*Of Domestical Duties,* pp. 434–35)

❧ *The nature of God*

NATHANIEL CULVERWELL (*bap.*1619, *d.*1651)
RICHARD CUMBERLAND (1632–1718)

The whole circulation of the blood, and every thing instrumental thereto, as the muscular force of the heart, and the individual contrivance of the valves in the veins, is at the same time subservient to the private nourishment of the individual and to the public good by propagating the species, whilst it sends off the material of the seed to the spermatic vessels.

(Richard Cumberland)[19]

These two Old Paulines lived in an age of deep religious controversy and responded by writing books to show that reason and religion belonged together and that both were reflected in the natural world.

Information about Nathaniel Culverwell is scanty, but we know that he was a fellow of Emmanuel College, Cambridge. There he mixed with a group of scholars now known as the Cambridge Platonists, many of whose ideas he shared, although he was the only one to base ethics on the laws of nature. His major work, *An Elegant and Learned Discourse of the Light of Nature,* was published after his death from papers prepared in the final years of his life.[20]

Culverwell's target was those who tried to demonstrate the 'miserable weakness of man's understanding'.[21] He used the Cambridge Platonists' favourite metaphor: human reason is 'the Candle of the Lord' with which man is born. Equipped with this light, we are able to appreciate and learn from the natural world. Man brings no knowledge into the world — in that sense Culverwell is not a Platonist — but 'sparks [...] fly from the variety of objects to the understanding, the mind, that catches them all, and cherishes them, and blows them, and thus the candle of knowledge is lighted'.[22] The laws of nature bubble forth from God and are there for good men everywhere, irrespective of religion: good men will hear the voice of pure reason, but the wicked 'sometimes will not hear it though it comes to them in thunder, nor take the least notice of it though it should flash out in lightning'. For Culverwell goodness and pleasure go together. The law of reason 'encourages men in obedience with a smile, it chides them and frowns them out of wickedness'.[23] However, his explanation of why spiritual pleasures are superior to physical ones is very strained:

The purer arts, the nobler sciences, have most pleasure annexed to them; whereas mechanical arts are more sordid and contemptible, being conversant about sensitive and corporeal objects [....] The ticklings of fancy are more delightful than the touches of sense [....] Catullus might easily find more sweetness in one of his epigrams, than in the lips of a Lesbia.*

In the end he is forced to conclude that man's light of reason, this Candle of the Lord, will only achieve happiness when after death it is transformed into 'a star that may drink in everlasting light and influence from its original and fountain light'.[24]

Richard Cumberland was at school with Samuel Pepys (see next entry), and indeed Pepys wanted his sister to marry him. At Cambridge, where it is said that he

---

* Much of the Roman poet Catullus's erotic verse was inspired by a woman he named 'Lesbia.'

The same reciprocal principle applies to society:

It is well known by the experience of all men that the powers of any single person, in respect of that happiness, of which from without he is both capable and stands in need, are so small, that he wants the assistance both of many things and persons to lead his life happily. Everyone can nevertheless afford many things for the use of others, which he himself does not need at all, and which therefore can be of no use to him. But seeing we are certain, from the known limit of our powers, that we cannot compel those whose aids we want [...] to cooperate with us in the procuring of our own happiness; the only method we have left to obtain this end, is to procure their good will by making a tender to them of our service, and by a faithful performance.

Cumberland's views look forward to utilitarianism and are surprisingly secular in approach, but he was clear that the laws of nature belonged to God and remained immutable simply because God would not contradict his own perfection. He went on to write other scholarly and religious works. In 1691 he became bishop of Peterborough.

Title page of Nathaniel Culverwell's Discourse, *privately printed 1661. © St Paul's School.*

Richard Cumberland, engraving by John Smith after Thomas Murray's oil painting. © *St Paul's School.*

invented the first mechanical model of the planets, he became particularly interested in mathematics and physics. His work on the laws of nature, *De Legibus Naturae Disquisitio Philosophica* (1672), went beyond Culverwell to argue that God's natural law could be discovered through experimental and theoretical science. He was writing in reaction to Hobbes's *Leviathan* (1651), which described man's life in a state of nature as 'solitary, poor, nasty, brutish, and short' and argued that moral laws could only be imposed by the magistrate.[25] Cumberland wanted to link the good of the individual with the good of the whole community.[26] His ideas evolved as he watched the Royal Society's experiments with an air pump:*

The air, which we have drawn into our lungs, we immediately breathe back again; or, if a small portion thereof be retained for some little time, for the refreshing of our blood and vital spirits, it is afterwards, along with the blood itself and vital spirits, as it were, with interest, restored by insensible perspiration to the common mass of the air; this reciprocal natural motion [...] thus resembles gratitude, and points out its necessity for the good of the whole.[27]

---

* Robert Boyle had presented his first vacuum pump to the Royal Society. Experiments were carried out to discover how much air animals needed for survival.

SAMUEL PEPYS (1633–1703)

Among others, my schoolfellow, Mr Christmas. Where very merry.[28]

Old Paulines and St Paul's School punctuate Samuel Pepys's life. During his tenure (1684–86) as president of the Royal Society, an honour reflecting his long administrative experience in the Admiralty as much as his enthusiasm for science, Pepys approved Old Pauline Edmond Halley's publication of Newton's *Principia Mathematica* (see later entry). His cousin Barbara married High Master Thomas Gale, with whom Pepys corresponded about ship-building.[29] He attended apposition at the school on more than one occasion, gave it books before and after the great fire, and was embarrassed to see High Master Samuel Cromleholme drunk. Most striking though is how many of his old schoolfellows appear in the pages of his diary.

Pepys's journal ran from 1 January 1660 until 31 May 1669, when he abandoned it because of deteriorating eyesight, which subsequently improved.

Pauline preachers got a mixed reception. Jonathan Radcliffe (born *c.*1635) was expected to be poor: on the king's birthday in 1661 he went to Walthamstow and 'heard Mr Ratcliffe [sic] (my former schoolfellow at Paul's, who is yet a mere boy) preach[…] he reads all, and his sermon very simple — but I looked for no better.'[30] Pepys heard

Samuel Pepys, oil by Sir Godfrey Kneller, 1689. Pepys left the Admiralty, where he had been secretary, in February 1689 after his patron, James II, was driven into exile by the 'Glorious Revolution' of 1688. © *National Maritime Museum, Greenwich, London.*

the bishop of Norwich, father of school-friend Edward Reynolds (1629–98) 'begin a very plain sermon' (presumably Pepys did not stay to the end).[31] Even Richard Meggott (*c.*1632–1692), whose 'commanding elocution' was eulogized at his funeral, failed to hold Pepys's attention on Christmas day 1664: 'I heard a good sermon of one that I remember was at Paul's with me, his name Maggett [sic]. And very great store of fine women there is in this church, more than I know anywhere else about us.'[32] On the other hand, he was favourably surprised at St Martin, Outwich: 'There I find in the pulpit Elborough [Robert Elborough (born *c.*1633)] my old schoolfellow and a simple rogue; and yet I find preaching a very good sermon, and in as right a parson-like manner, and in good manner too, as I have heard anybody; and the church very full — which is a surprising consideration.'[33]

Richard Cumberland (1632–1718) the philosopher (see last entry) became Pepys's preferred husband for his sister. Their fathers had been neighbours and fellow tailors when the two were at school, and Pepys became the dedicatee of Cumberland's book, *An Essay toward the recovery of Jewish Weights and Measures* (1686): 'A most excellent person he is as any I know, and one that I am sorry should be lost and buried in a little country town, and would be glad to remove him thence; and the truth is, if he would accept of my sister's fortune, I should give £100 more with him than to a man able to settle her four times as much as I fear he is able to do.' In fact she decided on Mr Jackson, 'a plain young man […] of no education nor discourse'. Pepys thought 'this plain fellow' good enough for his sister but for himself thought he would 'have no pleasure nor content in him, as if he had been a man of breeding and parts like Cumberland'.[34]

Pepys's meeting with Christmas (dates unknown) while visiting Sir William Batten, who 'lives like a prince', brought back guilty memories: 'Here dined with us two or three more country gentlemen; among the rest, Mr Christmas my old schoolfellow, with whom I had much talk. He did remember that I was a great roundhead when I was a boy, and I was much afeared that he would have remembered the words that I said the day that the king was beheaded (that were I to preach upon him, my text should be: "The memory of the wicked shall rot"); but I found afterward that he did go away from school before that time.'[35]

There was the occasion when he visited the school for apposition and took an alcoholic lunch break with two other Old Paulines, Benjamin Pulleyn (*c.*1632–90) and Edward Baines (dates unknown): 'Thence by and by with Mr Pullen [sic] and Baines (a great nonconformist) with several other of my old acquaintance to the Nag's Head Tavern and there did give them a bottle of sack; and away again and I to the school and up to hear the upper form examined.'[36]

Most evocative is a set of entries on Jack Cole, the only information known about this Old Pauline. Pepys first renewed his acquaintance in 1662: 'Met with Jack Cole in Fleet Street, and he and I went into his cousin Mary Cole's (whom I never saw since she was married) and drank a pint of wine, and much good discourse. I find him a little conceited, but he hath good things in him and a man may know the temper of the City by him, he being of a general conversation and can tell how matters go; and upon that score, I will encourage his acquaintance.' A year later Pepys discerned more pedantry in Cole but decided to keep in touch because 'he knows much of the temper of the City'. Then in July 1664 he makes a distressing visit to Pepys, 'his errand, in short, to tell me that he is giving over his trade. He can do no good in it, and will turn what he hath into money and go to sea — his father being dead and leaving him little, if anything. This I was sorry to hear, he being a man of good parts, but I fear debauched.' A year later he was dead of consumption, and Pepys 'mightily troubled in my sleep all night with dreams of Jack Cole my old schoolfellow, lately dead, who was born at the same time with me, and we reckoned our fortunes pretty equal. God fit me for his condition'.[37]

❧ *The greatest of Colet's Children*

JOHN MILTON (1608–74)

> O shame to men! Devil with devil damned
> Firm concord holds, men only disagree
> Of creatures rational, thought under hope
> Of heavenly grace; and God proclaiming peace,
> Yet live in hatred, enmity, and strife
> Among themselves, and levy cruel wars,
> Wasting the earth, each other to destroy.
>
> (*Paradise Lost*)[38]

John Milton's great epic about Satan's temptation of Adam and Eve, *Paradise Lost,* probably took its final form between 1658 and 1663. By this time he was completely blind. He worked on the poem in the winter months, composing lines during the night and on rising at four in the morning, when he 'wanted to be milked' by his amanuensis. Milton had an outstanding memory, but the diarist Aubrey believed 'that his excellent method of thinking and disposing did much to help'.[39] He would dictate about forty lines a day, preferring to sit with one leg thrown over the arm of his chair.

These were dangerous times for Milton. He described his situation in the opening lines of book seven:

> On evil days though fall'n, and evil tongues;
> In darkness, and with dangers compassed round,
> And solitude.[40]

On 29 May 1660 Charles II entered London triumphantly after years of exile during the civil war and Commonwealth. Milton was an outspoken enemy of the Stuart monarchy. While Charles I was being tried in Westminster Hall in January 1649, he wrote *The Tenure of Kings and Magistrates*, which set out to prove 'that it is lawful […] for any, who have the power, to call to account a tyrant or wicked king, and after due conviction, to depose, and put him to death'. The pamphlet was published on 13 February, two weeks after Charles's execution. A month later the council of state appointed Milton Latin secretary at an annual salary of £288 13s. 6½d., a post he held until 1660. He was now official apologist for the republic and wrote widely circulated tracts defending it and Cromwell against royalist attacks from the continent. Then, in the final days of the Commonwealth, he dictated two editions of *The Ready and Easy Way* (February and April 1660), hoping to arrest the headlong rush of a 'misguided and abused multitude' into the bondage of a restored monarchy.

Surprisingly, Milton escaped a death sentence at the

The walls of Ludgate Gaol falling during the great fire of London, aquatint by Jan Griffier, 1646–1718, published William Birch, 1792. In his revised version, published in 1720, of John Stow's Survey of London (1598), Old Pauline John Strype (1643–1737) described how the fire 'propagated itself so far before day, and with such violence, that it bred a kind of distraction and stupidity in the inhabitants and neighbours near it'. *Guildhall Library, City of London.*

'Satan with his angels in the burning lake, thunderstruck and astonished', illustration by John Baptiste de Medina, engraved M. Burgesse. John Milton, *Paradise Lost*, first illustrated edition, 1688. *Ken Lawson. © St Paul's School.*

Restoration, perhaps because it was felt that God had punished him by striking him blind in 1649 as he wrote the second word of *Eikonoklastēs* ('image-breaker'), a pamphlet which compared serving the king to idolatry. Even so, copies of his books were burned by the public executioner, he spent some weeks imprisoned in the Tower of London and probably lost all his savings.

Milton's first portrait of Satan was in a Latin mini-epic about the gunpowder plot, *In Quintum Novembris*, which he wrote as a student at Cambridge, probably for a college feast.[41] After his return in 1639 from a grand tour of Italy, he outlined a tragic drama about the fall of Adam and Eve. His purpose in *Paradise Lost* was even larger, to use the highest form of poetic expression, classical epic, for 'Things unattempted yet in prose or rhyme'. At its centre is the familiar story of the fall, but its scope is truly cosmic, from the beginning of the universe to the end of time. It embraces the classics, the Bible and seventeenth-century learning. The language of the poem, its 'grand style', is extraordinarily powerful and subtle.

Paradise Lost was published in autumn 1667, a suitably apocalyptic moment after the great plague and fire of London. It is said that courtier and poet Sir John Denham came 'into the House [of Commons] one Morning with a Sheet Wet from the Press, in his Hand' exclaiming that it was 'Part of the Noblest Poem that ever was Wrote in Any Language, or Any Age'.[42] John Dryden obtained Milton's permission to 'tagge his verses' and put on a rhymed stage version at the new Theatre Royal in Drury Lane in 1674 just after its opening.[43] This rendering was printed in 1677 and easily outsold Milton's original, which attracted wide notice only when the sumptuous illustrated fourth edition was published in 1688.

Dryden turned the key figure of Satan into a portrait of Oliver Cromwell, whose execution of Charles I was echoed by Satan's failed attempt to overthrow God, the king of Heaven. This is a royalist misreading, but the poem is certainly political. Milton declared the purpose of his great argument was to 'assert Eternal Providence,/And justify the ways of God to men', and from the start readers argued over his reaction to a revolution he believed was God's will and yet had failed.[44] Some thought he had repented of his republicanism; others that he wrote Satan with such gusto because he was still a rebel at heart.[45]

Paradise Lost fascinated the Romantics. William Blake called Milton 'a true poet and of the Devil's party without knowing it',[46] the monster in Mary Shelley's *Frankenstein* read his creator's copy of the poem and compared his own wretched state to that of Adam. On the novel's title page are three lines spoken by Adam after the fall:

Did I request thee, Maker, from my clay
To mould me man? Did I solicit thee
From darkness to promote me?[47]

In the twentieth century critical voices on the poem were many and diverse. F. R. Leavis notoriously accused Milton of 'cultivating [...] complete and systematic [...]

callousness to the intrinsic nature of English'.[48] The American critic Stanley Fish argued ingeniously that readers of the poem are repeatedly seduced by Satan's rhetoric, just as Eve was by the serpent, and Milton keeps intervening to put them back on the right track.[49] In the trilogy *His Dark Materials* (1995–2000) Philip Pullman set out to produce a version of *Paradise Lost* for teenagers.

Milton's other work tends to be cast into shadow by his great epic, but of course there is much more. He saw in the biblical story of Samson an individual empowered by God to overthrow tyrannical rulers by pulling down the pillars of their temple and in 1671 published *Samson Agonistes,* his version of Greek tragedy, although it may have been written much earlier and was not intended for performance. He wrote tracts attacking the power of bishops, in favour of a free press and seeking a more liberal attitude to divorce. In early life he wrote Latin verses, the finest and last of these being an epitaph for his schoolfriend Charles Diodati (1609/10–38). His innovative court masque *Comus* was performed at Ludlow Castle in 1634. *Paradise Lost* was followed by *Paradise Regained* (published 1671), a four-book poem about the temptations of Jesus in the wilderness.

Among Milton's shorter English poems is the elegy *Lycidas*, commemorating the drowning in 1637 of Edward King, his near contemporary at Christ's College, Cambridge. The catalogue of the quatercentennial exhibition *Living at This Hour* at Cambridge University Library observed, 'Many regard [it] as the finest short poem in English, just as *Paradise Lost* is widely considered the greatest long poem.'

❧ *Latin poet, flatterer and turncoat*

PAYNE FISHER (1615/16–93)

Notwithstanding the poverty of his career, and his want of principles, Fisher [...] was a man of considerable attainments, and excellent talent for poetry.

(Robert Bell)[50]

Payne Fisher, or Pagani/Fitzpaganus Piscatoris, is almost forgotten now because he worked in Latin, and we see him through the partial eyes of seventeenth-century antiquary Anthony à Wood. He left school to be educated first at Oxford and then at Cambridge, but 'having a rambling head he threw off his gown' and went into military service.[51] He was on the losing royalist side at Marston Moor (1644), taken prisoner and put in Newgate gaol, where he worked on his poems about military events and great men of the day, converting to the parliamentarians, no doubt to secure his release. Wood observes that Fisher

'favoured by his pen the successful rebellion, and, as a true time-server (incident to most poets) ingratiated himself so much with the great men then in power, that he did homage to, and became at length poet laureate (or as he himself used to say, scribbler) to Oliver, the Protector of England'. Marston Moor was now a great victory and Cromwell the subject of several eulogies: 'With safe and gentle gales you change the Scene,/And make a State where Monarchy hath been.'[52] He seems to have received scanty recognition for such poetic flattery and at the Restoration quickly rediscovered his royalist principles.

'The death of Sir William Lambton at the battle of Marston Moor', oil by Richard Ansdell, 1842. A scene from the battle viewed through Victorian eyes. Payne Fisher fought on the royalist side, was taken prisoner and then turned parliamentarian to secure his release.
Photograph reproduced by kind permission of the Harris Museum and Art Gallery, Preston.

Much of Fisher's work was in effect poetic begging. 'His usual way when he had written and printed a book,' Wood relates, 'was to write many dedication papers to be put before them as occasion served, or his necessities required [...] and took all occasions to write epitaphs or sepulchral eulogies, purposely to present them to the sons, grandsons, and other relations of the party deceased, mostly for lucre's sake, and partly out of private ambition.' He turned from poetry to heraldic volumes with the same purpose of making money out of presentation copies. Pepys (see earlier entry) was handed by Fisher 'a book in praise of the king of France with my arms and a dedication to me, very handsome' — a fortnight later he was woken early in the morning with a message from the poet, begging for money.[53]

Despite these efforts, Fisher's finances were so precarious, especially after the Restoration, that he spent much of his time in the Fleet debtors' prison. His dedications brought him contempt more often than reward, and when he did have money he wasted it. He visited Oxford during the protectorate but 'a great part of the undergraduates [...] having received a sufficient character of the vain and conceited humour of the author, as being little better than a braggadocio, they did so much disturb him by humming, hissing, stamping, grinning, etc. that he was deterred from coming a second time'.

Witchcraft

JOHN WAGSTAFFE (1633–77)

He is described as a crooked, shrivelled little man, of a most despicable appearance. This circumstance, together with his writings against the popular belief in witchcraft, led his academical associates to accuse him, some of them in sport, but others with grave suspicion, of being a wizard.

(Charles Wentworth Upham, *Lectures on Witchcraft*)[54]

John Wagstaffe's most famous book, *The Question of Witchcraft Debated* (1669), launched a spirited and satirical attack on the widely held belief in witches. He denied any genuine scriptural basis for witchcraft; it was a myth orig-inating in pagan fables and exploited by the clergy for their own crooked purposes. He poured scorn on Catholic inquisitors:

How grossly the opinion of witchcraft hath been made to serve the corrupt ends and interests of men appears from nothing more than the strange examinations of inquisitors, so strange, that 'tis to me a wonder, if the inquisitors can hold their countenances and forbear from laughing at one another. This I am sure of, that [...] the confessions which they have extorted from some do savour of the Pontifical rack, and seem to have been dictated unto these miserable wretches by the very inquisitors themselves, with a design to advance the reputation of [...] their own church.[55]

Because men had fear implanted by nature as the strongest of their passions, he argued, echoing the ideas recently published in Hobbes's *Leviathan* (1651), it was only to be expected that their minds would create strange apparitions. He dismissed as mere coincidence claims that accidents happened to those under a curse and refused to accept the more objective approach to evidence increasingly valued in the late seventeenth century: 'It is far more easy, and far more rational to believe, that witnesses are liars and perjured persons, than it is to believe, that an old woman can turn herself, or anybody else, into a cat.'

There were fierce rebuttals of the book when it first appeared, so much so that he quickly brought out an expanded second edition, rejecting the accusation that he was an atheist. One writer did spring to his defence in *The Doctrine of Devils* (1676), declaring Wagstaffe's performance 'a judicious book, that contains more good reason,

true religion, and right Christianity, than all those lumps and cartloads of luggage, that hath been fardled up, by all the faggoters of demonologistical wintertales, and witch-craftical legendaries, since they first began to foul clean paper'.[56]

Nothing is known about his few remaining years.

Anthony à Wood relates, 'He died in a manner distracted, occasioned by a deep conceit of his own parts, and by a continual bibbing of strong and high-tasted liquors.'[57]

An execution of four witches, engraving, seventeenth century. *Time & Life Pictures/Getty Images.*

❧ *Mathematics of the universe*

EDMOND HALLEY (1656–1742)

He went to Paul's School, to Dr Gale: while he was there, he was very perfect in the celestial globes, insomuch that I heard Mr Moxon (the globe-maker) say that if a star were misplaced he would presently find it. He studied geometry, and at sixteen could make a dial, and then, he said, thought himself a brave fellow.

(John Aubrey, *Brief Lives*)[58]

Edmond Halley is a household name simply because of the comet he observed in 1682 and correctly forecast would reappear at Christmas 1758. As this would be after his death, Halley asked later astronomers to acknowledge that the comet's return was first predicted 'by an Englishman', but did not predict how it would hide his many other scientific achievements.[59] He has been called 'one of the virtuosi who changed our understanding of the world around us'.[60]

Despite a school career interrupted by St Paul's destruction in the great fire of London (it reopened in 1671), Halley was studying at Queen's College, Oxford, at the age of sixteen, accompanied by 'a curious apparatus of instruments, purchased by his father, who spared no expense to

encourage his son's genius'.[61] In his final year as a student (Halley left university without taking a degree, as was quite common then) this 'talented young man from Oxford' published papers on planetary orbits, sunspots and the moon's occultation of Mars.[62] When he was just twenty and with the support of Charles II, the East India Company sponsored Halley to travel to St Helena and study stars from the southern hemisphere. His *Catalogus stellarum australium*, published in 1679, was not superseded for fifty years.

In late 1680 he set off for a European tour with fellow Old Pauline Robert Nelson (1656–1715), known now for his *Companion for the Festivals and Fasts of the Church of England* (1704). The tour's highlight was observing a

A salvage operation on the sea bed using Edmond Halley's diving bell, March 1752, engraved for *Universal Magazine. MPI/Getty Images.*

and paid for it himself. Not only that: Halley's observations of the 1680 comet in France were key to part three of the *Principia.* Halley even provided a Latin ode in praise of Newton to preface the book. Halley said he was the Ulysses to Newton's Achilles.[†] Newton in his turn acknowledged his own debt at the beginning of the *Principia*: 'In the publication of this work, the most acute and universally learned Mr Edmond Halley not only assisted me with his pains in correcting the press and taking care of the schemes, but it was to his solicitations that its becoming public is owing.'[64]

Halley was elected clerk to the Royal Society in 1686 and presented many papers on an extraordinary range of topics. He had a facility for applying science to other areas of learning, used tidal records to calculate where Julius Caesar landed in Britain and suggested that a comet colliding with the earth might have caused Noah's Flood. He worked out tables to calculate expectation of life and determine the cost of life insurance: actuaries continue to use tables in this form. He devised an improved diving bell (and invented a diving suit) to salvage a cargo of ivory and gold lost off the Sussex coast. Halley went down in the bell himself and while he was there made observations of light below sea level which Newton used in his *Opticks.* There were learned mathematical presentations and work on thermometers and rainbows. Most significantly, he built on Newton's *Principia* to calculate the elliptical orbits of twenty-four comets and predict the return of the comet now bearing his name.

More voyaging followed in 1698. Just as in his youth Charles II had secured Halley's excursion to St Helena, so now he set sail for the Atlantic in the *Paramore,* a boat specially built for him by command of Queen Mary, with instructions from the Admiralty to 'improve the knowledge of the longitude and variations of the compass'.[65] The charts he produced showing magnetic variation are still important today. Another voyage in this boat led to a long-valued chart of tides in the English Channel.

High academic office came surprisingly late, but Halley was appointed Savilian professor of geometry at Oxford in 1704. At the age of sixty-nine he became the country's second astronomer royal. One final posthumous consequence of Halley's studies had to wait until 1769: his work on the transit of Venus and where it could be best observed in that year led to Cook's voyages of discovery.

brilliant comet (not the one that would bear Halley's name) with Cassini, director of the Paris observatory. It was comets that first brought Halley and Newton together on his return to England early in 1682, and led to his most momentous achievement.

Halley had been elected a fellow of the Royal Society ('a college for the promoting of physic-mathematical experimental learning') when he was twenty-two.[63] One evening in January 1684 he was conversing with the philosopher Robert Hooke and Sir Christopher Wren after a society meeting about the mathematics of planetary orbits: the outcome was a consultation with Newton in Cambridge.[*] This in turn led to Newton returning to some earlier work and writing the *Philosophiae naturalis principia mathematica,* among the most important works of mathematical science ever produced. It was Halley who realized the significance of Newton's book and drew it to the attention of the Royal Society's president, Samuel Pepys (see earlier entry). When the Society agreed to its publication, it was Halley who looked after the printing

* The specific question was whether orbits of the planets were under an inverse square law of attraction to the sun.

† Ulysses was instrumental in recruiting Achilles before the Trojan War.

❧ *Beetles and glow-worms*

BENJAMIN ALLEN (1663–1738)

eruditissimus et ingeniosissimus amicus noster
(John Ray)[66]

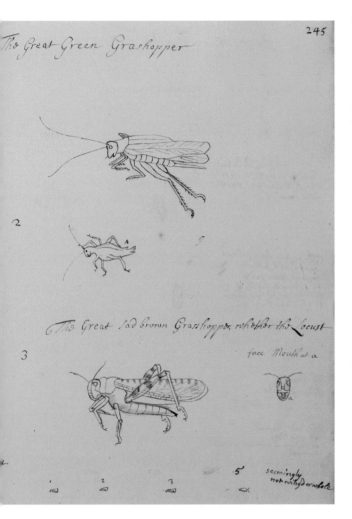

Benjamin Allen had a large medical practice in Braintree, Essex, but he was also one of the country's first beetle specialists. From eminent naturalist John Ray, who lived nearby, there is an account of Allen's discovering the male glow-worm in 1692:

I doubt not but that they are everywhere to be found, being nothing else but a kind of long-bodied beetle […] The reason why I mention this is because this gentleman, meeting with this beetle and finding by strict observations that the body of it answered exactly in figure to that of the creeping glow-worm, suspected it to be the male glow-worm; and, having some creeping glow-worms by him, put this animal into a box with one of them; which after some short time, coupled with it.[67]

Despite 'the fact that he never learnt to write intelligible English',[68] Allen published a minutely detailed account of his work on the death watch beetle, which he proudly showed 'to Mr Ray while it was yet alive and did beat'.[69] Towards the end of his life he began a commonplace book; it is filled with medical remedies, the ingredients including millipedes and sheep, horse and peacock dung: it also contains several hundred pen sketches of insects.

Written on Allen's tomb in Black Notley churchyard is the legend, 'As to his character, it may suffice to say that his learning, industry and integrity engaged the attention of the judicious and discerning part of mankind.'[70]

A page of grasshoppers from Benjamin Allen's commonplace book. Benjamin Allen Papers, MS0036/2, RCSEng Library.
Photograph reproduced by kind permission of the Royal College of Surgeons.

❧ *'The Hanging Judge'*

GEORGE JEFFREYS, FIRST BARON JEFFREYS (1645–89)

Judge Jeffreys […] was one of the most extraordinary specimens of ruffianism that the world ever produced; and if history — like Madame Tussaud — were to get up a chamber of horrors, Judge Jeffreys would certainly take his place in it by the side of Danton, Sawney Bean, Marat, Mrs Brownrigg and Robespierre.*

(*The Comic History of England*)[71]

George Jeffreys might have been remembered for his exceptional legal career. The historian Montgomery Hyde wrote:

His rise in the legal firmament can only be described as meteoric. By birth a Welshman of good family, he became common serjeant of London at the age of twenty-six, recorder of the City in his thirty-fourth year, lord chief justice of

England at thirty-eight and lord chancellor when he was forty; he remains the youngest occupant of the woolsack in history. He figured either as counsel or judge in almost every state trial of importance during the period.[72]

---

* Sawney Bean was a sixteenth-century Scottish mass murderer and cannibal, probably fictional. Mrs Brownrigg was executed in 1767 for torturing her female apprentices to death. Both appear in *The Newgate Calendar* (see entry on John Villette, Eighteenth Century.)

George Jeffreys as lord chief justice, engraving after Sir Godfrey Kneller's painting. This was published in London in 1694, five years after Jeffreys's death. © *St Paul's School.*

with four other justices, was to try 2,600 rebels alongside routine assize business. Some of them confessed, it seems on the understanding that they would be spared death penalties, but that still left 1,381 found guilty of treason and sentenced to death, although most of these were in the event transported, with 160–70 actually hanged.

By the standards of the day, it was a fair outcome. In any case, it was up to James II to exercise his royal prerogative and restrict the death penalty to a few ringleaders. Instead of this, he appeared openly delighted by the vast number of death sentences (too many for the hangman to cope with), and Jeffreys was to say on his death bed that he acted 'by express orders, and [...] was not half bloody enough for the prince who sent him thither'.[76] Why then has his name been blackened?

Jeffreys certainly had a reputation for being highhanded and aggressive in court, and he was seriously ill with a painful kidney stone throughout the assize, which did not help his temper. His first judgement in the 'Bloody Assize', condemning to death an elderly widow for sheltering a few rebels after their defeat, was fiercely attacked later. His wit at the expense of witnesses led one MP to say Jeffreys 'behaved himself more like a jack-pudding than with that gravity which beseems a judge'.[77] Nonetheless, the principal reason for Jeffreys's enduring bad name lay with the overthrow of the increasingly arbitrary and unpopular James II by his protestant son-in-law William of Orange in 1688. Jeffreys tried to escape the country disguised as a sailor but was apprehended and taken to the tower, where he died of natural causes in April 1689. A man so closely associated with James could not escape infamy. After his death his effigy was gibbeted and burnt by a London mob. There was a flood of pamphlets demonizing him: according to Dunton's 'character' of Jeffreys in his satirical *Merciful Assizes* (1689), 'If he excelled in one thing more than another, 'twas in his Haste to send Whigs to Heaven: For, Hang Men first, and try 'em afterwards was his Peculiar Talent.'[78] Comments like this, described by a modern historian as 'the reckless and largely fictitious attacks of this half-demented and fanatical scribbler', were accepted as true by the Victorian whig historians, Macaulay and others.[79] Jeffreys's loyalty, a rare quality among seventeenth-century statesmen, was his main enemy, and now it is his caricature that survives, in history and in the pages of novels.

Instead, history has condemned him for one month's work on the western circuit in September 1685, the so-called 'Bloody Assize'. Victorian writers were particularly vigorous in their attacks. Edward Foss could not bring himself to include Jeffreys in his *Judges of England*, because relating his life's 'disgusting details' would 'be but a repulsive repetition'.[73] In contrast, Charles Dickens thought that the young *should* learn about 'the enormous injustice and barbarity of this beast' and featured him in *A Child's History of England.*[74]

King Charles II had died suddenly on 6 February 1685, to be succeeded by his autocratic Roman Catholic brother James II. Jeffreys was not Catholic himself but during Charles's reign he was a loyal supporter of James, then Duke of York, and made a careful distinction between subversive Catholics and 'persons that profess the Romish religion [who] abhor those principles of murdering kings and subverting governments'.[75] His loyalty was rewarded when James made him the first Baron Jeffreys of Wem on 16 May and lord chancellor when he returned from the western assizes.

In June 1685 Charles II's illegitimate son the Duke of Monmouth landed in Lyme Regis, condemned James and claimed the throne for himself. His army was recruited from workers in the depressed cloth trade, farmers, craftsmen and common labourers. The rebels were easily routed by the king's artillery when they attempted a surprise attack on their camp at Sedgemoor. Jeffreys's task, together

SAMUEL JOHNSON (1649–1703)

Who ever called Queen Mary mad bitch? No, the courtesy of England has been shown, even to that treacherous and bloody woman, who deserved as ill of the Christian religion, as ever Julian did.[80]

Samuel Johnson's political pamphlet *Julian the Apostate* was published in 1682. Its message was simple: just as Christians of the fourth century had stood up against their pagan emperor Julian, so must the English prevent the Catholic James, Duke of York, from succeeding Charles II as king. Its effect was spectacular: 'The apostasy of Julian the emperor did not perhaps make a greater noise in the cities of the Roman empire than did the short account of his life, called *Julian the Apostate*, in the City of London at its first publication.'[81] Johnson's tone was scornful and provocative. If early Christians were ready to defy the law and die for their religion, then protestants, whose beliefs are protected by the law, should not just watch on when they are threatened:

Are we under the sentence of death, according to the laws of our country, if we do not presently renounce our religion? Poor men, they were! And though they died as glorious martyrs, in respect of their religion, yet they died as criminals, and malefactors, in the eye of the law. I hope many good protestants would make a shift to die for their religion, though it may be not with the gallantry that these soldiers did, if they were in the like sad circumstances, and had the laws against them; but till then, they throw away their lives, and are certainly weary of them, if they practise such passive obedience. And the truth is, we justly deserve to be so used, [...] and moreover to be loaded with the curses of all posterity, if we suffer ourselves to be brought into that condition. For that can never happen, but by our own treachery to our religion, in parting with those good laws which protect it, and in agreeing to such as shall destroy it.[82]

The tories, who favoured James's succession, flooded the market with rebuttals of this tract, and then Johnson's patron, Lord Russell, became implicated in the trials following the Rye House plot, a failed attempt to assassinate both Charles II and his brother James. Russell was executed but only after he addressed to the court an offensive farewell speech that was attributed to Johnson. Johnson found himself in front of fellow Old Pauline, Chief Justice George Jeffreys (see last entry), accused of seditious libel for *Julian the Apostate*. Remaining copies were burnt by the common hangman, and he spent four years in gaol.[83]

Johnson's efforts did not flag. While in the king's bench prison he wrote an address to prick the consciences of protestants serving in James II's army (he became king in 1685). For this he was stripped of his holy orders and

James, Duke of York, later King James II, oil by Henry Gascar, 1672–73. In this Baroque portrait James is wearing a Roman costume and represents Mars, the god of war. Before being excluded from office as a Catholic in 1673, James was lord high admiral for his brother Charles II. The page boy is traditionally said to be the young John Churchill, later Duke of Marlborough. © *National Maritime Museum, Greenwich, London.*

flogged from Newgate to Tyburn. With the accession of William and Mary he was released and reinstated as priest. Pamphlets continued to flow from his pen: Johnson kept to the improbable view that James II's departure vindicated the whole nation, who had resisted oppression and defended their legal rights.[84]

SIR JOHN TREVOR (*c.*1637–1717)

A gentleman that visited Mr Arthur Trevor, at his going out, observed a strange-looking boy in his clerk's seat (for no person ever had a worse squint than he had), and asked who that youth was: a kinsman of mine said Arthur Trevor, that I have allowed to sit here to learn the knavish part of the law!

(Roger North)[85]

The old House of Commons in the Palace of Westminster, from the River Thames, engraving, *c.*1790. © *St Paul's School.*

According to Bishop Gilbert, a commentator of the time, John Trevor 'was a bold and dexterous man, and knew the most effectual ways of recommending himself to every government'.[86] After a spell at the bar, where he became an expert in gambling transactions, he bought the pocket borough of Castle Rising for sixty pounds in 1673. A staunch and eloquent tory, he was quickly promoted and in 1685 was accepted unopposed as House of Commons speaker 'by reason of his great integrity, knowledge of the laws of the land and of the rules and orders of this House'.[87] This was in spite of 'his grotesque features and hideous squint [which] were far beyond the reach of caricature'.[88] In the same year he became master of the rolls, no doubt with the help of his cousin and fellow Old Pauline Sir George Jeffreys, recently appointed lord chancellor (see earlier entry). He successfully survived loss of favour when William and Mary began their reign: in 1690 he was reappointed speaker and three years later resumed his post as master of the rolls.

It was in 1695 that what the Victorian historian Macaulay called his 'mastery of the science of chicane' caught up with him. Trevor was discovered to have received a thousand guineas as a bribe for passing the London Orphans Bill, and found himself on 12 March presiding over the House of Commons while it resolved 'That Sir John Trevor [...] is guilty of a high crime and misdemeanour.'[89] He was not at parliament the following morning but sent a message explaining that he was suddenly taken ill with a violent colic and asked to be excused attendance. This happened again the next day, but by royal permission the House of Commons proceeded to choose a new speaker. On 16 March, when he was also found to have received bribes from the East India Company, Trevor was expelled.[90] He was however a survivor: an attempt to impeach him failed, and he continued as master of the rolls for life. He is buried in the Rolls Chapel in Chancery Lane with a monumental inscription 'wise in its brevity'.[91]

Macaulay, brimming with the moral confidence of 1856, dismissed Trevor as 'a man in whom craft and profligacy were united in a high degree', but it is easy to forget the role influence and partisanship played 150 years earlier.[92]

A life of controversy

CHARLES BOYLE, FOURTH EARL OF ORRERY (1674–1731)

He was short-sighted; and two or three other celebrated wits happening to have the same blemish, the fops of the town, who had an ambition to be thought wits, all of them affected to appear short-sighted.

(Eustace Budgell)[93]

Charles Boyle was a man of great learning who left a library of ten thousand volumes and collection of scientific instruments to Christ Church, his Oxford college, but his life was filled with controversy. His title lives on as patron of the clockwork devices invented by clockmaker George Graham in the early eighteenth century to represent planetary motion.

Boyle was the only nobleman at Christ Church to take a degree in the course of thirty years and was asked to show off his scholarship by translating letters supposedly written by the fifth-century BC Sicilian cannibal Phalaris. Unwisely, he complained in his prefatory remarks to the published edition (1695) that it was incomplete because the king's librarian, Richard Bentley, showed 'singular humanity' in refusing to let him 'have the further use of the manuscript'.[94] Bentley, who was a notable Cambridge scholar, fought back with two dissertations, the second conclusive, disputing the authenticity of 'Phalaris': the letters 'were nothing more than a fardle of common places and such an heap of insipid lifeless stuff that no man of sense and learning would have troubled the world with a new edition of them'. In response to the first of these attacks, and with the help of friends, Boyle wrote a lightweight reply for popular consumption, described by Bentley's editor Alexander Dyce as 'a tissue of superficial learning, ingenious sophistry, dexterous malice and happy raillery'.[95] The episode became a centrepiece of the Oxford versus Cambridge argument about the merits of ancient writers versus the moderns, a less solemn version of the heated 'querelle des Anciens et des Modernes' shaking the Académie Française in Paris in the 1690s. Swift incorporated it into his *Battle of the Books* (1704).[96]

Boyle entered parliament when elected to his family seat Charleville, county Cork, in 1695. In 1701 he won a seat at Huntingdon, but was in trouble when the result was disputed and he ridiculed the borough recorder in the House of Commons: a duel followed in a gravel pit in Hyde Park, with both men seriously injured. On his brother's death in 1703 he became an Irish peer, fourth Earl of Orrery, and his broadly tory sympathies led to Harley's elevating him to the Lords as Baron Boyle of Marston in 1711. He turned away from Harley two years later and for a short time was loyal to the newly-ascended George I but soon fell from

favour. By the end of 1717 he was a confirmed Jacobite (he wanted the descendants of James II restored to the throne) and found himself imprisoned in the Tower when his Oxford tutor Atterbury's plot to capture the royal family was discovered in 1722.

His body languished, and his health was impaired every day, till at last he was reduced to such an extremity, that Dr Mead went boldly to the council and told them, that unless the Earl of Orrery was immediately set at liberty, he would not answer for his life twenty-four hours, […] Upon this remonstrance, his lordship was at last admitted to bail, after having been kept in the tower about six months.[97]

Recovery from his ordeal was a slow process. Orrery continued activities for the Jacobite cause, but achieved little before his death on 31 August 1731. Even at the end there was controversy. In 1727 he had quarrelled with his son and determined not to leave him his library and instruments because he lacked 'inclination either for entertainment or knowledge which study and learning afford'.[98] They were reconciled later, and but for his sudden death the will would have been changed back.

'A Philosopher giving that lecture on the Orrery, in which a lamp is put in place of the Sun', oil by Joseph Wright of Derby, exhibited 1766. © *Derby Museum and Art Gallery.*

❧ *Judge and murder suspect*

SPENCER COWPER (1670–1728)

It was not for blood, shed in an angry brawl — it was not for vindicating his honour by his sword in defiance of the law, that Spencer Cowper was arraigned. He was accused of having deliberately murdered a woman, whose only fault was having loved him too devotedly, and trusted him too implicitly. He was called upon to plead to a charge which, if proved, would not only consign his body to the gibbet, but his name to eternal infamy.

(*Blackwood's Magazine*, 1861)[99]

Spencer Cowper was called to the bar in 1693 and in due course enjoyed a successful legal career, despite having been accused of murder in 1699.

Sarah Stout belonged to a local Quaker family which supported the Cowpers' political careers: Spencer Cowper's brother and father were the two whig MPs for Hertford. He was at her house late one evening before she was found drowned in the river. Despite a coroner's verdict of suicide, Cowper was tried for murder at the Hertford assizes, together with three other men who had been with him that day. Cowper had been married for more than ten years, and the likely explanation is that she killed herself because her love for him was unrequited, but the case attracted great attention. Pamphlets were issued by both sides, and the case was still being discussed more than 150 years later.

Cowper conducted his own defence and claimed that the prosecution was motivated by an alliance of Quakers defending their way of life and tories keen to unseat his relatives:

Spencer Cowper, oil by Sir Godfrey Kneller. *By kind permission of the provost and fellows of Oriel College, Oxford.*

It seems, they [the Quakers] fancy the reputation of their sect is concerned in it; for they think it a wonderful thing, nay absolutely impossible […] that one, who was by her education entitled to the light within her, should run headlong into the water, as if she had been possessed with the devil; of this they think their sect is to be cleared, though by spilling the blood of four innocent men. The other sort of people that concur with the Quakers in this prosecution, I shall mention […] are possessed with much prejudice against me, upon feuds that have risen at the elections of my father and brother in this town.[100]

The case was also notable as one of the first to make extensive use of expert medical evidence, with much of the trial concentrating on the difference between the state of a body that had been drowned and one that was already dead before entering the water. In his authoritative *History of the Criminal Law in England*, 1883, James Fitzjames Stephen commented that the judge showed little interest in the case or the evidence, and that justice was threatened by the habit at that time of finishing cases in a single day:

The judge, Baron Hatsell, behaved with a languid indifference which even now raises a feeling of contempt. He continually grumbled at the length of the trial. 'Do not flourish too much, Mr Cowper.' 'Mr Cowper, do you mean to spend so much time with every witness?' He ingenuously confessed that he could make nothing of the medical evidence (which was quite easy if he had only given his mind to it), and he modestly concluded his summing up thus: 'I am sensible I have omitted many things. But I am a little faint, and cannot repeat any more of the evidence.'[101]

Cowper and his associates were acquitted, but that was not the end of the story. Sarah Stout's heir-at-law moved to set the verdict aside by means of the wager of battle, a centuries-old right of appeal by single combat but one that had fallen into disuse. The appeal was first allowed but then set aside on a technicality.[102] In one sense the prosecution did have a victory. Cowper's brother was forced to find a new parliamentary seat, but he did so quickly and eventually became lord chancellor.[103]

❦ Military leader

JOHN CHURCHILL, FIRST DUKE OF MARLBOROUGH (1650–1722)

Oh! MARLB'ROUGH! I am raised! I'm all on Fire!
And if my Strength could answer my Desire,
In speaking Paint, thy Figure should be seen,
Like *Jove* thy Grandeur, and like *Mars* thy Mien,
And Gods descending should adorn the Scene.

(Timothy Harris, *The Pomp of Death*, 1722)[104]

Marlborough was a survivor who negotiated his path skilfully through a very turbulent period of British history. Recognition of his ability as a soldier came early. In 1673–74 John Churchill as he was then fought against the Dutch in the French army's Royal English Regiment commanded by King Charles II's bastard son the Duke of Monmouth. His bravery at the siege of Maastricht, where he saved Monmouth's life and was first to plant the fleur-de-lys on the enemy defence works, secured him personal thanks from King Louis XIV. Ironically, his next military campaign, eleven years later, was to suppress the Duke of Monmouth's west country rebellion when he sought to depose the newly-crowned James II (see entry on Jeffreys), and his finest hours on the battlefield would be fighting in an alliance with the Dutch against the French.

Churchill's talents as a courtier and politician equalled his military skills. In the final years of Charles II's reign he served the future Catholic King James II and conducted

The first Duke of Marlborough, detail from oil by Jan Van Hughtenburg.
Ken Lawson.
© St Paul's School.

valuable diplomacy with the protestant William of Orange (the Dutch were allies after the peace of Nijmegen in 1678) while retaining the confidence of Charles II. As James II's short reign became more extreme and unstable, Churchill again managed to balance his loyalties and defected to William's camp only when James's position was hopeless. Two days before William and Mary's coronation in 1689, he was created Earl of Marlborough.

Even so, he had to wait until Queen Anne's reign (1702–14) before embarking on his major military campaigns. He had been too close to James II to escape suspicion, and an anonymous pamphlet *The Dear Bargain* (September 1690) accused him of contacting James, now in exile. For once his political touch was less than certain. In 1692 he was briefly held in the Tower of London on suspicion of high treason, and historians have uncovered a letter, supposedly written by Marlborough in 1694, informing James of an impending landing by King William's forces at Camaret Bay near Brest. Winston Churchill refused to accept this letter as genuine, but it is possible that Marlborough was still trying to hedge his bets, frustrated by his current lack of responsibilities.[105]

Reconciliation with William took time, but in 1701 Marlborough was appointed ambassador-plenipotentiary to negotiate a treaty of grand alliance with the Dutch republic, Austria and other powers, to counter France's attempt to alter the shape of Europe by taking control of Spain and its empire. His excellent diplomatic skills proved invaluable and then, despite his relative inexperience on the battlefield, Marlborough was chosen as captain-general of the allied forces.

The War of the Spanish Succession was to be a long one, and when in 1704 Maximilian of Bavaria became a French ally it was at a critical point. Marlborough responded with his celebrated march to the Danube followed by the battle of Blenheim. The march itself has been called 'a masterpiece of military organization', and the battle marked the first major French defeat in forty years.[106] Casualties were very high, but Marlborough's talent for making his forces work together over a broad front, reacting to events as they unfolded, won the day. The most dramatic moment came when 3,000 French cavalry drowned in the Danube, prompting poetic effusions linking it with God's destruction of Pharaoh's hosts in the Red Sea:

> As th'*Egyptians* perish in the flood,
> O'er which their Leader stretch'd his Hand.
> *Miriam* her thankful Voice to Heav'n did raise;
> It was a woman sung the Hymns of Praise.

> So, whilst Great Marlborough thro'the Danube drives
>   The Armies of our Foes,
>   'Till the chok'd Stream the Bank o'erflows,
> Our pious QUEEN to Heav'n the Glory gives.[107]

Blenheim did not end the war, but it cemented the Grand Alliance. It also made Marlborough's fortune when he was granted by Queen Anne the very lucrative manor of Woodstock, birthplace of the Black Prince, funds to build Blenheim Palace and a substantial income for life.

Another celebrated victory came at Ramillies in 1706 and another flood of panegyrics, including a Miltonic effusion from one Mr Paris of Trinity College, Cambridge:

> Swift as the Light'ning Glimpse he wings his Way
> Impetuous, nor can ought restrain his Course
> Where Danger calls; o'er Heaps of prostrate Slain
> He rides intrepid, not regarding Death
> That covers all the Plain in hideous Hue;
> […] Ball from Hostile Tubes,
> Instinct with Motion from the Nitrous Grain
> Inflam'd, with dismal Hiss play round his Head
> Innocuous, the Messengers of Fate,
> Part single, part with Chain connexive link'd
> In conjugal Destruction. Thrice his Steed
> Sunk under him.[108]

Two years later quick thinking enabled the allies to confuse the enemy and enjoy another fine victory at Oudenarde, but it was compromised by the long and costly siege of Lille that followed. In 1709 came Marlborough's final large battle, Malplaquet: the whigs in parliament pronounced it his greatest victory, but in fact there was no clear outcome apart from immense loss of life. Back in England, panegyrics were being replaced by satirical attacks. There was a change in London to a tory ministry, and Jonathan Swift published his *Conduct of the Allies*, a highly influential attack on Britain's involvement in the war and on Marlborough for being motivated by fame and 'that unmeasurable love of wealth, which his best friends allow to be his predominant passion'.[109]

On 30 December 1711 Queen Anne removed Marlborough from power. Three years later the exhausting war was at last over, and when George I ascended the throne he received Marlborough with the words, 'My lord Duke, I hope your troubles are now over.'[110] He was restored as captain-general of the land forces. It was too late for him to enjoy influence while alive, but he was awarded the rare honour of a state funeral. His estate has been valued at about one million pounds.[111]

The Eighteenth Century

❧ *Professor of astronomy*

ROGER COTES (1682–1716)

Sir Isaac Newton, speaking of Mr Cotes, said 'If he had lived we might have known something.'[1]

Roger Cotes went up to Trinity College, Cambridge, where in his uncle's eyes he was already married to mathematics:

[your father] showed us your letter in which you expressed a feeble inclination to come and see us in the country, we thank you for it, and count it a favour if you can spare us any share of your affection from your dear Mrs Mathesis; I am glad to hear it she so easily yields to your courtship.[2]

At the age of twenty-three he was nominated the first Plumian professor of astronomy and experimental philosophy, a position that brought with it an observatory and quarters over the great gate at Trinity College. Here he famously observed the total eclipse of 22 April 1715, or at least some of it: he 'had the misfortune to be oppressed by too much company, so that though the heavens were very favourable, yet he missed both the times of the beginning of the eclipse and that of total darkness'.[3] He sent drawings to Newton of the event, mentioning that his assistant had timed it by a method of his own: 'I do remember that I hear him call out to me, "Now's the Middle", though I knew not at that time what he meant.'[4]

Cotes is best known now for his work on the second edition of Newton's *Philosophia naturalis principia mathematica*. The first edition, brought to fruition through the efforts of Old Pauline Edmond Halley (see chapter two), was out of print. Newton thought that Cotes, who admired this work greatly, would simply read proofs and check for clerical errors. Instead, he carried out a thorough revision, entirely unpaid, which entailed four years of very detailed correspondence. Newton clearly felt this was unnecessary interference but did at least plan brief recognition of Cotes's labours in his preface: 'In publishing all this, the very learned Mr Roger Cotes, professor of astronomy at Cambridge, has been my collaborator: he corrected

the errors in the former edition and advised me to reconsider many points. Whence it came about that this edition is more correct than the former one.'[5] He then withdrew even this acknowledgement when it seems he discovered an error carried over from the first edition. Six months after the book's publication Newton sent a further list of corrigenda and addenda. Cotes was not pleased and wrote a letter which for a time halted their correspondence:

After you have now your self examined the book and found these twenty, I believe you will not be surprised if I tell you that I can send you twenty more as considerable, which I have

Roger Cotes, marble bust signed P. Scheemakers. The Wren Library, Trinity College, Cambridge. The bust was presented to the library in 1758 by Robert Smith, master of the college. Smith had been Cotes's assistant in the Plumian Observatory, and presumably timed the total eclipse in 1715. Peter Scheemakers made his name in England with the Shakespeare memorial in Westminster Abbey. His workshop specialized in library commissions. *By kind permission of the master and fellows of Trinity College, Cambridge.*

casually observed, and which seem to have escaped you: and I am far from thinking these forty are all that may be found out, notwithstanding that I think the edition to be very correct. I am sure it is much more so than the former, which was carefully enough printed; for besides your own corrections and those I acquainted you with whilst the book was printed, I may venture to say I made some hundreds, with which I never acquainted you.[6]

Eventually, a preface by Cotes appeared in the third edition of the *Principia* (1726), expounding his ideas about the study of natural philosophy, but by this time he was dead. Cotes's cousin, Robert Smith, edited a posthumous collection of his mathematical works. Among its subjects are angles, curves and error theory. The methods and solutions are elegantly printed but often with no explanatory text, and it is not for the faint-hearted. It does however establish him as 'probably the most talented British mathematician of the generation after Newton'.[7]

❧ *The South Sea bubble*

EDWARD GIBBON (1666–1736)

All were condemned, absent and unheard, in arbitrary fines and forfeitures, which swept away the greatest part of their substance.

(Edward Gibbon's grandson on the punishment of South Sea Company directors after its collapse)[8]

In 1720 Edward Gibbon, grandfather of the historian, was a very wealthy man. He had made a fortune of more than £100,000 in the City, much of it through a bill-broking business. He was also a customs commissioner and apparently had an unrivalled understanding of 'the commerce and finances of England'. We know that in 1711 he was given a concession to sell lottery tickets, and made £4,500. He was a director of the East India Company, and in 1716 he had joined the board of the notorious slave-trading South Sea Company.

Early in 1720 the South Sea Company struck a deal with the government whereby government debt stock (mainly in the form of interest-bearing annuities) was transferred to the company in exchange for its own readily marketable stock and a large cash payment. To make this work, South Sea stock needed to be overvalued. It was talked up through press releases and coffee-house gossip. Subscribers were seduced by generous terms and the chance to borrow against the security of their shares. Early profit-taking was blocked by delaying the issue of share certificates. As a result stock went up from 128 on 1 January to the point where a new issue was successfully sold in June at 1,000, a price that bore no relationship at all to the company's trading situation.

Satire on the South Sea Bubble, engraving by James Cole, 1720. 'The Bubblers bubbl'd, or the Devil take the hindmost' depicts the interior of the Stock Exchange, with many figures showing pleasure or dismay and holding leaflets which describe their profit or loss. In the centre a stand bearing a scroll inscribed with a list of 'bubbles'. *Guildhall Library, City of London.*

A speculative wave had spread through Europe that year. When a similar operation, the Mississippi scheme, collapsed early in the summer, it was not long before stock markets fell again, first in Paris, then in Amsterdam and then in London. By December the South Sea Bubble had burst, and stock was down to 130, with many investors ruined. Blame was shared between the company directors and members of parliament who had been bribed with secret share options to support the deal over government debt. James Cragg, the postmaster-general, committed suicide, and the chancellor of the exchequer, John Aislabie, resigned. As the company's chief cashier, Robert Knight,

had fled to Europe with his 'Green Book' itemizing corrupt transactions, only rough justice was possible, and a special act of parliament stripped the directors of almost all their assets. Those, like Gibbon, not directly implicated in corrupt practices, were allowed to keep £10,000. Edward Gibbon thought his grandfather, a well-known tory, was victimized by the whig government and suffered arbitrary justice, 'a pernicious violation of liberty and law'. As it happened, he recovered very quickly, and by the time of his death Gibbon's second fortune 'was not much inferior to the first'.[9]

✒ *The only Old Pauline prime minister*

SPENCER COMPTON, EARL OF WILMINGTON (*bap.*1674, *d.*1743)

A plodding, heavy fellow, with a great application, but no talents. [...] He was always more concerned for the manner and form in which a thing was to be done than about the propriety or expediency of the thing itself [...] so he was much fitter for a clerk to a minister.

(Lord Hervey on Wilmington)[10]

The only Old Pauline to become prime minister, Spencer Compton was among the least distinguished holders of that office. Despite his tory roots, he entered parliament in 1698 as a whig after quarrelling with his brother, the fourth Earl of Northampton. Membership of the Kit-Cat Club enabled him to cultivate the friendship of Robert Walpole, and his career moved forward when he was appointed treasurer, first to Prince George of Denmark, Queen Anne's consort, and then in 1715 to the future George II. In the same year he was elected unanimously as speaker of the House of Commons, a post he held until 1727. A mannered and uninspiring orator, Compton did at least have an encyclopaedic knowledge of the rules and conventions of the house, but he was said to be a lax disciplinarian. When one MP demanded the right to be heard during a noisy debate, Compton replied: 'No sir, you have a right to speak, but the house have a right to judge whether they will hear you.'[11]

Walpole became the country's first prime minister under George I in 1721, but the Prince of Wales warned him that his efficient treasurer, Compton, would take over when he succeeded his father on the throne. Walpole kept Compton out of harm's way by seeing that he remained speaker and bribing him with the extremely lucrative post of paymaster-general (he probably amassed £100,000 over eight years in the position). George I died in May 1727, and as promised the new king told Walpole 'go to Chiswick and take your directions from Sir Spencer Compton'.[12]

Compton proved totally incapable of discharging his new responsibilities and after a few days declared the burden would be too great, a humiliating outcome he blamed on Walpole, who retained office.

Compton became Baron Wilmington in 1728 and the Earl of Wilmington two years later. His 'slow-burning hatred of Walpole was never extinguished', and he became associated with a group of whig discontents waiting for the chance to topple the prime minister.[13] Surprisingly, he

'The Political Vomit for the Ease of Britain, 1742,' drawn by D. Paulicino. Spencer Compton appears in just two political cartoons. Here he is wearing a tricorn hat and kneels at Walpole's feet, grabbing the power falling from his mouth. *Courtesy Lord Baker.*

became lord privy seal and then lord president of the council in 1730, but this might have been the king's decision. Walpole remained in power for another twelve years, and for almost all this time Wilmington was a quiet and loyal minister, at least on the surface, to the disgust of Lord Chesterfield: 'The president is as contemptible and subservient as ever.'[14]

On 2 February 1742 Wilmington was invited to become prime minister. Walpole's cabinet had become increasingly divided, especially over policy towards Spain, and Wilmington had been working on a new broadly-based ministry. His appointment was greeted with public ridicule:

The wits and satirists of his day made merry at his Lordship's expense. He accepted the offices of first lord of the treasury and president of the council, at an advanced period of life, when it was asserted, that in his prime he had acknowledged himself incompetent to the proper discharge of such arduous duties. Here the frequenters of the coffee houses, the wits and politicians of the day, brim full of political gall, overflowing with the rancour of party malignity, took their stand, and assailed him with countless squibs and pasquinades.[15]

As it turned out, he was little more than a figurehead, with Carteret the *de facto* leader. Wilmington died in office in 1743.

❦ Architect of the Mansion House

GEORGE DANCE (1694–1798)

[I was shown] a gentleman who every year is said to go up to London from his country seat in one of the Northern counties, with no other view but to enjoy the pleasure of p-ss—g upon this ridiculous edifice.

(P. J. Grossley, *Tour of London*, 1772)[16]

George Dance, or George Dance the Elder, was the son of a mason and freeman of the City of London. This, together with his active involvement in London freemasonry, doubtless helped him to make his way in the City, becoming clerk of the works in 1735, a position which strengthened his hand when he successfully beat serious

competition to become architect of the Mansion House (1739–52).

This is by far Dance's most important work, although several other London buildings were constructed to his design. The Mansion House was to be a tangible statement of the City's political and financial power. It had to

View of the front and west side of the Mansion House with views down Cornhill and Lombard Street, drawn by John Maurer, *c.*1750. *Guildhall Library, City of London.*

combine on a cramped site grand mayoral accommodation, sumptuous rooms for civic receptions and a justice room when the lord mayor acted as chief magistrate of the City. Dance's structure reflects the contemporary Palladian fashion, with a giant Corinthian portico that looked even more spectacular with its original forecourt and double flights of steps. At the same time, the nearness of other buildings left the lower storeys very dark, and the Mansion House's critics complained that it was cumbersome and out of scale, an effect worsened by the two transverse attic storeys Dance added to create more internal space.[17]

This edifice was erected by the City of London for the residence of their chief magistrate for the time being. No expense was spared to make it useful and magnificent. [...] This fabric is built with Portland stone, has many decorations, and is disposed in various commodious, and elegant apartments; particularly, a large Egyptian hall, ninety feet long and fifty feet wide, in which the first nobility, gentry and merchants of this city, are frequently entertained in a superb and magnificent manner.

(*Vitruvius Britannicus*)[18]

The City of London cannot be accused of any great display of taste and judgment in the erection of their Mansion House. [...] They have crammed this massy edifice into a corner where it cannot be seen, among buildings which are admirably placed to seclude the light from the apartments, and the architect, to second their intention, has loaded the front with a portico, which as effectually shades the windows on that side. In fact, when we contemplate the structure, its heavy ponderous appearance, its want of elegance, and a certain air of clumsiness that pervades the whole, give us very little reason to regret its being placed out of sight.

(William Nicholson)[19]

❧ Masters of the King's Musick

MAURICE GREENE (1696–1755)
WILLIAM BOYCE (1710–79)

The lives of these two composers were closely intertwined. William Boyce was one of Maurice Greene's first articled pupils when he became organist of St Paul's Cathedral. Both were composers and organists at the Chapel Royal. On Greene's death Boyce succeeded him as Master of the King's Musick, and realized Greene's project of assembling a historical collection of church music to be presented to every English college and cathedral. Both produced a very wide range of compositions, Greene being remembered now for anthems such as '*O clap your hands together*' and Boyce for his anthem '*The King shall rejoice*' and '*Eight Symphonys*' compiled from ode and opera overtures.

Their personalities, however, appear to have been very different. Greene had a tempestuous relationship with Handel: they became friends when Handel took a liking to the organ at St Paul's and Greene would pump the bellows, but the friendship ended abruptly when Greene began to favour the newly arrived Bononcini, a rival to Handel in opera composition. Bononcini's success was short-lived — links with leading Jacobites led to his downfall — but from that time Handel never spoke of Greene 'without some injurious epithet'.[20] According to the eighteenth-century music critic, Sir John Hawkins, he blotted his copybook a second time by endorsing Bononcini's fraudulent claims to a madrigal written by Lotti and performing it at the newly formed Academy of Ancient

William Boyce, oil by Thomas Hudson, 1745–50. *The Bodleian Library, University of Oxford.*

Music, which despite its name included contemporary works in its repertoire. Hawkins also had little time for Greene's organ voluntaries, which he thought vulgar and demeaning.

Meanwhile, Boyce's life as performer, composer, teacher and philanthropist (he composed works to benefit several charitable foundations) won posthumous praise in 1788 from Hawkins. It is relevant perhaps that Boyce's final composition was a setting of one of Hawkins's poems. Boyce suffered from increasing deafness and came to concentrate more on musicology and theory. Given what happened to a more famous composer just a decade later, there is sad irony in Hawkins's comment, 'Who ever heard of a deaf musician?'

Mr Handel and Dr Greene

Greene […] courted the friendship of Mr Handel with a degree of assiduity, that, to say the truth, bordered upon servility; and in his visits to him at Burlington House, and at the Duke of Chandos's, was rather more frequent than welcome. At length Mr Handel discovering that he was paying the same court to his rival, Bononcini, as to himself, would have nothing more to say to him, and gave orders to be denied whenever Greene came to visit him.

In the disputes between Handel and Bononcini, Greene had acted with such duplicity, as induced the former to renounce all intercourse with him; and from that time no one was so industrious in decrying the compositions of Handel, or applauding those of his rival. He was a member of the Academy of Ancient Music, and, with a view to exalt the character of Bononcini, produced in the year 1728 the madrigal 'In una siepe ombrosa' ['Beneath a shady hedge'], which gave rise to a dispute that terminated in the disgrace of his

friend. Not able to endure the slights of those who had marked and remembered his pertinacious behaviour in this business, Dr Greene left the academy and drew off with him the boys of St Paul's Cathedral and some other persons, his immediate dependents; and fixing on the great room called the Apollo at the Devil Tavern, for the performance of a concert, under his sole management, gave occasion to a saying not so witty as sarcastical, viz., that Dr Greene was gone to the Devil.[21]

The late Dr Boyce

As a musician Dr Boyce was doubtless one of the first of his time, if we except Mr Handel, whom the sublimity of his genius has placed above all comparison. Dr Boyce's merit consisted in the union in his own person and character of the various excellencies of former church musicians. […] In a word, it may be said that in skill and in powers of invention, he was not surpassed by any the most celebrated of his predecessors or contemporaries. […] He possessed a great degree of that modesty peculiar to real artists, arising from a comparison of their works with their ideas, and the inferiority of the former to the latter, that rendered him ever indifferent to applause and even commendation. He declined composing an anthem on occasion of his present Majesty's coronation, to the words 'Zadok the priest etc.,' alleging that it would be presumption in him to attempt it after Mr Handel; his excuse was accepted, and he made one to other words, which was performed. [...] He was endowed with the qualities of truth, justice, and integrity, was mild and gentle in his deportment, above all resentment against such as envied his reputation, communicative of his knowledge, sedulous and punctual in the discharge of the duties of his several employments, particularly those that regarded the performance of divine service, and in every relation of life a worthy man.[22]

✢ Eighteenth-century antiquarians: letters, travels in disguise, coins and a severed head

ROGER GALE (1672–1744)
SAMUEL GALE (1682–1754)
GEORGE NORTH (1707–72)
RICHARD RAWLINSON (1690–1755)

Roger and Samuel Gale were sons of Thomas Gale, high master and a scholar and antiquary of considerable repute: one of Roger Gale's publications was an edition of his father's work on Roman Britain. Like others of their time, both brothers were enthusiastic antiquarian travellers. Roger was also a keen correspondent, 'an indefatigable receiver and purveyor of antiquarian information and one

of the principal participants in the learned letter-writing which was so notable a feature of the revival of antiquarian studies in the first half of the eighteenth century'.[23] Samuel preferred smoking pipes to writing and used to travel incognito with another scholar, Dr Andrew Coltee Ducarel:

They usually took up quarters at an inn; and penetrated into the country for three or four miles round. After dinner, Mr Gale smoked his pipe, while Dr Ducarel took notes, which he regularly transcribed. [...] They were accompanied only by their footman and coachman, the latter being directed, in the spirit of his employers' playful anonymity, to tell any enquirers 'it was *a job*; and that he did not know their names, but that they were civil gentlemen'.[24]

George North collected principally coins, and he too was regularly in contact with Ducarel. The literary editor John Nichols described him as a 'well-looking jolly man', but his correspondence suggests otherwise. A journey to the west country in Spring 1750 was nearly ruined when he was told about a coin he knew nothing of:

You have greatly alarmed my curiosity by mentioning in your letter a coin of Henry III, with *Villa Bereweci* on the reverse; which I never saw or heard of, and informs us of what I cannot find in our histories, that Berwick was in the English possession in that reign. As I believe it will be seven months before I shall be in London, I should esteem it a high favour, would you enclose that particular piece in any book or pamphlet, that I might see it here; and the next return of the Hitchin waggoner should re-convey both of them to you safe, with thanks.

Three months later, health had become his obsession:

I have not enjoyed three days of good health for much above a year, and the languor which continual weakness and pain has occasioned leaves little ability, or even inclination, to get to the press; even this moment tormented with rheumatism and gravel, which succeeded the cessation of my piles, besides an almost daily chilliness and stagnation for a while, which too much threaten an epilepsy.

North became an active fellow of the Society of Antiquaries for many years, but in 1765 hypochondria and paranoia again took over, when he thought he was dying and ordered the majority of his papers should 'be indiscriminately burnt [...] from a conviction how ungenerously such things are commonly used after a person's decease'.

Richard Rawlinson was a staunch Jacobite and nonjuring bishop (he believed in the Stuart succession and refused to take the oath of allegiance under George I). His intense opposition to the established church made him unpopular among his contemporaries, and a year before he died he was removed from the council of the Society of Antiquaries, where he had been vice-president. Rawlinson's response was to delete the society from his will, an act which provoked an attack in the press, suggesting that his antiquarian pretensions were motivated by

'sheer hatred to the present generation'. In fact he was an exceptional collector of manuscripts and papers: he left Oxford's Bodleian Library an immensely important set of material he had discovered and put into order. A special interest was the history of non-jurors, presumably to give more substance to his own beliefs, and it led to rumours of one strange item he sought out, the head of Christopher Layer, another Jacobite, which was placed on the customary spike at Temple Bar after his execution for high treason in 1723:

When the head of Layer was blown off Temple Bar, it was picked up by a gentleman in the neighbourhood [Mr John Pearce, an attorney] who showed it to some friends at a public house, under the floor of which, I have been assured, it was buried. Dr Rawlinson, meanwhile, having made inquiry after the head, with a wish to purchase it, was imposed on with another instead of Layer's, which he preserved as a valuable relic, and directed it to be buried in his right hand.[25]

Samuel Gale, oil by School of Kneller, early eighteenth century. © *Society of Antiquaries of London.*

SIR PHILIP FRANCIS (1740–1818)

Thicknesse always mentioned Philip Francis and Philip Rosenhagen as the most naturally clever and the best scholars of his whole career as high master, but Rosenhagen, he said, had neither perseverance nor moral conduct, while Francis had both.

(Michael McDonnell, *A History of St Paul's School*)[26]

Despite a promising start — at the age of twenty he was private secretary to William Pitt the elder — Philip Francis's own career in public life was frustrated. At one point he hoped to become deputy at the war office, but this fell through; he was nominated to an extremely lucrative position on the supreme council in India but never fulfilled his ambition of becoming governor-general; in later years he was unproductive as an MP. In these respects he is a minor figure.

However, Francis is also by far the most likely candidate for authorship of the pseudonymous and highly influential Junius letters (1769–72) published in the *Public Advertiser*.[27] Junius strongly disliked what he thought of as the corrupt administration of Grafton, formed when Pitt's health forced him from office late in 1768, and several of the letters are direct attacks on Grafton for his weakness

and lack of principle. Other victims of his satire were Grafton's cousin, the Duke of Bedford ('Can grey hairs make folly venerable?' Junius asks him), and Lord Chief Justice Mansfield: 'Instead of acting that open, generous part which becomes your rank and station, you meanly skulk into the closet, and give your Sovereign such advice as you have not spirit to avow or defend.'

Junius's letters are not merely invective. They no doubt played a role in bringing about Grafton's resignation in January 1770, and their vigorous advocacy of higher principles in government meant that they were known widely and frequently republished. Their style is very much of their time, often elegantly turned but not afraid of blunt language.

To His Grace the Duke of Grafton, 30 May 1769

If the measures in which you have been most successful had been supported by any tolerable appearance of argument, I should have thought my time not ill-employed in continuing to examine your conduct as a minister, and stating it fairly to the public. But when I see questions of the highest national importance carried as they have been, and the first principles of the constitution openly violated, without argument or decency, I confess I give up the cause in despair. […] Relinquishing, therefore, all idle views of amendment to your Grace, or of benefit to the public, let me be permitted to consider your character and conduct merely as a subject of curious speculation. There is something in both which distinguishes you not only from all other ministers, but all other men; it is not that you do wrong by design, but that you should never do right by mistake. It is not that your indolence and your activity have been equally misapplied; but that the first uniform principle, or, if I may call it, the genius of your life, should have carried you through every possible change and contradiction of conduct, without the momentary imputation or colour of a virtue; and that the wildest spirit of inconsistency should never once have betrayed you into a wise or honourable action.[28]

Sir Philip Francis, engraving by Freeman after painting by J. Hoppner. © *St Paul's School.*

HENRY WOODFALL (1739–1805)

Intriguingly, two other Old Paulines, both very near contemporaries of Philip Francis, are associated with the Junius affair. Henry Woodfall was editor of the *Public Advertiser*, which enjoyed a surge in circulation when it printed letters from Junius. Several letters were indeed addressed 'To the Printer of the Public Advertiser', and one, containing a lengthy address to the sovereign ('Lay aside the wretched formalities of a king, and speak to your subjects with the spirit of a man, and in the language of a gentleman'), led to a lawsuit: Woodfall was in effect acquitted with a verdict of 'printing and publishing only'. He always claimed not to know the identity of Junius.

PHILIP ROSENHAGEN (*c*.1737–98)

His life was not exactly that which would suit our modern evangelists. When chaplain of a regiment he was the gayest man at mess. In aftertimes Francis met him in Paris, in hat and feather silk coat, red-heeled shoes, and all the foppery of a *petit-maître*. He took F. to his lodgings, up a hundred steps, where he found a little room with a bed in it that nearly filled it; the remaining space was occupied by a chair and a box containing the tenant's wardrobe, on which he seated himself, complimenting his visitor with the honours of the chair, and telling at the same time that yesterday the Duke of — occupied it; the day before, and before, the Marquis, the Comte, the Chevalier, etc. If he was to be believed, half the nobility of France had ennobled his bedroom by their presence.

(Lady Francis)[29]

As befits a lifelong friend of Philip Francis, Philip Rosenhagen's story is enveloped in rumour. After ordination in 1765 his time was spent mainly abroad, as a 'very inattentive' chaplain in America, and on the continent, living it seems a rakish existence financed by cards and his admirers. At one time he was said to be Junius, at another he was said to have sought favours from Lord North (prime minister, 1770–82) by revealing Junius's identity, but the first is almost impossible and the second impossible to prove, as is his eyecatching claim that he refused to marry the Prince of Wales to his mistress Mrs Fitzherbert, a few weeks before this illegal match actually occurred. In 1782, after his return to England, Rosenhagen was watched by government agencies as a possible French spy. He spent his final years as archdeacon of Colombo, where the date of his death was also a subject of rumour.[30]

Town and Country Magazine published a vivid portrait of Rosenhagen in 1776, which endorses Thicknesse's assessment of him at school (see above), but then this publication was driven by scandal as much as fact.

Extract of a Letter from Paris

We have a phenomenon here, an English parson, the descendant of a German minister. His name is R-s-h-gen. He was chaplain to an English regiment; but being a very active man, and abusive writer on the side of opposition, he found himself under the necessity of retiring, and commenced chevalier d'industrie at large. He was not unacquainted with the finesses at play, and availed himself of them upon every occasion. However, as this commerce is not the most certain in the world, he found it expedient to extend his credit upon paper to a very considerable amount. When the bills became due, he sought refuge in the verge of the court; but even here his liberty became perilous, and he judged it prudent to make a trip to the continent. He went to the south of France, and sojourned for a considerable time at Lyons; here it was necessary to call his adroitness into play, by which, under the sanction of Mrs P—t (Lady L-g-n-r's mother), who was his patroness, and with whom he lived on the strictest intimacy for some time, his hours glided in ease and luxury. But a disagreeable discovery of an operation at Lansquenette induced him to quit that city à la sourdine, and to repair to this metropolis. He had not been here long before he made acquaintance with Madame L— , who being upon the haut-ton of demireps, she was caressed by persons of the first rank. Her house is now the belle assemblée of first-rate ladies of her complexion, and wherever they resort the men will go. Cards form the greatest part of the enjoyment of these parties. Deep play is the word every night; the ladies fleece their male friends with impunity, and the parson has a fellow-feeling. […] Notwithstanding these nocturnal revels, R— is seen every forenoon reading his Tacitus in the Tuilleries or the Palais Royal, with as much gravity and composure as if the whole night had been devoted to study.

❧ *An amiable and convivial bookseller*

JOHN LOCKYER DAVIS (1717–91)

This warm appreciation published by John Nichols (father of the Old Pauline publisher John Bowyer Nichols mentioned in chapter four) on the occasion of John Lockyer Davis's sudden death captures not only his character but the spirit of eighteenth-century obituaries.

Mr Davis went out of existence, April 23 1791, in a manner singularly calm, and devoid of sickness. He had been indisposed for some time with the gout; but was thought to be quite recovered; and, a few moments previous to his death, had been diverting himself with playing at draughts with one of his daughters; but suddenly dropping his head, and remaining for a second or two in that posture, Miss Davis, imagining he had a sudden twinge of the gout, said, 'Are you in pain, sir?' No answer being made, she flew to his assistance, but found all assistance vain. He was no more. Mr Davis was much valued as an honest and intelligent individual. He had read much, and to the purpose. Some little matters he had written; but they were principally, I believe, *jeux d'esprits*, arising from temporary circumstances, and dispersed in the public papers, particularly the *St James's Chronicle*. The only volume of which I recollect his having acknowledged himself the editor was a valuable collection of the 'Maxims of Rochefoucault,' 1774, 8vo. Few men, however, knew more of books, or more of the world; and fewer still were equally willing to advantage others by a free communication of that advice which, being the result of experience, was the more valuable. He always wished to know his man before he opened his mind to him; but, once knowing him sufficiently to think him worthy of his confidence, he would communicate freely, and urge the party to exert himself sufficiently to be able to make the best use of his friendship. In every society he mixed with, he may be said to have been the life and soul, as he had the happy talent of rendering himself beloved equally by the young and by the aged, and that without the least departure from the strictest decorum of manners. Temperate in the extreme himself both in eating and drinking, few men enjoyed more heartily the conviviality of a select party; and scarcely any one excelled him in those minute but useful attentions to a mixed company, which lead so usefully to support conversation, and to render every man better pleased with his associates. His intimates were those of the first rank in life and literature; and his politeness in facilitating the researches of literary men has been the theme of many a writer. He was of amiable manners in private life; and his long management of an extensive business had made known to many of the first characters in the kingdom, and to almost all literary men, his integrity as a tradesman, his extensive information as a scholar, and his real value as a man.[31]

❧ *Fine handwriting*

JOSEPH CHAMPION (1709–*c*.1768)

The origin of PENMANSHIP, or first invention of LETTERS, has been much controverted; but next to GOD, the Author and Giver of all science, it seems rational to think it was derived from *Adam*.

(Joseph Champion)[32]

Joseph Champion's enthusiasm for fair handwriting was unbounded, but it owed more to the time he spent as a boy at Sir John Johnson's Free Writing School in Foster Lane than to his education at St Paul's. By the age of twenty-two he was advertising in the *New Craftsman* 'a new and most convenient Writing School (intended entirely for St Paul's School) being two doors on this side of the said school', and seven years later after changes of premises he claimed in another advertisement to be 'accomptant and writing master' at the school.[33] His exact relationship with St Paul's is unclear (he competed without success for the official post of writing master in 1741), but it must have been close for his pupils' script, which varied little, to become known as the 'Pauline hand'.[34] Champion's major work, *The Parallel*, contains a sumptuous range of scripts and is a magnificent celebration of the lost art of elegant handwriting.

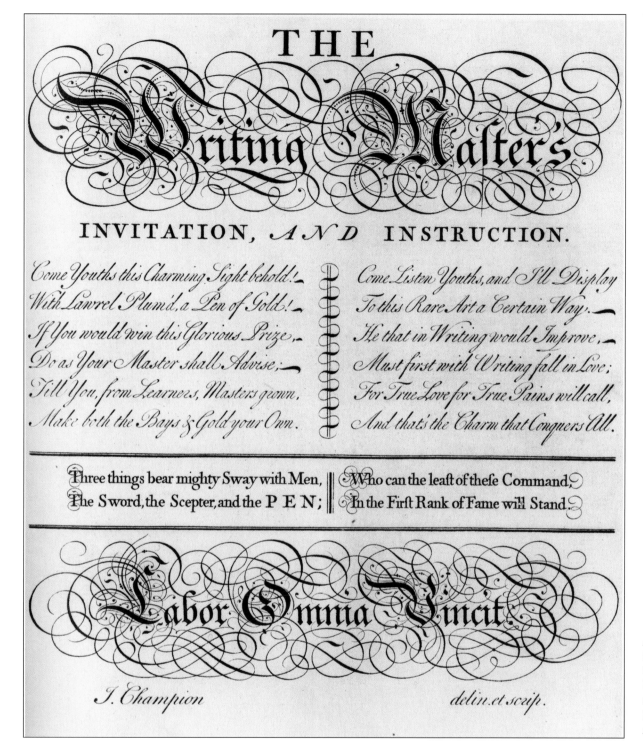

THE Writing Masters INVITATION, AND INSTRUCTION.

Come Youths this Charming Sight behold!,
With Lawrel Plum'd, a Pen of Gold!,
If You would win this Glorious Prize,,
Do as Your Master shall Advise,;
Till You, from Learners, Masters grown,
Make both the Bays & Gold your Own.

Come Listen Youths, and I'll Display
To this Rare Art a Certain Way.,
He that in Writing would Improve,,
Must first with Writing fall in Love;
For True Love for True Pains will call,
And that's the Charm that Conquers All.

Three things bear mighty Sway with Men, ‖ Who can the least of these Command,
The Sword, the Scepter, and the P E N; ‖ In the First Rank of Fame will Stand.

Labor Omnia Vincit

J. Champion   delin. et scrip.

A page of calligraphy (1734?) by Joseph Champion from *The Universal Penman*, engraved by George Bickham, 1733–41. *Ken Lawson.*

❧ *Magistrate and man of letters*

CHARLES COOTE (*bap.*1760, *d.*1835)

He did not devote his hours with zeal to the perusal of the Code and Digest, or inspect *con amore* the pages of a Grotius, a Bynkershoek, or a Domat; he either gave way to a habit of indolence, or dissipated his attention on general literature.

(Charles Coote)[35]

The tantalizingly little evidence we have about Charles Coote comes mainly from his *Sketches of the Lives and Characters of eminent English Civilians.* He had the odd conceit of including himself in what forms the longest and easily the liveliest portrait in the book. A shy and eccentric man, he was on his own admission a poor speaker. He was clearly not cut out for a career as an advocate but had the integrity when acting as a magistrate 'to adopt the legitimate conclusions of equity [rather] than the deductions of blind formalism or the *dicta* of jejune technicality'. Coote published several volumes of history which did not all sell well; his first work was *Elements of the Grammar of the English Language* (1788), a book that despite its dry subject matter is interesting to dip into. His choice of examples is high-minded: about the article he writes, 'The article is also omitted before nouns that imply the different virtues, vices, passions, qualities, sciences, arts, metals, herbs, etc. as, prudence *is commendable*; falsehood *is odious*; anger *ought to be avoided*, etc.'[36] There are no risky juxtapositions such as William Cobbett allowed himself in his *Easy Grammar* of 1818, where the list of 'nouns of number' reads 'Mob, Parliament, Rabble, House of Commons, Regiment, Court of King's Bench, Den of Thieves.'[37] Instead, Coote deconstructs parts of speech such as the preposition 'on' in a beguilingly patient fashion:

On, or *upon*, relates to the situation of a person or thing considered as higher than another, or as placed on the upper part of another; as, *he is lying* on *or* upon *the ground; he has a good coat* on *or* upon *his back; they were branded* on *or* upon *the forehead*. With some allusion to this primitive signification, it is used on several other occasions; as, *it happened* on *Saturday, that is* while Saturday was still passing; *they agreed* upon (that is, *with respect to*) *that point; he returned* on (that is, *at or soon after the time of*) *the receipt of your letter;* on (that is, *in consequence of*) *the news of their arrival, she came to town; my hopes of success are founded* on (that is, *have for their foundation*) *that circumstance; the parliament imposed an additional tax* on (that is, *to arise from*) *windows, which was a heavy burden* on (that is, *to be borne by*) *the people; he wrote a commentary* on *the Scriptures; that is, for which the Scriptures served as a groundwork or foundation*.[38]

✢ *Duty, suffering and the fires of Hell*

DANIEL BELLAMY (*bap.*1717, *d.*1788)

Daniel Bellamy was ordained in 1741 and worked in several parishes in the home counties. His father was a religious writer, and Daniel Bellamy revised his formidably titled *Ethical Amusements*.[39] His own great work is *The Family Preacher*, first published in 1754 and revised in 1776. It comprises 'Practical Discourses for Every Sunday throughout the Year'. As befits a man who had early in life published a paraphrase of the book of Job, the choice of topics for the family is often severe: two Sundays are devoted to intemperate drinking, there is a lengthy sequence on family duties, and there are discourses on the miseries of this life and the advantages of temporal afflictions. The most dramatic group begins with a week on 'The Certainty of a Day of Judgment', progresses to a vast sermon entitled 'A Description of the Torments of Hell', which Bellamy dismisses as a sketch ('it is rather outlines only, than a finished piece'), and concludes with the sequel 'Hell torments eternal'.

The flames of Hell

It is a fire prepared for the Devil and his angels; who (as we suppose) are mere spirits, and therefore it is such as is able to afflict a spirit with a sense of pain and torment. And such too it must be, that it may affect and punish the separate souls of men, while their bodies yet remain mouldering in the grave.

Frontispiece of Daniel Bellamy, *The Family Preacher*, drawn by Boitard, engraved Scotin. The family is remarkably calm as it receives the book's severe religious message. *Reproduced by kind permission of the Syndics of Cambridge University Library (7100.d.37).*

H. Gravelot Inv. et del.

G. Scotin sculp.

'Pagan, Jewish, Christian and Mohammedan' religion, drawn by H. Gravelot, engraved Scotin. Frontispiece of Broughton, *Bibliotheca historic-sacra, or, An historical library of the principal matters related to religion, antient and modern*, 1737. This compendious work was the major achievement of Old Pauline Thomas Broughton (1704–74). Among his other publications were translations of Voltaire and Don Quixote, and the libretto to Handel's *Hercules. Ken Lawson.* © *St Paul's School.*

It is also a fire which in its nature is everlasting, and must be therefore of a different kind from ours. The latter is a transient, perishing flame, which consumes its own fuel, and then expires; but the former will not only exceedingly torment; but will never waste the fuel on which it feeds; will never consume those wicked men, those devils, who shall be thrown headlong into it; nor will it ever languish, or go out. It is a peculiar fire, calculated for a peculiar purpose; it is something which the divine wrath has ordained to be his instrument to punish and torment his rebellious subjects; to afflict the souls as well as bodies of wicked men, and even such intellectual beings as have no bodies. We must suppose then, the wretched creatures who are thus thrown into this abyss of endless misery, to be plunged into a lake of *fire*, a mighty sea of ever-burning brimstone. We may suppose, that these damned wretches are not only scorched, not only singed externally, but are glowing all within, like metals in a fiery furnace. Oh, how terrible a place and punishment is prepared for impenitent sinners! How fearful a thing is it, to fall into the hands of the living God! Who of us can dwell with devouring fire? Who can endure everlasting burnings?[...] No part of the body shall be free from agonizing pains, and the whole soul shall be filled with misery. This will be the sad catastrophe of guilty mirth and pleasure. This will be the final reward of that which is at present prosperous, and much envied wickedness.[40]

⚘ *Hangings: an arsonist and thief, a chaplain at Newgate and the execution of a spy*

WILLIAM JOBBINS (1769–90)

William Jobbins, as far as we know, was the only Old Pauline to be hanged as a common criminal. Together with one Edward Lowe, he was convicted of setting fire to a house in order to plunder it and duly executed on 20 November 1790. Jobbins chose not to give evidence himself, but his father, John Jobbins, spent much of his time in the witness box painting his son as a young scholar, studious and attentive with a fine understanding of Latin. Jobbins appears to have exaggerated his son's youth (he claimed that William was nineteen, but if St Paul's admission registers are accurate he would have been twenty-one) and made the point that he still kept his school books in a case that had cost the significant sum of sixteen guineas (£16.80). This had no impact on judge or jury of course: largely as the result of evidence from an accomplice who gave testimony in return for a pardon, Jobbins was found guilty, and the recorder went on to address them in the strongest of terms:

I hardly know how to find words to express the abhorrence that I feel, or that the public entertains, of the crime of which you stand convicted. The setting fire to houses in the dead of night, for the purpose of plunder, at the risk of the lives of the inhabitants of a great city, is a crime not yet to be met with upon the records of villainy that have been brought forward in this court. As the crime is singular, so the punishment must be marked. I take it that it will be so marked, and hope the example will be such that if there should be left any persons of the same wicked intentions they will take example from your fate. As your crime is singular and novel, I hope it will be the only one brought into this court of the same description. You therefore must prepare to die, and consider yourselves as men without hope in this world. And give me leave to assure you that it is my decided opinion that, for an offence so very atrocious as yours, you can never expect salvation in the world to come unless you make some reparation to your injured country, and to God, whom you have offended, by a sincere confession of all the offences of which you have been guilty, and by a disclosure of the names of all persons who either have engaged, or are about to engage, in crimes so detestable as that of which you stand convicted. Nothing therefore remains but that I should pray to Almighty God, and it is now my earnest prayer to Him that you may all obtain forgiveness and remission of your sins.[41]

Anthony and Emanuel de Rosa and Mr William Fullager murdering Mr Fargues in the night near the Barking Dogs Hoxton 1752, etching, engraving by Valois, 1774–78. This is typical of the graphic illustrations in *The Annals of Newgate*. *Courtesy The Royal Pavilion and Museums, Brighton and Hove.*

JOHN VILLETTE (1747–99)

John Villette spent most of his adult life as chaplain or ordinary of Newgate Prison, and may well have witnessed Jobbins's trial and execution. One of the privileges of the ordinary was to publish accounts of trials and confessions, and Villette was the principal author of *The Annals of Newgate, or Malefactors' Register*, 1776:

A particular and circumstantial account of the lives, transactions, and trials of the most notorious malefactors, who have suffered an ignominious death for their offences […] calculated to expose the deformity of vice, the infamy and punishments naturally attending those who deviate from the paths of virtue, and intending as a beacon to warn the rising generation against the temptations, the allurements, and the dangers of bad company.

It is doubtful whether either the text or its often gruesome illustrations ever achieved these high-minded aims.

MAJOR JOHN ANDRÉ (1750–80)

At length the awful period arrived; and on the morning of the second of October this unhappy victim of the errors of others was led out to the place of execution. As he passed along, the American army were astonished by the dignity of his deportment and the manly firmness and complacency of countenance, which spoke the serene composure of his mind; a glow of sympathy pervaded the breasts of the soldiers, and the tears of sensibility were visible in every eye.

(Joshua Hett Smith)[42]

The romantic story of John André, executed as a spy during the American War of Independence, makes a striking contrast to the sordid world of Newgate Prison. He may well have chosen a military career in reaction to an unhappy love affair with a poet, and when sent out to Quebec it was the social life, collecting books and sketching that most appealed: 'We dine, dance rondes, toss pancakes, make a noise, and return, sometimes overturn, and sometimes are frostbit.'[43] The reality of the campaign made more impact when he was captured by the Americans in November 1775 and kept on parole for a year in the remote wilderness city of Lancaster, Pennsylvania. Once released, he witnessed several actions and in October 1779 was made adjutant-general to the commander-in-chief of the British forces in America, Sir Henry Clinton. This was to prove his downfall.

Among André's duties was liaison with American spies, including General Benedict Arnold, who was planning to betray West Point to the British. Improbably, they used a crockery dealer, Joseph Stansbury, as their go-between. In due course André went up the Hudson in the British sloop *Vulture* to meet Arnold, but there was a great deal of muddle before the rendezvous occurred, and by the time André had seen the general and collected details of the West Point defences, the *Vulture* had been compelled to retreat under enemy fire.

Although stranded behind the American lines, André had a pass signed by Arnold and proceeded back on foot disguised as a civilian, which meant that if he were caught he would be treated as a spy rather than just taken prisoner.

His companion for some of the journey back was surprised to hear André waxing lyrical about 'the richness of the scenery' and 'adopting the flowery colouring of poetic imagery'. He was captured in sight of the British lines, but the details remain obscure. One version has André blithely greeting three 'ragged knaves', who turned out to be American soldiers, in the belief that they were British. In their own account the captors unconvincingly claimed that, despite large bribes offered to release him, they cried out patriotically, 'No, by God, if you give us 10,000 guineas, you should not stir a step!' The papers from Arnold that condemned him were found hidden in a boot.

André was tried in New York and sentenced to execution by hanging. He rose to the occasion. At the trial his judges concluded that he 'carefully concealed everything that might involve others' while frankly admitting 'all the facts relating to himself'. He wrote a famous letter to General Washington, which made no difference, requesting that he should not die on the gibbet but that the mode of his death should be adapted 'to the feelings of a man of honour'. On the day of his execution he doffed his hat to reveal 'a long and beautiful head of hair which, agreeable to the fashion, was wound with a black ribbon and hung down his neck'. His last words were reported to be, 'I have nothing more to say, gentlemen, but this: you all bear witness that I meet my fate as a brave man,' sentiments that led to 'a wailing […] from the crowd'. André's stylish appearance was set off by the hangman, 'a frightful-looking creature', his face covered in soot 'taken from the outside of a grease pot'.

John André, engraving by Hopwood from a drawing by André. *Ken Lawson © St Paul's School.*

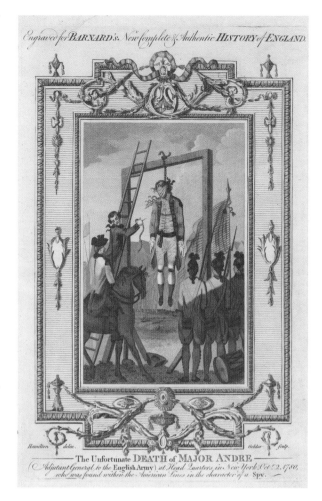

'The Unfortunate Death of Major André', drawing by Hamilton, engraved Goldar, for Barnard's *New and Authentic History of England*, 1790. *Courtesy Lord Baker.*

Modern readers are tempted to see this as a performance — André had put on theatrical productions during his service in America — but there is no reason to doubt his integrity, courage and charm. Such was the admiration he earned that George III caused a monument to be erected to his memory in Westminster Abbey.

❧ *Bringing back from the dead*

WILLIAM HAWES (1736–1808)

The custom of hastily laying out the persons supposed to be dead, and rashly interring the same, has been opposed, by men of learning and philanthropy, in this and other countries. The testimonies of learned authors, and the attestations of living evidences, have proved that many who were consigned to the grave were possessed of the vital principle. It is a sad and melancholy but notorious truth, that mankind has remained almost invincibly attached to this custom, engendered by ignorance and nursed by superstition.

(William Hawes)[44]

It was in 1773 that William Hawes began to attract attention. He wanted to show that the apparently drowned or otherwise asphyxiated could often be revived. There was much scepticism at first, but when he offered financial rewards, often from his own pocket, to anyone who rescued persons from the Thames between Westminster and London bridges and brought them quickly to a place where they could be treated, the response was strong and a large number of lives saved.[45]

The next step was to form, with a number of friends, 'The Institution for affording immediate relief to persons apparently dead from drowning', known from 1776 as the Humane Society and from 1787 as the Royal Humane Society. This organization recruited voluntary medical aid, continued to reward those responsible for rescues and carried out research and publicity. Hawes worked tirelessly for the society first as registrar and then as treasurer. His enthusiasm for its aims never faltered, and he lost no opportunity to promote it wherever he went. His philanthropic energy can readily be seen in the *Transactions of the Royal Humane Society* (1795), which he edited. It is packed full of high-minded editorials, records of Hawes's copious correspondence and evidence of resuscitation, as well as poems, addresses to parliament, and lists of those who have attended the drowned or suffocated without fee. Not all his recommendations would go down well today — there is a strange section on the effectiveness of tobacco as a treatment — but there is no mistaking his fervent commitment to saving life.

Tobacco considered as an aid to resuscitation

Impelled, therefore, by a most zealous solicitude for the advancement of that cause wherein we have the happiness of cooperating, I hope you will excuse me in thus requesting your most serious attention to the propriety of tobacco, applied in the enematic form, as one of the media of eliciting, the *abditae vires naturae*, [the suspended powers of nature]. You need not be informed of the high and deservedly illustrious medical characters and authorities, who have declared in favour of it; nor need you be informed of the *felices casus vitae restitutae* [happy cases of life restored], wherein this herb has been successfully applied [...] In the case of W. Smith, who had remained 'above an hour' in the sea, 'spirits were applied to his temples and nostrils, and friction, with mustard etc., were employed in vain' but [...] on fumigation of tobacco being used, and in its enematic form, by the repeated applications of its fumes, convulsive motions were produced, with the return of sense and life.[46]

'Young Man lifted from a River Apparently Drowned', oil by Robert Smirke.
© *Crown copyright: UK Government Art Collection.*

'Resuscitation by Dr Hawes of Man Believed Drowned', oil by Robert Smirke.
© *Crown copyright: UK Government Art Collection.*

Hawes was a medical zealot. He was unsparing in his condemnation of John Wesley's *Primitive Physic*, and once wrote, 'I have made quacks of all denominations my enemies, but what medical man of honour and reputation would wish to be upon tolerable terms with the murderers of the human race?'[47] He rightly became highly respected and was honoured by humane societies from Edinburgh to Massachusetts.

JOHN CLARKE (1760–1815)

The influence of the practitioner in midwifery is very great: they may be said to rule the nation very much in the way that the headmaster of Westminster School, Dr Busby, said he did. 'I rule the boys,' said he; 'the boys rule the mothers, the mothers the fathers.'

(Unus Quorum)[48]

Clarke trained at St George's Hospital medical school, and his 'Notes taken from Mr Hunter's lectures on surgery 1781' are the only surviving version signed by Hunter himself, the 'founder of scientific surgery'. His decision to specialize in midwifery was unusual for the time, but he soon had a very successful practice. Clarke was said to possess 'an acuteness of perception superior to most of his competitors, and rather a brilliance of talents'.[49] Among his patients was Mary Wollstonecraft, when she was dying after the birth of her second child (see later entry on Thomas Taylor).[50] He attended at the General Lying-in Hospital and the Asylum for Female Orphans, lectured and wrote on obstetrics.

Later in his career Clarke focused more on diseases affecting women and children. He revealed how one private lying-in hospital masked its high mortality rate from puerperal fever by burying two women in each coffin.[51] He began now to see a political side to his work. A nation's prosperity depended on lowering infant mortality, and strict quarantine was essential for the good of the community: 'A man, in a state of society, must be content to surrender some proportion of his own liberty for the advantage of the community in which he lives; and he is only to enjoy so much as is compatible with the good of his neighbour.'[52] Clarke left his midwifery practice to his younger brother Charles Mansfield Clarke and nephew Thomas Stone. His life was summed up in a pseudonymous collection of mementos 'in stone-cutters' verse' published by William Wadd in 1827:

Beneath this stone, shut up in the dark,
Lies a learned man-midwife, y'clep'd Doctor Clarke.
On earth while he lived, by attending men's wives,
He increas'd population some thousands of lives:
Thus a gain to the nation was gain to himself;
And enlarg'd population, enlargement of pelf.
So he toil'd late and early, from morning till night,
The squalling of children his greatest delight.
Then worn out with labours, he died skin and bone,
And his ladies he left all to Mansfield and Stone.[53]

View of the City of London Lying-in Hospital, City Road, Finsbury, engraving *c.*1830. *Guildhall Library, City of London.*

There is an intriguing group of eighteenth and early nineteenth-century Old Pauline actors and actor-managers (see also chapter four). Key information on them comes from another Old Pauline, Stephen Jones (1763–1827), whose revised *Biographia Dramatica, or a companion to the playhouse* (Jones updated it from 1782–1811) remains a standard work on the theatre of the period.

JAMES SOLAS DODD (1720/21–1805)

James Solas Dodd's father was Jago Mendozo Vasconcellos de Solis, who had to flee Barcelona after duelling with the governor's son and leaving him for dead. He was rescued by a sea captain, lodged with him in London, married his daughter and adopted his wife's name. James Dodd also started on a naval career, training as a ship's surgeon (one of his early publications was *An Essay towards a Natural History of the Herring*) before deciding to settle in London and concentrate on what he called 'the literary line'.

He wandered the west country and Ireland in search of literary employment and was engaged in 1769 by another Old Pauline, William Parsons (see next entry) to re-read Garrick's Jubilee Ode to Shakespeare in Birmingham Theatre. Odd incidents punctuated his life: in 1767 the London house where he lodged suddenly collapsed; in 1781 he was tricked by the bogus Baron Weildmester (in reality Major John Savage) to embark on a trip to Russia, where they would apparently act as ambassadors, enter a treaty of alliance and come away with decorations and £1,000 per year pensions. It was only when the expedition reached Riga, with Dodd paying all expenses, that he realized his mistake. Dodd died in Mecklenburgh Street, Dublin, where the myth was current that he had reached the age of 104.

In 1766 Dodd performed on several occasions his *Satyrical Lecture on Hearts: to which is added A Critical Dissertation on Noses*. The lecture was delivered in three parts, and echoes the fascination with noses Laurence Sterne had displayed in his recently published *Tristram Shandy*. It is a laboured text, which might have come alive in performance, when it was supported by props, representations of hearts and noses of different colours and shapes, but seems to confirm the view of a contemporary that Dodd 'had but small wit himself'.[54]

On Hearts

There is the heart of a British sailor (showing a wainscot-coloured heart) made of the same stuff as the ship's bottom, solid English oak: this is truly an heart of oak. We found several cavities in this heart differently filled; in one, was courage; in another, inconsiderate prodigality; in a third, downright honesty; and a fourth was filled with flip, and his Wapping landlady's daughter.

There's a white heart, the heart of a coward […], one Tom Bubblefool, card sharper and Hogarthian deceiver of young heirs […] he was a brave fellow! For he could bully a parson, and lift up his foot against a petticoat, till at last he died of a fright, at seeing the mistress of an alehouse, where he had sconced a Welsh rabbit and a pint of two-penny, take up the kitchen poker to oblige him to pay his reckoning.

This great lubberly overgrown heart was once that of Mynheer *Van Gotten Gelt*, burgomaster of *Scheidam*, and merchant of herrings and whale-oil. One of the cavities of this heart was filled with ducats, and the other with butter, which had so covered its whole substance, that it was impenetrable to any thing but gain; and the sharpest stings of conscience were blunted by the unctuosity of his darling food. *Sacramenteen Ich can well de gelt holden*, said he one day, and clapping his hand upon his pocket, *Sdonder and Blixen, here been mine Got*. If you wanted to buy of him on credit, *Ich can nich forstand Mynheer*. But shew him the money, and he would open his mouth as wide as that of Gargantua, and roar out, *Why yaw, Hogan well geborn Heer dat is goodt*.[55]

WILLIAM PARSONS (1736–95)

I […] became sensible how painful laughter might be, when such a man as Parsons chose to throw his whole force into a character.

(James Boaden)[56]

William Parsons served his acting apprenticeship under Garrick and was admired as an immensely versatile actor whose whole body spoke eloquently to the audience. He could make a great deal of unpromising parts and seems to have had the rare comic gift of reducing an audience and even his fellow actors to helpless laughter. He suffered badly from asthma, but made the difficult breathing part of his acting, and received a fine tribute from John Litchfield when he died:

In speaking of the merits of PARSONS, the critic unfortunately has no means of comparing them with those of another, that he may tell in what they excelled, and where they were surpassed; since there is no living actor who can possible be *lugged* into any competition with him. He was an undoubted ORIGINAL, both in conception and manner; and if any performer could be said to found a *school of acting,* PARSONS would be the first to lay claim to such an honour; with a fund of genuine *English* HUMOUR, he combined the *Italian* GESTICULATION, and the *French* LOCO-MOTION. His whim was incessant, eliciting in a thousand different ways, and productive of mirth through a thousand different channels. Such was the eccentricity of his humour, that the laugh he *once* provoked, he could prolong by a variety of stratagems, apparently unforced, till the audience were absolutely *convulsed,* and the actors in the same scene with him incapable of conducting its progress. The difficult *aspirations,* which no doubt were the consequence of the disease that brought him to the grave, he soon learned to adapt to his professional capacity, and thus, what an irritable mind would have made the plea of peevishness and complaint, PARSONS, with as much good humour as ingenuity, converted to a source of innocent hilarity.[57]

William Parsons as Moneytrap in Vanbrugh's *The Confederacy,* watercolour drawing by Robert Dighton. *By kind permission of the Garrick Club/Art Archive.*

🌿 *Old Paulines and early Romantic poetry: a song for Coleridge and a friendship with Blake*

WILLIAM LINLEY (1771–1835)

William Linley, aged eighteen, oil by Sir Thomas Lawrence, 1789.
The painter was a friend of the Linley family.
© *Dulwich Picture Gallery.*

Lines to W. Linley, Esq. While he sang a Song to Purcell's Music

While my young cheek retains its healthful hues,
  And I have many friends who hold me dear,
  Linley! methinks, I would not often hear
Such melodies as thine, lest I should lose
All memory of the wrongs and sore distress
  For which my miserable brethren weep!
  But should uncomforted misfortunes steep
My daily bread in tears and bitterness;
And if at death's dread moment I should lie
  With no beloved face at my bed-side,
To fix the last glance of my closing eye,
  Methinks such strains, breathed by my angel-guide,
Would make me pass the cup of anguish by,
  Mix with the blest, nor know that I had died!

(Samuel Taylor Coleridge, 1797)

Coleridge was inspired to address a sonnet to William Linley, one year his senior, just before he began his finest series of poems. Linley's own career as writer and composer did not glitter. In 1796 he composed incidental music for *Vortigern*, a Shakespeare text fraudulently written by W. H. Ireland and so bad that it ran for only one night: when J. P. Kemble, the principal actor, delivered the line 'And when this solemn mockery is ended', the audience dissolved into riotous laughter. Linley attempted comic opera and wrote two novels, but his only significant publication was an anthology of Shakespearian songs by several composers including himself. Linley continued to sing: he belonged to several Catch and Glee Clubs. In 1810, he was elected to the Sublime Society of Beefsteaks.[58]

THOMAS TAYLOR 'THE PLATONIST' (1758–1835)

'Pray, Mr Taylor,' said Blake one day, 'did you ever find yourself, as it were, standing close beside the vast and luminous orb of the moon?'

'Not that I remember, Mr Blake: did you ever?'

'Yes, frequently; and I have felt an almost irresistible desire to throw myself into it headlong.'

'I think, Mr Blake, you had better not; for if you were to do so, you most probably would never come out of it again.'

(Recollection of Alexander Dyce, friend of Thomas Taylor)[59]

At school Thomas Taylor's 'contemplative turn of mind' as he put it marked him out as a philosopher in the eyes of at least one master. In fact he left St Paul's early, 'disgusted' by the 'arbitrary manner in which the dead languages' were taught there and 'in all other public schools' and for a time turned his mind to mathematics, but it was not long before his enthusiasm for ancient philosophy was rekindled. Routine employment was not to Taylor's taste: early marriage to his childhood sweetheart Mary Morton obliged him to forego university and work first as an usher, a situation he found 'extremely disagreeable', and then for six years as a bank clerk, where he was 'disgusted with the servility of the employment'.

In a typically eccentric move, he decided to emancipate himself from the slavery of paid employment by dazzling the world with a perpetual lamp made on ancient principles and fuelled by a combination of oil, salt and phosphorus. His first and only demonstration of the lamp was a disaster: the phosphorus caught fire and in Taylor's own partial words 'raised a prejudice against the invention, which could never afterwards be removed'.[60] However, the event did lead to his finding patrons who gave him enough to devote his time to literary work, and over his life he produced many translations of ancient philosophy, including the first English version of Plato's complete works and numerous translations of the later neo-Platonists.

Taylor's strongest influence was probably on Blake, who appears to have been a close friend for a time, and it is very likely that Blake learned from him to turn away from the material world and Newtonian physics in favour of the Pythagorean tradition, where number expresses the order of the soul.[61] Taylor's observation in his early commentary on the neo-Platonist Proclus that 'the brutal hand of commerce has blinded the liberal eye of contemplation' sounds very much like Blake.[62] Coleridge and Shelley both owned copies of Taylor's translations even though they read Greek fluently. Shelley sympathized with Platonism, and his words 'the One remains, the many change and pass'[63] are very close to Taylor's own 'Platonic Philosopher's Creed'. Mary Wollstonecroft, mother of Shelley's second wife, lodged with Taylor for three months, together with her intimate friend Fanny Blood, but her radical feminism was too much for the Platonist's sense of order. He responded to her *Vindication of the Rights of Woman* with a laboured sarcastic defence of animal rights, *A Vindication of the Rights of Brutes* (1792), which some later readers have taken seriously.

Taylor's versions of Plato received caustic reviews: Coleridge observed that he translated from 'difficult Greek into incomprehensible English',[64] and a critic in *Blackwood's Magazine*, 1825, wrote, 'The man is an ass, in the first place; secondly, he knows nothing of the religion of which he is so great a fool as to profess himself a votary; and thirdly, he knows less than nothing of the language about which he is continually writing.'[65] In America his translations were embraced enthusiastically by the writer Emerson and his disciples.

ADMIRAL SIR THOMAS TROUBRIDGE (*c*.1758–1807)

Whenever I see a fellow look as if he was thinking, I say that's mutiny.

(Sir Thomas Troubridge)[66]

Despite humble origins for a naval officer (his father was a baker), Thomas Troubridge rose to be one of the most senior of Nelson's Band of Brothers. He played his part in the wars against France with extraordinary enthusiasm. In 1794 he was captain of the *Castor*, part of a convoy captured by the French. Troubridge was taken on board the French flagship *Sans Pareil*. Three weeks later the *Sans Pareil* came under attack. Locked in the boatswain's storeroom during the battle, he 'amused himself in pouring forth every invective against the French and the man appointed to guard him' and 'began to jump and caper with all the gestures of a maniac' when he heard the ship's mainmast fall overboard.[67]

The *Culloden* was his next command. After leading the action against the Spanish at the battle of Cape St Vincent, he was devastated to run aground at the battle of the Nile: in his haste to join the fight he cut a corner and hit a shoal. The failure haunted him for months and was worsened by hearing news of his wife's death. Writing to condole with Captain Darby of the *Bellerophon* (who was

wounded), he 'added that had his suffering been fifty times as much, he had rather been in his place than have borne the anguish he felt from running aground, and being kept out of the action — that he had found great difficulty from shooting himself, and that he even then frequently shed tears'.[68]

His next task, assisting Nelson in repulsing the French from the Kingdom of Naples, was to try his patience even more. The Neapolitans were feeble and treacherous. By the time Troubridge arrived the government had been led by Nelson to safety in Sicily, and the 'war […] of extermination as long as a Frenchman is left alive' he had been anticipating was not to happen. He described the 'Neapolitans as the worst of intriguing enemies; every hour shows […] their infamy and duplicity'. Troubridge's grim humour showed when he scribbled 'A jolly fellow' on a letter accompanying the head of a Jacobin that was sent him by the killer as proof of his loyalty. But anger dominated his cascade of letters to Nelson, even when Naples was eventually made secure. The Sicilians would not help

The British Fleet at anchor in the Bay of Naples, 17 June 1798, watercolour with body colour by Giacomo Guardi, *c*.1800. © *National Maritime Museum, Greenwich, London.*

the starving islanders in the bay. 'The distress for bread in Ischia is so great, that it would move even a Frenchman to pity,' he wrote, and then seized grain ships from Palermo harbour. The behaviour of Neapolitan officers damaged his health: 'I am really very ill. I must go to bed. This treachery fairly does me up.' Then there was the problem of meting out justice to traitors among the clergy: 'The judge appears to me to be the poorest creature I ever saw [...] talks of it being necessary to have a bishop to degrade the priests before he can execute them. I told him to hang them first, and if he did not think the degradation of hanging sufficient, I would...!'[69]

And there was Nelson's private life. Troubridge's morality was naïve and patriotic: he could never accept the *ménage à trois* comprising Nelson, Sir William Hamilton and his theatrical ex-courtesan wife Emma that began in Palermo and continued in England. 'A gambling woman in the eyes of an Englishman, is lost,' he advised Nelson.[70] They had been friends since the age of fifteen, when they joined the *Seahorse* within a few days of each other, but when Troubridge became a junior lord of the Admiralty in 1801, Nelson became convinced that his postings were designed to separate him from Lady Hamilton. No amount of correspondence from Troubridge would convince him otherwise. At the Admiralty Troubridge transferred his relish for punishing rebels into the pursuit of corruption in the naval department. He was made rear-admiral of the blue in 1804, but this only led to a frustrating time at the East India Station — he sailed from

Admiral Sir Thomas Troubridge, drawing by W. Evans, engraved M. Bourlier, after Sir William Beechey's painting.
© *St Paul's School.*

Madras in January 1807 and on 1 February was caught in a cyclone off Madagascar and drowned.

Nelson once said of Troubridge, 'I know he is my superior.'[71] On the other hand, Admiral Pellew, with whom he fell out in Madras, dismissed him as 'un garcon patisser [sic] from St Martin's Lane [...] a weak man, entirely commanded by his passion'.[72] In the end the navy could not forget his humble origins.[73]

The third school, aquatint, drawn by Thomas H. Shepherd, engraved William Deeble, published 1827. This building for all its classical grandeur was in essence little different from the school it replaced. © *St Paul's School*.

The Nineteenth Century

❧ *Abolishing the slave trade*

THOMAS CLARKSON (1760–1846)

In the vessel of eleven tons, the length of the room for the thirty slaves was twenty-two feet. The greatest breadth of the floor was eight, and the least four. The whole height from the keel to the beam was but five feet eight inches, three feet of which were occupied by ballast, cargo, and provisions, so that two feet eight inches remained only as the height between the decks. Hence, each slave would have only four square feet to sit in, and when in this posture, his head, if he were a full-grown person, would touch the ceiling or upper deck.

(Clarkson's description of a pleasure-boat built for six persons to sail on the Severn and now refitted for the slave trade in Africa)[1]

THOMAS CLARKSON'S enormous contribution to the abolition of slavery has only recently received due credit. He was unfairly cast in the shadow of William Wilberforce when the latter's sons published their father's biography in 1838, and a recent historical fashion for assigning economic causes and little else to the collapse of slavery marginalized all the abolitionists for a time. However, in 1996 a sesquicentennial tablet in his name was placed in Westminster Abbey, and the bicentenary of the British parliamentary act abolishing the slave trade in 1807 brought him further into the public eye.

His story has an epic quality, beginning with the Latin essay prize won at Cambridge in 1785. Clarkson entered what he in retrospect called 'an innocent contest for literary honour', but the more he researched the set topic, 'Anne liceat invitos in servitutem dare' ('Is it right to make slaves of others against their will?'), the more he was affected by the evils of slavery. He stopped to rest his horse at Wadesmill in Hertfordshire when riding to London after reading out his essay in the Senate House and experienced a kind of Damascene conversion: 'A thought came into my mind, that if the contents of the essay were true, it was time some person should see these calamities to their end.' A monument now marks this place.

The essay was published in 1786 by a Quaker contact (the Quakers were already actively against slavery), and it led to the recruitment of Wilberforce and creation of an anti-slavery committee. Clarkson went on to publish twenty-three works, predominantly on this cause, and

threw himself unsparingly into the campaign. Between 1786 and 1794, when he took temporary retirement to recover his health, he travelled 35,000 miles round the country collecting evidence and inspiring groups to form and petition government, although his attempt to involve the national assembly in revolutionary Paris did not go down so well. A second campaign and more travel began in 1804, leading to the act of 1807. Eventually, after enormous efforts on paper and on horseback, including international diplomacy, he saw slaves emancipated in the British empire by the act of 1833.[2]

Clarkson lived on well into old age, but one is still struck by the extraordinary effort and self-sacrifice that went into his activities. Wordsworth honoured him in a sonnet written in 1807 (Dorothy Wordsworth was a close friend of Clarkson's wife): 'thy zeal shall find/Repose at length, firm friend of human kind!'[3]

A nasty incident in Liverpool.

(Falconbridge was a former slave-ship doctor, and invaluable source of evidence. Peter Green was a steward savagely murdered on ship — one of Clarkson's concerns was to show how many British seamen died in the slave trade.)

The temper of many of the interested people of Liverpool had now become still more irritable, and their hostility more apparent than before. I received anonymous letters, entreating me to leave it, or I should otherwise never leave it alive. The only effect which this advice had upon me was to make me more vigilant when I went out at night. I never stirred out at

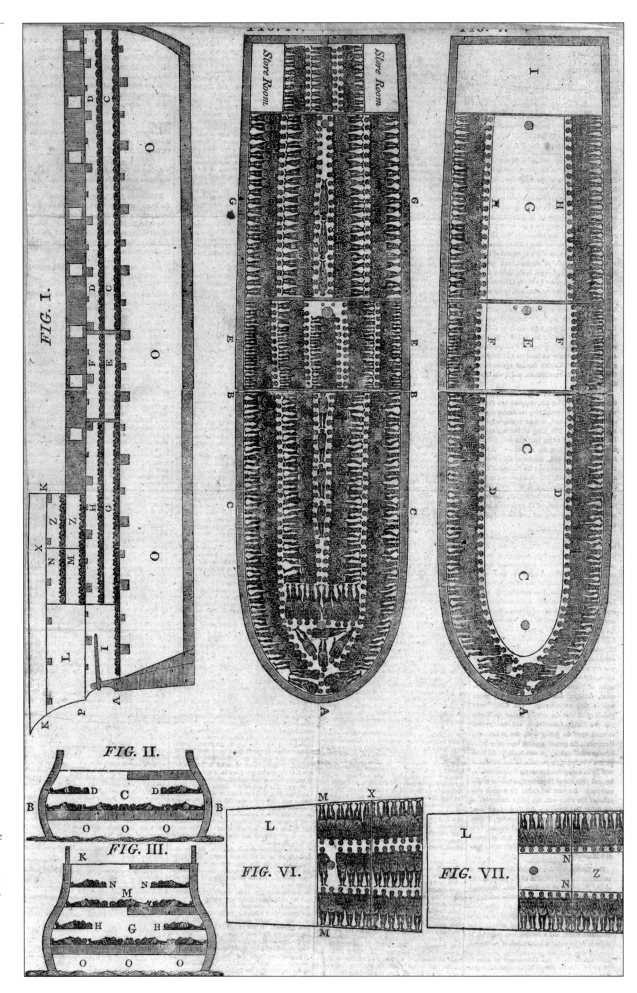

A late variant of the well-known and widely copied set of stowage plans for the Liverpool slave ship 'Brooks', first published in 1789. The original drawing was commissioned by abolitionists in Britain in 1788 and distributed widely.
© *National Maritime Museum, Greenwich, London.*

this time without Mr Falconbridge. And he never accompanied me without being well armed. Of this, however, I knew nothing until we had left the place. There was certainly a time, when I had reason to believe that I had a narrow escape. I was one day on the pier-head with many others looking at some little boats below at the time of a heavy gale. Several persons, probably out of curiosity, were hastening thither. I had seen all I intended to see, and was departing, when I noticed eight or nine persons making towards me. I was then only about eight or nine yards from the precipice of the pier but going from it. I expected that they would have divided to let me through them; instead of which they closed upon me and bore me back. I was borne within a yard of the precipice, when I discovered my danger; and perceiving among them the murderer of Peter Green, and two others who had insulted me at the King's Arms, it instantly struck me that they had a design to throw me over the pierhead; which they might have done at this time, and yet have pleaded that I had been killed by accident. There was not a moment to lose. Vigorous on account of danger, I darted forward. One of them, against whom I pushed myself, fell down. Their ranks were broken. And I escaped, not without blows, amidst their imprecations and abuse.[4]

❧ Attack on high society

JOHN OWEN (1766–1822)

This passion for diversions renders the Sunday particularly irksome to persons of any sort of *ton* in the Fashionable World. A dose of piety in the morning is well enough, though it is somewhat inconvenient to take it quite so early; but then it wants an opera, or a play, or a dance, to carry it off. There are indeed some *esprits-forts* among the ladies, who are trying with no little success to redeem a portion of the Sabbath from the insufferable bondage of the Bible and the sermon-book; and to naturalize that continental distribution of the day, which gives the morning to devotion, and the evening to dissipation.

(John Owen, *The Fashionable World Displayed*)

The Reverend John Owen's most distinguished achievement was working as unpaid principal secretary of the British and Foreign Bible Society from a few weeks after it was founded in 1804 until his death, but he also wrote a curious work under the naïve pseudonym of Theophilus Christian, *The Fashionable World Displayed,* published in several editions from 1804. Owen was regarded as an abrasive and short-tempered person, and in this book he launches a cynical and irritated attack on high society, its inverted values and disregard of religion. He attached an ironic glossary to later editions.[5]

A fashionable glossary

(Vernacular terms) (Fashionable sense)

Age	An infirmity which nobody owns
Buying	Ordering goods without present purpose of payment
Conscience	Something to swear by
Courage	Fear of man
Cowardice	Fear of God
Day	Night
Debt	A necessary evil
Decency	Keeping up appearances
Dinner	Supper
Dressed	Half-naked
Duty	Doing as other people do
Economy	(Obsolete)
Enthusiasm	Religion in earnest
Fortune	The chief good
Friend	(Meaning not known)
Home	Everybody's house but one's own
Honour	The modern Moloch, worshipped with licentious rites and human victims
Knowing	Expert in folly and vice
Life	Destruction of body and soul
Love	(Meaning not known)
Modest	Sheepish
New	Delightful
Night	Day
Nonsense	Polite conversation
Old	Insufferable
Pay	Only applied to visits
Play	Serious work
Protection	Keeping a mistress
Religion	Occupying a seat in some church or chapel
Spirit	Contempt of decorum and conscience
Style	Splendid extravagance.
Thing (the)	Any thing but what a man should be
Time	Only regarded in music and dancing
Truth	(Meaning uncertain)
Virtue	Any agreeable quality
Vice	Only applied to servants and horses
Undress	Complete clothing
Wicked	Irresistibly agreeable
Work	A vulgarism

John Owen, oil. *With the kind permission of the master and fellows of Corpus Christi College, Cambridge.*

❦ Royal tutor, bishop and patron of Constable

JOHN FISHER (1748–1825)

I had a great horror of *bishops* on account of their wigs and *aprons*, but recollect this being partly got over in the case of the then bishop of Salisbury by his kneeling down and letting me play with his badge of chancellor of the Order of the Garter.

(Queen Victoria writing in 1872)[6]

'Salisbury Cathedral from the Bishop's Grounds', oil by John Constable, *c.* 1825. In 1822 John Fisher commissioned a view of the cathedral from Constable but rejected this canvas because it had a stormy sky. A second version with a bright sky was painted in 1826 and is now in the Frick Collection, New York. The figures on the left are Bishop Fisher and his wife. © V&A Images/Victoria and Albert museum, London.

three or four times a week and held the appointment until 1817, the year of Charlotte's early death, but she did not take to him, and Fisher found her manners irksome: 'Her nose requiring to be *wiped*,' he complained, 'she did not apply her handkerchief, but wiped her nose with *her sleeve*, as vulgar people do.'[8] The prince regent asked him to talk sense into Charlotte but to no avail: 'our jilt' he called her when in 1814 she broke off her engagement to the Prince of Orange and fell in love with Prince Frederick of Prussia.

Fisher held an impressive number of ecclesiastical appointments: he was nominated by George III to a canonry at Windsor, in 1803 he moved on to become bishop of Exeter, and four years later he succeeded Old Pauline Bishop John Douglas (1721–1807) at Salisbury. Of great interest was his post as titular rector of Langham in Essex. It was in nearby Dedham, then a popular resort for visitors of rank and fashion from London, that he met the painter John Constable. A capable sketcher himself (some of his drawings can be seen at Windsor), he was one of Constable's most influential patrons, introducing him to the London art world and inviting him to Salisbury: this is why the Cathedral features in several paintings. John Constable and Bishop Fisher's nephew John (archdeacon at Salisbury) became very close friends and conducted a lengthy, colourful and sometimes scurrilous correspondence about art and artists, but the bishop wrote disappointingly brief and factual letters.

Fisher was also an unpretentious and capable bishop who lived on his private means and used official revenues for acts of charity.[9]

John Fisher had a talent for cultivating royalty. His patron, Bishop Richard Hurd, recommended him to George III as tutor to Prince Edward, an appointment he held from 1781–85. He also taught Princess Elizabeth drawing and was popular in fashionable circles: 'A charming creature, generally known in society as "the King's Fisher"' (Mrs Piozzi).[7] But when he returned in 1805 to see to the troublesome Princess Charlotte of Wales's education, things went less well. By this stage he was middle-aged and married, rather than the dashing young bachelor who had impressed the court ladies twenty years earlier. He visited

❦ Old Paulines and the later Romantics: a fantasist, a friend of Keats and parodist of Wordsworth, a victim of Byron

ROBERT FINCH (1783–1830)

Of Mr Finch I must give an account — he was a kind-hearted generous and I believe a perfectly upright man, but these qualities were sadly spoiled by the infirmity I cannot give it a worse name, of braggadocio lying. His untruths were the offspring of mere vanity.

(Crabb Robinson)[10]

Robert Finch was a man whose self-image regularly outran reality. A clerical career was his first plan, but when he dismissed as 'contemptible' the society in Maidstone

where he held a curacy, it was clear it would not work out. He developed big literary ambitions but published very little. He claimed acquaintance with the major Romantic figures, sprinkling his journals and letters with phrases such as 'my dear friend Byron' and 'our friend Coleridge', but there is no evidence that he ever saw Coleridge, and Byron has just one passing reference to him. He became a fellow of the Society of Antiquaries, but his own collecting was haphazard — a few good paintings, and coins and medals described as 'a fair collection of the jackdaw variety'.[11]

In 1814 he decided to live on the continent, and this was when his fantasy life took a more bizarre turn. Apparently with the intention of making it easier to cross borders, he awarded himself the title of lieutenant-colonel, a fiction he came to believe in himself. Mary Shelley described his Falstaffian bragging in a letter from Rome in 1819, comparing the episode to Thomas Moore's recently published novel *The Fudge Family in Paris*, in which Biddy thinks Colonel Calicot is the king of Prussia in disguise, when actually he is a draper's clerk:

Yesterday evening I met at a Conversazione [...] an Englishman with 'the dear Corsair expression half savage half soft' — with the beautiful mixture of 'Abelard and old Blücher' — and his forehead 'rather bald but so warlike' and his mustachios on which the lamp shone with as fine an effect as the sun did upon Biddy's Hero — that when I heard his [him?] called Signore Colonello I could not retain a smile which nearly degenerated into laughter when I thought that we had Colonel Calicot in Rome. Presently he began in very good Italian which although Englishly pronounced yet is better spoken than any other Englishman that I have heard — to give an account of his warlike feats and how at Lisbon he had put to flight thirty well armed and well mounted robbers (he on foot) with two pistols that never missed their aim. — There can be one such man in the world as you will be convinced when I tell you that while I was admiring his extraordinary prowess Clare whispered to me *It is Colonel Finch*.[12]

Finch liked to cultivate important people and to dominate conversation. Writing in 1829, a year before Finch died, Crabb Robinson related, 'He amuses himself with buying books and talking about them, and having lived in good company in England is himself an entertaining companion — he is somewhat of an invalid and is very glad to give me tea in return for my literary gossip.'[13] In his defence, Finch did give generous help to English artists in Italy, entertaining them, writing letters of introduction and commissioning work for which he paid generously. Tantalizingly though, he was always at one remove from the great figures. He lived in the house that would later become Keats's last home for example, but his closest contact appears to have been a second-hand description of his death which was passed on to Shelley, who was affected by 'the heart-rending account of the closing scene of the great genius'.[14]

The final fantasy had to wait for Finch's own death: a large monument in Rome's English cemetery, where Keats and Shelley already lay buried, and an extremely long epitaph from Dr Nott which eloquently mythologizes his failures.

Sacrificing views of ambition to the love of knowledge he travelled a contemplative and deep observer through many kingdoms of Europe and Asia everywhere seeking the good and the learned, everywhere sought for and honoured by them. [...] No poor man ever solicited his charity in vain, no scholar sought that he did not derive, no artist needed that he did not receive: instruction from his learning, from his liberality assistance.

JOHN HAMILTON REYNOLDS (1794–1852)

Reynolds's quicksilver quality, which led Keats to compare him to the god Mercury, showed indeed that he was not a poet but a brilliant imitator.

(Robert Gittings)[15]

Words, images — sometimes even thoughts — crowded in and were heaped up beyond measure. He dashed off what occurred to his fertile mind and had not enough patience in revision or power of self-criticism to prune down and perfect his work.

(George L. Marsh)[16]

John Keats and John Hamilton Reynolds were near contemporaries (Keats was born in 1795). When they met first in October 1816 both were struggling between poetic ambition and the need to earn a living. Reynolds was already a full-time writer who contributed to several journals, had published three volumes of verse and was about to see his fourth, *The Naiad: A Tale with other Poems*, in print; Keats was a young apothecary, a profession he would shortly abandon, and had published almost nothing. There followed a close friendship until Keats left for Italy in September 1820 (he died in Rome six months later). It was a poignant relationship. Some of Keats's most profound ideas about poetry were expressed in his letters to Reynolds, and they would walk together on Hampstead

John Hamilton Reynolds, copy of a miniature by Joseph Severn, 1818. *London Metropolitan Archive.*

went through three editions in two months, and ironically contributed to the subsequent high sales of Wordsworth's piece. 'The ante-natal Peter' with its own preface and critical apparatus convincingly mocks Wordsworth's fondness in *The Lyrical Ballads* and its preface for sentimentalized Lake District peasants. The satirical eye is very sharp, whether it is ridiculing Wordsworth's self-important prose or his poetry's bizarre imagery, verbosity and moments of banality. It is certainly unfair to Wordsworth (that is part of the point) but has been called 'one of the greatest parodies of all time'.[18] Reynolds would not have wished to be remembered in this way: his later years were not happy ones, and on his tomb is engraved in letters as large as his own name 'The Friend of Keats'.

From 'Peter Bell, a Lyrical Ballad'

It is written in that pure unlaboured style, which can only be met with among labourers; — and I can safely say, that while its imaginations spring beyond the reach of the most imaginative, its occasional meaning falls far below the meanest capacity.

4   Beneath the ever blessed moon
      An old man o'er an old grave stares,
      You never look'd upon his fellow;
      His brow is covered with grey hairs,
      As though they were an umbrella.

      . . . . .

6   'Tis Peter Bell — 'tis Peter Bell,
      Who never stirreth in the day;
      His hand is wither'd — he is old!
      On Sundays he is us'd to pray,
      In winter he is very cold.

7   I've seen him in the month of August,
      At the wheat-field, hour by hour,
      Picking ear, — by ear, — by ear, —
      Through wind, — and rain, — and sun, — and shower,
      From year, — to year, to year, — to year.

      . . . . .

10   He is rurally related;
      Peter Bell has country cousins,
      (He had once a worthy mother)
      Bells and Peters by the dozens
      But Peter Bell he hath no brother.

11   Not a brother owneth he,
      Peter Bell he hath no brother;
      His mother had no other son,
      No other son e'er call'd her mother;
      Peter Bell hath brother none.

      . . . . .

Heath enthusing about Shakespeare. Reynolds praised Keats's work in print and gave him reviewing opportunities. Keats dedicated himself to poetry, but when Reynolds became engaged to Eliza Powell Drewe, he sought financial security by taking a legal apprenticeship. He may also have been all too conscious of Keats's superior talent, both factors provoking his 'great renunciation' of the poetic muse on St Valentine's Day 1818, when Keats was just moving towards his finest period of writing:

    I have no chill despondence that I am
    Self-banished from those rolls of honouring men
    That keep a temperate eye on airy Fame
    And write songs to her with golden pen.[17]

This was not exactly the watershed he thought it would be, but increasingly Reynolds wrote more light-hearted and ephemeral pieces. His greatest success came with parody. When he saw a forthcoming poem, *Peter Bell*, advertised by William Wordsworth, he wrote his own version with the same title. Shelley called it 'the ante-natal Peter' because it was published before the real one. Composition was almost instantaneous. Keats recorded that Reynolds 'wrote it as soon as thought on', and it may well have been composed and sent off to the printer within twenty-four hours. The parody was enormously popular,

14   The hand of Peter Bell is busy,
     Under the pent-house of his hairs;
     His eye is like a solemn sermon;
     The little flea severely fares,
     'Tis a sad day for the vermin.

15   He is thinking of the Bible —
     Peter Bell is old and blest:
     He doth pray and scratch away,
     He doth scratch, and bitten pray
     To *flee* away, and be at rest.

16   At home his foster child is cradled —
     Four brown bugs are feeding there;
     Catch as many, sister Ann,
     Catch as many as you can
     And yet the little insects spare.

17   Why should blessed insects die?
     The flea doth skip o'er Betty Foy,
     Like a little living thing:
     Though it hath no fin or wing,
     Hath it not a moral joy?

WILLIAM ROBERTS (1767–1849)

I send you a letter to Roberts, signed Wortley Clutterbuck, which you may publish in what form you please, in answer to his article. I have had many proofs of men's absurdity, but he beats all in folly. Why, the wolf in sheep's clothing has tumbled into the very trap! We'll strip him.

(Letter from Lord Byron to his publisher John Murray, 23 August 1819)[19]

William Roberts was nephew to Old Pauline High Master Richard Roberts. A barrister by profession, he also edited the *British Review* from 1811 to 1822. In this tory and evangelical periodical Roberts was naïve enough to attack Byron for deploying his humour and poetic skill to pollute upright English men and women with continental debauchery:

Put feeling, and virtue, and the interests of human happiness out of the question; assume the hypothesis of a world without souls, level man to the consideration of brutes; […] and this little poem of *Beppo*, which, it is said, but which we are slow to believe, Lord Byron, an English nobleman, an English husband, and an English father, hath sent reeking from the stews of Venice, is a production of great humour and unquestionable excellence.* In all seriousness then, we mean to say, that the way in which the writer of this bantering poem has treated the sin of adultery, and all the sanctions by which marriage is made holy and happy, designates it as the product of a mind careless, cold, and callous; for who but a man of such a mind could, at a distance from his country and home, with a full knowledge of what makes that country great and prosperous, her families honourable, her sons manly and true, and her daughters the objects of delicate and respectful love, send among us a tale of pollution, dipped in the deepest dye of Italian debauchery, relieved and recommended by a vivacity and grace of colouring that takes from the mischief its apparent turpitude and disarms the vigilance of virtue.[20]

Byron's revenge came in Canto I of *Don Juan* (1819), where he mockingly suggested that he had bribed the editor of what he insultingly called 'my grandmother's review' to write a favourable article only to find Roberts 'smear his page with gall instead of honey,/All I can say is that he had the money'.[21] Of course Roberts took this seriously and was unwise enough to publish an indignant response:

No misdemeanour, not even that of sending into the world obscene and blasphemous poetry, the product of studious lewdness, and laboured impiety, appears to us in so detestable a light as the acceptance of a present by an editor of a Review, as the condition of praising an author; and yet the miserable man (for miserable he is, as having a soul of which he cannot rid) who has given birth to this pestilent poem has not scrupled to lay this to the charge of the *British Review*.[22]

Byron scented victory and sent a pointedly ironic 'Letter to the Editor of My Grandmother's Review' by one 'Wortley Clutterbuck' to his publisher John Murray, but Murray would not touch it. It was published eventually in *The Liberal*, but it is not clear that Roberts read it: Arthur Roberts was unaware of its existence when he wrote his father's life in 1850.[23]

---

* *Beppo: a Venetian Story* (1818) was the first of Byron's mock-heroic romances in *ottava rima* and prepared the way for *Don Juan*. It describes Beppo's return to Venice in disguise after a long absence and confrontation with his wife and her new partner. Everybody is reconciled over a cup of coffee, something which deeply offended Roberts's morals.

CHARLES MOLLOY WESTMACOTT (1787/8–1868)

[He] keeps a Sunday newspaper as a reservoir for the filth of the week; he lets out a cabinet d'aisance for any man who wishes to be delivered of a lie. No trader of the kind can be more obliging or more ill-savoured: his soul stinks of his profession, and you spit when you hear his name. Sneak has run through all the circle of scoundrelism: whatever is most base, dastardly, and contemptible, Sneak has committed. Is a lie to be told of any man? Sneak tells it. Is a Countess to be slandered? Sneak slanders her. Is theft to be committed? Sneak writes to you, 'Sir, I have received some anecdotes about you, which I would not publish for the world if you will give me ten pounds for them.'

(Edward Lytton Bulwer's description of Westmacott, whom he dubbed Sneak)[24]

Charles Molloy Westmacott's own life gave rise to plenty of gossip. In St Paul's admission registers he appears as the son of Richard Molloy, a merchant of Lambeth Marsh, and his enemies called him 'a brat of old MOLLOY', a chimney-sweeper, but he was probably the illegitimate son of Richard Westmacott, a sculptor, and Susannah Molloy, an innkeeper.[25] His métier was satirical and scandalous journalism, and he became very wealthy, partly by extortion. His victims would have to pay to keep their names out of his publications. It was even said that he once received £5,000 to suppress evidence which supported the claims of Princess Sophia's illegitimate son Captain Garth that his father was not Equerry-General Garth but Sophia's brother, the Duke of Cumberland, who had raped her.

Westmacott's first organ, the *Gazette of Fashion*, ran a feature on gambling dens, where he laid claim to a list of over two hundred people he was intending to name, not (he disingenuously protested) because he sought hush money but because they 'merited chastisement'. Subsequently he purchased *The Age*, which went on to flourish as a sensational and scandalous tory journal: by 1830 it probably had the highest circulation of any newspaper in the country, daily or weekly. *The Age* is populated by absurd caricatures, and their very absurdity dilutes the satire. The Duchess of St Albans, a former actress made extremely wealthy by two marriages and desperate to become established in high society, appears as 'Her Grease'. After unwisely dubbing Westmacott 'Sneak', the independent radical MP Lytton Bulwer (he was very proud of the 'Lytton' and later wrote novels as Lord Lytton) found himself turned into 'Edward Liston Wifewhack Whiggett'. Westmacott was reviled by his victims and opponents but did not always escape unscathed. After some nasty remarks about his daughter Fanny, a fashionable actress, the actor Charles Kemble sought him out at a performance in Covent Garden and beat him with a stick: *The News* gleefully reported that he was left to 'roll about the floor and roar'.[26] Westmacott was unabashed: in *The Age* he ridiculed Kemble, 'an athletic man, full six feet high' for taking on 'a pigmy [...] a *defenceless* dwarf [Westmacott was famously small]'.[27]

It was claimed that a number of other works published under the pseudonym of Bernard Blackmantle were in fact written entirely by Westmacott, but the degree of his involvement has never been determined. One of these, the *English Spy*, is filled with the gossip he enjoyed, as in the account of a Venetian Carnival at the Argyll Rooms:

'Who is that dashing looking brunette in the turban, that is just entering the room?' inquired Transit, who appeared to be mightily taken with the fair incognita. 'That lady, with the

Charles Molloy Westmacott, engraving by Daniel Maclise, published 1834. *National Portrait Gallery, London.*

mahogany skin and *piquant* appearance, is the favourite mistress of the *poor* Duke of Ma**b***h,' responded Crony, 'and is no other than the celebrated Poll Pshaw! Everybody has heard of the *Queen* of the *Amazons*, a title given to the lady, in honour, as I suppose, of his grace's fighting ancestor. Poll is said to be a great voluptuary; but at any rate she cannot be very *extravagant*, that is, if she draws *all her resources* from her protector's present purse. Do you observe the *jolie dame* yonder sitting under the orchestra? That is the well-known Nelly Mansell, of Crawford Street, called the *old Pomona*, from the richness of her *first fruits*. [...] Do you perceive the swarthy amazon waddling along yonder, whom the old Earl of W—d appears to be *eyeing* with no little anticipation of delight? That is a lady with a *very* ancient and most fish-like flavour, odiferous in person as the oily female Eskimos, or the more *fragrant* feminine inhabitants of Russian Tartary and the Crimea; she has with some of her admirers obtained the name of *Dolly Drinkwater*, from her known dislike to anything *stronger* than pure French Brandy.'[28]

If Charles Molloy Westmacott hoped that his exploits would win him social recognition, he was disappointed. Later in life he simply sank into obscurity.[29]

❧ *Actors, managers, and playwrights*

JOHN FAWCETT (1769–1837)

This gentleman is an actor of great original merit, and whether his character be ancient or modern, his style of playing is peculiar to himself.

(Thomas Gilliland, *The Dramatic Mirror*, 1808)

John Fawcett caught Garrick's eye at the age of eight and, despite his father's hope that St Paul's School would knock him into shape, he ran away ten years later to Margate, where he adopted a pseudonym and launched his stage career. After spells in Maidstone and York he decided to concentrate on low comedy and enjoyed his London début in 1791. He appeared regularly at the Haymarket and Covent Garden, often in plays written by George Colman with him in mind, and even turned his hand to writing pantomimes and melodrama.[30] *Obi* or *Three-Fingered Jack*, set on a West Indian slave plantation, was apparently a huge success. For Gilliland, Fawcett's acting was the best of his time:

Fawcett's Lingo is as good a piece of acting as we have on the stage. Pangloss is a character as finely drawn as any in the whole range of the drama, and he unites in his delineation of the pedant, all the richness of the author's humour, with a chaste and classical colouring. There is a wide and opposite cast of characters, which he sustains with the happiest effect; indeed his acting is as near perfection as the efforts of human art can possibly reach. The physical properties of this gentleman are certainly highly advantageous to his line of acting, which, though in no way singular or disagreeable as a private gentleman, make a very effective figure, either as a countryman, pedant, old man, Quaker, or Jew, etc. His voice too, has an agreeable harshness, which well accords with the whimsical sentiments of the Comic Muse, without lessening the force of a pathetic passage.[31]

John Fawcett, engraving after portrait begun by Sir Thomas Lawrence in 1828. © *St Paul's School.*

ROBERT ELLISTON (1774–1831)

For thee the Pauline Muses weep. In elegies, that shall silence his crude prose, they shall celebrate thy praise.

(Charles Lamb's elegy to Elliston, 1831)[32]

Like Fawcett, Robert Elliston ran away to the stage, in his case to Bath, and like Fawcett he had a spell in Yorkshire before returning to Bath:

He made his appearance in the character of Romeo. [...] The indisposition of several performers now afforded him the long-wished-for opportunity of calling into action a versatility of powers which was before unknown, even to himself. He appeared in tragedy, comedy, opera, and pantomime, with such success, that he declined the promised engagement at New Drury, and retained his situation at Bath.[33]

A move to Drury Lane was finally made in 1804 after a benefit performance in Bath where 'the torrent was so impetuous, that the door-keepers, money-takers, and assistants, were overwhelmed, and a scene of great confusion ensued, which none but those who witnessed it can conceive'.[34]

It was the mellow, romantic character in his repertoire that most impressed Elliston's audiences, although Gilliland, writing in 1808, was very critical of his dress sense:

In the support of early English characters, in which the costume is, in a great degree, regulated by fancy, Mr Elliston is more happy in the arrangement of his dress; but when he appears as a modern gentleman, he displays no taste in either the clothes he wears, or in putting them on. White *small clothes* with a blue coat and white waistcoat, constitute the dress of *his private gentleman,* either in winter or summer, which gives him more the appearance of a holiday fop, or a smart hair-dresser, than an elegant gentleman. Mr Elliston we think is less excusable for this negligence of attire than many of his brethren, because he mixes in the gay circles of fashionable life, where he must see men of elegant dress and deportment in a drawing room. With a little more attention to the dressing of his hair, and to the costume of a private gentleman, he would appear to considerably more advantage before the public than he has ever yet done. Nature has given him a good figure, and while he continues to offer himself to public notice, it is a duty he owes to the consequence of his public character and to his audience to give the most decisive effect to whatever character he takes upon himself to assume.[35]

When Drury Lane was burnt down in 1809, Elliston turned his hand to theatre management. So fast did he move in leasing theatres throughout the country that he became known as the 'Napoleon of the theatre'.[36] His apogee came when in 1819 he became manager of the new Drury Lane, which he ran until declared bankrupt in 1826. He found out that the Regency audience wanted spectacle and amusement: even Edmund Kean as King Lear, allowed now for the first time since King George III's madness and death, was not successful without a risqué afterpiece. It was an age of theatre rather than drama. Elliston's final years were spent as actor-manager of the Surrey Theatre, where despite failing health he made a superb Falstaff in *The First Part of King Henry IV*, at least in the retrospective eyes of the *New Monthly Magazine* (1836): 'We fear that few, very few, critics crossed the bridge to see the fat knight, which, it is our faith, was the highest triumph of Elliston as an actor, inasmuch as it combined, heightened, and enriched all the qualities which he severally displayed in other parts.'

Robert Elliston as Duke Aranza in Tobin's comedy *The Honey Moon*, oil by Samuel de Wilde. The duke has pretended to his wife that he is a lowly rustic rather than the noble she thought she had married. The black plumes on his wide-brimmed felt hat and his fur-trimmed jerkin are not normal rustic dress. *By kind permission of the Garrick Club/Art Archive.*

RICHARD HARRIS BARHAM (1788–1845)

My wife goes to bed at ten, to rise at eight, and look after the children and other matrimonial duties. I sit up till three in the morning, working at rubbish for *Blackwood*. She is the slave of the ring, and I of the lamp.

(from Richard Barham's diary)[37]

Richard Barham's appetite for humour and practical jokes surfaced early, before he became a Pauline at the age of eleven:

He was chief or president of a school and juvenile association in his native place [Canterbury], who assumed to themselves the title of The Wig Club, and who, disguised in legal, clerical, and sporting wigs of every sort, from the judge's full-bottom to the pedagogue's scratch, besides other masquerade habits, were wont to meet [...] and play such fantastic tricks as more frequently attend the inventions of the cleverest men, when seeking recreation from severe studies and toils, than could be expected from the sallies of youth.[38]

His friend at St Paul's, Charles Diggle, was given to stealing shoelaces and throwing jam tarts at Quaker meetings,[39] and Barham's time at Oxford is famed for the way he dealt with his tutor Hodson's complaint about absence from early morning chapel:

'The fact is, sir,' urged his pupil, 'you are too *late* for me.'
'Too late!' repeated the tutor, in astonishment.
'Yes, sir — too late. I cannot sit up till seven o'clock in the morning: I am a man of regular habits; and unless I get to bed by four or five at latest, I am really fit for nothing next day.'[40]

So it was to continue in later life. One enduring friend was the notorious hoaxer, Theodore Hook.* Another was 'the facetious Sydney Smith', canon at St Paul's Cathedral, where Barham was a minor canon.[41] The two were famed for their contests in wit. When Smith declared at dinner, 'Nothing should ever induce him to go up in a balloon, unless indeed it would benefit the Established Church', Barham 'recommended him to go at once, as there would at least be a chance of it'.[42] At the Garrick Club, where he was a founder member, 'the literary man would find all that was agreeable and delightful in the society of the Reverend Richard Barham, Charles Dickens, William Makepeace Thackeray, Charles Reade'.[43]

Barham was an active parish priest throughout his adult life, first in East Kent ('The World is divided into Europe, Asia, Africa, America and Romney Marsh') and subsequently in London.[44] He wrote for several periodicals and formed a close link with another old school-friend, publisher Richard Bentley (see next entry). It was in *Bentley's Miscellany* (from 1837) that the popular *Ingoldsby Legends* first made their appearance. Writing as Thomas Ingoldsby of Tappington Everard in Kent, Barham pretended to be publishing authentic extracts from his family memoranda, discovered in an old oak chest within an 'antiquated manor

---

If any one lied, —or if any one swore,—
    Or slumber'd in pray'r-time and happened to snore,
    That good Jackdaw
    Would give a great 'Caw!'

'The Jackdaw of Rheims', illustration by Arthur Rackham, from *The Ingoldsby Legends* by R. H. Barham, 1907 edition. © *Bridgeman Artists' Copyright Service.*

---

* In the Berners Street Hoax, 1809, Hook took out his grievances on a Mrs Tottenham by sending to her house wagonloads of falsely ordered goods and several falsely invited dignitaries, including the lord mayor of London.

house of Elizabethan architecture, with its gable ends, stone stanchions, and tortuous chimneys'.[45] The benign hoaxer was at work again.

The legends are mainly in verse and from a variety of sources, including Sir Walter Scott, Kentish legend and medieval tales. Barham would compose 'while waiting for a cup of tea, a railroad train, or an unpunctual acquaintance, on some stray cover of a letter'.[46] The poetry is striking for the ease with which he uses extraordinary compound rhymes and 'verbal pyrotechnics' equal to the best of Byron.[47] Barham's comic treatment of Gothic subject matter was less welcome to the straight-laced Victorian reviewer:

A sly, laughable, and merry tale, at the expense of cunning friars, and licentious monks, and frail vestals of the cloister, may do a vast deal of irreparable mischief. [...] But of all the wild audacities of the spirit of mockery, none is so astounding as that which makes sport of the infernal and malignant agency, perpetually at work for the ruin of the human race [...] And we are grieved that the Rev. R. H. Barham should have suffered his native propensity for the ludicrous to betray him into so unseemly and perilous an indiscretion.[48]

The Ingoldsby Legends have been frequently reprinted, and their illustrators include Tenniel, Cruikshank and Rackham.

❧ *Publishers*

JOHN BOWYER NICHOLS (1779–1863)
SAMUEL BENTLEY (1785–1868)
RICHARD BENTLEY (1794–1871)

John Bowyer Nichols and his cousins Samuel and Richard Bentley were members of a powerful publishing dynasty. Samuel Bentley and Nichols were civilized men, interested in antiquities and the art of typography. Nichols published many significant early nineteenth-century county histories; Samuel Bentley's major achievement was *Excerpta Historica*, a scholarly compilation of early documents, and he was a skilled pioneer of incorporating relief woodcuts into a text.

Nichols was respected for 'his honourable dealings and mild manner'.[49] This could not be said of his other cousin Richard Bentley, who became enmeshed in the less savoury aspects of the book trade. After a period working with his brother Samuel, in 1829 Richard Bentley went into partnership with an unscrupulous publisher, Henry Colburn, and began a sequence of projects for the new popular market. The Standard Novels, six shilling (30p) one-volume reprints of fiction, were highly successful and have been called 'the most remarkable cheap reprints of the century',[50] but other enterprises failed, and an inordinate amount of money for the time (£27,000) was spent 'puffing' or promoting their publications.[51]

In 1832 the two publishers parted company and became rivals, ridiculed in Thackeray's *Pendennis* as Bacon and Bungay (a reference to two medieval magicians). Bentley's appetite for self-publicity was legendary: in 1833 he managed to be made 'publisher in ordinary to his majesty' but his firm published nothing for William IV or for Victoria. The American publisher Jared Sparks wrote:

Erasmus, *Concio de Puere Jesu*, published 1818. An example of fine printing by John Bowyer Nichols and Samuel Bentley. In his statutes Colet laid down that all the children at his school would attend St Paul's Cathedral annually to hear a sermon by the boy bishop. Erasmus's volume contains an address about the boy Jesus to be given by a boy from the school founded by John Colet. *Ken Lawson. © St Paul's School.*

DES. ERASMI ROT.

CONCIO

𝔇𝔢 𝔭𝔲𝔢𝔯𝔬 𝔍𝔢𝔰𝔲

OLIM PRONVNCIATA A PVERO

IN SCHOLA IOANNIS COLETI

LONDINI INSTITVTA

IN QVA PRAESIDEBAT

𝔍𝔪𝔞𝔤𝔬 𝔓𝔲𝔢𝔯𝔦 𝔍𝔢𝔰𝔲

DOCENTIS SPECIE.

LONDINI

TYPIS I. ET I. B. NICHOLS, ET S. BENTLEY.
M.DCCC.X.VIII.

Next to Colburn he [Bentley] has the character of being the most familiar of any publisher in London with the small tricks of his trade. He has lately had the vanity to get himself made 'Publisher to her Majesty', which is mere vapour. Now there are divers 'Leather Breeches Makers to the Queen' in London, though it is not positively known, that her majesty ever wore leather breeches; but she has certain equerries, huntsmen, and grooms, who sometimes bedeck themselves in that habiliment, and Albert may now and then want a pair when he goes upon his sporting excursions; so that the tailors make some good account of the office of royal breeches makers. But who ever heard of the queen or any of her household publishing a book? Yet Bentley attaches this foolish appendage to all his title-pages.[52]

Another notorious incident in his career was Bentley's brush with Charles Dickens. In 1836 he signed up Dickens to edit a new periodical. The original title was *The Wit's Miscellany* and when that was changed to *Bentley's Miscellany* his schoolfriend Richard Barham (author of *The Ingoldsby Legends* — see last entry) commented 'Why go to the other extreme?'[53] The serialization of *Oliver Twist* was a success, but editorial and financial arguments soon surfaced and, despite nine agreements renegotiating terms in Dickens's favour, they parted in 1839. Typical of Dickens's distrust (he once accused Bentley of 'offensive impertinence') was this comment:

Mr Bentley in his advertisements and hired puffs of other books with which I never had and can have any possible connection, has repeatedly [...] used my name and the names of some of my writings in an unwarrantable manner [...] calculated to do me serious prejudice.[54]

Although he lost the most lucrative author of his age, Bentley prospered for a time. The Standard Novels sold well, and he revelled in *Miscellany* dinners attended by 'all the very *haut ton* of the literature of the day'.[55] However, he was losing edge and judgment in a tough market and nearly went insolvent, although a late success with Mrs Henry Wood's racy novel *East Lynne* helped to repair his fortunes. Contemporary judgments of Bentley varied, but on his death *The Bookseller* wrote of Bentley's 'fine taste' and 'integrity' while also observing that 'he frequently over-estimated the value of works offered him'.[56]

Architects and builders

DANIEL ASHER ALEXANDER (1768–1846)

Daniel Alexander became a highly successful architect and attracted much comment with his radial design (1810) for Dartmoor prison, which was to hold French and American prisoners of war. Only in 1850, after more than thirty years of disuse, did it become a civilian prison.

Among his other projects were two new wings to accommodate naval asylums, joined by open colonnades to Inigo Jones's Queen's House at Greenwich, work which earned praise from Sir John Soane, then professor of architecture at the Royal Academy, for its finely conservative spirit.

View of The Queen's House at Greenwich showing additions by Daniel Alexander, aquatint by J. T. Lee, published J. Gold, 1811. *Guildhall Library, City of London.*

GEORGE RENNIE (1791–1866)

George Rennie shared his father John Rennie's interest in arches and bridges and studied extensively on the continent. He claimed authorship of the original design for London Bridge (1820) and made elaborate notes and drawings of Waterloo Bridge, both projects of his father. The railway age suited him perfectly, and he was responsible for planning several lines. One project he recommended was the London Grand Junction Railway, a line to run on an arched viaduct from Camden Town following the route of Farringdon Road to terminate just by what is now Holborn Viaduct. Rennie commented, 'The eye dwells with pleasure on the undulating line of the arches, and when the series is of some length the effect is still better. The admiration excited by the aqueducts at Rome and Lisbon is proof of this.'[57] It was never built. Interestingly, another Old Pauline, the antiquary and architect John Pridden (1758–1825), had already submitted a scheme to the corporation of London which anticipated Holborn Viaduct.

Rennie and his younger brother John set up a shipbuilding yard in the 1830s. They supplied steam engines for the British navy and Spanish government, and in 1840 built the first British navy vessel with a screw propeller. The yard also manufactured railway locomotives.[58]

The proposed London Grand Junction Railway, lithograph by George Remington, published G. S. Tregear, c.1835. *Guildhall Library, City of London.*

THOMAS GRISSELL (1801–74)

Together with his cousin Samuel Morton Peto, Thomas Grissell became London's leading public works contractor. Among their commissions were several London clubs, Nelson's Column and Clerkenwell Prison. The Lyceum Theatre was constructed by Grissell and Peto in sixteen weeks and St James's Theatre in just ten. They worked on the river front of the new Houses of Parliament but as costs increased decided not to take up contracts for the rest of the building. Grissell became very wealthy. He lived in a Kensington Palace Gardens mansion constructed of surplus stone from the Houses of Parliament and went on to buy a Georgian estate in Surrey.[59]

Nelson's Column under construction by Grissell and Peto, April 1844. Salt paper print from a calotype negative by William Henry Fox Talbot. Grissell published an account of the scaffolding used on this project.
National Media Museum/Science & Society Picture Library.

❧ *Gothic revival*

BENJAMIN WEBB (1819–85)

His dress was very peculiar and intended to designate ultra-highchurchmanship.

(Joseph Romilly, fellow of Trinity)[60]

Benjamin Webb was still a freshman at Trinity College, Cambridge, when he founded with fellow undergraduate John Mason Neale the Cambridge Camden Society. Unlike the parallel high-church Oxford Movement, which focused on theological questions, Webb and Neale were interested in architecture and liturgy, and before the 'Blessed Benjamin' graduated in 1841 they had produced important pamphlets for churchwardens and church builders and launched a monthly magazine, the *Ecclesiologist* (edited by Webb 1841–68).

The mid-nineteenth century was an extraordinary period for church architecture, with 1,727 new churches constructed between 1840 and 1876 and over seven thousand restorations.[61] The Camden Society, later reconstituted as *The Ecclesiological Society*, wanted eighteenth-century box pews and triple-decker pulpits swept away, and the altar and chancel returned to the centre of worship. The Anglican architect 'for his own style should choose the glorious architecture of the fourteenth

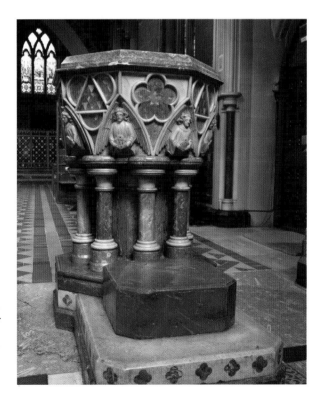

The font at All Saints, Margaret Street, an example of William Butterfield's use of polychromatic materials. *Amanda Denny.*

century'.[62] Webb's speciality was continental churches and his first independent publication *Sketches of Continental Ecclesiology, or Church Notes in Belgium, Germany and Italy* (1848). He was one of the first to recommend brick for church construction and enthused over the Venetian style before Ruskin published *The Stones of Venice.*

Webb's view was that 'in God's house everything should be real'. He believed in the use of indestructible materials, polychromatic brick, marble, alabaster and fresco. The architect he most admired was William Butterfield, to whom he almost certainly introduced Italian Gothic. Butterfield's All Saints, Margaret Street, London (1849–59), was planned as a model church under the auspices of the Ecclesiological Society,[63] and praised by Webb for showing that 'red brick is the best building material for

London, and [...] compatible with the highest flights of architecture'.[64]

Despite the sartorial excesses of his undergraduate days, Webb was a moderate figure among the tory high-church ritualists, and remained a convinced Anglican:

At all events, in an investigation into the differences between ancient and modern church architecture, the contrast between the ancient and modern builders could not be overlooked, and it is not too much to hope that some, at least, may be struck by the fact, that the deeply religious habits of the builders of old, the hours [set times of prayer], the cloister, the discipline, the obedience, resulted in their matchless works; while the worldliness, vanity, dissipation, and patronage of our own architects issue in unvarying and hopeless failure.[65]

❧ *'The Modern Luther'*

WILLIAM GOODE (1801–68)

Satan can inspire men to speak either known or unknown languages.

(William Goode)[66]

William Goode, photograph 1855–68. *Guildhall Library, City of London.*

In 1825, when William Goode began his work as curate at Christ Church, Greyfriars, fashionable London was just recovering from the sensational arrival of Edward Irving, a preacher from Dumfriesshire. Irving's sermons at the Caledonian Chapel were packed out with cabinet ministers, peers, the rich and the famous, who had come to hear an intoxicating mixture of stern religion and Romantic idealism. His popularity did not survive the increasing length of his addresses, sometimes over three hours, but Irving remained a force to reckon with. His views became apocalyptic — the world would end in 1868. He was denounced for the heresy of believing Christ to be fully human and capable of sin. Then, at a time when England was in the grip of election-reform fever, he turned to charismatic worship. There was an outbreak of speaking in tongues. His church was attracting the seriously disturbed, and the result, some said, was bedlam. It was at this point that Goode published *The Modern Claims to the Possession of the Extraordinary Gifts of the Spirit* (1833), a lengthy and learned denunciation of glossolalia as the work of Satan:

When there suddenly rise up in the Church those who, with a high moral character, and all the appearances of sincerity, zeal, and religious devotedness, profess to have received the extraordinary gifts of the Spirit, admonish men against Satan, preach Christ, and urge upon the Church the duty and neces-

sity of seeking higher powers and attainments, it seems to Christians in general a harsh and improbable supposition, to imagine that Satan can have had any hand in bringing about such an occurrence.

But when we turn to facts, and ascertain that such cases have been constantly occurring in the Church, and confessedly due, if not to Satanic power, yet certainly to nothing more than human enthusiasm, or excitement, under Satanic influence, the charm is dissolved, the only evidences upon which the delusion stands at once dissipated, and we are able to estimate it at its real value. He who knows how often, and how perfectly Satan has acted his part, as an angel of light, in producing such delusions, will want nothing further to prepare him for their recurrence, with all the plausibility with which the subtle ingenuity and supernatural power of the great enemy can invest them.[67]

Goode was growing in reputation as spokesman for the evangelical branch of the Church of England and was referred to as 'the modern Luther', with whom he shared a birthday. As it happened, Irving died in December 1834. Ironically, his successor as chief pastor in what was now known as the Catholic Apostolic or Irvingite Church was an Old Pauline, Christopher Heath (1802–1876), whose name appears next to Goode's own in the school admission registers. The Irvingite Church gradually metamorphosed, becoming more international and elaborately ritualistic. Goode too changed focus and turned his formidable learning and powers of debate against the emerging Oxford Movement and its Romanizing tendencies. One of his critiques extended to three volumes. As far as he was concerned, the slightest unnecessary gesture or ornament in church could trigger a slide into wholesale popish ritual:

It ought not to be forgotten, that if [...] additional ceremonies are to be allowed in the public ministrations of the Church, because they are not expressly forbidden, other ceremonies must be permitted on the same ground. For instance, in the ministration of the sacrament of baptism, the use of oil, tapers, spittle, and other popish ceremonies, may be introduced, and defended on the same grounds as those we have been considering [...] And so, in short, almost the whole mass of popish ceremonies [...] may be re-introduced into our Church by the Romanizing party that have lately sprung up among us.[68]

Goode served in several London parishes before becoming president of Sion College and finally dean of Ripon.[69]

Two Victorian headmasters

JAMES PRINCE LEE (1804–69)

Lee was the greatest man I have ever come within the influence of — the greatest and the best.
    (E. W. Benson, later archbishop of Canterbury and one of Lee's pupils at King Edward's School, Birmingham)[70]

Kept at a distance, and treated [...] like schoolboys.
    (Comment in the *Manchester Guardian* on Lee's management of clergy when bishop of Manchester)[71]

The puzzle of James Prince Lee's life is why such success as a schoolmaster was followed by such failings as a bishop.

After eight years' teaching at Thomas Arnold's Rugby, he became headmaster of King Edward's Birmingham at the early age of thirty-four. He took over an expanded school and massive new Gothic buildings, designed by Charles Barry, which were used until 1936. Classes were generally taught in groups in the great hall, as was true of many schools, and at one end Lee would sit at a massive desk thought to have been designed by Pugin and superscribed with the word 'Sapientia' — a piece of furniture still visible in the twentieth-century school hall. Round him sat his own classical scholars, many of whom went on to win high honours at Cambridge: eight of his pupils were elected fellows of Trinity College.

Lee wove a remarkable spell as a teacher, E.W. Benson said, admittedly in a memorial sermon:

For about ten years at Birmingham [his scholars] came to him and left him in even flow; their intercourse with him was hourly, and their loyalty absolute. The love of him was always at the height; they were bound together by it then and ever since: it was the perfection of affection for him which has made so many of them seek his own profession.[72]

His combination of cultural breadth and rigorous attention to language was in turn passed on by his pupils to their own students, even to the extent of their adopting a similar abstruse and pedantic written style.

James Prince Lee, engraving, published 1853 by John Clowes Grundy.
© *St Paul's School.*

But there was a problem. Towards the end of his time at Birmingham, Lee fell victim to Thomas Gutteridge, a local surgeon and it seems serial scandal-monger, who blamed Lee as a governor of Birmingham General Hospital for blocking his appointment as surgeon there. Among his allegations were specific charges of drunkenness, once when visiting a dying Blue Coat boy and once at divine service, and a general accusation that Lee meddled in Birmingham's civic institutions, 'exhibiting a most officious, insolent, and domineering behaviour and an intriguing and ill-natured disposition which dishonoured his character as a clergyman'.[73]

Gutteridge was found guilty of criminal libel, but the strain on Lee, whose health was never good, can only be imagined. It seems that his pupils knew little or nothing of the verbal attacks until Lee had been appointed to the new bishopric of Manchester, a post he assumed in early 1848, but when they did hear, their loyalty did not waver: Benson called Gutteridge a 'dog, for whom hanging is too good'.[74]

Lee's move to Manchester opened the second half of his career. A new diocese, with a paucity of churches and a growing, in places overcrowded, population, was a much bigger challenge than a school, but he worked tirelessly to build churches and recruit clergy. It was his management style that caused problems. Early on he fell out with the Dean and Chapter over their property. As a low-church-man fearful of 'popish' incursions he used his deans to spy out churches with inappropriate fittings. When one vicar complained of Lee's interference, the bishop's dismissive reply began, 'Reverend Sir. I have to acknowledge the receipt of your letter. I have neither time nor inclination to undertake the, I fear, needless task of commenting on it.'[75] Such incidents turned Mancunian clergy against Lee, and Lee against them. He would hide away in his palace, Mauldeth Hall, so that 'his whole way of living and ruling was such as would have become a cardinal of the Renaissance'.[76] Finally, there was an echo of the Gutteridge episode. Lee became involved with Manchester's learned societies; in doing so, he somehow offended James Crossley, a very eminent local antiquary who took revenge by exposing flaws in Lee's only published piece of scholarship, an edition of Isaac Barrow's *Sermons and Fragments*. Unlike Gutteridge, Crossley was

The great hall at King Edward's School, Birmingham, designed by Charles Barry. James Prince Lee taught his classical scholars from a massive desk at the far end. *Courtesy King Edward's School, Birmingham.*

right, and he pressed home his advantage by publishing an unpleasant lampoon when Lee died.

The paradox then is of a teacher loved and revered for his piety, understanding and knowledge who became a bishop reviled for duplicity, overbearing behaviour and poor scholarship. The 'domineering' manner with adults that so irritated Gutteridge may be partly to blame, and it is easy to cast him as the kind of schoolmaster who liked to be didactic and completely in control, but perhaps he was simply unfortunate.[77]

ALFRED JAMES CARVER (1826–1909)

Well, I do not want an Eton or Harrow here, but if there be anything greater, better, and more useful than an Eton or Harrow, that I wish to have here.

(Carver on Dulwich College)[78]

In 1884 Frederick William Walker led a St Paul's that had grown rapidly since he became high master seven years earlier into Waterhouse's grand new school in West Kensington. In 1870 Alfred James Carver had seen Dulwich College into Charles Barry's lavish new buildings, financed by £100,000 obtained from selling estate land to the Crystal Palace Company and to several rail-

ways for their lines into London. Both moves symbolize the new prosperity of academic London day schools. Carver had spent six years at St Paul's School as surmaster before being appointed Master of Alleyn's College of God's Gift at Dulwich in 1858. The statutes of Alleyn's original foundation for 'twelve poor scholars', dating back to 1626, had recently been altered by a private act of parliament to provide for two schools. One establishment, soon known as Dulwich College, became more elitist both socially and academically; the other, Alleyn's School, concentrated on boys intended for careers in commerce. Carver was head of both schools.

With the idle members of the class he did not much concern himself: shortsighted, buried in his author, declaiming ever and anon in that sonorous voice of his some passage that took his fancy, he might not observe that some youths on the back benches were reading novels or writing letters. It was to the earnest student that his lessons were addressed, and of these there were always enough to reward his care.[79]

He believed in academic elites and fought a long battle with William Rogers, chairman of the governors, and the Charity Commissioners, who wanted Alleyn's endowment used to set up middle-class schools in London parishes. Rogers was a friend of Old Pauline Benjamin Jowett at Balliol (see next entry), and his educational work had included creating schools for poor children in the City of London. A compromise was finally reached in 1882, the year before Carver retired, when Alleyn's moved into new buildings under its own separate head.[80] Meanwhile, Dulwich grew faster than any of its competitors and was one of the 'leading schools of England' invited to the first meeting of the Headmasters' Conference in 1869.[81]

Carver's legacy is evident from the league table of Oxford and Cambridge Scholarships (1885–92), inevitably led by St Paul's with one hundred awards over that period. Dulwich appears eighth, ahead of Westminster, and was the top London school without closed awards. He wanted Dulwich to be academic but had a broader view of education and the curriculum. 'The most successful intellectually were also in general the most manly in character and the most robust in health,' he stated at speech day, an occasion to which he imported from St Paul's the tradition of prize declamations.[82] The new buildings were the most advanced of their day in terms of science provision, and he encouraged art, drama and music.

Carver approved of examinations for the Civil Service and those of the Oxford and Cambridge Schools Examination Board, founded in 1873 (in 1877 Dulwich came fourth in the board's results, after Eton, Rugby and Marlborough), but he also saw their dangers.[83] His comments one speech day have a surprisingly modern ring:

There are many boys here who have been nearly three weeks under examinations, during which they have taken between thirty and forty papers. Besides that, several of the head boys here had to go in for other competitive examinations. The fact remains that during a term of some twelve or thirteen weeks a boy may be kept five or six weeks under actual examinations.[84]

Dulwich College from the South East, photographed York and Son, 1870–1900. The new buildings were designed by Charles Barry. *Reproduced by permission of English Heritage. NMR.*

BENJAMIN JOWETT (1817–93)

He always had a dislike for small-talk and trivialities, and never talked unless he had something to say. I have heard of his excusing his silence and saying: 'If I say nothing, it is not because I am out of temper, but because I have nothing to say.'

(Lord Hobhouse on Benjamin Jowett)[85]

Benjamin Jowett,
photograph by
H. H. H. Cameron, 1893.

High Master John Sleath thought Benjamin Jowett the best Latin scholar he ever sent to college.[86] He won school prizes in both Greek and Latin; in later life he became Oxford regius professor of Greek and renowned for his translation and analysis of Plato. As a theologian he gained some notoriety for his radical interpretation of St Paul's Epistles and belief that each age should read the Bible in its own way. Above all, Balliol College, Oxford, was the centre of Jowett's life: he lived there for fifty-seven years as undergraduate, tutor and in due course master.

From his early days as a student, Jowett made a lasting impression on those who met him. A contemporary recalled:

I looked upon Jowett as the freshest and most original mind I had come across; and I still think that I have never held converse with anyone who was more thoroughly original, or more careful to say only what he made his own.[87]

The word 'careful' is significant here: as a tutor, and one who without doubt took great personal interest in his pupils, his economy with language was legendary. Conversation was punctuated by alarming silences:

'I well remember his ways,' commented W. L. Newman, editor of Aristotle. 'When one took him composition, he used commonly to seat himself in a chair placed immediately in front of the fire and close to it, and to intersperse his abrupt, decided and pithy comments on one's work with vigorous pokes of the fire. Occasionally he would lapse into silence, and say nothing whatever perhaps for two or three minutes; but, if one rose to go, one often found that his best remarks still remained to be uttered. The silent interval had been a time of busy thought.'

This appears not to have been simply shyness. A follower of Socrates, Jowett believed that his pupils needed to think for themselves. As he put it, 'The chaos of ideas has to be moulded by every one in his own fashion.' Rather than detailed criticism, undergraduates could expect comments such as, 'That is not so Greek as the last you did,' or on one worrying occasion, 'Have you any taste for mathematics?'

Jowett detested systems. 'How I hate learning,' he said. 'How sad it is to see a man who is learned and nothing else, incapable of making any use of his knowledge.' He also believed that Oxford should open its minds to new subjects and its doors to a wider social range of undergraduates: before becoming master of Balliol he wrote to his friend Florence Nightingale:

I swore horribly at the master and some of the fellows of Balliol on Friday internally but fortunately no oath escaped me [at college meeting]. Having more room than I want, I offered to take a poor and distinguished scholar into my rooms who could not otherwise come up to the university. They objected, first that he would have 1/200 of the servants of the college gratuitously waiting upon him at dinner; secondly that he would pay nothing, not for coals but for having them carried to him. At last, after nearly an hour's discussion in which I said nothing, the majority graciously consented. Is there any red tape in the War Office worse than this? [88]

On becoming master of Balliol, Jowett set about creating a liberal Christian meritocracy, and the college established itself as the country's pre-eminent academic institution. He wrote to Lord Russell about the importance of 'giving the best education to the best intelligences in every class of society'.[89] Students were recruited from a wider range of schools and indeed from many countries overseas. Despite his liberal views, Jowett was also very good at building connections in high places and using them to position Balliol men. When three graduates became successive viceroys of India, it did begin to look as if Balliol were fulfilling his ambition, expressed to Florence Nightingale, of governing the world.[90]

There was a naïve side to Jowett. Lord Russell called him 'a schoolboy of magnificent proportions'. His understanding of society did not extend to the working class: when passing a drover with his sheep he asked, 'Why is it that those who have to do with animals become so degraded?'[91] During his spell of duty as university vice-chancellor there was aloofness again, driven of course by conviction, as he sought to convert other colleges to the Balliol model.

Convert them he did. At Jowett's funeral seven of the pallbearers were Balliol men, now heads of other colleges.

꽃 *Oxford tutor and bishop*

EDMUND ARBUTHNOTT KNOX (1847–1937)

To turn a rather idle college into a reading college is a very difficult proposition.

(Edmund Knox)

Edmund Knox's career culminated with seventeen effective years as bishop of Manchester, the see that had given Old Pauline James Prince Lee so much difficulty (see earlier entry). He was an undergraduate at Corpus Christi College, Oxford, and became a fellow of Merton aged just twenty-one. He was to stay there for seventeen years, as dean, tutor and then chaplain. Merton was not a model college. There were no resident tutors and, from two p.m. until nine o'clock the following morning, undergraduates were left to their own devices. Knox, who quickly won the soubriquet 'Hard Knox', set out to 'check extravagance and idleness, and to increase as far as I could the ranks of the industrious'. He found a few brilliant pupils but also dull men who could barely write English. Among such familiar undergraduate misdemeanours as illegal horse-racing and climbing into college dangerously during the night, he had one more interesting disciplinary problem to solve:

The college had erected a three-storey set of new buildings with a wealth of windows looking out on a gravelled quadrangle. For some reason it had become the habit of the idle to smash these windows with stones, or with small loaves left over from meals. It was a cheap form of amusement to the wealthy, for the college practice was to divide the cost of repairs among all the undergraduates resident, and to enter the charge in the battels, or bills sent in to parents. The £2 or £3 extra on battels which ran up to £60 or £70 a term passed unnoticed by wealthy parents, but it was a heavy extra in the bills of a poor man who was trying to scrape through on £30 or £40 a term. He resented this extra charge for the privilege of having his windows broken by men with whom he had little in common. The problem presented to me was to stop this practice without either espionage or informing. With the approval of my colleagues I determined to divide the glazier's bill among the six men whose battels were highest for the term. [...] The result was that the window-breaking came to an end.[92]

꽃 *Eccentric monk and preacher*

JOSEPH LEYCESTER LYNE (1837–1908) [*known as* Father Ignatius]

He [Ignatius] allows that a man must be of a very rare and peculiar temperament to become and remain a monk. A monk he says must either be a philosopher or a 'holy fool'. He also allows that monkery has a strong tendency to drive people mad.

(Francis Kilvert)[93]

Joseph Lyne was an extraordinary child. Tormented by the fear of Hell almost from birth, he spent his time at prep. school converting his schoolfellows. Lyne claimed to have been thrashed at St Paul's within an inch of his life by J. P. Bean, the surmaster (a 'Squeers-like old man') for bringing into the classroom some representations of the Temple at Jerusalem.[94] Exaggerated or not, the event did lead to the first of Lyne's many nervous breakdowns. He went to spend time on his uncle's ship, HMS *Undaunted*, where he entertained his cousins with dramatic stories of Christian martyrs and their violent ends.

It comes as no surprise that this pious, unstable dreamer sought a religious career. Lyne combined 'the evangelistic fervour of Moody and Sankey and General Booth with the monastic aspirations of Newman and Pusey'. While training at Trinity College, Glenalmond, he imagined

founding an order of Anglican monks, and by 1861, when as a deacon he became responsible for the mission church of St Saviour's in East London, he had assumed the religious title Father Ignatius and wore a Benedictine habit. His evangelizing knew no limits: one Saturday evening he strolled on to a dance floor populated by drunken couples, still in his monastic dress, and announced, 'We must all appear before the Judgement Seat of Christ.'[95]

For several years Ignatius gave immensely popular sermons in London churches, but his focus now was on establishing a monastic order. After a false start at Claydon in Suffolk, he moved to a former Dominican priory at Elm Hill in Norwich. It was a chaotic place, peopled with religious down-and-outs, and the church authorities did not take to him: the bishop of Oxford reprimanded Ignatius for 'a puerile imitation of a past

Father Ignatius with Black Bear and Hoop Hawk at Forepaugh's Wild West Show in Philadelphia.

an instant when his mother ridiculed Ignatius's tonsure.

He survived a mutiny in Norwich, but eventually financial disagreements drove him to a new life, this time as the Monk of Llanthony, an abbey he built at Capel-y-Ffin. Preaching tours produced money, and the community settled into its strange routine. Monks took turns to be led into the cloister with a halter, where the rest of the community spat and walked over them; lateness for meals was punished by eating off the floor; reading other than the Bible meant wearing the offending work round your neck for two days. Then there were apparitions, hard to credit, centred upon the holy rhubarb bush, from which leaves were said to work a miraculous cure.

When Ignatius's health failed him again in 1890, he was ordered a rest-cure in America, but he seized the chance to preach to the Sioux Indians brought to Philadelphia in Forepaugh's Wild West Show. He returned to England convinced that Anglo-Saxons were the lost tribe of Israel and that the earth was flat.

Ignatius had been a deacon since 1860, because no-one in the Church of England was prepared to ordain him priest. His final and perhaps greatest folly came in 1898, when he accepted 'ordination' from a bogus Syrian prelate, His Grace the Archbishop Mar Timotheus, metropolitan for the Old Catholics in America, otherwise René Vilatte, described in the *Church Times* as a man without 'fixed religious principles' whose consecration as bishop was 'gangrened with fraud'.

After Father Ignatius's death the *Church Times* commented, 'As a religious founder he accomplished nothing, less than nothing.' As a preacher 'he wielded such a power as few have exercised since John Wesley ceased from his labours'.[97]

phase of service which it is just as impossible [...] to revive in England as it would be [...] to resuscitate an Egyptian mummy and set it upon the throne of the Pharaohs'.[96] At the same time, his chapel was so full that admission was by ticket, interest fuelled by stories of his cures and curses: one boy was reported to lose his hair in

A secret mission in China

WALTER MEDHURST (1796–1857)

Walter Medhurst began working for the London Missionary Society when he was twenty. He spent time in Penang and Batavia (now Jakarta); when Shanghai was opened to British merchants in 1842, he established there what quickly became the most important LMS station in China. After leaving St Paul's he had been apprenticed to a printer, and he profited from this experience by setting up China's first modern press and publishing many items for the mission in both English and Chinese. He was a formidable linguist himself, and among his own writings were thirty-four books in Chinese and sixty-two Malay volumes, as well as translations and work in English.[98] It

was said that Medhurst was a difficult man who inspired respect more than affection, but that is not borne out by his most approachable work, *A Glance at the Interior of China*, which describes a dangerous clandestine journey through the silk and green tea districts in 1845. The writing is lively and personal and wears its religion lightly. There are many moments to enjoy, including one when his artificial pigtail becomes detached and he is nearly discovered.

Eating with the Chinese.

In partaking of food, also, great care must be taken to eat as others do; not only is it necessary to eat with chopsticks, but to handle them in such a way, that the instrument may appear to be in the hand of an adept. […] The stranger must take care to hold firmly the piece he wishes to secure for himself, and convey it safely to his mouth, without letting it slip or fall on the table, or the ground; a thing which seldom happens to the Chinese themselves, and which, occurring in his case, would not fail to stamp him as a novice in the use of the instrument. It would not be worth while for the stranger to feel fastidious about eating out of the same basin with his Chinese friends; as it is not uncommon for them (particularly when they profess to entertain the least respect or affection for their guests) to use their own chopsticks, and take out one of the nicest pieces of meat or fish they can find, and place it in the stranger's own basin; lest he should complain, however, of the chopsticks not being sufficiently clean, the host previously draws them very carefully through his own lips, and gives a good suck before performing the operation. […] When the rice bowl is placed before the guests, it must be taken up in the left hand, and held by the thumb being placed over the rim of the basin, the fore-finger on one side, the little finger on the other, and the two middle ones at the bottom. The Chinese, however, frequently leave the rice basin on the table, and put down their mouths to it; when, by the help of the chopsticks, they poke the rice into their mouths very dextrously. […] The more slobber and noise made during this operation, and the more rice a man can get into his mouth at one time, even at the risk of choking himself, is, in the Chinese estimation, the better; but he must be careful not to spill any of it on the table or ground, nor to leave any in the basin when he has done; as this would be a mark of waste, from which the Chinese ideas of economy revolt; and would show the individual to have been brought up in some outlandish extravagant school.

When one basin is finished, and the guest wishes another, he must ask for a whole or half a basin full, as he feels his appetite inclines him; or if he has too much, he may shove a

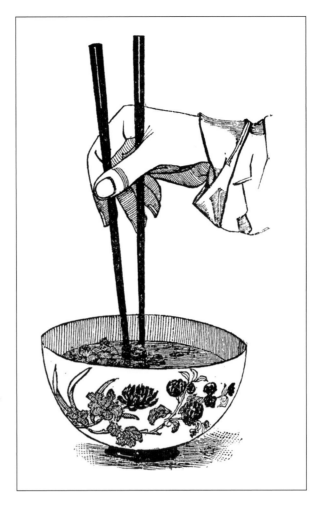

The use of chopsticks, illustration from Chambers' Encyclopaedia, 1881. *Courtesy FCIT.*

portion of it into his neighbour's basin, which would be taken kindly; but he must not leave anything. As for the dogs, they must content themselves with the bones which are thrown down, or put up with such coarse food, as may be prepared on purpose for them and the pigs.[99]

❧ *Searching for Franklin*

RICHARD KING (1810–76)

They died of official pigheadedness and Admiralty neglect.

(*The Atlas* on the fate of Franklin's voyage in search of the north-west passage)[100]

Discovering a north-west passage between the Atlantic and Pacific Oceans had for centuries been one of explorers' supreme ambitions, and Sir John Franklin's expedition in the *Erebus* and *Terror*, which sailed down the Thames in May 1845, was crewed by men of the highest quality and had on board the latest equipment and supplies to last three years. There were 1,000 books, fine silverware and cut glass. Whalers sighted the ships in Baffin Bay on 26 July that year, and then they were not seen again.

Richard King took great interest in Franklin's voyage. He was familiar with the problems as he had been surgeon and naturalist on an expedition in 1832 to find John Ross, who was away for three years, also searching for the north-west passage. (King did not find him, but Ross returned safely in 1833.)

So it was that King volunteered in 1847 to deliver fresh provisions to Franklin's party, but all that resulted was a dismissive memo from the North-American department of the Colonial Office: 'Richard King [...] is a person who omits no opportunity of directing public attention upon himself, so that it would be scarcely safe to follow his views on the subject.'[101] King had to sit by and watch other search parties mounted. He was convinced that they were looking in the wrong places and choosing maritime routes that would be icebound, but when he again offered his own services for an expedition in 1848, he was arrogantly referred to the Admiralty if he sought employment.

In October 1854 John Rae's expedition returned with the sensational news of Franklin's fate, but it took more than a year for the Admiralty to admit grudgingly that King had been right:

It is impossible not to admit that Dr King, in the year 1848, volunteered his services to proceed down the great Fish River, and to the very spot indicated by Dr Rae where the relics of the lost expedition have been found. The last spot that any

one but Dr King [...] considered it *likely* that traces would be found, happens most unfortunately to be the spot of all others that, if searched, might have led to the safety of some of the party, and is the only spot unsearched.[102]

In 1859 the remains of Franklin and his party were found exactly where King had proposed eleven years previously. He received no proper credit for this, and complained justifiably that others were 'showered with honours and emoluments' for their Arctic service while he remained 'unhonoured and unrewarded'.

King's assessments were dismissed as inspired guesswork rather than scientific, and his youthful impetuosity and self-confidence did not go down well with the older grandees at the Admiralty and Colonial Office. He made his views very clear in the book *Franklin Search from First to Last* (1855) and then took no further part in Arctic exploration.

❧ *Three attorneys-general and a serjeant-at-law*

THOMAS WILDE, FIRST BARON TRURO (1782–1855)

He was probably one of the most laborious and painstaking men that ever practised.

(Ballantine)[103]

Thomas Wilde rose steadily to the top of his profession: solicitor-general, attorney-general, chief justice of the court of common pleas, lord chancellor. His capacity for hard work was legendary, and he had the largest common law practice in England. He first practised as a solicitor and was called to the Bar twelve years later. Wilde loved detail: he was articled to his father and reportedly once ran away and was found 'busily engaged in the Long Room at the Custom House, making himself acquainted with the mysteries of tare and tret, cocquets and averages'. It was for his professionalism and acuteness in analysing and applying the law that he was admired. As a speaker he was monotonous and uninspiring, often taking recourse to synonyms to mask a speech impediment. St Paul's School has cause to recognize in him one of its most generous benefactors. Legal historians, however, have been reluctant to forgive him his start in the less glamorous branch of the profession:

His mind [...] was so intensely fixed on details at the age when our faculties are most expansive and supple, that he had not afterwards the full power of embracing the entirety of a great subject, which even at the Bar was often required of him, and which his station made afterwards indispensable to perfect success. It was his misfortune [...] to have practised as an attorney so long as he did; no doubt it conduced in many ways to his early and great success, but it prejudiced him when that success was attained.[104]

Thomas Wilde, Baron Truro, oil by Sir Francis Grant. *David Bussey.* © *St Paul's School.*

SIR CHARLES WETHERELL (1770–1846)

A member of the House of Commons declared that in his speech made upon Catholic Emancipation, standing with his hands in the waistband of his breeches, he had but one lucid interval, which was that between his breeches and his waistcoat.

(Michael McDonnell, *A History of St Paul's School*) [105]

Despite becoming solicitor-general and attorney-general, Charles Wetherell hardly brings glory to the Old Pauline community. He was an arch-reactionary who stood firmly against any kind of reform, parliamentary, university, municipal or religious. His effectiveness in parliament was limited, first by his notoriously slovenly dress and secondly by his manner of speaking: he was 'treated by both sides as a whimsical pedant rather than a formidable debater'.[106]

In October 1831 he visited Bristol as city recorder to open the autumn assizes and provoked the worst of all the parliamentary reform riots. He had not helped himself by declaring in the House of Commons that the people of Bristol had no interest in reform. Wetherell was stoned on arrival and had to escape over the roof of the Mansion House, fleeing the city in disguise and leaving his wig and robe to the mercy of the mob.

With this record, it is surprising that he successfully defended James Watson, a leader of a minor riot for parliamentary reform at Spa Fields in 1816. Watson was a fanatic moved by the spirit of the French Revolution — he exhorted the crowd in the language of Desmoulins before the storming of the Bastille and set off (unsuccessfully) for the Tower of London brandishing a tricolour. He and four others were charged with high treason, but Wetherell showed that the only evidence against Watson came from one Castle, a government informer: Watson was acquitted and charges dropped against the others. It is hard to see how anything other than legal ambition motivated Wetherell in attacking a tory government, although ironically the verdict led to the so-called 'Gag Acts'. Wetherell's defence was used as a model by Charles Dickens for the trial of Charles Darnay in *A Tale of Two Cities*.[107]

If you bear in mind who is the principal (I should say the only) witness in this case — a man of the name of Castle; if you bear in mind what he has proved to have done in the course of these transactions; if you bear in mind for whom he is a witness, from what place he comes, what he has been, and what he now is [...] you will hereafter consider whether Mr Castle is not the man who has made these persons his dupes; whether he has not alone invented, organized and framed the whole of the projects which he represents were moulded into a system of conspiracy; whether, according to every fair and rational presumption, he is not the author and parent of all these transactions, forming an ideal conspiracy for purposes of his own.[108]

SIR (JONATHAN) FREDERICK POLLOCK, FIRST BARONET (1783–1870)

When Frederick Pollock entered St Paul's in January 1800, he had already walked away from three other schools, and his daughter Mary revealed later that it almost happened a fourth time:

One day he had some difference with the headmaster, Dr Roberts, and came home and told his parents that he did not intend to go there any more. They acquiesced. But the headmaster, who was also a friend, called and remonstrated, and when he found he could not succeed in altering their decision, said angrily: 'That boy will live to be hanged.'[109]

Roberts was wrong. The boy stayed on, rose rapidly in the legal profession and lived to be attorney-general and lord chief baron of the exchequer, presiding over the court for a quarter of a century. His judgments were praised for their 'high moral tone', although he liked quick decisions and had little appetite for legal detail. This was clear from his earlier days as a barrister on the northern circuit:

At the time to which the story relates he was the leader of the northern circuit. Chief Justice Abbott, afterwards Lord Tenterden [lord chief justice, 1818–32], was presiding at the Yorkshire assizes, which were held at York only, and Pollock had to open the case for the plaintiff in a very heavy dispute about a colliery contract. He was called at five o'clock in the morning in order to read his brief, but happened to take up *The Heart of Midlothian* [the novel by Sir Walter Scott] and was so interested in it that he never touched the papers until breakfast time. The court in those days sat at nine, and there was therefore no chance whatever of his mastering the case so as to present it in a proper form to the jury; he found, too, that two or three hundred letters had passed between the parties. Accordingly, with greatest coolness, he said to the

Sir Frederick Pollock, oil by F. R. Say. *David Bussey.* © *St Paul's School.*

jury: 'I could not better present the facts of the case to you, gentlemen, than by using the language of the parties themselves, and I shall therefore read to you the correspondence which has passed in chronological order.'

This he proceeded to do, and had continued reading for nearly an hour, when Chief Justice Abbott, who was very much afraid of Pollock, thought it was time to intervene. 'Mr Pollock, is it absolutely necessary for you to read all this correspondence? Cannot you condense it a little?' To which Pollock replied: 'Absolutely necessary, my Lord, for I never read it before.' Of course, in the face of such sublime impertinence there was nothing more to be said, and the case proceeded.[110]

It was said that one of Pollock's few shortcomings was partiality to his son-in-law's arguments in court.[111] Theirs was a close and high-achieving Pauline family. His brother, Sir David (1780–1847),[112] became chief justice of Bombay; one son, Sir William Frederick (1815–88), was the queen's remembrancer, and the other, Sir Charles Edward Pollock (1823–97), the last baron of the exchequer.

WILLIAM BALLANTINE (1812–87)

They were all tyrants — cruel, cold-blooded, unsympathetic tyrants.
(Ballantine on his teachers at St Paul's)[113]

As a young man William Ballantine, serjeant-at-law, frequented London's literary taverns and met several Victorian novelists, including Thackeray ('very egotistical, greedy of flattery, and sensitive of criticism to a ridiculous extent') and Dickens ('there was a brightness and geniality about him that greatly fascinated his companions'). In places his autobiography, *Some Experiences of A Barrister's Life*, published when he was seventy, also reads like fiction. There are melodramatic descriptions of his cruel masters at St Paul's. Among his court cases, stories of the first murder on a British train, the Tichborne claimant and the unscrupulous Gaikwar of Baroda would sit readily in the pages of a nineteenth-century three-decker novel.

In 1864 Ballantine's brilliant prosecution, with the solicitor-general Sir Robert Collier, secured the conviction of Franz Müller for murder and theft on the North London Railway. The case attracted widespread attention because of fears about rail safety and led to the compulsory communication cord. One of its more exotic elements came from Müller's choice of John Death, a Cheapside jeweller, to exchange a gold chain stolen from his victim. It was a box labelled 'Death' that attracted the attention

of a London cabdriver who provided crucial evidence. Arresting Müller also involved a transatlantic chase.

The preposterous story of the Tichborne claimant has entered cultural history and received the final accolade, an episode of *The Simpsons* ('The Principal and the Pauper') based on the case. The heir to the Roman Catholic Hampshire family's title and estate had disappeared in a shipwreck in 1854, but his mother would not accept that he was dead, and in response to worldwide enquiries a lawyer from Sidney replied that a butcher living in Wagga Wagga fitted the description of her son. In fact he did not. The real heir, Sir Roger Charles Doughty Tichborne, was slim, sharp-featured, black-haired and mainly spoke French. The pretender, who turned out to be Arthur Orton, a butcher's son from Wapping, was plump, had round features and light-brown hair, and spoke no French. Despite this, the desperate Lady Tichborne acknowledged him as her son, and it was only after her death that other members of the family were able to begin proceedings. Ballantine's talent as Orton's counsel may explain why the trial lasted 102 days: more than a hundred witnesses vouched for his client's identity as the genuine Sir Roger

Tichborne, and Orton dealt resiliently with the innumerable discrepancies in his story. Eventually, however, Ballantine gave up the battle, and the case collapsed. Orton was subsequently charged with perjury and after another mammoth case, this time lasting 188 days, sentenced to fourteen years' hard labour.

Ballantine's final major case was just as extraordinary. He went out to India to defend Malhar Rao, the Maharaja Gaikwar of Baroda, against the charge of attempting to murder the British resident, Colonel Phayre, by spicing a cup of pomelo juice with arsenic and ground diamonds, a suitably lavish method of poisoning he had already used to dispatch his brother and predecessor. Partly through his brilliant cross-examination of Phayre, Ballantine somehow saved the Gaikwar from the death penalty, but so much imperial corruption emerged during the trial that Malhar Rao was deposed and imprisoned. Ballantine received a near-record honorarium of £10,000.[114]

On retirement Ballantine tried to imitate Dickens with a tour of public readings in America, but it did not make money, and he seems to have died in poverty. The obituary in the *Law Times* (15 January 1887) said harshly that he 'left behind him scarcely any lesson, even in his own poor biography, which the rising generation of lawyers could profitably learn'.

Serjeant Ballantine, published in *Vanity Fair,* 5 March 1870. *Lordprice Collection.*

❧ *Zoologist*

SIR (EDWIN) RAY LANKESTER (1847–1929)

He is the most powerful human being I ever came into contact with; he is like those winged beasts from Nineveh at the British Museum. What you feel is just immense force.

(Olive Schreiner)[115]

Ray Lankester's formidable talents as a zoologist were quick to emerge. A young Oxford graduate on a travelling fellowship, he was greeted by the sceptical professor of zoology at Leipzig in 1870, 'What, are you Ray Lankester, the author of the "Earthworm" and other papers? I thought you were a middle-aged man!' He was a tutor at Exeter College, Oxford, two years later, and appointed professor of zoology by University College, London, at the age of twenty-eight.

There was another, less desirable, talent that emerged equally quickly. His obituarist in *The Times* wrote,

He had almost a genius for putting himself in the wrong by explosive and unconsidered action in a just cause, or at least in an otherwise completely tenable position. The mistake once committed, Lankester would concentrate his attention exclusively on the justice of his cause, while those who were opposed to him would see nothing but the violence of this conduct.[116]

During his brief stay at Exeter College, he managed to irritate the authorities by clamouring for changes to Oxford science teaching. In 1876 he determined to unmask a fashionable medium, Henry Slade, and saw him sentenced to three months' hard labour. There was an appeal, and Old Pauline barrister Serjeant Ballantine (see last entry) had the conviction quashed on a technicality, but Slade had to stay out of the country.

Lankester was in London for sixteen years, apart from a characteristic episode when he accepted a professorship at

Sir Ray Lankester, water-colour by Sir Leslie Ward, published in *Vanity Fair*, 12 January 1905. © *St Paul's School*.

Honduras Turkey, 1829, engraving by Old Pauline Edward Griffith (1790–1858) for *The Animal Kingdom*. Griffith was controlling editor of the ambitious eleven-year project to publish in fifteen volumes an expanded English version of Cuvier's *Règne animal* (1816). *Ken Lawson*. © *St Paul's School*.

Edinburgh, secured with the assistance of friends, decided he did not like the conditions there, caused much annoyance by resigning and returned to University College. His lectures were memorable occasions, illustrated by meticulous diagrams, even if he surveyed his audiences so that, in one student's words, 'we felt somewhat as if we were cockroaches'.[117] UCL was turned into a foremost centre for evolutionary studies.

In 1891 he was unwisely tempted back to Oxford by the Linacre chair of comparative anatomy. He was outspoken in his attacks on university privileges and in his letters yearned for the superior London life:

There [in London] you walk to your lecture-room through the streets, and see a thousand kinds of people, lovely women, old swells, dirty children, country cousins […] Here I walk to my lecture-room. I meet two or three stiff, pert, ugly-looking Oxford ladies and perhaps a broken-down old don or a beefy-looking parson. […] Then dinner in London — the club, or with a friend at a restaurant, or a dinner party with amusing people. Here either solitary mastication or a company of silly, pompous fools with nothing interesting about them.[118]

Becoming director of what is now the Natural History Museum in South Kensington in 1898 should have been the ideal appointment for him. It was not. His changes to the displays were popular, but Lankester could not accept that the museum was subordinate to the British Museum in Bloomsbury. He demanded autonomy, was deeply offended when the administration suggested he was taking longer holidays than were permitted and considered he was 'subject to plots and devilries'.[119] Relations became so sour that he was forced to retire at sixty, an injustice he thought merited plenty of letters to the press.

Lankester wrote over two hundred scientific articles, the first published when he was fifteen. For over thirty years he edited the *Quarterly Journal of Microscopical Science*, turning it into a leading scientific journal. In retirement he wrote a very popular weekly column in the *Daily Telegraph*, 'Science from an easy chair'. He was a civilized man with artists and writers as his friends, and would have risen even higher in his career if only he had been more tolerant of authority and officialdom. A strange example of this character trait came in the small hours of Saturday 6 October 1895. Lankester thought a prostitute was being roughly treated by the police in Piccadilly Circus, sprang to her defence and found himself 'bound over' for 'resisting the police'. His letters to *The Times* (he wrote two) were uncompromising:

I ask whether it is tolerable that a man perfectly well known, talking to another person in the street […] should be ordered to move on, and that on his remonstrating — even if angrily — he should be liable to be seized and treated as the vilest criminal?[120]

Boomerang theory

SIR GILBERT THOMAS WALKER (1868–1958)

Through the kindness of Mr O. Eckenstein, I have recently had the opportunity of seeing and throwing some boomerangs made by him, in which rounding was present, but no twisting; the angle between the arms was considerably more obtuse, the size increased, and the weight doubled.

(Sir Gilbert Walker, 'On Boomerangs')[121]

When Gilbert Walker made a serious linguistic blunder in a classical exercise at St Paul's, he was in his own words 'sent in disgrace' by the high master to the mathematical side. This proved an excellent decision: he won a scholarship to Trinity College, Cambridge, was senior wrangler (gained the highest mark) in parts one and two of the mathematical tripos, and was elected to a college fellowship. Senior wranglers were university celebrities, but it was prowess at throwing boomerangs on the Backs that made 'Boomerang' Walker a Cambridge legend for decades. He could send a boomerang 175 yards in one direction and perform double loops with those that were meant to return. Close theoretical analysis of projectile design and his own technique led to a well-known paper, 'On Boomerangs', which he presented to the Royal Society in 1897. This study, a mixture of heady mathematics and basic advice about the best shape for a boomerang and how to throw it, led on to an encyclopaedia article, 'Spiel und Sport', where he extended his analysis to billiards, ball games and bicycles.[122]

Walker left Cambridge in 1904 to spend twenty years in charge of the Indian state meteorological service, wrestling with the problem of predicting monsoons. He became fascinated there by the gliding skills of Himalayan birds, an interest that led him in retirement to encourage the growing English sport of human gliding. A paper was published in 1934 on gliding and the weather: he regretted that at sixty-five he was too old to be a good glider pilot. Whatever he did, Walker's mind turned to science. After his undergraduate exertions his health broke down, and he spent three winters skating in Switzerland. This led him to create ice rinks in Simla, the only complaint being that the ice was too hard. He played the flute, thought about its construction and suggested additional fingerings which some instruments still employ.[123]

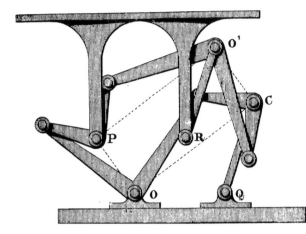

An apparatus for parallel motion from *How to Draw a Straight Line, a Lecture on Linkages*, 1872, by Old Pauline Sir Alfred Bray Kempe (1849–1922). He also published an important, though incorrect, solution to the four colours problem. *Courtesy Cornell University Library, Historical Math. Monographs Collection.*

Sir Gilbert Thomas Walker, photograph by Maull and Fox. © *The Royal Society.*

🎜 *Comic verse and a novel detective*

EDMUND CLERIHEW BENTLEY (1875–1956)

When the old high master of St Paul's School ran his eye through a version of the Dog in the Manger, which described the cattle as being prevented 'from refreshing their inner cows', he went into unearthly convulsions of his own extraordinary laughter which, like the other movements of his extraordinary voice, began like an organ and ended like a penny whistle. 'That boy looks at the world standing on his head.'

(G. K. Chesterton, *Autobiography*)[124]

Edmund Clerihew Bentley has the unique distinction of inventing a verse form while in the eighth form at St Paul's. 'There is no record of the coming into existence of the sort of nonsense verse that was afterwards to be let loose on the public as *Biography for Beginners*,'[125] he wrote, but it seems that the clerihew as it became known later was born with the following example, which apparently reached Bentley in a Coleridgean moment of inspiration:

Sir Humphrey Davy
Detested gravy.
He lived in the odium
Of having discovered Sodium.

Bentley was at school with a particularly precocious group, including G. K. Chesterton (see chapter five). They formed a junior debating club which even published its own magazine filled with ambitious and serious articles. Chesterton was to comment later, 'I fear there is something incurably conscientious and solemn about the nature of Paulines.'[126] The 'biographies' were an antidote. Bentley wrote a number of examples 'at a sitting one evening: and when GKC and others got hold of the idea there came to be a large output among us. Nothing quite so preposterous had occupied our attention before'.[127] The original collection of clerihews was transcribed by Bentley, who had composed most of them, into a notebook illustrated by Chesterton before 'the joke began to pall'. The book had its own identification code, with Bentley's contributions indicated by a dodo. One page features three literary figures:

That you have all heard of Hume
I tacitly assume.
But you didn't know, perhaps,
That his parents were Lapps.

I weep over John Bunyan
As though he were an onion.
If I knew a wicked ogress
I would lend her "The Pilgrim's Progress."

Daniel Defoe
Could tie himself in a bow.
He thought it was rot
Tying one's self in a knot.[128]

When Bentley decided to find a publisher for *Biography for Beginners* (1905), he thought the original notebook was lost and put down from memory a number of verses of his own devising, again illustrated by Chesterton. More volumes followed in 1929 and 1935, but it was only after publication of *The Complete Clerihews of E. Clerihew Bentley* in 1981 that the notebook's significance was realized: it was now in the Rare Book Room at St Paul's and contained ninety unpublished examples.[129]

The other claim to fame of Bentley, who spent most of his career as a leader writer for the *Daily Telegraph*, was his detective story, *Trent's Last Case*. The genre in 1910 was dominated by Sherlock Holmes, whose 'exaggerated unreality' Bentley had turned against.[130] His own 'exposure of detective stories' featured a hero, Trent, whose meticulously correct solution of the murder mystery turned out to be completely wrong. Bentley saw this as 'a detective story of a new sort' and it still holds its distinctive place,[131] but it is telling that in the dedication to Chesterton, Bentley looked back to his schooldays, 'when we were purely happy in the boundless consumption of paper, pencils, tea, and our elders' patience'.[132]

A page from the original *Dictionary of Biography*. Verses by E. Clerihew Bentley and artwork by G. K. Chesterton, 1893. *Verses reproduced with permission of Curtis Brown Group Ltd, London, on behalf of the estate of E. Clerihew Bentley.* © *E. Clerihew Bentley 1983. Artwork* © *St Paul's School.*

That you have all heard of Hume
I tacitly assume.
But you didn't know, perhaps,
That his parents were Lapps.

Weep over John Bunyan
As though he were an onion.
If I knew a wicked ogress
I would lend her "The Pilgrim's Progress."

Daniel Defoe
Could tie himself in a bow.
He thought it was rot
Tying one's self in a knot.

The south front of the fourth school in the 1960s. Waterhouse's buildings were opened in 1884, and G. K. Chesterton was admitted three years later. © *St Paul's School*.

The Twentieth Century

PART ONE 1900–1945

❧ GKC

GILBERT KEITH CHESTERTON (1874–1936)

Walking down Fleet Street some day you may meet a form whose vastness blots out the heavens. Great waves of hair surge from under the soft, wide-brimmed hat. A cloak that might be a legacy from Porthos floats about his colossal frame. He pauses in the midst of the pavement to read the book in his hand, and a cascade of laughter descending from the head notes to the middle voice gushes out on the listening air. He looks up, adjust his pince-nez, observes that he is not in a cab, remembers that he ought to be in a cab, turns and hails a cab. The vehicle sinks down under the unusual burden and rolls heavily away. It carries Gilbert Keith Chesterton.

(A. G. Gardiner)[1]

G. K. Chesterton in the garden of his home in Beaconsfield, *c.*1932. *Getty Images.*

G K. CHESTERTON was writing and drawing incessantly even at school. He was equally at home illustrating clerihews for his lifelong friend E. C. Bentley (see chapter four) or giving political papers as chairman of the Junior Debating Society, an exclusive group which continued to meet in members' houses after they had left St Paul's: Leonard Woolf's memory of him is 'standing very upright at the table, tearing sheets of paper into tiny pieces and dropping them on the table, while he spoke at immense length on some subject like taxation or bimetallism or the Irish question'.[2]

Drawing remained a hobby for Chesterton and his friends, but he quickly gathered a public reputation for idiosyncratic essays and reviews. In 1903 his first major work was published, a 'singularly luminous' study of Robert Browning, 'liberally adorned with those audacious paradoxes, fantastic comparisons, and explosive antitheses which those acquainted with the always clever and interesting work of its author were entitled to expect' (review in *The World*).[3] He was not a man for precise detail — his final report from St Paul's described his Greek and Latin composition as 'quite futile' — but revelled in ideas and colourful phrasing, concluding his book on George Bernard Shaw (1909) with the unlikely image of GBS slaying 'the polysyllable, that huge and slimy centipede which has sprawled over all the valleys of England like the "loathly worm" who was slain by the ancient knight'.[4]

Most widely read now are Chesterton's many stories about the fictional detective Father Brown, a Roman

Catholic priest whose experiences in the confessional sharpened his grasp of the criminal mind, and his first two novels. *The Napoleon of Notting Hill* (1904) is a futuristic fantasy where London is ruled over by a jester-king and one borough goes to war against the others. Chesterton came to see in it the genesis of his opposition to large-scale government. When published it was dismissed by *The Times* as 'a facile extravagance'.[5] *Vanity Fair* praised the book's 'device of presenting huge philosophic ideas in a dress of brilliant and exaggerated and exuberant humour', but then this review was written by Chesterton's brother Cecil.[6] In *The Man who was Thursday* (1908) Chesterton enjoys the paradox of writing about a cell of anarchists, all but one of whom turn out to be police detectives in disguise spying on the others. Again, comments at the time were often dismissive: the *Academy* called Chesterton 'the provoker of a certain kind of giggle among a certain kind of red-tied, hirsute, nut-chewing babblers'.[7]

The Man who was Thursday ends with Sunday (the one member of the cell not a covert policeman) appearing as an enigmatic religious figure, so enigmatic that when it was explained to him, Bentley commented to Chesterton, 'Who shall understand but you?'[8] His interest in religion was strong. In 1922 he became a Roman Catholic and published *St Francis of Assisi*, another book about paradox, this time the unworldly saint in love with the created world. His later years as an eminent lay Catholic apologist began to rob his work of its provocative unpredictability, but there were still linguistic fireworks: in 1927 he attacked contraception: 'The nearest and most respectable parallel would be that of the roman epicure, who took emetics at intervals all day so that he might eat five or six luxurious dinners daily.'[9]

Chesterton adored toy theatres and puppet shows. The most treasured souvenir of his final trip to Spain was a new miniature theatre complete with electric lights. 'The affairs of the world,' he wrote just before his death, 'still mean less

to me than Punch and Judy on Campden Hill.'[10] If his fiction and the declamatory extravagance of his non-fiction tasted of the theatre, so did his appearances in public. Wyndham Lewis recalled his role in an improvised satire on the cheaper press, *The Witch of Fleet Street*, in 1923/4:

We got along rather lamely […] until GKC came on and lifted the whole thing at once into brilliant fantasy, as you might expect. […] For some reason I forgot, his enormous figure was swathed in black muslin rags and tinsel, and he was supposed to represent Famine, flying from Fortnum and Mason. All I remember of his performance is an attack on the *Daily Mail* for reducing him to a skeleton. The audience loved it all.[11]

Ernest Howard Shepard (1879–1976) at work, photograph published by the *Evening Standard* just after his death. Among his drawings are the definitive illustrations to A. A. Milne's *Winnie the Pooh* and its successors, and some engaging images of his time at St Paul's, where his uncle was surmaster. *Getty Images.*

AUSTIN FREDERIC HARRISON (1873–1928)

Well, some of us may remember an illustration of Du Maurier in *Punch* some years ago, which depicted an old maid very much shocked by the sight of some bathers on the distant side of a lake. 'But they are too far off to be indecent,' remarked her companion. 'Not if you use a glass,' objected the old maid.

(Austin Harrison's riposte to *The Spectator's* discovery of bad moral influence in the pages of the *English Review*)[12]

From 1909–23 Austin Harrison was editor of the *English Review*, a monthly literary and political magazine. He liberalized its pages by including new writers, women, and

work from the continent, and when in June 1911 it claimed to be the 'Great Adult Review' and published an article by Frank Harris which appeared to encourage sexual promiscuity among both men and women, there was uproar. The article suggested that youthful indulgence would be followed by the self-control of maturity, but it was easy to quote selectively, and *The Spectator* focused on these lines:

It is certain that a little excess in youth in the gratification of natural desire is less harmful than the abstinence generally recommended in England. [...] Temporary excesses are not harmful; sometimes, indeed, they are positively beneficial. Our vagrant nature is impatient of rigid limits. And the tolerance already accorded to one sex should be extended to the other.[13]

The Spectator thought this was 'a receipt to make a harlot' and launched a vigorous attack on the *English Review's* moral tone, accusing it of dumping 'garbage [...] on the nation's doorstep'. It also threatened to boycott the magazine's advertisements, something Harrison called 'rather a sour grape', as they had not been offered any recently.[14]

There were plenty of writers ready to spring to the *English Review's* defence, including Arnold Bennett and Ford Madox Ford. Harrison claimed to be the victim of 'a simple act of persecution', and Frank Harris himself ended a furious letter to *The Spectator* with two scathing sentences:

English morality indeed: Piccadilly Circus at night and *The*

A NUISANCE.

Miss Priscilla. 'YES; IT'S A BEAUTIFUL VIEW. BUT TOURISTS ARE IN THE HABIT OF BATHING ON THE OPPOSITE SHORE, AND THAT'S RATHER A DRAWBACK." *Fair Visitor.* "DEAR ME! BUT AT SUCH A DISTANCE AS THAT—SURELY——"
Miss Priscilla. "AH, BUT WITH A *TELESCOPE*, YOU KNOW!"

Spectator as censor. There is a pit fouler than any imagined by Dante, a cesspool bubbling and steaming with corruption and all shining with putrid iridescence of hypocrisy — that pool is English morality, and one of the foul bubbles on it *The Spectator*.[15]

Cartoon from *Punch*, 8 October 1892, p. 162. Despite some inaccuracies, it was clearly this cartoon to which Austin Harrison referred in his attack on *The Spectator. Reproduced with permission of Punch Ltd, www.punch.co.uk.*

❧ *The hyphen in Rolls-Royce*

CLAUDE GOODMAN JOHNSON (1864–1926)

In 1896 London's first exhibition of motor cars was organized by Claude Johnson in the grounds of South Kensington's Imperial Institute, where he was a clerk. One man was especially impressed, Frederick Simms, who had negotiated British patent rights to the Daimler internal combustion engine and in effect founded the British motor car industry. Simms appointed Johnson secretary to the Automobile Club (now known as the Royal Automobile Club) when it was established in 1897. Johnson went on to promote the motor car at exhibitions and in contests, culminating in the thousand-miles trial of April and May 1900. During this event cars stopped every night and were displayed in a new location. The gold medal in the trial was awarded to the Hon. C. S. Rolls, who reached forty-two mph in the speed section; Johnson, driving a six hp Daimler, took the silver with a creditable twenty-seven mph. He was to write, with typical modesty:

I crave the indulgence of my readers if I attach too much importance to the thousand miles trial [...] Very probably the writer overrates its value. But it must be borne in mind that no public demonstration of motor vehicles had previously been held in England in which a long distance was covered by a number of vehicles.[16]

Early motoring was for the upper classes, and Johnson had to warn club members about the damaging social consequences of number plates, which might become compulsory if they ignored the convention of giving way to horse-drawn vehicles:

The Committee are certain that the compulsory numbering of motor vehicles would seriously damage the industry of this country, as ladies and gentlemen would refuse to adopt motor vehicles as their private carriages if these carriages are to be disfigured by labels, and their owners are to be placed on a level with drivers of hackney carriages.[17]

In 1903, after a failed attempt at producing electric cars, Johnson joined Rolls at his motor agency, which sourced vehicles for high society. A year later Rolls discovered

Claude Johnson demonstrating the capacity of a heavily loaded Rolls-Royce to negotiate Sydenham Hill, photograph dated 23 January 1906. *Courtesy the Sir Henry Royce Memorial Foundation.*

The Rolls-Royce 40/50hp AX 201. This car was used extensively by Claude Johnson for trials and demonstrations. In strict terms the name Silver Ghost belonged solely to AX 201, but it was widely applied to the 40/50hp model. *Courtesy the Sir Henry Royce Memorial Foundation.*

Henry Royce ('I have found the greatest engineer in the world') and struck the deal that created the famous company. Royce provided the chassis, Rolls the bodywork and Johnson the publicity before being made managing director (he called himself 'the hyphen') in 1906.

His advocacy of the Rolls-Royce marque was tireless. He bettered the record his rival car retailer Charles Jarrott, veteran of 'Homeric inter-country races', set for driving from Monte Carlo to Boulogne.[18] When he heard it was said that a Rolls-Royce was a fine racer but hopeless for touring in hilly districts, Johnson took a car to Sydenham and met the press: 'Then he loaded the car with nine of the heaviest journalists he could find, drove them all up the hill, starting and stopping on the steepest section, with no difficulty at all.'[19]

Johnson's most important decision was to concentrate on producing one model, the famous Silver Ghost 40/50 hp, from 1907–22. He proved its reliability in a 15,000 mile trial, during which there was just one involuntary stop, of thirty seconds, to rectify a petrol tap. 'The best object lesson on the durability of the modern motor car that could possibly be given,' according to *The Motor.*[20]

CJ, as he was known, moved in an exclusive world. He would visit Rolls-Royce owners to discuss any points they or their chauffeurs might have. He did not expect to see women behind the wheel: 'There were quite enough hazards on the road without adding lady drivers!'[21]

During the First World War, Lawrence of Arabia used Rolls-Royce 40/50 hp armoured cars in the desert and said they were above rubies. By 1918 the company was also the world's largest manufacturer of aero-engines.

Johnson was a genial and civilized employer who had permanent large block bookings at Derby's Grand Theatre for his workforce. He was always modest and self-effacing, declining a knighthood after the war and horrified to find himself described as the 'Chief instigator of the House of Rolls-Royce'. After his death Royce said, 'He was the captain, we were only the crew.'

❧ Aircraft pioneer

SIR (EDWIN) ALLIOTT VERDON-ROE (1877–1958)

Being eager to get on with the building of my new machine, I remember cycling back to the workshop with long lengths of timber balanced on my shoulder. I was so proud of this specially selected wood which I had acquired [...] and the thought certainly never entered my head that a time would come — and not so many years ahead either — when a firm bearing my name would be buying timber for aeroplane construction not by the piece but by the ship-load, and that approximately 15,000 lumbermen would be engaged in cutting down trees to be converted into Avro aircraft.

(Sir Alliott Verdon-Roe)[22]

Alliott Roe was on the science side at St Paul's. He left at the age of fifteen to become an engineer, and it was while working as third engineer on the SS *Ichanga* in 1902 that he 'used to spend hours, in a state of fascination, watching the albatross glide majestically with motionless wings' and 'became convinced it was possible to construct an aeroplane'. News of the Wright brothers' successful powered flights in 1903 spurred him on. Roe wrote to *The Times* in 1906 about his belief in heavier-than-air flight. The letter appeared in an engineering supplement, but with an editorial health warning:

It is not to be supposed that we can in any way adopt the writer's estimate of his own undertaking, being of the opinion, indeed, that all attempts at artificial aviation on the basis he describes, are not only dangerous to human life, but foredoomed to failure from an engineering standpoint.[23]

First prize (£75) in a powered model aeroplane competition the following year gave him the funds to build a full-size version of his winning design, and permission was granted, with reluctance, to use Brooklands motor track as a test runway. It was a makeshift existence. Roe lived in the aircraft hangar, survived on five shillings' (25p) worth of food a week and manoeuvred his aircraft out on to the track single-handed. Sympathetic motorists willingly towed him off the ground for some short straight 'hops', although they often held on with 'embarrassing tenacity' when the machine began to swerve in the air, resulting in damaging crash-landings. Another hazard was the local sewage farm to which the aircraft seemed drawn by magnetic attraction on landing.[24] Even so, in 1908 he had to his credit the first flights when 'a British-designed and British-built aeroplane had risen from the ground under its own power, piloted by the designer and constructor'.[25]

With the backing of his brother, who had made a fortune out of 'Bullseye Braces', Roe went on to design a triplane and then founded A. V. Roe & Co. in Manchester. Here he produced the first enclosed cabin aeroplane, which in October 1912 set up the British flying record of seven and a half hours. Next came the revolutionary Avro 504, a two-seater training machine designed in 1913. It was manufactured in thousands during the First World War

The AVRO 504, photograph 1913? The inset portrait is not Alliott Verdon-Roe. *Courtesy Avro Heritage Centre.*

and has been called the 'best aeroplane ever produced'. It was used for the first-ever air raids, on the Zeppelin sheds at Friedrichshafen in November 1914, but Roe hated the 'strange paradox that creative brains should be so busily engaged on the design of apparatus whose sole aim is destruction and death — the reverse of creation'.[26] Declining sales in the 1920s led Roe to sell out to Armstrong Siddeley Motor Company and form a new partnership with the Cowes boat builders Saunders Ltd.

Saunders-Roe built a reputation on its flying boats.

Roe was a visionary who foresaw supersonic flight and pressurized cabins decades in advance. He also predicted 'flying-machines [...] able to [...] rescue people from ships in distress, or from burning buildings'.[27] Appropriately, it was Saunders-Roe that manufactured the Saro Skeeter, the first helicopter to be used by the British Army Air Corps.

Inventor

ARCHIBALD MONTGOMERY LOW (1888–1956)

The telephone may develop to a stage where it is unnecessary to enter a special call-box. We shall think no more of telephoning to our office from our cars or railway-carriages than we do today of telephoning from our homes.

(Archibald Montgomery Low, 1937)

Archibald Low, a self-styled professor, was an extraordinarily gifted inventor who lacked the concentration and discipline to capitalize on his discoveries. He has a place in the International Space Hall of Fame at the New Mexico Museum of Space History but never received in this country the recognition he deserved.

Low spent his childhood building steam turbines at home and irritating the neighbours with his chemical experiments. St Paul's, he felt, did not allow enough for his individualism, although he won two science prizes before leaving the army class aged sixteen (Montgomery was a

Archibald M. Low demonstrating a TV system which he developed in London, March 1928. *Fox Photos/Getty Images.*

fellow pupil — see chapter six) to attend Central Technical College. There he designed a drawing device that was marketed by Thornton's and anticipated by more than thirty years gear pre-selector mechanisms.

From college he entered 'The Low Accessories and Ignition Company', his uncle's engineering firm. There was never enough money to fund his inventive genius, but Low's whistling egg-boiler, 'The Chanticleer', was marketed with great success. In May 1914 he gave a presentation to the Institute of Automobile Engineers called 'Seeing by Wireless', in which he introduced *TeleVista*, in the words of the *Daily Chronicle*, 'a new apparatus [...] by which it is possible for persons using a telephone to see each other at the same time'.[28]

The First World War interrupted further work on this precursor of television. Low was put in charge of the Royal Flying Corps Experimental Works and by 1918 had invented a wireless-controlled rocket guidance system. The British authorities did not see how important this work was, but the Germans did: twice they attempted to assassinate Low, and then in World War Two they borrowed his ideas for their V-2 rockets.

After the war he opened the Low Engineering Company, and there was an unstoppable flow of new inventions. His Norlow motor scooter sold well; his rocket-propelled bicycle controlled by deflection shields did not. Many of Low's ideas were again well ahead of their day: a mechanism for converting print into Braille through photo-electric cells, an audiometer for high-speed sound photography, a portable x-ray machine and a device for copying photographs by radio. He cultivated the image of the eccentric professor, a 'young man with a shock of black hair, a pale impish face, a stoop, and a nervous blink. A sort of scientific Shelley' (Beverley Nichols).

In his final years Low's health was poor, but he still had some intriguing ideas for Second World War armaments, including a water bomb: 'It floated below the surface, came up when wanted, and spread a kind of umbrella, which when touched operated the fuse.' As president of the British Interplanetary Society in 1950, he was confidently predicting men on the moon before the end of the century and the launch of space stations.

Low believed in popular science. He wrote innumerable articles and forty books, including four pieces of science fiction for children: 'Had he persevered with his television research (1914), his guided missile (1917), and so many other of those inventions which *he saw first*, he might have been the greatest genius of his time' (Ursula Bloom).[29]

❧ Survivor of Scott's final Antarctic expedition

(GEORGE) MURRAY LEVICK (1876–1956)

We experienced strange sensations as we examined the cheerless hole that had been the only home of six of our hardiest men. No cell prisoners ever lived through such discomfort.

(Murray Levick)[30]

When Scott's ship the *Terra Nova* reached the Antarctic base camp and one party prepared its assault on the South Pole, Murray Levick joined a separate group of six men (led by Victor Campbell) as surgeon and zoologist. It was to spend almost two years (1910–12) on the Victoria Land coast. While searches were made for Scott and his men, Levick's party was enduring the exceptional winter of 1912 in a snow cave at Evans Cove, living off seal and penguin, but their extraordinary story of survival has been overshadowed by the literature and legends of Scott's disastrous return from the pole.

Although Scott came to recognize that Levick had a 'really charming nature', he was not impressed by his 'vacant smile' and said early on, 'I am afraid there is little to be expected of him.' As it happened, his straightforward optimism and good sense proved key ingredients for survival: Atkinson, his cabin mate on the *Terra Nova*, found him 'slow to move and act, but wise at bottom' and possessed of 'a magnificent fund of anecdote'.[31]

The group's first objective, King Edward VII land, had to be abandoned because of heavy ice. The *Terra Nova* took them on to make a scientific survey of Cape Adare. On the way they encountered the Norwegian explorer Roald Amundsen preparing his own successful polar expedition. Life at Cape Adare passed in the relative comfort of a prefabricated hut, where the men kept up standards by dressing for dinner, listening to a wind-up gramophone and even publishing their own newspapers. It proved impossible to survey the interior, but for Levick it was an opportunity to take some valuable photographs and study the Adélie Penguin. His book *Antarctic Penguins*, though superseded now, brings the

Murray Levick during the British National Antarctic Expedition, 1910-13. *Courtesy Scott Polar Research Institute, University of Cambridge.*

subject to life with an engaging mixture of science and empathy:

Suddenly those that walked would flop on to their breasts and start tobogganing, and conversely strings of tobogganers would as suddenly pop up on their feet and start walking. In this way they relieved the monotony of their march, and gave periodical rest to different groups of muscles and nerve-centres.[32]

In January 1912 the *Terra Nova* transported the team to a new location for six weeks' work, but bad ice prevented the ship from relieving them. Without proper equipment or provisions, Levick and his companions were facing an Antarctic winter. They spent more than six months in an ice and snow cave. Conditions were cramped and airless; their diet was very limited and had unpleasant side-effects; at one point they nearly died of asphyxiation. Even so, Levick's memories reflect extraordinary optimism, a necessary complement to Campbell's strict regime, which required the cave to be divided by an imaginary line into the 'messdeck' and the 'quarterdeck'. Levick devoted sixty-four nights to reading *David Copperfield* to his companions, and his diary records with pride their ingenuity as supplies ran short:

We have a very little tobacco which we eke out with every possible substitute. The tea leaves we have used have all been boiled three times and are now being smoked. We all smoke wood shavings, a piece of teak proving the best flavoured, but I have at the present moment some raisin stalks mixed with an old pipe heel burning merrily in my pipe, and it is very passable.[33]

After the long winter they journeyed the 230 miles back to base camp by sledge, only to find everyone else out looking for the bodies of Scott's polar party.

In later life Levick founded what is now known as the British Schools Exploring Society. He also worked tirelessly to help blind and physically handicapped children learn useful skills. C. F. Spooner, a fellow expedition leader for young people, said of him, 'He was always so full of life and enthusiasm and he made everything such enormous fun; even a setback became the cause of greater enjoyment with him, as it simply offered a greater challenge.'[34]

❧ *Geography, racism and beauty*

VAUGHAN CORNISH (1862–1948)

Vaughan Cornish married a trained engineer with money and at the age of thirty-two gave up work as director of technical education for Hampshire county council to concentrate on research. They lived in a cliff-top house, and his first area of interest was waves, of water, sand and snow, which the couple travelled the world to study. He wrote several books about his findings and in 1901 shot the first film of the Severn bore. His travels also gave him a taste for political debate: he began to see geography as a medium for safeguarding imperial values. Books were published with titles such as *Imperial Military Geography* (1920) and *A Geography of Imperial Defence* (1922). Then in 1925 he began to argue for something much more sinister. 'The method of the geographer', he stated in the *Eugenics Review*, 'is to study all mankind in relation to the regions of the world, and he therefore enquires which nations are now the most useful part of the human community.' Cornish was certain that the white peoples were the most useful, and he seems to have put the British at the head of the list. He encouraged British married couples to have at least four children and ended his essay with an exhortation:

Let me point out in conclusion that the resolve to people our own lands with British stock and to maintain the present proportion of our numbers in the world is essential to the achievement of our highest ethical ideas, for only by maintaining the British as a great and populous people can we ensure that our conception of righteousness shall receive its normal development in our lands and continue to command the respectful attention of the rest of mankind.[35]

Alongside such outmoded thinking, Cornish developed another and more sympathetic aspect of his subject, aesthetic geography. He came to regard beauty of environment as 'no mere luxury but an essential factor in the spiritual welfare of the nation'.[36] The landscape was still part of his concern for Britishness, but in strangely overwritten passages, a mixture of scientific exactitude and romantic decadence, the experience also became religious:

The pageant of the sunset passed with the fading of the last touch of carmine, and the western sky took on the tint of sober blue which comes between the cobalt of the day and the indigo of night, a colour chosen by Italian masters for the background of devotional scenes. Venus riding high, a solitary silver spur, shone steadily, the *descant* of the twilight, seeming to make the silence musical with angelic voices.[37]

The self-styled 'Pilgrim of Scenery', Cornish also campaigned for national parks and very actively supported the Council for the Preservation of Rural England. He gave his own stretch of cliffland near Salcombe Regis for public use in perpetuity — 'great stretches of our cliff-lands may yet be saved from villadom' — and left a bequest to Oxford University so that graduate students could study the beauty of scenery.

✿ A passion for plants

FRANCIS KINGDON-WARD (1885–1958)

If I ever travel again I'll make damned sure it's not with a botanist. They are always stopping to gape at weeds.

(Lord Cawdor, Frank Kingdon-Ward's travelling companion)

Son of a botanist and strictly brought up, Frank Kingdon-Ward quickly discovered his passion for collecting plants. Had his father's early death not forced him to leave Cambridge without a degree for financial reasons, he might have enjoyed the security of an academic career. As it was, commissions from nurseries and sponsors enabled him to embark on a series of very fruitful expeditions, mainly in Burma, Assam and Tibet.

Kingdon-Ward's rigid upbringing perhaps gave him the physical toughness, adaptabilty and reserves of patience to survive rough territory. His quests for new species sometimes read like epic battles:

To say that I progressed two yards in five minutes up that accursed slope would convey no inkling of the struggle. It was a fight all the way, through frozen tangle. To go straight up was impossible. I dodged which way I could. After pushing in vain against an unyielding barrier, I would seek passage to right or left, at the same time trying to keep my eye on the prize. Yet so steep was the face, that I as often lost sight of the goal, struggling up to my neck in the thicket. Heaving against the stiff upsweeping branches which fended me off breast high, I finally overbalanced and fell back against the more yielding branches behind; which gave way, so that I broke through the tangle and collapsed amongst snow and vegetation, half supported, in a helpless position. All the while my hands were being lacerated by the steely branches.

Not surprisingly, the discovery itself, in this case of the 'Tea Rose' primula, was a moment of ecstasy:

I can recall several flowers which at first sight have knocked the breath out of me, but only two or three which have taken me by storm as did this one. The sudden vision is like a physical blow in the pit of the stomach; one can only gasp and stare. In the face of such unsurpassed loveliness, one is afraid to move, as with bated breath one mutters the single word 'God' — a prayer rather than an exclamation [...] I stood there transfixed on the snow-cone, in a honeymoon of bliss, feasting my eyes on a masterpiece.

Kingdon-Ward preferred to travel alone, and companions found their patience tested by his silent ruminations and dedication to his task. Lord Cawdor complained, 'I'm bound for Lord knows how long to wander this damned country with a man who can only shuffle along like a paralytic. [...] In the whole of my life, I've never seen such an incredibly slow mover.' His reflections were interesting.

Once he thought of turning papaya seeds into ersatz caviar, and he was ahead of his day in realizing that 'man has altered the vegetation of the globe and continues to do so at an ever-growing rate. How many square miles under tea, coffee, rubber etc? Destruction of forest for pulp.'

From his most successful expedition, 1924–25, Kingdon-Ward collected ninety-seven different rhododendrons and the first viable seed of the spectacular blue Himalayan poppy, which made a sensational impact at the 1926 Chelsea flower show. When he died there were over 23,000 plant numbers to his credit. His own epitaph was modest:

Sometimes I ask myself, is it right to spend so much time, energy and money, not to mention thought, and wear, and tear, and effort, to achieve what appears to be so little? Say half a dozen first-class plants. But why not. How else would one spend the time? These plants may give pleasure to thousands for many years. It is a justifiable way of spending one's life.[38]

Francis Kingdon-Ward on his travels in the East. *© Royal Geographical Society.*

❧ *Museum director*

SIR SYDNEY CARLYLE COCKERELL (1867–1962)

I found it a pigsty; I turned it into a palace.
(Sir Sydney Cockerell)[39]

Sydney Cockerell was director of the Fitzwilliam Museum in Cambridge for twenty-nine years from 1908, in Wilfred Blunt's words transforming 'a dead-alive, almost static little provincial gallery into one of the most vital, best-displayed and choicest museums in the country'. Cockerell would have agreed wholeheartedly with this assessment: he was not a modest man. The museum was more than doubled in size, its collections were much enriched, and it became a much more open and interesting place to visit.

Cockerell's testimonial from John Ruskin characterized him as 'an earnest reader with considerable knowledge of art — wonderfully neat and careful in his work and in collecting and arranging things admirable — and with a love, a power, of keeping things in beautiful order — always genial and pleasant'. This high regard for order led him to dismiss the Egyptian departments at the Fitzwilliam as 'a complete and repellent muddle', and the tough side of his character came through also in his ruthless quest for donations of money and artefacts to the museum. Thomas Hardy wrote, 'How you manage to squeeze £1,000 out of a dinner table passes my understanding. It is ...better than big game shooting.' Stories abounded about his sudden appearance at the deathbeds of the wealthy, and on Cockerell's retirement the chancellor of Cambridge University said, 'There is no collector in the world who feels his treasures safe so long as Sir Sydney is in the land.'

He had a remarkable circle of friends and acquaintances. Before coming to Cambridge he had travelled with John Ruskin and worked as William Morris's secretary. Christopher, Cockerell's only son (and inventor of the hovercraft), mentions Bernard Shaw, Joseph Conrad, Freya Stark and T. E. Lawrence among their houseguests. He became a friend of Thomas Hardy, and in due course his literary executor, after asking him to contribute a manuscript to the museum (Hardy in fact gave two). Letter writing was part of his phenomenal capacity for work: he wrote thirty-nine letters to T. E. Lawrence alone.

Cockerell was a discriminating collector of books and expected his visitors to appreciate this. Of David Knowles, regius professor of modern history, he wrote, 'No doubt an excellent fellow [...] but I was rather unfavourably impressed by his way of looking at the books I showed him, which did not seem to indicate appropriate enthusiasm.' In 1956 and 1957 he sold his collection, which included a rare vellum copy of the finest work produced by the William Morris press, the Kelmscott Chaucer, and realized over £80,000.

When one young woman mentioned an 'unforgettable' evening at his house, Cockerell responded, 'I have no recollection whatsoever of the evening you mention', but the young woman was right: his evenings were unforgettable. Siegfried Sassoon was invited to Cockerell's home several times while he was on officers' training in Cambridge during 1915:

On those Sunday nights in the quiet candle-lit room he seemed a sort of bearded and spectacled magician, conjuring up the medieval illuminated missals and psalters on which he was a famous expert, and bringing my mind into almost living contact with the Pre-Raphaelites whom I had worshipped since my dreaming adolescence. Brusque and uncompromising, his light-blue eyes regarded me somewhat austerely as he handed me yet another treasure to gloat over. People were sometimes offended by his plain-spoken manner; but to be contradicted by Cockerell was an education; and no doubt I offered him numerous opportunities to do so.[40]

Sydney Cockerell's father died when he was ten, and instead of going up to university he left St Paul's at the age of seventeen and spent seven years in the family coal business. This makes his achievement all the more special.[41]

Sir Sydney Cockerell in the Manuscript Room of the Fitzwilliam Museum, photograph by Lafayette Ltd, 1933. *Fitzwilliam Museum, Cambridge.*

Sums and talk

JOHN EDENSOR LITTLEWOOD (1885–1977)

In his younger days incompetent research students reminded him of a general in *War and Peace* who, disturbed by the groans of a soldier, calls to him: 'My good man, do try to die more quietly!'

(Béla Bollobás)

Writing about a mathematical genius is a challenge, especially one who took pride in divorcing his pursuit of ideal theory from anything of practical value. When asked what God was doing before the Creation he replied, 'Millions of words must have been written on this; but he was doing pure mathematics and thought it would be a pleasant change to do some applied.'

John Littlewood's life largely sheltered him from the ordinary world. When he sat the mathematical tripos at Cambridge in 1905, after just two years' study, there was still an order of merit (it was abolished in 1910) and he duly came first, earning the title of senior wrangler, which he shared with a Manchester post-graduate. There was a short spell lecturing in Manchester, but then Littlewood returned for life to his old college, Trinity. He occupied the same set of rooms, apart from service in the First World War working on the mathematics of gunnery, from 1912 until 1977.

The most celebrated mathematics of Littlewood came in about a hundred works written with G. H. Hardy, many on number theory. The Nobel prize-winning Soviet physicist Landau thought 'the mathematician Hardy-Littlewood [...] the best in the world, with Littlewood the more original genius, and Hardy the better journalist'.

His view of life was undoubtedly that of a Cambridge don, but Littlewood was more than just a mathematician and teacher, and a fuller flavour of his attractively idiosyncratic personality comes from his book *A Mathematician's Miscellany*. In this collection, a kind of mathematician's commonplace book, he mixes theory, autobiography, anecdote, humour and aphorism, in places turning a straightforward problem (how to survive in a lion's den) into a very complex formula, in places illuminating mathematical immensities, such as the concept of large numbers, by simple analogies. In the *Miscellany* is glimpsed Littlewood, the civilized and cultured conversationalist.

Autobiographical

When Trinity once (before 1914) had some wine at lowish price, but not satisfactory and also not selling, they doubled the price, whereupon the idle rich bought it all up.

John Littlewood teaching at Cambridge. *By kind permission of the master and fellows of Trinity College, Cambridge.*

An example of genuine mathematical reasoning with minimal material

Three ladies, *A.B.C.* in a railway carriage, all have dirty faces and are all laughing. It suddenly flashes on *A*: why doesn't *B* realize *C* is laughing at her? — Heavens! *I* must be laughable. (Formally: if I, *A*, am not laughable, *B* will be arguing: if I, *B*, am not laughable, *C* has nothing to laugh at. Since *B* does not so argue, I, *A*, must be laughable.)

Large numbers

There is a stone, a cubic mile in size, a million times harder than diamond. Every million years a very holy man visits it to give the lightest possible touch. The stone is in the end worn away. This works out at something like 10^{35} years; poor value for so much trouble, and an instance of the 'debunking' of popular immensities.

An unconscious assumption

Schoolmaster: 'Suppose x is the number of sheep in the problem.'
Pupil: 'But, sir, suppose x is not the number of sheep.' (I asked Prof. Wittgenstein was this not a profound philosophical joke, and he said it was.)[42]

❧ *Royal Physician*

BERTRAND EDWARD DAWSON, VISCOUNT DAWSON OF PENN (1864–1945)

The king's life is moving peacefully towards its close.

(Lord Dawson's wording of the final bulletin on George V, written on a menu-card at Sandringham,
9.25 p.m. 20 January 1936)

The Lying in State of King George V, Westminster Hall, 24–28 January 1935. *Nealf.*

Bertrand Dawson administered a fatal injection of morphia and cocaine to ease George V's death. This he admitted was partly driven by his wish that the first announcement should appear 'in the morning papers rather than the less appropriate evening journals', and he had asked his wife by telephone to recommend *The Times* to delay going to press until there was an announcement from Sandringham.[43] However, it is clear from his own notebook that Dawson's motives were primarily humanitarian. He felt that protracting the king's final hours did not comport 'with that dignity and serenity which he so richly merited'. Later in 1936 he went on to speak against the Voluntary Euthanasia (Legalization) Bill stressing that this was 'something which belongs to the wisdom and conscience of the medical profession and not to the realm of law'.[44] His decision in January, which the queen and Prince of Wales were happy to leave in his hands, precisely reflected his beliefs: Dawson was at once deeply religious and influenced by the free thinking he encountered as an undergraduate. As well as looking after the royal family's health (in 1929 his prompt action may well have saved the king's life), he was a vigorous advocate of improving national health, coined the phrase 'health centre' and masterminded the Dawson report, published in 1920, which in many ways foreshadowed the Beveridge report and National Health Service legislation of the 1940s.

❧ *Fighting for rights in South Africa*

SIDNEY PERCIVAL BUNTING (1873–1936)

Socialists with a genuine interest in the working class as a whole during the formative years of apartheid needed to be resilient characters with a strong sense of purpose. Such was Sidney Percival Bunting, one of the founders of the first Communist Party in Africa. Bunting fought not only for the rights and interests of the white working class, but he actively participated in the struggles of black people in South Africa during the years when it was treachery to side with the blacks.

(Chris Hani, general secretary of the South African Communist Party, assassinated in 1993)[45]

Sidney Bunting trained as a lawyer and settled in Johannesburg after serving in the colonial irregular forces during the Boer War. He was also a director of the family wattle plantation in Natal. Interest in politics began in 1910, when he joined the white South African Labour Party, but it was events three years later that opened his eyes. A dispute affecting Rand gold miners had turned into a general strike in July 1913, and when the Rand Club (popular with mineowners) was threatened, British dragoons fired into the crowd and killed dozens. In *The*

Worker of 10 July, Bunting launched his considerable powers of rhetoric on the mining magnates and 'parasites of the town clubs', who had been praying that the rioters would 'be butchered to make a Rand Club holiday'. He belonged to the club himself and was probably there when the shooting occurred, but throughout his life events would radically change his views. 'Bunting was always condemning his own past.'

Other changes came with the First World War. Bunting had gone out to South Africa believing strongly in the values of empire but led now a War-on-War faction in the Labour Party. He broke away entirely after it voted to 'support the Imperial Government wholeheartedly in its prosecution of the war'. The Labour Party had only served the interests of relatively privileged white workers, and he became a foundation member of the Marxist International Socialist League of Africa, fighting for recognition of all workers, including the black underclass.

Bunting became a notorious figure and was charged with incitement to violence after a strike by native sanitary workers in 1918. He wrote passionate weekly articles for the *International* in his efforts to bring the interests of black and white workers together, but it was a naïve aspiration, and when the Communist Party of South Africa absorbed the ISL in 1921, it was almost exclusively white. His dilemma was graphically illustrated by the last great miners' strike or 'Rand Revolt'. White miners were in effect striking in order to protect the industry's colour bar, but the Communist Party supported it, and out of loyalty to the party Bunting persuaded himself that the 'true issue' was not race but the threat of lower wages for workers. However, by the end of 1924 the movement to emancipate black labour was openly supported by the Communist Party of South Africa, and momentum gathered.

Bunting had attended the Fourth Comintern Congress in Moscow in 1922 and came away confirmed in his duty to serve all workers. When he returned for the Sixth Congress (1928), Comintern had become much more

Mounted police dispersing strikers in Market Square, Johannesburg during the 1913 strike.
Courtesy Museum Africa, Johannesburg.

dogmatic and required the South African party to create an independent black republic which granted minority rights to white workers as a stage towards the overthrow of capitalism. In other words, Bunting was now faced with an anti-white party. 'We did not want to put the black man on top and the white man underneath. We wanted them to be equal,' he said. His attempts to explain the special conditions in South Africa only led to his being denounced as a white chauvinist.

Bunting stayed loyal to the party even when disagreeing with it, and stood as a Communist Party candidate for the rural seat of Tembuland in the 1929 elections. He was denounced now by the government for being anti-white and arrested more than once. His leaflets were confiscated and voters intimidated. 'All the forces at the disposal of the government were used to discredit him,' but he still won sufficient votes to save his deposit.

It was not enough to impress the communists. The CPSA conference in 1930–31 was run on strict Bolshevik lines: 'the party must be hewn from a single piece of stone'. Bunting was considered too unorthodox to remain on the committee and accused of reducing the movement for national native independence to a mere reformist struggle for equal rights. In September 1931 Comrade S. P. Bunting was classed as a right-wing agitator and expelled from the party altogether. The shock was compounded by a campaign to discredit him and his fellow 'Buntingites'. The CPSA became more and more Bolshevik with a completely unrealistic programme of peasant leagues, political training classes and so on, while he became the 'imperialist bloodsucker Lord Bunting'. In due course the party reverted to a more moderate stance, but it came too late. Bunting had not made much money from his legal practice (most of his clients were poor Africans) and was now in poor health. His final job was as a caretaker, and he died in 1936 after a stroke.[46]

❧ *Missionary in Johannesburg*

RICHARD ELLIOTT RAYNES (1903–58) [RAYMOND RAYNES]

He was nicknamed 'Kalofo' (Sesotho name for 'golfstick') [...] because he was tall and bent at the top, just like a golfstick. Father Raynes liked his nickname very much, and answered to it with great joy.

(Nicholas Mosley, *The Life of Raymond Raynes*)

In 1935 Raymond Raynes was an 'inexperienced, awkward young schoolmaster' teaching at St John's College in Johannesburg, an establishment for white boys modelled on the English public school which claimed to be 'the finest south of the equator'. He belonged to the Anglican Community of the Resurrection at Mirfield, which he joined in 1930 after a short period working as curate in a Lancashire parish. He was most at home in the common

Raymond Raynes in Sophiatown, Johannesburg. *Courtesy Mirfield, Community of the Resurrection.*

room at St John's and liked to reminisce about his days at St Paul's. With such a background, Raynes seemed the least likely person to take over a community mission in the black Johannesburg township of Sophiatown, but when invited he said he would 'like to have a stab at it'.

The outcome was remarkable. Helped by Dorothy Maud, a bishop's daughter already working in Sophiatown, he built in the space of six years three churches and ten schools. The hospital was expanded, and the township was given roads, lighting, water and sanitation. Raynes found himself regularly saving Africans from police oppression, clearing up after fights, dealing with emergencies. He once delivered a baby, baptizing it Gabriel because he said the angels assisted him. There were the schools to run and antagonistic government inspectors to cope with.

When Raynes went home on leave in 1938 he had become 'leader of one of the most important missionary works in Africa' and was spoken of as the next superior of the order. He returned to ever-increasing responsibilities in South Africa. Despite major surgery for a perforated ulcer, the consequence of neglecting sleep and food, he continued to expand the mission's work, especially when he realized his election as community superior at Mirfield was imminent.

The call came in 1943, and he returned to Mirfield so unwell that he was ordered to bed. A novice was deputed to look after him, a quiet man called Trevor Huddleston. In him Raynes discovered his successor at the Sophiatown mission. It was an inspired decision, and Huddleston became known and admired as parish priest and a formidable opponent of apartheid. During his fifteen years overseeing the Community of the Resurrection, Raynes's most-criticized action was recalling Huddleston in 1956. The reasons for this can only be guessed. Developments in South Africa meant that Huddleston had become a prominent political figure in danger of arrest, but Raynes was not a man to bow to political pressure or worry about physical risk. Possibly he felt that the publicity was damaging Huddleston's monastic vocation.

Following years of poor health, Raynes died after suffering a coronary thrombosis during a visit to Hurstpierpoint in 1958.[47]

❧ *Religious thinking*

AUSTIN MARSDEN FARRER (1904–68)

Of all my able pupils he was the most aloof and most difficult to know.

(Austin Farrer's tutor at Balliol)[48]

There was one occasion when as a boy at St Paul's Austin Farrer 'hired an organ grinder to play outside his classroom, ensuring that when the form-master flung up the window the blind would fall on his neck', but for the most part he was very serious. His speech on 'feminism will result in the extinction of chivalry' to the Union debating society 'brought wrinkles to the faces of the light-hearted and by his seriousness appalled even the most irresponsible'. It comes as no surprise that at Balliol College, Oxford, his fellow undergraduates, whose intellectual pretensions disgusted him, told Farrer he was born old.

He was to spend the last thirty-seven years of his life in Oxford, twenty-five of them as chaplain of Trinity College. Farrer's interest lay in the relationship between theology and philosophy. In books such as *Finite and Infinite* (1943) he set out to show that the existence of God was consistent with a world that had its own observable scientific logic, and in doing this he hoped to rebut those philosophers around him who as logical positivists thought that what you saw and reasoned about was all that had meaning. These ideas are undoubtedly difficult, and

Farrer's elegant allusive style was at times illuminating and at times simply obscure. The same was true of his teaching.

Austin Farrer, acrylic by George Speake, 1970.
By kind permission of the warden and fellows of Keble College, Oxford.

As one former pupil put it, 'His lectures rarely attracted queues', but like-minded students who knew him well discovered not only intellectual inspiration but also a sympathetic chaplain whose austere and lapidary sermons were balanced by surprisingly relaxed and convivial evenings in his college rooms.

'Faith and Evidence', published in 1964, illustrates Farrer's gift for using metaphor to illuminate his beliefs:

There is a stock scene of Victorian fiction — I do not know how many times it occurs. The seeming orphan, brought up by a hard-faced aunt, is suddenly confronted by his real mother. The mother does her best not to give herself away; but a sort of warm, pinkish wave of sentimental electricity tingles through the child; he is strangely moved, he knows not why. Nonsense, I say; ten to one, the child would experience nothing. Undisclosed, actual mothers can be encoun-

tered by seven-year-olds with equanimity. What cannot be a subset of indifference to them is the suggestion of a possible mother, if it actually comes to mind. Our orphan child, let us assume, has some access to normal families. He knows what a mother is. Then one day he says to himself, 'Goodness! Suppose I really have got a mother! They say she disappeared in the Revolution, when I was brought to America. They say she was killed, but I wonder!' The child's mind alternates between hope and resignation. The suggestion that there might be a mother is not an isolated factual hypothesis; it is a picture of the world, with an attitude built in; it is a filial existence in place of orphan existence. […] For the child to think of a possible mother is to experiment in having a mother; to try filial existence. The experiment takes place in the realms of imagination, but it is real enough to the heart. And similarly to think of a possible God is to experiment in having God.[49]

❧ *Political extremist and sage*

ARAVINDA ACKROYD GHOSE, (1872–1950) [SRI AUROBINDO]

Grave with intensity, careless of fate or opinion, and one of the most silent men I have known, he was of the stuff that dreamers are made of, but dreamers who will act their dream, indifferent to the means.

(*Manchester Guardian* journalist H. Nevinson after meeting Sri Aurobindo)[50]

Sri Aurobindo spent his first few years in Bengal, but his anglophile father, a civil medical officer, wanted him to join the Indian Civil Service and sent Aurobindo and his brothers to England for their education. He won a foundation scholarship to St Paul's, an open scholarship in classics to King's College, Cambridge, and a high pass in the extremely competitive ICS examination, but he was to say later that even at school he was turning against British rule

Sri Aurobindo at Pondicherry.
© *Sri Aurobindo Ashram Trust.*

in India and towards political action, inspired by Shelley's French Revolution poem, *The Revolt of Islam*.[51]

Torn between loyalty to his father and loathing of his prospective career (he described the men he would be working with as 'unmannerly, uncultivated, unintelligent'), Aurobindo decided to engineer rejection from the ICS by failing the compulsory riding test that followed the final written examination: on the first occasion he fell off his horse, and he ignored six appointments for a retest. There was a tragic sequel. Dr Ghose was overjoyed when his son passed the written papers and ordered him back to India on an early steamer, which sank off Portugal. Delayed by the horse-riding, Aurobindo was not on the boat, but his father was unaware of this, took to his bed broken-hearted and died.

Aurobindo's first employment came from a fortuitous meeting in London with the Maharaja Gaikwar of Baroda, who offered him a post as his unofficial private secretary. He stayed with the maharaja for thirteen years from 1893, becoming professor in the state's college. It was a period of growing resentment against British rule. Aurobindo had little time for the Indian National Congress set up in 1885 'to release pent-up forces of discontent'. Just four months after his return he published a forthright article in Bombay telling Indians they 'must no longer hold out supplicating hands to the English Parliament, like an infant crying to its nurse for a toy, but must recognize the hard truth that every nation must beat out its own path to salvation with pain and difficulty'. He was also coming to see armed revolution as the road to freedom and with the maharaja's tacit consent began infiltrating the Indian army with revolutionaries.[52]

Little happened until Britain's controversial and it turned out temporary division of Bengal (1905–11). Aurobindo left Baroda for Calcutta, where he became principal of the newly-founded Bengal National College and wrote leaders for *Bande Mataram*, a revolutionary daily newspaper. At one point he was tried for sedition and acquitted, gaining a national celebrity he claimed he did not like, preferring to 'push people without their knowing it'.[53] He had also been setting up a network of secret revolutionary cells: one of these, run by his younger brother Barindraumar (born 1880), was trying to stir up popular enthusiasm through assassinations, all of which had so far gone wrong. Aurobindo claimed to disapprove of sporadic acts of terrorism, favouring instead full-scale insurrection, but he had overall charge of the group, certainly knew about Barin's 'childish' plots and did not try to prevent them. On 30 April 1908 two members targeted the carriage of an Indian Civil Service officer, Douglas Kingsford, who had presided over several press prosecutions. The bomb exploded, but it was the wrong carriage, and two Englishwomen were killed. One assassin shot himself rather than betray the group; the other was tried and executed. Aurobindo was among others arrested, but again he was acquitted: the chief witness against him, a member of the cell who had turned king's evidence, was murdered before the trial started.

Aurobindo's release was greeted with enthusiasm. He undertook a political tour and continued to write for the press. Then in February 1910 he left the political scene for ever. He has written that he was obeying a sudden divine command to go to French India, but he was also under threat of another prosecution for sedition, and the authorities were looking for a chance to deport him.

Spiritual experiences had featured in Aurobindo's previous life, 'the vision of the Godhead surging up from within when in danger of a carriage accident in Baroda in the first year of his stay', and he had been practising yoga for several years, feeling it gave him the spiritual power to execute his political ideas.[54] In Pondicherry (capital of French India) his life now encompassed writing and yoga, and a community grew up around him. His philosophy moved on from revolution and liberation to a step in evolution which would 'raise man to a higher and larger consciousness'. Mankind would be in contact with the 'supermind' — 'the truth of that which we call God'. 'A new spirit of oneness will take hold of the human race.'[55] In 1920 a Frenchwoman, Mirra Alfassa, joined him and became known as the Mother, his spiritual equal. When Aurobindo withdrew from the public eye in 1926, she looked after the spiritual community or ashram.

Within Aurobindo's vast corpus of writing, still keenly studied, his most important legacy may be the vision of integrating Western materialism with Eastern spiritual culture:

The hope of the world lies in the re-arousing in the East of the old spiritual practicality and large and profound vision and power of organization under the insistent contact of the West and in the flooding out of the light of Asia on the Occident, no longer in forms that are now static, effete, unadaptive, but in new forms, stirred, dynamic and effective.[56]

❧ *A man of many parts*

SIR (EDWARD MONTAGUE ANTHONY) COMPTON MACKENZIE (1883–1972)

We lunch or dine sometimes with Compton Mackenzie, and he is nice. But one feels the generations of actors behind him and can't be quite serious. What a queer thing the theatre is in its influence. He […] walks a sort of aesthetic figure […] in a pale blue suit to match his eyes and a woman's large brown velours hat to match his hair.

(D. H. Lawrence)

Compton Mackenzie (or Monty) came from a theatrical family. His father was actor-manager of the Compton Comedy Company, and his mother and four siblings all had stage careers. Mackenzie's own life — he described himself as 'Protean' — was a series of roles and reinventions, each played with theatrical gusto.

An extraordinarily prolific writer, he published 113 titles,

including a Scottish historical odyssey almost a million words long, *The Four Winds of Love* (1937–45),* and a ten-volume autobiography, *My Life and Times*, published in his eighties. His most successful work was shaped from his life. His second novel, *Carnival* (1912), was set in the world

---

* The manuscript was presented to St Paul's School.

Compton Mackenzie
dictating to James
Eastwood with Hamlet,
*c.*1918. Compton
Mackenzie, *My Life and
Times*: Octave 5, 1930–31,
Chatto and Windus, 1967.

of variety theatre, and such was its popularity that for six months the smart set talked the language of Jenny, its heroine: 'It was no longer Cockney but a "Jennyism" to say "don't be soppy" or "any old way" or "I must have been potty".' Mackenzie's third, *Sinister Street* (1913–14), was a *Bildungsroman* created from his childhood and adolescence. St Paul's became St James'; Walker appeared as Dr Brownjohn, 'huge of build, with a long grey beard to which adhered stale morsels of food and the acrid scent of strong cigars', Elam as the dried-up, eccentric and irascible Mr Neech, who nonetheless was 'almost the only schoolmaster with a positive personality whom Michael [the protagonist] ever encountered'.[57] *Sinister Street* was at once praised and reviled. The novelist Ford Madox Ford thought it 'possibly a work of real genius',[58] but its allusions to teenage sexual urges and homosexuality were considered so offensive at Eton that Cyril Connolly was beaten for reading it, and his headmaster wrote an outraged letter to *The Times*.

The First World War cast Mackenzie in the new role of intelligence officer in Athens. He enjoyed his work 'as a boy enjoys playing at pirates', ordered stylish white suits to parade the streets and had his code name Z stamped at the head of his stationery. He admitted later that he was motivated less by security than by Athens' 'infinite romance and excitement' and what he, 'an impressionable writer of fiction', wanted the secret service to be. His exploits have a flavour of the *Boys' Own Paper*: on one occasion he sailed into Smyrna with two sacks which he explained contained trussed Turkish hostages who would

be executed unless his chief agent was released. His finest moment came with recapturing the Cyclades islands, not the most challenging of assignments but celebrated by new stationery headed 'Director, Aegean Intelligence Service'.

After a spying career, Mackenzie's alter ego John Ogilvie said, 'I feel I shall never want to go back to writing, living is so much more enjoyable.' For Mackenzie himself, the reality of the secret service had not quite matched the dream, and he did go back, unwisely spilling some classified information in his book *Greek Memories* (1933): he was charged and typically felt 'rather tickled by the prospect' of being prosecuted by the attorney-general in person. The £100 fine was probably well worth it.

There were other parts to play. Disillusioned with life on the British mainland, he joined the colony of expatriate thinkers and artists on the island of Capri, until their pretensions tired him. For writer Francis Brett-Young, seeing 'Mackenzie enter the Café Morgano in a black or white sombrero and voluminous cape, lined […] with blue velvet, was one of the sights of Christendom. He managed it as the great Victorian actresses managed their gowns'. *Extraordinary Women*, 1928, was his attack on the lesbian element of Capri. The romantic history of Scotland drew him next. He settled on the Hebridean island of Barra in the thirties and after the Second World War wrote popular comedies about the island and the highlands: he liked to defend the inhabitants against outside interference, and *Whisky Galore*, the story of a cargo of Scotch salvaged by the islanders, became a huge Ealing Studios success. Mackenzie himself had a small part.

There was Mackenzie the horticulturalist. In 1909 he thought he would become a gardener, and so he wrote for gardening magazines and started travelling to flower shows. He saw himself as a classical music expert and founded *The Gramophone* magazine, still flourishing today, despite the disapproval of more-established critics: 'Monty's habit of reviewing records which he listened to while writing novels was not approved of, nor was his tendency to write of a flute "whistling like an errand boy", or a piano "rocking gently like a boat on a sea of strings".'

Finally, in 1952 he bought an elegant house in Edinburgh's Georgian New Town, settled to his remarkable memoirs and enjoyed becoming an *éminence grise* of Scottish culture.[59]

🎕 *A publishing revolution*

SIR VICTOR GOLLANCZ (1893–1967)

Victor exuded a greater dynamism than any man I've ever known. Even to see him coming through the front door was like a tempest coming in [....] I remember going in to see him one day. He was sharpening a pencil; it was like any lesser man hewing down an oak tree. Everything Victor did was done like that.

(Norman Collins, assistant managing director at Gollancz's publishing house)[60]

Victor Gollancz was a publisher of legendary energy and talent. From 1921 he served a stormy apprenticeship under Ernest Benn. He transformed the firm's list and marketing strategy, hiring newspaper critics as readers to guarantee the good reviews on which high sales depended, but hated answering to a mentor: 'the incredible little EJPB (he is *really* nasty— very!)'. When Benn offered him an exceptionally generous contract to stay on in 1927, he chose instead to set up his own publishing company.

Gollancz presented his books for maximum impact: 'Instead of the dignified list of twenty titles set out primly in a modest space, there was the double or triple column, with the title of one book screaming across it in letters three inches high. The forces of modernity had been loosed, the age of shouting, the period of the colossal and the sensational had arrived.'[61] His famed bright-yellow dust wrappers with black and magenta lettering could not pass unnoticed on the shelves. He used to boast that he sold in enormous quantities titles that would languish on other publishers' lists, but his motive was not just commercial.

Gollancz also set out to educate his readers in politics and particularly socialism, an ambition sharpened by events of the 1930s. In 1933 he published *The Brown Book of the Hitler Terror and the Burning of the Reichstag*, an early account (possibly instigated by Comintern) of the horrors of life in Nazi Germany which was translated into seventeen languages and sold several million copies world wide. His opposition to fascism drew him to Soviet communism despite its dictatorial nature, and he planned the *New Soviet Library*, a collection of twelve volumes, with the Soviet Embassy, also in 1933: the project foundered when one of his contributors, the public prosecutor Vishinsky, was responsible for the execution of another, Bukharin (editor of *Izvestia*). When asked by *Cavalcade* magazine

to nominate the 'man of the year' in 1937, he chose Stalin for 'safely guiding Russia on the road to a society in which there will be no exploitation',[62] but a year later he told Old Pauline Leonard Woolf (see later entry) that he had been wrong to accept Soviet censorship as a necessary evil on the road to a socialist society.[63]

His main weapon against Nazism and fascism was the Left Book Club, the first organization of its kind, which published political writing in cheap editions from 1936–48. George Orwell and Arthur Koestler were among its contributors, and at one point it had 57,000 members. The club spawned 1,500 discussion groups, held three large rallies and organized many educational activities. It was a major force behind Labour's dramatic victory in the 1945 general election. It also revealed Gollancz's gifts as a public speaker. He once spoke at the Oxford Union in favour of a more energetic and practical government policy 'toward the rescue of Jews in Europe', and was so persuasive that the motion's opposer and almost all his followers crossed the floor to join him.[64]

Old Pauline Norman de Mattos Bentwich (1883–1971), chairman of the National Peace Council (1944–46) and professor of international relations at the Hebrew University of Jerusalem (1932–51), wrote, 'Victor Gollancz was among the most forceful personalities in the country, combining the intensity of a prophet with an uncanny flair for publicity.'[65] Among the many causes he threw himself into were the Campaign for Nuclear Disarmament and Save Europe Now, a programme he set up for sending food to half-starved Germans after the war. He supported the founding of the state of Israel despite a dislike of nationalism which led him to say, 'Of all forms of patriotism Jewish patriotism seems to me the most detestable', in response to a letter complaining of anti-Semitism in

Victor Gollancz.
Courtesy University of Warwick Library.

Orwell's *Down and Out in Paris and London*, which he published.[66] Later, Gollancz was to call himself Judaeo-Christian and edit two religious anthologies.

However liberal and pacifist his political views, Gollancz was in his own business an autocrat and by the 1950s an intolerant one: 'Far too accustomed to being compared with Gandhi, Schweitzer, Ezekiel and Jesus Christ, Victor had come to regard criticism as a *lèse-majesté*, and his rows with authors and agents were the stuff of gossip and legend.' He was not a man to accept weakness or failure. Once, when losing at table tennis to his accountant, he thumped the table every time his opponent was about to serve, put him off his stride and retrieved the match. When an agent reminded him about a bonus he had forgotten, Gollancz shouted, 'How dare you, I am

incapable of error!' In everyday life he was notoriously tight-fisted, and yet the parties his wife Ruth hosted in the twenties were glamorously lavish, with the centrepiece on one occasion an ice-swan filled with caviar.[67]

Contradictory in almost everything he did — when embarking on an affair with a woman active in the Left Book Club, he obtained his wife's approval in advance — Gollancz was a figure larger than life but filled with humanity. After being exiled from Abyssinia by Mussolini, Emperor Haile Selassie stayed with the Gollancz family. His thank-you letter 'To the lady Gollancz, wise in kindness and motherhood', was also addressed 'To her most wise and dialectical husband kind in all things including the cigar and the brandy'.[68]

❧ *Fraudster turned bookseller*

CLARENCE CHARLES HATRY (1888–1965)

I have often tried hard to find excuses for Hatry on the grounds that 'Genius is akin to madness', but Hatry was not mad; he had however the supreme quality of dangerous optimism coupled with inordinate conceit. [...] his brain was honeycombed with crevasses into which unpleasant facts were allowed to slip, and there he permitted them to remain in the hope that the glacier would never reveal its secrets.

(The Marquess of Winchester)[69]

Hatchard's bookshop in Piccadilly, owned by Clarence Hatry after his release from prison. *Swiv.*

In 1930 Clarence Hatry was sentenced to fourteen years' penal servitude. He had an appetite for adventurous city deals and in 1929 sought to gain control of United Steel. The market was falling in the wake of a Labour election victory, and Hatry was unable to raise the money legitimately to buy all the shares he needed. Instead, he borrowed heavily on forged documents. He spent very large sums vainly trying to support the value of his other companies, and rumours began to circulate. Even so, one London bank gave Hatry a supportive reference a week before the crash, '[A] well-known City financier, at present engaged in big steel combine, backed by first-class people, and we think he should be good for his engagements.' On 20 September he confessed his fraud to the director of public prosecutions. It is thought that investors in Hatry's companies lost £15 million, money they attempted to recoup by heavy selling on Wall Street, where catastrophic price collapses came on 24 and 29 October.

Hatry was experienced in spectacular success and failure. In the illusory boom following the end of the First World War, he made an immediate fortune of about £350,000 by buying and reselling Leyland Motors. His wealth grew further through an eclectic mix of interests including glass, pig farming and cotton spinning. The *New York Times* said he 'inspired confidence by his amazing flair

The river front of Shell-Mex House, designed in 1931 by Old Pauline Ernest Marton Joseph (1877–1960). 'It is thoroughly unsubtle, but succeeds in holding its own in London's river front' (Nikolaus Pevsner). *Amanda Denny.*

for getting investors a quick return for their money'.[70] Hatry enjoyed being rich: he owned a yacht, racehorses and a Mayfair house famed for its nine bathrooms and glass-floored winter garden. When his bank, the Commercial Corporation of London, collapsed in 1923, he could cover personally its debts and guarantees (partly by pawning his wife's jewellery) and made an asset of his failure with the slogan 'The Man Who Always Pays'.[71] He went on to make money buying and selling department stores, but his activities on the stock market became byzantine in their complexity, and he was possibly in trouble before the United Steel débâcle.

At his trial Hatry did not deny his actions but thought of them as 'irregular' rather than 'criminal'.[72] He did however portray himself as an optimist and altruist: he acted 'in a moment of great and overwhelming temptation,

when great projects and great enterprises seemed near fulfilment, and it appeared that by taking the wrong step it would be possible to avert a disaster which would bring on many thousands of innocent people a loss that they could hardly bear'. The judge was unimpressed, telling Hatry he stood convicted of 'the most appalling frauds that have ever disfigured the commercial reputation of this country'. His plea for clemency was dismissed as 'nothing more or less than the threadbare plea of every clerk or servant who robs his master and says that he hoped to repay the money before his crime was discovered by backing a winner'.[73]

There was more enterprise to come. Hatry became librarian in Wandsworth Jail and on his release in 1939 began to advise the book trade. In the early 1950s he owned Hatchard's, the Piccadilly bookshop, as well as several London coffee bars.

❧ The circle of Keynes

RICHARD FERDINAND KAHN, BARON KAHN (1905–89)

We had great fun on Sunday mornings catching each one and weighing it in a home-made form of scales, devised by Keynes, to ascertain whether it was yet ripe for the bacon market.

(Kahn on pig-keeping during his visits to Keynes's house)[74]

While on holiday in the Austrian Tyrol in August 1930, Richard Kahn invented the revolutionary new theory that investment created ripples of demand spreading through the economy. This idea was christened 'the multiplier' and

became the centrepiece of John Maynard Keynes's *General Theory of Employment, Interest and Money* (1936), one of the most significant works of economic theory every written.

Keynes was a fellow of King's College, Cambridge. In

1930 he published *A Treatise on Money* but had doubts about its propositions soon afterwards and formed a discussion group, the famous 'Cambridge Circus', of brilliant young economists to debate his evolving ideas for the new book. Kahn was the key figure in this group, and he often visited Keynes and his wife at their Sussex home to examine early drafts of the *General Theory*.

Although Kahn's own publications were few, he had a powerful influence on other leading economists such as Joan Robinson and Nicholas Kaldor. During the Second World War he was at the Board of Trade, apparently relishing the administrative routine there, but otherwise his adult life was spent as a disciple of Keynes at Cambridge. He should be better known. It was suggested that his work deserved to be recognized by a Nobel prize, but in the view of his obituarist he was handicapped by 'some lack of extrovert warmth and an inability to delegate'.[75]

Lord Kahn in 1973, photograph by Ramsey and Muspratt. *Courtesy the British Academy.*

🦗 *Socialist*

GEORGE DOUGLAS HOWARD COLE (1889–1959)

When *Who's Who* first invited him to send in an entry he showed me a draft which ended, 'Recreation: *to diaphtheirein tous neous* [corrupting the young men].' When I suggested that this was possibly unwise, he said in an astonished voice, 'But of course I meant *politically*.'

(Margaret Cole)[76]

St Paul's, classics at Balliol and a prize fellowship at Magdalen College, Oxford, was not the conventional background for a radical socialist thinker, but Douglas Cole was no conventional socialist. William Morris was the fashion among his school-friends, and he was first inspired by *News from Nowhere* (1891), a dream fantasy of England freed from industrial squalor and centralized government and returned to a life of rural beauty and happy craftsmanship. Cole remained something of an aesthete: according to his wife Margaret, one of his sternest critics, his idea of rural life was utterly naïve: '[He] turned quite sick with horror the first time he laid eyes on a little white runt in a litter of pigs.' His Palladian rooms at Magdalen contained a fine collection of glasses: 'an atmosphere of patrician culture surrounded him; he had written a volume of poetry and edited two books called *Oxford Poetry*, but it was understood that he had given up verse-writing because more serious work was in hand.'[77]

Douglas Cole, charcoal and pencil drawing by W. Rothenstein, *c.*1940. *Reproduced with the kind permission of Nuffield College, Oxford.*

The more serious work was *The World of Labour* (1913), where he urged trade unions to rely less on central government and instead take direct action to create a new world of loose federations or guilds. This book was widely praised, but Cole had to find a forum for promoting his ideas further. He wrote regularly for the subversive London weekly the *New Age* despite appearing alongside anarchists, medieval revivalists and *laissez-faire* liberals. He then made a rash attempt to take over the Fabian Society but resigned in 'a silly display of temper' when the vote went against him.[78] According to his Oxford friend Maurice Reckitt, Cole was never easy to work with: 'He was impatient, not a little cussed, and apt to fly off the handle when things were not going as he liked.'[79] The two went on with other Fabian rebels to found the National Guilds League in 1915. A conscientious objector, Cole avoided conscription by assuming work of 'national importance' as a research officer at the Amalgamated Society of Engineers and continued to develop his theory. For a time after the war, guild socialism seemed to offer a way forward, and his work was especially admired in the United States, but rising unemployment and then the collapse of the 1926 general strike effectively killed off the movement and any chance of giving unions more power.

He was reader in economics at Oxford from 1925 to 1929, setting up the 'Cole group', a discussion circle which continued throughout the 1930s and had among its members future Labour leader Hugh Gaitskell and future cabinet minister Michael Stewart. Cole had now renounced his previous views as naïve, and in *The Next Ten Years in British Social and Economic Policy* (1929) he optimistically set out a vast programme of government reforms, reorganizing industry, education and commerce. The thirties saw the publication of much more broadly based works on labour history, including his most popular book, *The Common People* (1938), written with his brother-in-law Raymond Postgate. In conjunction with his wife, Cole produced twenty-nine detective novels between 1923 and 1945. They were overlooked at the time but are now collectors' items.[80]

For a brief period the prodigal Cole was back in the main socialist fold, but the collapse of Ramsay MacDonald's Labour government (1931) in the wake of the world depression marked a return to much more radical thinking. After the Second World War he became Chichele professor of social and political theory at Oxford (his successor would be Old Pauline Isaiah Berlin — see chapter seven) and now sought to reconcile central control with his earlier beliefs in the importance of diversity. Cole never stopped writing articles. Many were for the *New Statesman*, but he also contributed to such diverse journals as the theosophical *Aryan Path* and the *Library Assistant*.

A poem by Reckitt began, 'Mr G. D. H. Cole/Is a bit of a puzzle.' One puzzle is why he never became an active Labour leader despite his ability to inspire others. In its obituary, *The Times* suggested why: 'He did not find it easy to work patiently with or under other people, and he never repressed his distaste for the pretences and pomposities of ordinary public life.'[81] He has been criticized for the changing face of his politics, but arguably this was in response to the altering political landscape around him. His manner could be aloof and intolerant, but underlying commitment showed through in decades of tutoring for the Workers' Educational Association. In his *Memoirs*, Harold Wilson (Labour prime minister) wrote, 'It was G. D. H. Cole as much as any man who finally pointed me in the direction of the Labour Party.'[82]

❧ *A devoted husband*

LEONARD SIDNEY WOOLF (1880–1969)

I know that V. [Virginia] will not come across the garden from the lodge, and yet I look in that direction for her. I know that she is drowned and yet I listen for her to come in at the door. I know that it is the last page and yet I turn it over. There is no limit to one's stupidity and selfishness.

(Note evidently made by Leonard Woolf after Virginia's suicide 28 March 1941 and discovered on his death)[83]

Dearest, I want to tell you that you have given me complete happiness. No one could have done more than you have done. Please believe that.

(From a note written by Virginia Woolf to Leonard on the morning of her death)[84]

A man of great modesty and integrity, Leonard Woolf claimed shortly before he died that his long career writing to promote socialist economics and international government amounted to '200,000 hours of useless work', but on the same page went on to say, 'In one's own personal life, in terms of humanity and human history and human society, certain things are of immense importance: human relations, happiness, truth, beauty or art, justice and mercy.'[85]

The Monk's House at Rodmell, Sussex home of Leonard and Virginia Woolf. *David Bussey.* © *St Paul's School.*

'Portrait of Martin Hardie', drypoint on paper by James McBey. Old Pauline Martin Hardie (1875–1952) spent thirty-seven years at the Victoria and Albert Museum, building up its collection of prints and drawings. In 1926 he was responsible for the exhibition that established Samuel Palmer's reputation. An artist in his own right, he produced in retirement a three-volume study of water-colour painting in Britain. © *Family of James and Marguerite McBey. Courtesy Aberdeen Art Gallery & Museums Collections.*

So it is that he is remembered most for his relationships with other writers and artists of the Bloomsbury Group and above all for his marriage to the novelist Virginia Woolf, née Stephen.

The couple's wedding was on 10 August 1912. Leonard Woolf had been serving with the colonial civil service in Ceylon, a career Virginia believed he sacrificed on the chance that she would agree to marry him, although his growing disillusionment with imperialism made it less of a sacrifice.[86] In contrast with his usual restrained style of letter-writing, his communications to her from the start were filled with emotion and a sense of his own unworthiness:

You are far finer, nobler, better than I am. It isn't difficult to be in love with you and when one is in love with anyone like you one has to make no allowances, no reservations. But I've many beastly qualities — though I've shown them to you deliberately often because I'm too fond of you not to want you to know that they do exist. For me to know that they do exist and to be in love with someone like you, that's where the pain comes in.[87]

His love never faltered, even when he realized the seriousness of the mental illness from which she suffered and how it would control their lives and indeed their marriage, which had to remain largely sexless. In September 1913 Virginia took an overdose: characteristically, Leonard took all the blame (he had not locked up the veronal tablets) and reflected afterwards:

I seem to be without a sense of sin and to be unable to feel remorse for something which has been done and cannot be undone — I seem to be mentally and morally unable to cry over spilt milk. In this particular case I felt that it was almost impossible sooner or later not to make a mistake of the kind.[88]

It was much later — almost thirty years — that the end came. Meanwhile, married life was sustained by the depth of their love, their shared ideals and passion for work and Leonard's strength, which complemented his wife's insecurities. The couple launched the Hogarth Press, publishing Virginia's fiction and works by many other key writers of the period, including the poet T. S. Eliot, the novelists E. M. Forster and Christopher Isherwood, the economist Maynard Keynes and the standard translation of Freud.

Those dreadful days in March 1941 were retold by Leonard with compelling frankness:

Desperate depression had settled upon Virginia; her thoughts raced beyond her control; she was terrified of madness. One knew that at any moment she might kill herself. The only chance for her was to give in and admit that she was ill, but this she would not do. [...] The terrifying decision [...] faced me. It was essential for her to resign herself to illness and the drastic regime which alone could stave off insanity. But she was on the brink of despair, insanity, and suicide. I had to urge her to accept the misery of the only method of avoiding it, and I knew at the same time that a wrong word, a mere hint of pressure, even a statement of the truth might be enough to drive her over the verge into suicide. [...] The memory of 1913 [...] haunted me.[89]

But nothing could prevent Virginia Woolf from walking down the lane from their house in Sussex to the river Ouse on 28 March, weighting her body with a stone and drowning herself. It was three weeks before her body was discovered: by the time of the cremation Leonard wrote that he 'was so battered and beaten that [he] was like some hunted animal which exhausted can only instinctively drag itself into its hole or lair'.

In fact he lived on into late old age, but increasingly his work became introspective and autobiographical.

Art, Bloomsbury and bohemians

DUNCAN JAMES CORROWR GRANT (1885–1978)

We liked Duncan Grant very much. I really liked him. Tell him not to make silly experiments in the futuristic line with bits of colour on moving paper.

(D.H Lawrence)[90]

When D. H. Lawrence and his wife Frieda visited Duncan Grant in January 1915, they found his paintings hopelessly bad and full of worthless ideas. David Garnett continues the story:

Finally, in despair, Duncan brought out a long band of green cotton on two rollers. I stood and held one roller vertically and unwound while, standing a couple of yards away, Duncan wound up the other, and a series of supposedly related, abstract shapes was displayed before our disgusted visitors. That was the worst of all.[91]

This work was his *Abstract Kinetic Collage Painting*, 1914 (now in Tate Britain, London), intended to be viewed in motion through a small rectangular window while listening to J. S. Bach. Grant's passion for painting began with the discovery of pre-Raphaelite artist Edward Burne-Jones at prep. school: 'For years I would ask God on my knees to allow me to become as good a painter as he.' He won seven art prizes at St Paul's (1899–1901) but learned more from lodging with the Stracheys, his cousins. Lady Strachey would regularly take him to visit leading artists. It was she who persuaded his army officer father that Grant was not suited for a military career and should enter art school instead.

His early work was relatively restrained, until that is Grant saw Roger Fry's exhibition, *Manet and the Post-Impressionists* at London's Grafton Galleries in 1910. On show were canvases by Gauguin, Cézanne and Matisse, artists Fry selected for their interest in colour and form rather than realistic illusion. Criticism was mixed: some felt that it was an exhibition of the mentally deranged, but the effect on Grant's own work was an explosion of colour and experimentation in portraits, still lifes and interiors, plus of course his abstract collage. In 1913 he joined Roger Fry and Vanessa Bell (Virginia Woolf's sister, with whom he was to live for the rest of his life) in founding the Omega workshops, where he designed trays, vases, rugs, even Christmas cards. The workshops closed in 1919.

In 1912 Rupert Brooke thought Grant's work 'always a trifle disappointing' and his genius 'an elusive and faithless sprite'.[92] His critical reputation was never secure, but when he mounted a one-man show in 1934, still broadly Post-Impressionist in manner, the *Sunday Times* described him

as 'a painter who, despite his own inequality and occasional wilfulness, has great powers of design and his own very beautiful sense of colour'.[93] Two years later three panels were commissioned from him for the *Queen Mary* and then rejected by Cunard in favour, according to Vanessa Bell's husband Clive, of 'titterings in paint, wood, glass, plaster and metal'.[94] He painted on until within a few days of his death, enjoying a late flowering as in his eighties he revisited the themes of his earlier work, adding a new quiet and inward quality.[95]

Grant was a central member of the radical set of artists, writers and thinkers known as the Bloomsbury Group. Their relationships were complex and intertwined. David Garnett, one of his many homosexual lovers, went on to marry Grant and Vanessa Bell's daughter Angelica, the only survivor of the set today. Virginia Woolf was Vanessa Bell's sister, and Leonard Woolf (see last entry) overlapped with Grant for one term at St Paul's. Lytton Strachey was Grant's cousin. Charleston farmhouse in Sussex, which Vanessa Bell set up for Grant, Garnett and herself, was only a few miles from the Monk's House, the Woolfs' country retreat.

It has never been agreed who exactly was in or out of the Bloomsbury Group, but the presence of figures such as the Woolfs, Maynard Keynes the economist, the novelist E. M. Forster and poet T. S. Eliot, have given it an air of

'Tulips (Parrot Tulips)', oil by Duncan Grant, 1911. Grant painted this colourful still life the year after seeing the Post-Impressionist exhibition at the Grafton Galleries. *Courtesy Southampton City Art Gallery/Bridgeman Art. © Estate of Duncan Grant.*

high seriousness. Grant however mentioned not only the Group's 'honesty and love of truth [...] but also their love of parties'.[96] The *Dreadnought* hoax of 1910 was the finest comic expression of their colourful and inventive taste for subversion. Grant, the future Virginia Woolf and four others dressed up elaborately (and very expensively) as Abyssinian princes and their entourage, and telegrammed the *Dreadnought*, the world's finest battleship, to prepare for a royal visit. The imposters were met at Weymouth and escorted to the ship and 'a full regiment of marines drawn up on deck playing Yankee Doodle, streaming flags in every direction'. Lacking Abyssinian, the 'princes' spoke muddled Latin interspersed with choruses of '*Bunga bunga*' and '*Chuck-a-choi, chuck-a-choi*'. They escaped detection, even though Grant's moustache was peeling off in the rain, and left hastily, declining an eighteen-gun salute, to catch the express train back to London. The story was leaked to the press, which had a field day. Shortly afterwards the real Emperor of Abyssinia arrived in London. He complained that boys ran after him in the street shouting '*Bunga bunga*' wherever he went, and when he requested to visit the Channel Fleet, the first lord of the Admiralty said regretfully that it was absolutely impossible.[97]

JOHN RUTHERFORD ARMSTRONG (1893–1973)

Apart from brief studies at St John's Wood School of Art, interrupted by war service, John Armstrong was a self-taught artist and struggled to become established until he formed a friendship in the 1920s with Elsa Lanchester, actor Charles Laughton's future wife, who ran *The Cave of Harmony*, a fashionably bohemian night club with avant-garde drama and cabaret. Armstrong was asked to design scenery and costumes for the club. Other commissions followed: art deco work for the Courtaulds' house in Portman Square, sets for the Lyric Theatre, Hammersmith, film and ballet designs. His costumes appeared in the film *Things to Come* (1938), and he produced several paintings in the famous sequence of Shell advertisements.

Armstrong's work at the easel had to take second place to these more lucrative commissions. In the 1920s his canvases were undoubtedly eclectic, but in 1933 Old Pauline Paul Nash (see chapter six) was sufficiently impressed to include him in his key surrealist and abstract exhibition, Unit One. He became an official war artist in 1940, when his painting took on a more sculptural quality. It also became more symbolic and political. *Victory*, an ironic depiction of the results of a nuclear holocaust, made a strong impact at the 1958 Royal Academy summer exhibition. His final paintings, known as the tocsin series, depict a church bell warning of the ever-increasing threats to civilization.[98]

'(*left*) Guests examining Epstein's sculpture of Adam at a Leicester Galleries private view in 1939. Old Pauline Oliver Frank Gustave Brown (1885–1966) was for most of his life a partner at the gallery, which held the first single exhibitions of many major contemporary artists. Henri Matisse was astonished to see how well his work sold in 1919: Brown recalled him crying 'Ils sont foux —les Anglais!' as the red spots were put up. © *Picture Post/Getty Images.*

(*below*) Theatre-goers use Shell' (1938). One of John Armstrong's five commissions for the famous series of Shell petrol advertisements. © *The artist's estate. Courtesy the Shell Advertising Art Collection.*

Cricketing records

PERCY GEORGE HERBERT FENDER (1892–1985)

Almost alone in cricket folklore the place held by Percy George Herbert Fender has depended on something he failed to do rather than what he did. 'The best captain never chosen to lead England,' has been the verdict passed down to later generations.

(R. Streeton)[99]

Percy Fender's earliest brush with sporting authority came before he reached St Paul's. He was about eleven and playing in a house football match at St George's College, Weybridge. He headed in the winning goal from a corner, to be told by his housemaster, 'That sort of goal is a professional's trick, Fender; no proper footballer scores a goal with his head.'

There was some football in later life, between cricket seasons. He kept goal for several non-league sides and represented the Casuals in the 1913 Amateur Football Association Cup Final at White City. Fender let in a ball passed back by one of his own defenders, but the Casuals still won 3–2.

His cricketing career was more distinguished. He first played for Sussex in his final summer at St Paul's and five years later, when he had moved to Surrey, was featured in *Wisden* as one of the 'five cricketers of the year'. He is credited with the fastest genuine century, in thirty-five minutes at Northampton in 1920, and in 1927 he became the first man in first-class cricket to take six wickets off eleven balls. Fender's appearance, tall and lean, with long sweaters, a short moustache, horn-rimmed spectacles and crinkly hair,[100] was a gift to cartoonists, and he admitted that, once Tom Webster began drawing him, he made a point of buying even larger sweaters and stretching them downward.[101]

He was entertaining and unpredictable in all his play. When batting he seemed to have strangely long arms, and 'what appeared to be the same shot would send similar balls flying in a variety of improbable directions'. His rapidly changing bowling style led one commentator to say it was as if Groucho Marx 'were suddenly to impersonate all his brothers in turn', and another to write, 'I have never seen better "bad" bowling if you can understand that. Every ball was different. There was some rubbish sent down, but you were aware all the time of his mind ticking over, and the ball might have been deliberate.'[102]

Fender captained Surrey for eleven years, showing great ingenuity in compensating for his side's bowling weaknesses. He also played in thirteen test matches and was vice-captain to F. T. Mann for the MCC South Africa tour of 1922–23. When he was not appointed England captain in 1924, Neville Cardus thought the reasons 'not apparent to the man in the street', but Fender could be a difficult man to deal with. Eccentric behaviour punctuated 1931, his final

Percy Fender, *Cricketers. Caricatures by 'RIP'*, issued by John Player and Sons, 1926. *Company copyright.*

Edgar Thomas Killick (1907–1953), *Cricketers, Second Series of 50*, issued by W. D. and H. O. Wills, 1928. As an undergraduate Killick batted for Cambridge University and Middlesex, and in 1929 he played in two test matches. He was ordained priest, becoming chaplain at Harrow School and later a vicar, commitments that prevented him playing regular first-class cricket after graduating, so that, in the words of his obituary in *The Times*, 'comparatively little was seen of one of the most classic batsmen of his age'. He died in an inter-diocesan clergy cricket match. *Company copyright.*

season as Surrey captain: chasing a difficult target against Kent for example, he promoted himself to open with Jack Hobbs, called an impossible single, was run out without facing a ball and then called off the chase in a fit of pique.[103]

It was suspected that Fender was behind the scheme to adopt bodyline bowling tactics for the MCC's controversial tour of Australia in 1932–33. He denied this, but 'his widespread recognition as the sharpest cricket mind in England made it inconceivable that he had no role in the matter'.[104]

Fender's playing career finished at the age of forty-four. He was in business as a wine merchant and became a cricket journalist, again causing a stir by being the first man to use a typewriter in the press box. His colleagues complained, and at Leeds so did a nearby woman spectator. 'Fender in his most charming manner offered to type the threatened letter of complaint to the club secretary for her.'

☙ *Tennis champion*

JOHN SHELDON OLLIFF (1908–51)

John Olliff's view of tennis takes us back to a more genteel age. His talent was such that he never bothered to train, but he still won the junior championship twice, beat Fred Perry at Wimbledon in 1929, and won British Hard Court and Covered Court doubles titles on several occasions between 1930 and 1939. He was refreshingly naïve about players who were not gentlemen: 'You will meet opponents who are not scrupulous, who will serve before you are ready, who will talk and chatter to distract your attention and who will argue decisions. It is even conceivable that you will be beaten by such an opponent, but it will only be a hollow victory for him.'[105] Foreign tennis events were as much about seeing the sights and meeting people as playing tournaments. His strongest memory of touring America with 'Bunny' Austin (the last UK player to reach a Wimbledon final) in 1928 was taking 'every meal at a different film star's house in Beverley Hills. Even breakfasts had to be arranged, as our other meals were so booked-up, and I remember in particular two breakfast parties at Charlie Chaplin's and Harold Lloyd's houses; on each occasion the meals were served at the side of their open-air swimming pools.'[106] Small wonder then that Olliff's expanding waistline obliged him to concentrate increasingly on the doubles game.[107]

Olliff became the *Daily Telegraph* lawn tennis correspondent after the Second World War, and published several books about the game. His death came suddenly during the 1951 Wimbledon Championships.

John Olliff demonstrating the smash.
J. Olliff, *The Groundwork of Lawn Tennis*, Methuen, 1934.

☙ *School stories*

HYLTON REGINALD CLEAVER (1891–1961)

He played his last game of rugby football at the approximate age of fifty; at half-time he called for a double brandy to augment the meagre slice of lemon that sufficed for his team-mates, and it was taken out to him under escort on a tray.

(*The Times*)[108]

In 1917 Alec Waugh (Evelyn Waugh's brother) published *The Loom of Youth*, a powerful and unremitting attack on 'Fernhurst', his fictional version of a complacent public school addicted to the cult of games. Such sentiments were anathema at the height of the First World War. The book was vilified, and its author stripped of his Old Shirburnian (Sherborne) tie. Early in 1920, *Brother O'Mine* appeared, the first of more than thirty school novels by Hylton

Cleaver. It has a passing comment to make on those who, like Waugh and his fellow cynics, leave a public school only to attack its values, but Cleaver insisted that he did not see glory on the rugby field as the only path to fulfilment there. Despite being 'marred by chronic asthma, acute short-sightedness, ugliness and a deplorable stammer', his schooldays were 'extraordinarily happy'.[109] Even so, with titles such as *The Harley First XV* and

Caught in the Slips, his novels still place games at the centre of the plot. In *Brother O'Mine* the corrupt captain of cricket is summarily expelled for a long list of offences that include drinking, bullying and libelling a popular master, but above all he is in disgrace for failing to set the honourable example belonging to his athletic position. Cleaver wrote in the Talbot Baines Reed tradition of moral entertainment for boys, a world where the bully is reduced to tears by the hero, practical jokes are played only on masters who deserve them, and the all-seeing head dispenses wise judgments. He was also a sports reporter for the *Evening Standard* and respected there for the same unfashionable belief in the high standards of honour and integrity that informed his novels.

"Mr. Mould was on his feet and counter-attacking with a handkerchief and a mortar board." Illustration by H. M. Brock to *Brother O'Mine*, a school story by Hylton Cleaver. *Courtesy Oxford University Press.*

꧁ *Stories of school*

ARTHUR CALDER-MARSHALL (1908–92)

Scene: New York City
My brother: What school did you go to?
Obvious Englishman: Westminster.
My brother: I went to St Paul's.
Englishman: To tell the truth, so did I.
      (Arthur Calder-Marshall)[110]

In 1934 the novelist Graham Greene edited *The Old School*, a collection of writers' schoolday reminiscences. Most of the contributions were about public schools. Greene thought that the public school was about to disappear and saw his book as a 'premature memorial', an epitaph to a 'vanished system'.[111] Arthur Calder-Marshall contributed a chapter on St Paul's. He had just abandoned a teaching career after two years at Denstone College to become a full-time writer. He went on to write novels, film scripts and biographies, ranging from a book on Donald McGill, the artist of saucy seaside postcards, to the definitive work on Old Pauline monk Father Ignatius, written after Calder-Marshall's own conversion to Christianity (see chapter four). In the thirties, however, his views were

clearly left-wing: in 1941 he looked back to this as 'the pink decade'.[112] The St Paul's piece focuses mainly on the Christian Union and is scarcely sympathetic despite Calder-Marshall's comment at the end that 'St Paul's is a very fine school'.[113] When *The Old School* was reprinted recently, this chapter was omitted.

From 'More Frank than Buchman'

There was a thing called the Pi-squash [Christian Union meeting] which this boy belonged to: I asked to go. I didn't think they wanted people like me. I felt like scum those days. But they let me go along one Friday evening to one of the rooms in the school. A lot of boys were there, scragging one another, and they got all covered with dirt. Then an

Arthur Calder-Marshall, bromide print by Humphrey Spender, 1935. *National Portrait Gallery, London.*

overgrown fellow came in, called Erb. Except for a dog collar he was dressed like an ordinary man. They said he was a rowing blue and everybody stopped slapping bottoms and Erb said a prayer. Then we sat down and a few chaps started pinching one another but mostly they were silent. Then Erb read a bit I knew out of the Bible and said it meant that we must play hard. He said he thought Christ would have played hard for His school, if He was at school today. Christ was a strong man, he said, not the sickly sort of man you saw in the pictures artists painted. He said, Christ might have rowed for the Varsity if there'd been any Varsity to row for. Then we stood up and said another prayer; and all the chaps round me got up and started scragging one another again and a boy called Nitbags went up and kicked Erb's bottom and ran away.

'How did you like it?' my friend said.

I'd been sitting next to him and I said, 'That was wonderful; I shall come next week.'*

❧ *Film actor*

DONALD ERNEST CLAYTON CALTHROP (1888–1940)

Calthrop was a true character actor. He had no particular 'line'. Blackmailers, Chinamen, journalists, gutter-rats, doctors, detectives, Frenchmen, Belgians — they all came alike to him.

(Laura Whetter)[114]

The story is told of a screen idol who was filming a scene which also included Donald Calthrop and a cat:

The hero […] protested that all the women in the audience would be looking at the cat — not at him. He complained, shouted, finally stormed into the producer's office and burst into tears […] saying that he would throw up his part unless the cat were taken out of the script. So out the cat went, leaving the matinée idol and Calthrop alone in the scene. The great lover, scenting more danger, insisted that Calthrop should face him all the time, with his back to the camera. And Calthrop, with fiendishly simply little gestures of the hands and shrugs of the shoulder, stole the complete scene. It was one of his most outstanding performances.[115]

Between 1918 and his death in 1940 he appeared in sixty-three films and made a habit of stealing scenes. A highly versatile character actor, he created some extraordinary cameo performances but rarely received the star parts he deserved. Of his Bob Cratchit in *Scrooge* (1935) it was written:

He must make you laugh at him; he must make you smile with him; and he must make you sorry for him. It calls for the skill of a Charles Chaplin to produce this particular blend of laughter and a lump in the throat; and Donald Calthrop has accomplished his task magnificently.[116]

But it was as a sinister villain that he became best known. A chance encounter with Hitchcock at Elstree led to a famously skulking performance in *Blackmail* (1929), the first British 'all-talkie', and a contract with British International Pictures. This proved a mixed blessing:

He was, in a sense, tricked into wasting away his career, and thrown a good part from time to time, as one throws a dog a titbit, to keep him happy doing the welter of bits he was called upon mostly to play, largely to bolster up other people's failing films.[117]

Calthrop entered the world of the cinema when stage actors regarded it as an entertaining means of earning some pocket money, and it was his misfortune that no one recognized he 'was the greatest character actor English films ever had'.

A scene from Alfred Hitchcock's *Blackmail* (1929). Donald Calthrop is on the right.
Lordprice collection.

* Frank Buchman was an American Evangelist. Calder-Marshall would have encountered him at Oxford, where he preached Moral Rearmament, 'world-changing through life-changing'.

Old Paulines and War

1890–1997

❧ *Victoria Cross in Mashonaland*

RANDOLPH COSBY NESBITT VC (1867–1956)

I had given up all hope of coming out of it alive.
  (R. A. Harbord, one of Nesbitt's troopers)[1]

THE EVENTS that led to Randolph Nesbitt's VC have been compared to a Hollywood western. He had joined the British South Africa Company Police and participated in the 1890 occupation of Mashonaland, now part of Zimbabwe. Six years later he was an inspector in the Mashonaland Mounted Police stationed at Salisbury when news came through of a violent native rebellion. Local residents who had survived the attacks were sheltering at Alice gold mine in the Mazoe Valley and were besieged by about a thousand rebels.

The police were very short of men, as many had been captured by the Boers in the disastrous Jameson Raid, and others were dealing with an uprising in Matabeleland. Nesbitt was ordered to make the thirty-five mile journey to Alice mine with a relief party of just twelve men. They got through despite being ambushed in a narrow pass. Without delay, he made a wagon bullet-proof by nailing iron sheets to its sides. In it travelled three women and the wounded. The party of forty-three set out. They were under fire for most of the route from a well-armed enemy, now swollen to at least 1,500. The natives had many vantage points from which to fire and could hide in the long grass. Nesbitt returned to safety with the loss of just three men, although most of the horses were killed. He estimated the enemy fatalities at a hundred. Nesbitt was embarrassed to be singled out for a VC and reported that all the men in his patrol, many of whom had not been under fire before, 'behaved splendidly'.

The First World War

Photographs of unknown Old Pauline soldiers in the First World War. All were probably casualties. © *St Paul's School.*

❧ *Letters from the trenches*

I think it will be summer soon, and perhaps the war will end this year and I shall see my Pretty One again.

(The last words of Robert Vernède's final letter home, 8 April 1917. He was killed the following day.)[2]

ROBERT ERNEST VERNÈDE (1875–1917)
KENNETH GORDON GARNETT (1892–1917)
DENIS OLIVER BARNETT (1895–1915)

Five hundred and six Old Paulines were killed fighting in the First World War. Letters from just three must represent the courage of many. Like Edward Thomas (see later entry), Robert Vernède was a writer and much older than most soldiers. He had written poetry and published several novels. His wife begged him to be candid about his experiences in the trenches. Kenneth Garnett had graduated from Trinity College, Cambridge, where he was a rowing blue; Denis Barnett left St Paul's in July 1914 with a scholarship to Balliol College, Oxford, but joined up immediately and was dead a year later. The letters are all the more poignant for their determined optimism. 'It is still impossible to pick them up without emotion' (Mead).[3]

A letter from Vernède to his wife, 23 August 1916:

The Push itself is done in hot blood: but the rest is horrible, digging in when you are tired to death, short rations, no water to speak of, hardly any sleep, and men being killed by shell-fire most of the time. [...] My dear, you never saw anything more dramatically murderous than the modern attack — a sheet of fire from both sides in which it seems impossible for any one to live. I saw it from my observer's post about 100 yards away. My observer was shot through the head in the first minute.[4]

Garnett, writing to his mother from Flanders, 1 November 1915:

Life is good out here, despite the great mud and the fact that we live in dugouts. It's just a great game of 'bears' and 'forts' such as we used to play. [...] I am enjoying trying to knock buildings down and stopping Bosch working parties [...] it really is great to be here. Mice are very prevalent, despite the fact that we have a cat and a tame pigeon — I suppose the pigeon isn't much use, now I come to think of it! But the mice or rats run all over one's bed and face at night time. I had one that seemed to want to build a nest on my face at our forward observing place two nights ago. Of course it may have been mere affection for me, or perhaps it was tired and wanted to sit down.[5]

Barnett, writing home from Flanders, 29 June 1915:

I've lately made the acquaintance of a great character here, the machine-gunner's goat. She's a most extraordinary beast, and has taken to M.–G. [machine-gun] tactics in a wonderful way. She *will* fall in with the gun teams; you can pull her away by main force, but she comes back at the double. She gets awfully excited at the command 'Action', and helps the gunners by running between their legs, and standing where they want to mount the gun. [...] When the guns are mounted she stands in front and licks their noses lovingly [...] we're all very fond of her [...] and now she bears the mystic sign M.–G. on the side of her, in emerald-green paint.[6]

❧ *Killed in Gallipoli*

CUTHBERT BROMLEY VC (1878–1915)

Bromley delivered a stirring speech to his men before leading them over the top. Wounded in the heel early in the advance, he refused to leave. For a time, he struggled forward using two Turkish rifles as makeshift crutches. Later, he ordered two stretcher bearers to carry him.

(Stephen Snelling, *Gallipoli*)[7]

A career soldier noted for his physical fitness, Cuthbert Bromley became adjutant of the First Battalion Lancashire Fusiliers three months before the outbreak of World War One. A correspondent to *The Times* wrote of his immeasurable personal influence over his men, which fostered the spirit to succeed in their part of the costly and abortive 1915 Gallipoli campaign. At six a.m. on 25 April 1915 his battalion led an assault on a small sandy cove, West Beach, between Tekke Burnu and Cape Helles, which had to be taken before the main forces could land. The Turkish defence seemed almost impregnable, but Bromley set an example of extraordinary bravery and was one of the first to reach the top of the cliff: 'Bromley appeared to be everywhere that morning; leading small leaderless parties forward, encouraging men to extra exertions, and always he appeared oblivious to the enemy's fire.'[8] That day's

Gallipoli west beach, later known as the Lancashire Landing. *Courtesy Imperial War Museum Q13660.*

action won him the Victoria Cross, but his indomitable courage was again in evidence later in the campaign, and on 28 June, at the battle of Gully Ravine, he insisted on staying with the advance even when seriously wounded, and only went to hospital after working through the night to consolidate his battalion's expensive gains.

He was evacuated to Egypt and made a point of returning to Gallipoli as soon as he could walk, but the troopship carrying him was torpedoed: Bromley was among the 866 to drown.

✃ *Two war artists*

PAUL NASH (1889–1946)

I am no longer an artist. I am a messenger who will bring back word from the men who are fighting to those who want the war to go on for ever. Feeble, inarticulate will be my message, but it will have a bitter truth and may it burn their lousy souls.

(Letter from Paul Nash to his wife from Ypres, 16 November 1917)

Paul Nash first went out to the front with the Hampshire Regiment in March 1917 and spent four months making drawings in the Ypres salient before being invalided home after an accident. He returned to Flanders that November as an official war artist under a new scheme devised by the department of information.[9] It was immediately after the battle of Passchendaele, in which almost half a million allied forces had been killed, and he found a sodden and desolate landscape punctuated by broken trees. The drawings he made in the field and the oil paintings that followed are probably Nash's most significant achievement.

His very early work had come from the imagination, often stimulated by poetry. One great ambition was to illustrate Yeats's poems, and so he sent some drawings to the poet:

In the course of time I was invited to a strange house in Woburn Place, where in a shadowy room upstairs I found Yeats sitting over a small dying fire. He […] probed me with a few languid questions, peering at the drawings the while and smiling at me with an amused air which I found disconcerting. 'Did you really see these things?' he asked.[10]

Nash was at the Slade when the strident colours and forms of Post-Impressionism were unsettling London artists, but unlike Old Pauline Duncan Grant (see chapter five) was barely affected by the daring continental canvases on display at the Grafton Galleries. Perhaps he heeded Slade Professor Henry Tonks's advice to stay away for fear of contamination. Then Sir William Richmond, the Victorian portraitist, told Nash, 'My boy, you should go in for Nature.' He did, but in the form of landscapes where imagination and observation came together in individual and often disturbing visions.

Nash saw his Flanders pictures as his chance to 'rob the

'The Menin Road', oil by Paul Nash, 1919. The painter suggested this inscription: 'The picture shows a tract of country near Gheluvelt village in the sinister district of "Tower Hamlets", perhaps the most dreaded and disastrous locality of any area in any of the theatres of war.' *Courtesy Imperial War Museum.*

seem to me to have been done in a kind of rational and dignified rage, in a restrained passion of resentment at the spectacle of what men suffer, in a fierce determination to transmit to the beholder the full horror of the war.

The Menin Road was commissioned from the ministry of information and painted immediately after the exhibition. There were commissions from other painters, and all the pictures were to be shown in a Hall of Remembrance, never built, celebrating heroism and sacrifice. Nash's aims were different. His canvas shows two figures finding their way through a devastated battlefield lit by sinister light while artillery fire sends up clouds of mud in the background.

After 1918 Nash described himself as 'a war artist without a war', but he discovered new themes in the landscapes of peace.[12] In 1933 he founded Unit One, a remarkable group of experimental artists including Henry Moore, Barbara Hepworth, Ben Nicholson and Old Pauline John Armstrong (see chapter five). Nash himself experimented uneasily with abstraction, his own brand of surrealism (St Paul's owns a canvas from this period), photography and design. In 1940, suffering acutely from asthma, he resumed as a war artist, but the anger and newness of his Flanders pictures was lost. Even so, *Totes Meer* (1940–41), which portrays a dump of wrecked German aircraft near Oxford as if it were 'a great inundating sea', has become his most famous painting.[13]

war of the last shred of glory, the last shine of glamour', and staged an exhibition, 'Void of War' at the Leicester Galleries in May 1918 (another Old Pauline, Oliver Brown, was a gallery director).[11] For Ezra Pound it was the best show of war art he had seen, and Arnold Bennett wrote in the catalogue's introduction:

He has found the essentials of it, that is to say, disfigurement, danger, desolation, ruin, chaos — the little figures of men creeping devotedly and tragically over the waste [....] But no one could explain the emotional force of the artistic individuality which has made these pictures what they are. They

ERIC HENRI KENNINGTON (1888–1960)

If I am of use, it is in depicting British soldiers in their truest and noblest aspect: of that work I shall never tire.

(Eric Kennington)[14]

Eric Kennington was an official war artist from 1917–19. He had fought in France and Flanders from the end of 1914 until invalided out of the army after an embarrassing incident when he shot himself in the foot while clearing a friend's jammed rifle. He spent the rest of that year producing a painting of his battle-weary platoon about to march off to billets after duty on the front line. The department of information found this work too bleak for an official war artist, but eventually agreed to take him on. Kennington felt he could not 'depict the horror and the tragedy […] it was too vast', but concentrated on linear drawings of individual soldiers, 'the nameless heroes of the rank and file'.[15]

After the First World War, he turned his attention mainly to sculpture. This may explain why his monolithic and often idealized work as a Second World War artist lacks the power of his drawings twenty-five years earlier.

'The Despatch Rider', chalk drawing by Eric Kennington, 1917–18. *Courtesy C. J. Kennington/ St Paul's School.*

Two war poets

(ROBERT) LAURENCE BINYON (1869–1943)

They shall grow not old, as we that are left grow old:
Age shall not weary them, nor the years condemn.
At the going down of the sun and in the morning
We will remember them.

(Laurence Binyon, 'For the Fallen')[16]

Four powerful lines from Laurence Binyon's poem 'For the Fallen' are carved on countless war memorials and read every year at Remembrance Day ceremonies. They were first published in *The Times* only weeks into the First World War. Binyon spent his whole career at the British Museum but always hoped to make his name as a poet. He was too old for active service and worked in a French military hospital in 1915 and 1916. 'Fetching the Wounded', his greatest war poem, describes these experiences. The manuscript was presented to St Paul's.

He was a prolific writer of poetry, plays and books on art throughout his life. Three of his war poems, including 'For the Fallen', were set to music by Edward Elgar in 'The Spirit of England', and Elgar conducted the incidental music he had composed for Binyon's verse-tragedy *Arthur* when it opened at the Old Vic in 1923.

(PHILIP) EDWARD THOMAS (1878–1917)

Lights Out

I have come to the borders of sleep,
The unfathomable deep
Forest, where all must lose
Their way, however straight
Or winding, soon or late;
They cannot choose.

Many a road and track
That since the dawn's first crack
Up to the forest brink
Deceived new travellers,
Suddenly now blurs,
And in they sink.

Here love ends —
Despair, ambition ends;
All pleasure and all trouble,
Although most sweet or bitter,
Here ends, in sleep that is sweeter
Than tasks most noble.

There is not any book
Or face of dearest look
That I would not turn from now
To go into the unknown
I must enter, and leave, alone,
I know not how.

The tall forest towers:
Its cloudy foliage lowers
Ahead, shelf above shelf;
Its silence I hear and obey
That I may lose my way
And myself.

Edward Thomas composed 'Lights Out' at the beginning of November 1916 while training as an officer cadet with the Royal Garrison Artillery in Trowbridge. The following month he volunteered for service overseas. On 9 April 1917 he was killed by a shell blast in the first hour of the battle of Arras. 'Lights Out', he wrote to his friend Eleanor Farjeon, 'sums up what I have often thought at that call. I wish it were as brief — two pairs of long notes.'[17]

Although brought up in London, Thomas was keenly interested in nature even as a schoolboy. Edmund Clerihew Bentley fancifully remembered him as 'an exceptionally reserved and quiet boy who usually had in his pockets a rat or so, and a few snakes, which he would shut in his desk with his books, and occasionally peep at

stealthily'.[18] His first book, *The Woodland Life* (1896), was inspired by long country walks and published at the age of eighteen, a year after he put behind him fifteen unhappy months at St Paul's. Holidays were regularly spent in Wiltshire, where he befriended an old gamekeeper and his wife, 'Dad' and 'Granny' Uzzell, two of the many traditional rural figures who permeate his work. His wife Helen recalled visiting the Uzzells' fairy-tale cottage in a wood just before Thomas went up to Oxford (they were to marry while he was still an undergraduate): 'Outside the owls hooted about the cottage, and bats twittered, and starlings stirred in the thatch. No other sound was to be heard, no trams, no people, no traffic.'[19]

To his father's dismay, Thomas decided to become a

Edward Thomas,
photograph by F.H. Evans.
*Courtesy estate of Edward
Thomas.*

'Lights Out' is a widely anthologized poem and often read as Thomas's acceptance of death on the battlefield. Since childhood a repeated experience when waiting for sleep had been groping slowly through 'vast unshapely towering masses', which he found 'somehow pleasant or alluring'.[25] He was often depressed. At St Paul's he had been 'sometimes in such wretchedness that I wanted to drown myself', and from their final decade living at Steep, near Petersfield, Helen Thomas remembered the day he put a revolver in his pocket 'and with dull eyes and ashen cheeks strode out of the house up the bare hill'.[26] His decisions to enlist and then volunteer for service in France took a long time to make, but once decided 'his old periods of dark agony had gone for ever [....] to the end his only fear was of being afraid'.

What 'Lights Out' does not illustrate is the characteristic voice of much of his poetry as he tried to grasp the essence of rural life strangely threatened and transformed by war across the channel. 'The sun used to shine' recalls a walk with Frost where they turned from men or poetry,

> To rumours of the war remote
> Only till both stood disinclined
> For aught but the yellow flavorous coat
> Of an apple wasps had undermined.

After Thomas's death Frost wrote to Helen:

There is no regret — nothing I will call regret. Only I can't help wishing he could have saved his life without so wholly losing it and come back from France not too much hurt to enjoy our pride in him. I want to see him to tell him something. I want to tell him, what I think he liked to hear from me, that he was a poet.[27]

Recognition of Thomas's significance as a poet has come slowly, but in 1991 *Elected Friends: Poems for and about Edward Thomas* was published with seventy-six contributions from writers including Robert Frost, Derek Walcott, Peter Porter, Elizabeth Jennings, Andrew Motion and Gavin Ewart.

professional writer and moved to rural Kent. Books about the countryside, such as *The Heart of England* and *The South Country*, were what interested him, but often the routine cycle of reviews, essays, anthologies, biographies and guide books needed to sustain his family made him feel like 'a doomed hack'.[20] He only began writing poetry after the outbreak of war. In 1913 he had enthusiastically reviewed *A Boy's Will*, the first collection of American poet Robert Frost, recently settled in England in search of a new life. The two met and formed a close friendship. It struck Frost that Thomas's latest country book *In Pursuit of Spring* (1914) was full of poetry 'but in prose form where it did not declare itself'.[21] Thomas had said to Eleanor Farjeon the previous year, 'I couldn't write a poem to save my life', but he did listen to Frost. In July 1914 he was telling her in his typically gloomy and self-deprecating way that with little prospect of other commissions during the war he 'may as well write poetry', and the first of more than 140 poems was written on 3 December.[22]

Thomas made Frost's reputation in Britain and America with his review of *North of Boston*, 'one of the most revolutionary books of modern times', and when Frost decided to return to America in 1915 he tried to persuade Thomas to come with him.[23] He failed, but Frost's influence was there in the rhythms of his verse and its natural imagery — and in the forest of 'Lights Out'. In *A Boy's Will* Frost had described 'dark trees' he wanted to stretch 'away unto the edge of doom'.[24]

🐦 *The story of Toc H*

PHILIP THOMAS BYARD CLAYTON (1885–1972)

In his twenties he was already the same jolly, fat, genial, boisterous, noisy, sentimental, impetuous, enthusiastic, warm-hearted creature that he is still. All his geese are swans, and always have been; and most of us, being geese, like him all the better for that. Without any enemy in the world and [with] friends all over the world, with malice toward none and a smile (or rather a roar, as from some infuriated elephant) for all, he remains humble and simple and devout, and absolutely sincere.

(Clayton's friend Trevor Braby Heaton, reader in anatomy at Oxford)[28]

In November 1915 a young volunteer army chaplain, already known to everyone as 'Tubby' Clayton, joined his fellow chaplain and friend from Oxford days, Neville Talbot in France. They were looking for a house where Clayton could establish 'some kind of homely club for a few of the multitudes of troops who pass to and fro'.[29] In the centre of the little town of Poperinghe, a few miles west of Ypres, they found a large empty mansion. On 15 December it opened as Talbot House, in memory of Neville's brother Gilbert Talbot, recently killed in action. T.H (or Toc H in Morse signallers' language) was visited by many thousands of men from all ranks during the remainder of the war and marked the birth of a movement that in revised form continues to this day.

Neville Talbot, who went on in 1916 to be assistant chaplain-general to the Fifth Army, said that Toc H was 'open to all the world, was full of friendship, hominess [sic], fun, music, games, laughter, books, pictures and discussion. And at the top, in the loft, obtruding upon no one, but dominating everything, was the Chapel — a veritable shrine, glowing with the beauty of holiness.'[30] The key to its success lay firmly in Clayton's character. To judge by the comments of a Pauline contemporary, from his schooldays status had never concerned him:

The thing which always filled me with wonder and admiration was to see you walking solemnly at the side of the Old Man [Walker] before prayers, apparently discussing the most abstract subjects as pal with pal. In the whole of my seven years at St Paul's, I never saw the like: and, when I heard later of 'Tubby's' failure to be awed in the presence of a field marshal, it did not surprise me.[31]

Accordingly, over the chaplain's room at Poperinghe was the notice 'All rank abandon, ye who enter here.' Clayton's methods of ice-breaking were effective rather than sophisticated, as those who entered these non-infernal gates discovered:

The room was crowded with men of all ranks, generals, majors, corporals, privates, some lolling against the mantelpiece, others perched on the window ledges or seated round the little table on which was arrayed the paraphernalia for afternoon tea. Over the whole hilarious company presided a rubicund gnome in a clerical collar whose jests and repartee had the room rocking with mirth. And the humour was not only verbal. The nervousness of a Devon lad standing beside a brigadier-general would be completely forgotten when Tubby offered him a box of matches, in which all the matches were stuck to the bottom; and across the room a purple-faced major of artillery, having also received a box, elicited yelps of glee as he tried to light his pipe with matches that were only intended to smoulder.

From Toc H Clayton regularly visited the troops at the front or as he put it 'went slumming'. He did not travel light: luggage could include hymn books, the 'groan-box' or portable harmonium — even a portable cinema, screen and films. Again it was his gift of lightening the mood that most remembered:

Tubby Clayton, 1966.
By kind permission of Toc H.

Wrapped in a greatcoat (sometimes sizes too large, for it was not always his own) with horn-rimmed glasses bestowing a deceptive innocence on an impressive face, he would arrive at some battery position and announce to the commander that he had a guest for the night. Within two minutes the place was in an uproar, and even the proximity of shell-fire could do little to restrain the enthusiasm.[32]

It was said of Clayton that during his time in France he appeared incapable of thinking ill of anyone, and as a result men felt at their best in his company. His optimism seemed unbounded: he wrote to his mother that being in France was 'altogether like living in a pheasant preserve, and the sounds of the guns […] like Beaulieu on the first of September'.

After his return to England Clayton founded Toc H in London. All Hallows by the Tower became the movement's guild church in 1923. It was no longer just for serving men but became an ecumenical Christian movement based on fellowship, service, fair-mindedness and the kingdom of God. At its peak there were a thousand branches in Britain, hundreds abroad and a parallel women's association. Even today, there are 150 Toc H groups.

That Toc H survived as it did is a surprising tribute to a man who seems to belong in the masculine world of the early twentieth century. Clayton became one of the country's best-known Anglican clergymen, caricatured by Max Beerbohm and regularly featured in the pages of *Punch*. However, he never felt at ease with women unless they were of very high rank. He often visited the Dowager-Duchess of Devonshire at Chatsworth (although he seems to have most enjoyed long conversations with her flunkeys) and thought Queen Mary and the Queen Mother the two most remarkable women he had met.

Addicted to excruciating jokes, incurably scruffy, infuriatingly unpunctual (he said 'the only way to arrive in time is to start out late'), Clayton could be difficult company, but such was his dedication, interest in others and power of speech that memories of him are almost universally warm.

Between two wars

✻ *Military history*

SIR BASIL HENRY LIDDELL HART (1895–1970)

The study of war has been my life's work. The study of costume has been a recreation, providing a light relief to the sombre effect of my principal study. Yet to describe it as 'light relief' may be to take its importance too lightly. For the continuance of the human species depends on sex attraction, in which dress is a major element, whereas the most that can be claimed for the study of war, even in the largest sense, is that it may possibly help to curtail the destruction of the human species.

(Sir Basil Liddell Hart, 1944)[33]

Basil Liddell Hart was a prolific writer who revelled in ideas and his own intellectual powers. Tall, thin and elegantly dressed, he had a remarkable head, 'literally bulging with brain'.[34] Before he was ten Liddell Hart was obsessed by war games and avidly reading reports from the Russo-Japanese War (1904–05). St Paul's proved uninspiring and the history tripos at Cambridge largely irrelevant to his military interests, but active service on the Somme (where he was gassed) and promotion to the rank of captain gave him the impetus to write about army training and tactics.[35] Two years later he was ready to reflect on his first twenty-five years. He put on record that his own intellect was 'deeper, clearer and more agile' than 'the pick of our regular soldier brains', and concluded that 'with experience' he could prove himself 'one of the "masters of war"'.[36] This was not to be: in 1923 the army placed him on half pay; four years later he was officially retired, ostensibly on the grounds of 'ill health caused by wounds' but possibly also because the authorities disliked his forthright military views.[37]

These views developed in Liddell Hart's books and journalism, and in 1932 he claimed to have become 'the best-known military writer in the world'.[38] An addict of war games, he saw the horrors of 1914–18 being replaced in the future by 'techno-thrillers' where quick-thinking generals would use light well-equipped forces to bamboozle the enemy:

The land 'punch' of the future will be delivered by fleets of tanks, their communications, maintained by cross-country and air vehicles, offering no fixed and vulnerable target for an enemy blow […] Speed, on land as in the air, will dominate the next war, transforming the battlefields of the future from squalid trench labyrinths into arenas where surprise and manoeuvre will reign.[39]

He thought his most important theory was the indirect approach, which he presented as a whole philosophical system:

We have only to reflect on love to realize the superior effectiveness of the indirect approach — it is fundamental to sex life. Again, every worldly-wise subordinate in a service or other organization will testify to the fact that the quickest and surest way of winning support for a step or change is to persuade the chief man concerned that it is his own idea.[40]

Such stylish and provocative writing attracted much attention. In 1935 he became defence correspondent of *The Times* and for the next three years advised two successive defence secretaries, Duff Cooper and Leslie Hore-Belisha. One historian described him as 'a strategic Jeeves to Hore-Belisha's political Bertie'.[41] However, as the army council was revitalized with new blood, so was it felt that the forces should not be run by journalists, and Liddell Hart's influence declined. He came to believe neither in war nor appeasement but in the primacy of defence, a policy that was identified with defeatism, especially after the allied collapse in spring 1940.

After the war he thought of concentrating all his energies on ladies' fashions, his other interest, but then re-emerged in his final years as an international military *éminence grise*: his trip to Israel in 1960 attracted more attention than any other foreign visitor apart from Marilyn Monroe.

It is hard to reconcile Liddell Hart's rational and humane commitment to restricted warfare with his visionary writing and romantic belief in the great general. It is also hard to think of a war correspondent penning articles, often under a pseudonym, on fashion, but recent biogra-

Sir Basil Liddell Hart, oil by Hein Heckroth, 1939. This portrait includes references to the impending war. Maps of Europe appear as a cloud and within a bubble, referring to the instability of the continent. The 'listening' ears were included by the artist in the belief that Liddell Hart might be connected with the Secret Services. © *National Portrait Gallery, London.*

phers have not resisted the temptation to discover imagery of containment in his obsession with wasp waists and corsets, and the rhetoric of destabilizing the enemy's psyche in the time he devoted to choosing his first wife's clothes and controlling the public impression she made.[42] His military archive is at King's College, London, appropriately so as he did much to promote the academic study of war, and his fashion library at Liverpool John Moore's University.

The Second World War

❧ *Captain of England*

FIELD MARSHAL BERNARD LAW MONTGOMERY, FIRST VISCOUNT MONTGOMERY OF ALAMEIN (1887–1976)

Last Saturday I was at Wembley. I was introduced to a young man called Wright. I was told that he was the captain of England. I said to him, 'I was captain of England myself at one time.' Wright asked me, 'When were you captain of England, sir?' I replied, 'In the war. In the war.'

(Lord Montgomery)[43]

On 15 May 1944 Bernard Law Montgomery gave a final presentation in the Board Room at St Paul's of his grand plan for the invasion of Normandy, Operation Overlord. He was allied land forces commander, and in his audience were King George VI, Churchill, Eisenhower (supreme allied commander) and senior members of the forces. His briefing was a characteristically methodical list of points and delivered, his military assistant Lieutenant-Colonel

Meeting in the Board
Room at St Paul's School
of the Supreme Command,
Allied Expeditionary Force
leaders, 1 February 1944.
Eisenhower is seated at the
head of the table with
General Montgomery at
his left. British official
photographer.
*Courtesy Imperial War
Museum TR1629.*

Dawnay recalled, in 'supremely confident' fashion.[44] Montgomery had a talent for making complex ideas clear and had worked out how the battle would proceed on both sides from day to day. He had definite views on the enemy command — 'Rommel [...] is best at the spoiling attack; his forte is disruption; he is too impulsive for the set-piece battle' — and was equally clear about what the allies must rely on: '(a) the violence of our assault; (b) our great weight of supporting fire, from the sea and air; (c) simplicity; (d) robust mentality'.

Montgomery spoke as a professional. Army routine was in his bloodstream, and he was a very experienced military instructor. Like his regular correspondent and fellow Old Pauline, the military historian Liddell Hart (see last entry), he saw the physical and psychological aspects of warfare as equally important. For both men too, the language of games and the language of war belonged together, but whereas Hart was ahead of his time in visualizing the battlefield as a large-scale computer game, Montgomery looked back to an older set of values, where valour and discipline on the rugby field were the prelude to heroism in the First World War. He had almost been killed on the Marne and watching the appalling losses at Passchendaele in 1917 convinced him the generals 'forget that the whole art of war is to gain your objective with as little loss as possible'.[45] Sporting metaphors continued to colour his concept of war, just as military discipline permeated his everyday life.

Games and battles were to be won. At school he relished fierce rugby matches, where he 'happily made his first battle plans'.[46] On being commissioned into the Royal Warwickshire Regiment (1908) for service in India, Montgomery was ordered to field a weak soccer team against the crew of the German battleship *Gneisenau*, making a friendly visit with the crown prince on board. Instead, he played all his best men and was unrepentant when the result was forty–nil. 'I was taking no risks with those bastards,' he told his colonel.[47] After Alam Halfa (August–September 1942), his first victory in the desert war, he wrote to a friend, 'My first encounter with Rommel was of great interest [...] there was no difficulty in seeing him off. I feel that I have won the first game, when it was his service. Next time it will be my service, the score being one-love.'[48] When the battle of Alamein itself was finally won, on the twelfth day as he had predicted, Montgomery wrote it was by two well-directed 'hard punches'.

If battles were to be won, then soldiers were not to be squandered on futile campaigns. He was responsible for

General Montgomery during his first press conference for
allied correspondents following the allied landings, 1944.
Courtesy Imperial War Museum B5337.

he is absolutely certain of success'.) Nevertheless, as a sportsman, Montgomery ended his press briefing in January 1945 by saying, 'Let me tell you that the captain of the team is Eisenhower. I am absolutely devoted to Ike; we are the greatest of friends.'[50] This did not stop Eisenhower attempting to cut him out of the final action, the march to Berlin, by taking away the two American armies under Montgomery's control and confining him to sealing off the Danish peninsula. Even so, one historian thought this was his greatest victory, and Montgomery savoured every moment of the surrender ceremony at Lüneburg Heath, on 2 May 1945, three days before the Berlin surrender.[51] A special tent was erected and the BBC summoned. The Instrument of Surrender, which the German delegation had to sign without delay, was phrased as a personal surrender to Montgomery himself, and he kept the document as a treasured memento, only sending photostat copies to Supreme Headquarters.

In later life he played up to the image of a retired field marshal. He was a governor of St Paul's and told High Master Tom Howarth (who had been a liaison officer with Montgomery in 1945), 'If you have any trouble with the other governors ring me up and I'll bring up the heavy artillery.'[52] He issued a numbered set of orders for two boys who wanted to visit him. ('They can wear any old clothes they like. They must get their hair cut.') When he took a walk through a Swiss village with a young man he had befriended, it was like a military inspection, with piles of firewood 'meticulously checked for rectilinear alignment'.[53] There was certainly a human side to Montgomery. His wife Betty died of septicaemia in 1937 after ten years of marriage, and in his own words he 'was utterly defeated'.[54] He had entered fully into family routine: when his son David was born he would move a china rabbit from one side of the bed to the other to remind Betty with which breast to start her next feed. But biographers still struggle to make sense of this 'wiry, scholarly, intense, almost fanatical personality', whose life was dominated by soldiering.[55]

the third division of the British Expeditionary Force in the first months of the Second World War but was convinced that an allied catastrophe was inevitable and therefore concentrated on training his men for what became the Dunkirk retreat rather than for offence. In December 1944, when a broad-front strategy commanded by Eisenhower was collapsing, it was Montgomery's defensive battle of the Ardennes that saved the day.

He thought Eisenhower's 'ignorance as to how to run a war [...] absolute and complete'.[49] (Eisenhower thought Montgomery too conceited 'to make a single move until

❧ *Escaping the enemy*

MAJOR-GENERAL WILLIAM MAURICE BROOMHALL (1897–1995)

If it had not been for the fact that Broomhall entered a little too wholeheartedly into his new role, he and his fellow escapers would certainly have got clear of Eichstatt.

(*The Times*, 17 January 1995)

There were several British professional actors in the prisoner of war camp Oflag VIIB at Eichstatt in Bavaria, and this may have inspired the most audacious of William Broomhall's attempted escapes. He had been captured in

1940 during the German invasion of France. Arriving at the camp he found his Savile Row tailor already there, and he helped with the disguise. Broomhall was to impersonate a German Wehrmacht general on an inspection visit,

A group of British prisoners of war celebrating Christmas at Colditz Castle. Among them may be William Broomhall. Note the tree and streamer. German official photographer. *Courtesy Imperial War Museum HU20276.*

accompanied by a staff of four. There had already been escapes by inmates masquerading as German soldiers, and so it was necessary to increase the rank of the escapers in order to overawe suspicious guards. A great deal of work went into creating uniforms from red cross blankets. Casing strings from the double bass in the camp band provided silver cords for the officers' hats.

Broomhall decided to make his general gruff and bad-tempered, a piece of acting brio that proved his downfall. Decked out in red tabs, Iron Cross and jackboots, he set off with his party to the camp's little-used back gate, where he barked a carefully-rehearsed German order at the sentry, 'Schnell, machen Sie das Tor auf!' ('Hurry up and

get that gate open!') The party were let out, but once the sentry had saluted smartly, he telephoned through to the front gate, warning the sentry there to look out as an irritable general was on the prowl. It did not take long for them to grasp this was a ruse, and the escapers were recaptured in a nearby wood half an hour later.[56]

Broomhall was moved on to Colditz, where he became senior British officer. After the war his continued escape attempts and morale-boosting work there were rewarded with a DSO. The thespians at Oflag VIIB gave the world première of Noel Coward's anti-war play *Post-Mortem* in January 1943.

AIR CHIEF MARSHAL SIR LEWIS MACDONALD HODGES (1918–2007)

An extremely efficient and gallant flight commander, whose leadership and unfailing devotion to duty have proved inspiring.

(Citation for the award of the Bar to Sir Lewis Hodges's DFC, 1943)[57]

When he heard that Lewis Hodges had gained entry to the RAF College at Cranwell, High Master John Bell said, 'They seem to be taking anyone these days.' Hodges went on to become one of the force's most highly decorated pilots. He joined Bomber Command in 1938. Two years later he was forced to crash-land his plane in Brittany

when returning from an attack on Stettin. Together with an air gunner, he was given civilian clothes by a farmer, helped by a fisherman, and given more clothes, shoes and money by a château owner. They reached Marseilles but were caught by the Vichy police and imprisoned in a fort near Nîmes. This did not detain him long. He used a potato to create authentic-looking stamps on a forged pass and made his way to Spain, where he was arrested again and this time sent to Miranda del Ebro concentration camp — the British Embassy stepped in and he was repatriated a few weeks later.

Hodges returned to his squadron in June 1941 and was decorated for his attack on the German battle-cruisers *Scharnhorst* and *Gneisenau* in the Channel. He was then chosen for special operations and began picking up agents in occupied Europe, hazardous assignments that required landing by moonlight or with the guidance of a few hand-torches. Among his passengers back to England were two future French presidents, Vincent Auriol and François Mitterand. He finished the war based in Calcutta, flying clandestine missions over Japanese-operated territory.

The air force remained his life. In the 1950s his role was to build up Britain's fleet of V-bombers. He rose steadily, and his final appointment was as deputy commander-in-chief, allied air forces, central Europe. In retirement Hodges became president of the RAF Association and saw through the renovation of its club in Piccadilly. Possibly what meant most to him were twenty-one years as the last president of the RAF Escaping Society, a charity that gave financial aid to those who assisted members of the RAF to evade and escape, and their dependants.[58]

Sir Lewis Hodges signing copies of 'Loire Rendezvous', a limited edition print published as a tribute to the Special Operations Executive in 2002. *Courtesy SWA Fine Art Publishers.*

✵ *Second World War casualties*

He was a very fine soldier and commander, and his men would have followed him anywhere. His loss to the regiment is irreplaceable.

(Letter from his colonel on Major Michael Antony Thomas Burke, 1920–43, killed in North Africa)[59]

Two hundred and fifty-nine Old Paulines died in the Second World War, and within the pages of *The Pauline* are many stories of courage and self-sacrifice that are even more moving for their brevity. Here is a small sample.

PETER DONALD MACALISTER (1917–41)

After leaving school he went abroad for a bit and also had some experience of journalism, but it was the arrival of the war that enabled him to find himself. He went to Finland to fight against Russia, made his way to Norway with difficulty, joined the Norwegian forces and, though he had never even been in an aeroplane before, did some air fighting; he was wounded but in due course escaped by a sort of miracle in an old machine to Scotland, where he entered the RAF. At first he was a fighter pilot and did some night fighting in the spring of 1941, but later transferred to bombers and was lost in a raid over North Germany on 2 July 1941.[60]

Spitfire Mark VB of No. 92 Squadron RAF. It was shot down in June 1941. G. Woodbine. *Courtesy Imperial War Museum CH2929.*

CHARLES ROBERT KENNETH FAY (1921–43)

He lost his life in the Mediterranean […] when the aircraft of which he was co-pilot and bomb aimer was forced down by engine failure. He and two other members of the crew managed to leave the aircraft, but they drifted apart; one of them was saved, one was never seen again, and Fay was picked up dead. The survivor, whose arm was broken when the aircraft struck the water, declared that he undoubtedly owed his life to Fay's tireless efforts to assist him.

CHARLES GORDON GWYNN (1908–43)

He won first eight swimming colours at school. Accepted for the Royal Naval Volunteer Reserve, he 'saw service in the Atlantic and the Mediterranean, including the Salerno landing. When HMS *Charybdis* was torpedoed in the Channel, he used his swimming powers to go from raft to raft helping others to get on; after some hours he was picked up by a destroyer, but the oil poisoned him and he died two hours later, giving his life to the service of others as he had always done.'

HMS *Charybdis* underway. Royal Navy official photographer. *Courtesy Imperial War Museum FL5201.*

JOHN ANTHONY WELLING-LAURIE (1917–44)

Vehicles disembarking from a pontoon raft after crossing the Irrawaddy. No. 9 Army Film and Photographic Unit. *Courtesy Imperial War Museum SE3167.*

He was engaged at the time of his death (December 1944) in ferrying his brigade, with all their transport and heavy equipment, across the Irrawaddy. At this point the river (1,000 yards wide) flows swiftly at 8 to 9 knots. […] A brother officer writes that he 'was doing his best to save the craft, and gave his orders with coolness and decision up to the very end'.

MAJOR-GENERAL ROBERT ELLIOTT [ROY] URQUHART (1901–88)

It was interesting meeting the actor who plays my role — Sean Connery. I liked him as a chap. He is very similar in shape, and when in uniform not unlike my appearance thirty-odd years ago.

(Roy Urquhart on filming *A Bridge Too Far*, 1976)[61]

In January 1944 Montgomery (see earlier entry) appointed Roy Urquhart GOC 1st airborne division. He was a career soldier with a distinguished record and won a DSO and Bar for his commands in Sicily and North Africa, but the appointment was a surprise. He knew nothing about the parachutists and 'had no idea at all how these chaps functioned'.[62] As a fourteen stone forty-two year old he was declared unfit for parachute training, and he suffered from severe air-sickness. Despite being 'clearly a military landlubber' and 'not a man to court popularity', he very soon won the men's 'complete respect and trust' as they prepared for operation 'Market Garden', which had the objective of capturing key bridges in Holland so that the British Second Army could outflank the Siegfried Line.[63]

Having been given the order 'Arnhem Bridge and hold it' just one week in advance, on 17 September 1944 Urquhart flew into Arnhem by glider. Eight days of desperate fighting followed, but the strength of the enemy troops had not been anticipated, and on 25 September he had to withdraw his forces across the Rhine. The operation was fraught from the start. Perhaps unwisely, Urquhart had agreed to his troops being flown out over a period of three days and dropped at a distance of several miles from the bridge to keep clear of anti-aircraft fire. The Germans secured the plans of 'Market Garden' when they were found on the body of an American soldier who was involved in another part of the operation and carrying them against orders. The radios rarely worked, and when Urquhart set off to make personal contact with his troops, he narrowly escaped death and was separated from his headquarters for thirty-six hours.

Urquhart led his men by example. A glider pilot, Sergeant Roy Hatch, called him 'a bloody general who didn't mind doing the job of a sergeant'. During the battle a signalman sought his help to move some heavy radio batteries, and when he realized his helper was a general, Urquhart just said, 'That's all right, son.'[64]

Urquhart ordered his men to break out rather than surrender, and his close knowledge of the evacuation at Anzac beach in December 1915 taught him how to sustain apparent opposition to the last. 2,163 men managed to cross the Rhine, 6,450 were taken prisoner and 1,350 killed in battle. On 28 September Montgomery handed him a note of

thanks at his tactical headquarters near Eindhoven: 'There can be few episodes more glorious than the epic of Arnhem, and those that follow after will find it hard to live up to the standards that you have set.'[65]

Major-General Robert Urquhart plants the Airborne flag outside his headquarters, the last British stronghold in the Arnhem area, before the evacuation. D. M. Smith, Army Film and Photographic Unit. *Courtesy Imperial War Museum BU1136.*

SEFTON DELMER (1909–79)

As I listened to the playback […] the bit I liked best was the denunciation of Churchill as a 'flat-footed bastard of a drunken old Jew'. Here, with one phrase, which cost no one any broken bones, we had won credibility as a genuinely German station. No member of the great German public, I felt convinced, would ever suspect that British propagandists could be capable of using such outrageous language about their beloved prime minister. This was a phrase, I decided, which was well worth repeating in other broadcasts.

(Sefton Delmer)[66]

Sefton Delmer's special responsibility in the Second World War was so-called 'black propaganda' broadcasts to Germany, designed to undermine the enemy by spreading fabricated information and rumours. He was in a good position to do this, having been brought up in Berlin (he attended school there as an enemy alien before his family were allowed to go to England) and having spent several years living in the Weimar Republic as a reporter for the *Daily Express*. He became very familiar with the Nazi regime, to a point where the Foreign Office thought he might be a German agent, and he walked at Hitler's side through the burning Reichstag.

His first war venture was a shortwave station, *Gustav Siegfried Eins*, which began broadcasting in 1941. It featured an old-fashioned Prussian officer, Der Chef, whose prurient disgust with invented acts of misbehaviour among minor Nazi officials was ingeniously intended to set a bad example the German people would follow. Delmer writes:

In one of his transmissions for instance, Der Chef denounced by name the wives of a number of high party officials in the Schleswig-Holstein area who, he said, had rushed to the clothing stores (also named) and bought up all the woollen goods and textiles to which they were entitled by their clothing coupons. Why? Because these traitorous whores had learned from their obscenity husbands [sic] that the Fatherland's supplies of textiles were running out owing to the needs of the army in Russia, and that any folkcomrade who did not cash his clothing coupons now, would not be able to buy anything at all a little later.

Sure enough, about six weeks later when I was looking through a Kiel newspaper which had been published shortly after The Chief's Philippic, there it was, the report of a run on the clothing stores. And to my great satisfaction the editor made things worse by reiterating The Chief's most effective argument. 'If everyone behaves like this,' he wrote, 'there will be nothing left for anyone, and the clothing coupons will be valueless.'

The broadcasts were spiced up with the most salacious details of the Nazi officials' private lives, a feature that Delmer reports required extensive research into German sexual aberrations via the works of Magnus Hirschfield, founder of the world's first sexology clinic, and added greatly to the station's listener appeal.

Not everyone approved of Delmer's methods. After one very explicit attack by 'Der Chef' on the habits of a German admiral, the left-wing politician Sir Stafford Cripps raced indignantly to the Foreign Office to see Anthony Eden and protest. 'If this is the sort of thing that's needed to win the war,' he stammered in his fury, 'w-w-why I'd rather lose it!'* Nevertheless, *Gustav Siegfried Eins* and other initiatives such as *Soldatensender Calais*, an imitation German forces radio station, and *Radio Livorno*, which pretended to come from the Italian 'Resistance' (and in Delmer's view did much to engineer the surrender of the Italian navy), played a significant part in weakening enemy morale.

* Cripps also announced he wanted to resign in September 1942, when he did not like the way Churchill was running the war.

Sefton Delmer making a propaganda broadcast to Germany from the BBC, 1 November 1941. *Getty Images.*

‰ *Code-breaker and writer of the film 'Peeping Tom'*

LEOPOLD SAMUEL MARKS (1920–2001)

The only really satisfactory way to dispose of *Peeping Tom* would be to shovel it up and flush it swiftly down the nearest sewer.

(Derek Hill, *Tribune*)[67]

Leo Marks's father was an antiquarian bookseller whose shop, 84 Charing Cross Road, became the setting for a best-selling novel and film. Seeing a first edition of Edgar Allan Poe's *The Gold Bug* for sale first fired Marks's enthusiasm for codes and code-breaking at the age of eight:

The book's tale of hidden treasure, the whereabouts of which was concealed by a cipher, entranced Leo, and he set about breaking his father's own secret pricing code, a series of letters pencilled inside the cover of each book. Within minutes he had found the key (the ten letters of Marks Cohen, the two partners in the business, each corresponded to a number) and gained two ambitions: to become an expert on codes and, like Poe, to write horror stories.[68]

Because of ill-health, Marks was not at first called up for service, but in January 1942 a genius for breaking codes placed him in the Special Operations Executive (SOE), which controlled all the Resistance movements in Europe. Despite his youth, he was soon head of agents' codes and ciphers. He found they used codes which could be 'read like daily newspapers',[69] being based on familiar poems which agents memorized: 'one poor chap had chosen the National Anthem'.[70] His first move was to require the poems where possible to be less decipherable original compositions, many of which he wrote himself. The most famous of these was written in memory of girlfriend Ruth Hambro, daughter of his boss and killed in an air crash in December 1943. He gave the poem to the agent Violette Szabo, and it featured in *Carve her Name with Pride* (1958), the film of her wartime activities:

> The life that I have
> Is all that I have
> And the life that I have
> Is yours.[71]

Marks's next step was to devise the 'silk code' with the aid of Colonel Elder Wills, surely a prototype for 'Q' in the James Bond films, whose inventions to assist agents included exploding animal dung, nuts and bolts as well as a vast array of false documents and items with secret cavities.[72]

Leo Marks demonstrating an example of his silk code. *AP/PA Photos.*

If an agent was caught in the field their code poem could be tortured out of them, and all their traffic read. It took me twelve months to convince SOE that every single agent must have a code printed on silk, every single one of them different, so that as they sent the message they could cut it away from the silk, burn it, and because they couldn't remember them, the codes could *not* be tortured out of them. But if they lost their silk codes, they had to have a poem in reserve.[73]

When asked what difference these new codes would make to agents (who were equipped with suicide pills), Marks simply replied, 'It's between silk and cyanide.'[74]

As a boy he became interested in Freud, who would visit his father's bookshop. Marks missed seeing him by five minutes and was given signed copies of two works by Freud in compensation. He said that the unconscious was 'the greatest code of all'.[75] It was his understanding of how agents thought and their proneness to errors under stress that correctly convinced Marks the Dutch SOE network had been penetrated by the Germans, but he was not listened to, and up to fifty unnecessary deaths resulted.

After the Second World War Marks wrote film scripts. In the most influential of these, *Peeping Tom,* a voyeuristic young cameraman is driven by the urge to film terrified women as he kills them, until in the end he films his own suicide. It was conceived in the code room, Marks said, and he intended his audience to read the visual clues and 'discover the clear text of this man's code for themselves'. As a child the cameraman in the film was the victim of his psychiatrist father, an expert on fear who terrified and photographed him day and night; Marks thought code-breakers and agents were 'basically voyeurs' as well as the victims of enemy scrutiny. The women's suffering was meant to reflect the wartime torture of allied agents. *Peeping Tom* was hated by critics, effectively ended the director, Michael Powell's, British career and left Marks's parents filled with shame, but recognition has come more recently. Watching the film again after a gap of thirty-four years, Dilys Powell of the *Sunday Times* found 'extraordinary quality' that lay concealed by her earlier 'efforts to express revulsion'.

❦ *War crimes prosecutions*

SIR HENRY DAVIES FOSTER MacGEAGH (1883–1962)

The evidence flowed in like a deluge and we were submerged by it [...] Our efforts then and later were like a man standing at the edge of the sea dropping lumps of sugar into it, and saying: 'Behold it is sweet.' We were failing because the wave of criminality was so great and our resources were so inadequate.'

(Colonel Gerald Draper, member of the judge-advocate-general's office, working on the Belsen Concentration Camp case)[76]

As judge-advocate-general, a position he held from 1934–54, Henry MacGeagh was responsible for military justice, which after the Second World War extended to prosecution of those responsible for crimes committed against British nationals in British-occupied territory.

MacGeagh's office had been cleared by the Oliver committee, set up in 1938 to investigate allegations of military miscarriages of justice. This result led him to say he would now blow his 'office trumpet', and he continued to resist any criticisms or interference in its work.[77] Britain's war crime trials were slow and ineffective:

[Macgeagh] was old, pedantic, conservative, tired out by the war and totally oblivious to conditions in Europe. He had, in fact, never crossed the Channel [...] The Department was not eager to do anything about war crimes, but it was quite ready to devote its legal and bureaucratic skills to preventing anyone else encroaching on its territory in order to get something done.

Within the British zone there had been eighty-one Belsen-like concentration camps, but the attorney-general, Sir Hartley Shawcross, discovered that only three were being investigated. MacGeagh required each potential witness at Belsen to make a sworn statement and then remain in the vicinity while it was decided whether the evidence would be used. This process took two months, and not surprisingly 'former inmates, after years of suffering, did not want to wait around any longer'. Many witnesses disappeared, but MacGeagh would not brook criticism: he 'rejected in no uncertain terms' a proposal from Viscount Bridgeman of the War Office to streamline bureaucracy, writing, 'I am responsible for the collection of evidence against and the prosecution of war criminals [...] I have yet to be persuaded that the present system is not efficient or that it causes or is likely to cause unnecessary delay.' The letter went on to say that any solution would have to be deferred until his return from leave.

Trials fell behind schedule. It was intended to complete

Two guards awaiting trial after the liberation of Bergen-Belsen concentration camp, 1945. Silverside. No. 5 Army Film and Photographic Unit. *Courtesy Imperial War Museum BU9745.*

500 cases involving 2,000 individuals by 30 April 1946, but by that deadline only 199 people had been tried in seventy-seven cases. Shawcross thought that at this rate the trials would 'go on until the crack of doom', but MacGeagh was satisfied his department was doing its best, and told him, 'It is very disturbing to those engaged in this work to be constantly pressed.' The Belsen trial (September–November 1945) resulted in some surprising acquittals and light sentences, for which MacGeagh was partly blamed by James Dean, legal adviser to the Foreign Office:

The judge-advocate-general insists on trying to prove in concentration camp cases that each of the accused was personally responsible for at least one murder. This is a ridiculous method of procedure, since the victims or potential victims who could have proved the necessary facts are themselves dead or vanished long ago.

MacGeagh has to take some blame for the inefficacy of British war trials, but it is also true that the allied powers' determination to pursue criminals 'to the uttermost ends of the earth' faded with peace. Victor Gollancz, the Old Pauline Jewish publisher (see chapter five), led a campaign for reconciliation rather than vengeance, and by 1947 Churchill thought killing the leaders of the defeated 'had exhausted any usefulness it ever served'.[78]

❧ War correspondent, writer and maker of television documentaries

EDWARD SAMUEL BEHR (1926–2007)

As an example of fact's being stranger than fiction, I can do no better than recall my first visit to Cuba just after the 1962 missile crisis [...] there were grim stories of suspected spies being arrested and held in dungeons for weeks at a time with no one the wiser. After clearing Cuban customs, I called in the apartment of a British diplomat in Havana who had had advance warning of my arrival. I expected the mood to be grim and conspiratorial. Loud music could be heard on the landing. The diplomat's wife opened the door. 'I'm so glad you could come,' she said. 'Mr Castro is teaching us how to tango.'

(Edward Behr)[79]

War shaped the course of Edward Behr's life from his schooldays. He was born into a Russian-Jewish family and lived in Paris until the German occupation of 1940, when they were betrayed by their concierge and fled to London.

There was a period of service with the Indian army before going up to Magdalene College, Cambridge, to read history, and already his taste for the absurd showed in a stratagem for obtaining supplies from a small Indonesian island:

Suddenly I had a brainwave. Promising to replace a Monopoly set, I bought it off the Royal Navy. I then explained to the island headman that I could let him have some of the new currency that was being introduced elsewhere in Indonesia, but that — since the release date of the currency was to come only in a few days' time — he was not to mention this to anyone.

The Monopoly money looked a good deal more genuine than anything he had seen during the Japanese occupation, and he parted with a sizeable amount of chickens and vegetables in exchange for some Monopoly bills [...] There is a happy ending to the story. Six months later, when an acquaintance went back to the island, the Monopoly money was in circulation there and had completely driven out not only the plummeting Japanese-occupation guilder but the Japanese yen as well.

In the 1950s and 1960s Behr reported on fighting and unrest throughout the world. Behr never glamorized his work: 'In real life,' he wrote, 'notebooks are lost, tape recorders jam, taxis break down in remote places and on the way to the revolution noisy children throw up in crowded planes. It's a world of Woody Allen rather than Joel McCrea [star of the Hitchcock thriller *Foreign Correspondent*].'[80] In the second half of his career he concentrated on books and television documentaries, which gave more scope for analysis and assessment. Notable among these were his films and writing on Hirohito and the way in which post-war propaganda had protected him from being held to account for atrocities earlier in his reign:

One of the most hated men in history went on to become constitutional monarch, pre-war and war role forgiven. Not only the sheer longevity of his reign, but the way he managed to extricate himself from responsibility for any of the pre-war and wartime decisions leading to millions of deaths, make him without doubt the ultimate survivor of all times.[81]

Behr always had an eye for the ridiculous — he relished describing how the Rumanian dictator Ceaucescu and his party stole anything they could lay their hands on when making a state visit to Paris — but his career was deeply motivated:[82]

What possible explanation was there for my aged Russian grandmother's horrible death in a Nazi concentration camp?

[…] folly, greed, and hypocrisy seemed to me, at a very early age, to be fairy godmothers presiding over the destinies of our planet, and little has occurred since to make me change my mind […] The only recourse, it seemed to me, was to try, where possible, to anatomize such instances, and what better way of doing so than by becoming a journalist?[83]

⚘ *Heroic action in Sierra Leone*

LIEUTENANT-COLONEL LINCOLN PETER MUNRO JOPP (1968–)

Lieutenant-Colonel
Lincoln Jopp.

Lincoln Jopp received the Military Cross for bravery during the military coup of 1997 in Sierra Leone. He was in charge of a UK team training Nigerian forces supporting the legitimate government when their temporary headquarters, a seaside hotel, came under fire from rebel forces armed with missiles, heavy machine guns, and a helicopter gunship. The odds were overwhelming, and Jopp, the only serving British officer in Freetown, also had to defend 800 British, American and European civilians taking refuge in the hotel. He directed operations from the hotel roof-top, defending his position for seven hours until the Nigerian force ran out of ammunition. Following a ceasefire arranged by the Red Cross, he was evacuated on the USS *Kearsarge* the following day together with the British High Commission and 1,300 others. Jopp received a number of shrapnel wounds and burns. His citation states, 'Captain Jopp undoubtedly contributed towards the saving of hundreds of civilian lives. His performance throughout the events over ten days, his courage, without regard for personal safety, dedication, leadership and ability deserve to be recognized.'

❧ *Chairs for the Festival of Britain*

ERNEST DAWSON RACE (1914–64)

The Antelope was less comfortable than the Springbok to sit on, which may have been due to a deliberate request by the organizers to prevent people lingering too long on them.

(H. Conway)

THE 1951 Festival of Britain on London's South Bank featured two innovative chairs by the young designer Ernest Race, the Antelope and the Springbok. Both were intended for outdoor seating and constructed from thin steel rod. Of the two it was the Antelope, with its white ball feet and moulded plywood seat (a new material readily available), that caught the public imagination:

Its gaiety, elegance and wit seemed to encapsulate [...] the Festival. [...] The lightness and strength of the Antelope, which could only have been achieved with the particular materials used, seemed to typify what 'contemporary' design should aim for. From the stylistic point of view the slightly splayed steel rod legs came to be one of the characteristics associated with 'contemporary' design as the 1950s progressed.[1]

Race was trained in interior design. At the end of the Second World War he responded to an advertisement from Noel Jordan, an engineer who was planning to set up a furniture company. Despite the scarcity of hardwoods, Jordan foresaw enormous opportunities for a resourceful designer:

The demand for furniture, particularly that of first-class artistic merit, will be tremendous. It therefore follows that an original designer, prepared to utilize new materials, such as steel, plywood, plastics (not necessarily the moulded type), aluminium, together with the new methods of finish of such materials, is presented with a unique opportunity for developing his work.[2]

The result was Ernest Race Ltd, with Jordan as managing director and Race as chief designer. Their first success was the 'BA' dining chair (1945) made of aluminium and holoplast, a laminated plastic with mahogany veneer. More than 250,000 were produced over nearly twenty years, and the chair's light elegance won Race the first of his gold medals at the Milan triennale. Another striking design came in 1953, the Neptune lounger for P&O cruises. It comprised two identical curved plywood forms which folded into each other.[3]

One reason for Race's impact was that his work adapted well to small domestic spaces. He embraced scientific approaches to design: the rods and spheres on his Antelope chair were triggered by a course he had attended on crystallography and industrial design.[4] At the same time, he was irritated by those who thought that 'anthropometrics and ergonomics' would clear 'the jungle in which designers have been endlessly thrashing for years'.[5] For Race good design

The Antelope chair, designed by Ernest Race for the Festival of Britain. *Courtesy Race Furniture Ltd.*

came before the new or the fashionable, which may explain why his later work was less successful and certainly explains why he was one of the few British designers to gain international recognition. Shortly before his early death he received a medal from The Society of Industrial Artists and Designers. The citation read, 'The complete originality of his work could claim to be genuinely indigenous to this country: there was nothing pseudo-Scandinavian about it.' The Antelope chair is still being manufactured by Race Furniture Ltd in 2009.

✣ *A car for Cruella de Vil*

ROBERT JANKEL (1938–2005)

Take along a £100,000 Roller and, for a further £100,000, they will lengthen it to give a conference-style rear section that looks like a cross between a branch of Dixons and a Berkeley Square cocktail bar.

(Jeremy Clarkson, *Sunday Times*, 25 April 1993)

In the 1974 film of *101 Dalmatians* Cruella de Vil preferred to travel in a Bugatti-style Panther De Ville, one of the rare and exotic creations of Panther Westwinds during its brief life under Jankel's control. The De Ville cost twice as much as a Rolls-Royce Silver Shadow, and among its purchasers were Elton John and Oliver Reed.

Jankel built his first car, an adapted Austin 7, while a sixteen-year-old at school. He began work in the family textile industry, but his real interest was car engineering. In 1970 he travelled round Spain in a 1930 Rolls-Royce he had completely reconstructed, and sold it to a bullfighter for £10,000. This inspired Jankel to found Panther Westwinds and design unusual sports cars. His most suc-

cessful models were the fibreglass Lima (1,000 produced) and the all-aluminium J72 (300 produced). The six-wheeled Panther Six turned heads at the 1977 London Motorfair, but only two were ever built.

Panther Westwinds went into receivership in 1979, but Jankel also had a small coachbuilding company, which he founded in 1955, the year he left St Paul's, and turned his attention back to special versions of luxury cars. Latterly the Jankel Group focused on stretch limousines, police vehicles and armoured cars. Such was its success that Jankel bought back the Panther marque in 2001. When he died he was designing yet another sports car.

The Panther De Ville, designed by Robert Jankel. *Courtesy Panther Enthusiasts Club.*

(HANS WERNER) JOHN WEITZ (1923–2002)

Dress is a form of tribalism. People wear what their tribe wears — executives, blue-collar workers, undertakers, accountants.

(John Weitz)[6]

At school it was said of John Weitz that his grades would only improve if he paid less attention to the cut of his collar and more to French declension.[7] He was always a model of elegance: in 1971 he entered the International Best-Dressed List Hall of Fame and remained there for the rest of his life. Weitz made his fortune as an American menswear designer. He was a pioneer of the designer label. John Weitz Clubs, as they were called, were established in stores throughout America and Europe, featuring clothes and accessories in a 'yacht club chic' style, aimed, as he put it, at the man who 'buys a Jaguar on time [i.e. in instalments]'.[8] He designed everything himself: shirts for the perfectly flat stomach, the 'Classic Men's Sock 12–pack' in aubergine and pumpkin race-flag checks, alphabet-patterned ties and pyjamas imitating motor-racing or golfing kit. A tall and distinguished figure, he appeared in many of his advertisements; others generated humour and business from his signature: one poster on the back of New York buses read, 'She ditched him, John Weitz ties and all.'[9]

The sporting motifs were not a coincidence. Weitz recalled that in his time at St Paul's 'it was the "snappy" thing to go to formal events in sports cars, wearing a white tie, topper and all – and there was something really young and rakish and debonair about it'. Before business interests intervened, he competed regularly in what he called the 'fashionable, poloesque sport' of motor racing.

In 1955 he completed 145 laps of Florida's Sebring in a Morgan Plus 4.[10] He published *Sports Clothes for Your Sports Car* in 1958. Of course he was a member of several exclusive yacht clubs.

Weitz's writing included a tough novel about the rag trade, *The Value of Nothing* (1970), and *Man in Charge: the executive's guide to grooming, manners and travel* (1974), but his final books reflected another side of his character. *Hitler's Diplomat* (1992) was a study of von Ribbentrop, and in 1998 he published a portrait of Hitler's banker, Hjalmar Schacht. Of the former Weitz said, 'Who but a fashion designer would understand a social climber? I wanted to write about the Nazis through the eyes of somebody I might have met at a cocktail party.' There was more to it than that. His parents had fled from Germany to the United States in 1938. Weitz became a member of the Office of Strategic Services (OSS), forerunner of the CIA, and undertook what he called 'sensitive' work in Germany between 1944 and 1946. It is thought that he liaised with the group planning the failed plot to kill Hitler. He was one of the first troops to liberate Dachau, an experience that led him to lose his Jewish faith.[11]

The tradition of high achievement has continued with Weitz's sons, Paul and Chris, both very well known in the film industry. Chris Weitz is an Old Pauline (see later entry).

John Weitz, impeccably turned out for the school swimming team photograph in 1939. Next to him is the coach, Sergeant Pagley. © *St Paul's School.*

✣ *Haute couture*

JOHN BRYAN CAVANAGH (1914–2003)

A new star shines in the London couture sky. Seldom has a more beautiful and discreet collection been seen than that of John Cavanagh.

(Alison Settle, fashion journalist)

John Cavanagh joined the House of Molyneux straight from school. By January 1952, when he opened a dress shop in Mayfair, he had also worked for Pierre Balmain and knew Christian Dior well. He was ideally placed to bring Parisian chic to London, and despite King George VI's death ten days after he opened (it was decided to curtail official mourning) Cavanagh's first collection was a great success. His reputation was for style and quality: he designed wedding dresses for both the future Duchess of Kent and Princess Alexandra, as well as many of the guests. However, the days of haute couture were numbered, and he was not comfortable with the transition to a ready-to-wear world.[12]

June Clarke, left, wearing a chiffon embroidered dress designed by John Cavanagh, centre, at a private fashion show at Claridges hotel, London, 18 November 1952. *Getty Images.*

✣ *Traveller*

(GEORGE) ERIC NEWBY (1919–2006)

He was a glorious combination of idiosyncrasy and beautiful manners, all the time bubbling with vitality and gob-smacking gusto.

(*Guardian*, 23 October 2006)

Eric Newby.
Courtesy Wanda Newby.

'Nobody was better qualified to produce his own obituary than travel writer Eric Newby,' wrote Edward Mace George in the *Guardian* when he died. He had an extraordinary gift for deriving entertainment from his travels and incident-filled life. Even at school, where his habit of dissolving into helpless hysterics was already getting him into trouble, managing a scout patrol became a source of farce:

On one occasion, when there was a danger of our losing one of the outdoor games known as 'wide games' (which necessitated covering large tracts of ground on foot), [a] member of my patrol whose family owned a huge limousine in which he used to arrive at wherever was the meeting place, summoned the chauffeur, who was parked round the corner, and six scouts whirred away in it to certain victory.[13]

Newby's poor mathematics ensured an early departure from St Paul's. After eighteen pointless months at an advertising agency, where he survived only because he was paid too little to be worth sacking, he went on holiday, saw the wreck of a four-masted barque half buried in the sand at Salcombe and immediately signed up for service as the only Englishman on a Finnish sailing ship. The *Moshulu* carried grain and went on to win the last grain race with Newby aboard. His escapades, published in 1956, included burning a fellow sailor with boiling gutta-percha as he attempted an amateur repair to his broken tooth during a gale after a riotous Christmas dinner.

He joined the Special Boat Section in the Second World War, was captured in Sicily and was sent as a prisoner of war to Northern Italy. *Love and War in the Apennines* (1971), his most substantial and serious book, is a powerful account of Italian peasant life when guerrilla warfare was at its height and of his meeting Wanda, a young Slovenian who helped him to escape to the remote Appenines, where eventually he was betrayed and recaptured. They married in 1946 and became inseparable: 'When he was asked in a magazine article to name the one indispensable item with which he always travelled, rather than choose a run-of-the-mill article like aspirin or a Swiss army knife, Newby chose his wife.'[14]

After his marriage he spent ten improbable years in the fashion business before sending a cable to his Embassy friend, Hugh Carless — 'CAN YOU TRAVEL NURISTAN JUNE?' The two set off, prepared only by a brief course on rock-climbing in Wales, to tackle 18,000ft peaks North-East of Kabul. *A Short Walk in the Hindu Kush* (1958) was the result. The book delighted the heart of Evelyn Waugh, who wrote a preface, and remains his most popular. In its final paragraphs the two amateurs meet seasoned explorer Wilfred Thesiger. Newby spends the evening tantalized by all his luggage. Eventually, they turn in: 'The ground was like iron with sharp rocks sticking up out of it. We started to blow up our air-beds. "God, you must be a couple of pansies," said Thesiger.'[15]

Earlier in the book Newby hands over his brand-new Rolex watch to entertain a group of tribesmen:

'Tell the headman,' I said to Hugh, 'that it will work under water.'

'He doesn't believe it.'

'All right. Tell him it will even work in that,' pointing to the cauldron which was giving off steam and glogging noises.

Hugh told him. [...] Before I could stop him he dropped it into the pot.

'He says he doesn't believe you,' said Hugh.

'Well, tell him to take it out! I don't believe it myself.'

By now I was hanging over the thing, frantically fishing with the ladle.

'It's no good,' I said. 'They'll have to empty it.'

This time Hugh spoke somewhat more urgently to the headman.

'He says they don't want to. It's their dinner.'

At last somebody hooked it and brought it to the surface, covered with a sort of brown slime. Whatever it was for dinner had an extraordinarily nasty appearance. The rescuer held it in the ladle. Though it was too hot to touch, it was still going. This had an immense impression on everyone, myself included. Unfortunately, it made such an impression on the man himself that he refused to be parted from it and left the bothy.

'Where's he going?'

'He's going to try it in the river.'

From 1964–73 he was travel editor of the *Observer*, then owned and generously financed by the Astor family, a good thing given the legendary size of Newby's expense claims. But the routine of the job bored him, and he was becoming disaffected with the way travel had turned into tourism. This may be why his later books (he wrote twenty-five altogether) lack the earlier ones' sparkle. Newby seemed to yearn for an earlier age of travel and adventure. He even ordered his first pair of boots from an advertisement in the 1878 edition of Murray's *Handbook to Switzerland*.

The founding father of trainspotting

IAN ALLAN (1922–)

Ian Allan was a boy with a passion for railways, and he left St Paul's to work in the office of the general manager of Southern Railway at Waterloo. He had lost a leg at the age of fifteen and spent the Second World War in the company's publications department, where his near-encyclopaedic knowledge of engines and rolling stock won him the job of answering public enquiries. Discovering there was wide interest in locomotive names and numbers, he produced at his own expense 2,000 copies of a pocket book listing this information, and to his surprise it sold out rapidly. The hobby of trainspotting was born. A reprint, *ABC of Southern Locomotives* (1942), was followed by books on the other four major railway companies. A similar pub-

lication on London Transport sold 20,000 copies in days. Books were produced on ships and civil aircraft.

By now the operation was far too large for Allan and his friends and neighbours to handle, and in 1945 the publishing company Ian Allan Ltd was created. Ian Allan Group, as it is now called, has a wider range of business interests but remains 'the world's leading transport, aviation and military publisher and retailer'. A permanent reminder of the founder's ruling passion is a 1922 Pullman car previously used by King George VI, which was acquired for the company board room.[16]

Ian Allan.

<figure>✒ *Architectural photographer*</figure>

ERIC SAMUEL DE MARÉ (1910–2002)

Eric de Maré changed the way we see.
(Peter Davey, *Architectural Review*)[17]

In 1948 Eric de Maré set out with his wife in a converted army pontoon to explore England's canals. The result was a special edition of the *Architectural Review* filled with his photographs of canalside buildings and bridges. He had trained as an architect and saw photography as 'building with light'; like architecture it was 'concerned with constructing forms, lines, tones, textures, and possibly colours, into a sculptural unity'.[18] A Swede by birth, he was attracted to the functional qualities of contemporary Scandinavian design and discovered in the simple and elegant architecture of the canals another kind of functionalism. The *Architectural Review* had since 1930 been

searching for an alternative tradition of English building to counterbalance its distaste for over-decorated Victorian and Art Deco architecture. The canals issue was part of this quest, as was its sequel, an edition dedicated to 'The Thames as Linear National Park'. In 1958 de Maré's images formed the main content of an important book, *The Functional Tradition*, with text by the review's editor.[19] These industrial photographs have been extremely influential: architects have found in them a native, less aggressive, context for modernist ideas, and they have helped to conserve warehouses, mills and other structures previously ignored.

The Barton Aqueduct opened to allow a vessel to pass on the Manchester Ship Canal, Eric de Maré, 1945.
Reproduced by permission of English Heritage. NMR.

The darker side of life

RICHARD PETER TREADWELL DAVENPORT-HINES (1953–)

Goths choose to stand on the giddy edge of things: they take the riskiest path up the volcanic slopes to peer into the crater.

(Richard Davenport-Hines, *Gothic*)[20]

On 18 May 1922 Violet and Sydney Schiff, 'a rich, cultivated and cosmopolitan English couple', held a famous party in Paris to celebrate the first night of Igor Stravinsky's burlesque ballet *Le Renard*.[21] Among the guests were Picasso and James Joyce. Marcel Proust made an entrance in the early hours. The carefully planned meeting of Proust and Joyce turned into a fiasco, and Richard Davenport-Hines's book *A Night at the Majestic* (2006) weaves around it a series of reflections on Proust and his final years. In the end the party becomes an image of Proust's reputation, part modernist and cosmopolitan, part a return to the style of the nineteenth century.

Davenport-Hines is a prolific writer and reviewer. His earlier work focused on business history and business biography, but *A Night at the Majestic* is the latest in a series of more adventurous books. In 1990 he published *Sex, Death and Punishment*, and in 1999 *Gothic: Four Hundred Years of Excess, Horror, Evil and Ruin*, an imaginative piece of aesthetic history ranging from seventeenth-century Naples to photographs of Damien Hirst in a mortuary: 'The studies in putrefaction have been presented by some journalists as flagitious, exploitative experiments in modernity, but in fact his exploration of the aesthetics of putrefaction reaches back to old Gothic revival

Richard Davenport-Hines.

antecedents.'[22] His important biography of W. H. Auden was published in 1995.

Perhaps his most fiercely argued book is *The Pursuit of Oblivion* (2001), a detailed social history of drugs over two hundred years, which also criticizes 'the war on drugs', both here and in the USA, as ineffectual cultural imperialism.[23]

Disc jockey

PETE MURRAY (PETER MURRAY JAMES) (1925–)

Welcome aboard the *6.5 Special*. We've got almost a hundred cats jumping here, some real cool characters to give us the gas, so let's get on with it and have a ball.

(Pete Murray launches the *6.5 Special*, 16 February 1957)

In the early years of television there would be a break in broadcasting between six and seven in the evening so that mothers could put their young children to bed undisturbed. It was in this gap that Pete Murray hosted the *6.5 Special*, a skiffle-based magazine programme for teenagers. The opening sequence was a film of a steam train accompanied by Don Lang's Frantic Five performing the show's theme song, 'The 6.5 Special's comin' down the line', and a smiling Murray would announce, 'It's time to jive on the

old 6.5.' He went on to be a regular panellist on *Juke Box Jury*, which ran from 1959–67. In this very popular weekly programme celebrities would give their verdicts on the latest pop releases, sometimes with the artists listening from behind a screen, and then the chairman, David Jacobs, would declare the disc a hit or a miss by sounding a bell or klaxon. Murray was also to be seen as guest DJ on Independent Television's rival programme *Thank Your Lucky Stars*. He was one of the first hosts of *Top of the Pops*.

Pete Murray in 1967.
© *BBC.*

Few people growing up in the fifties and sixties will have forgotten him.

As his television career waned, Murray worked for over ten years presenting BBC Radio 2's *Open House*, a two-hour weekday magazine programme, but in 1983 he was dropped because his style was thought too old-fashioned.[24] He continued until 2002 as a presenter for LBC, a London commercial radio station.

In his autobiography (1975) Murray describes his wax model for Madame Tussaud's:

The modelling was quite fun, but I never had the nerve to go and see my effigy. And now I never will. Madame Tussaud's remains; the Murray model has been demolished, melted down a couple of years later at the same time as Harold Wilson, who had, I think, fallen from power.[25]

❧ *Blues musicians*

ALEXIS KORNER (1928–84)

The father of modern British rhythm and blues.
(Peter Gammond)[26]

(DONALD) CHRISTOPHER BARBER (1930–)

If you are looking for the Godfather of British Blues, the *Capo di Capi*, the man who made it all happen, then look no further than Donald Christopher Barber.

(Harold Shapiro)[27]

Interviewed in 1988, Chris Barber recalled being at St Paul's with Alexis Korner.[28] Korner had in fact left three years earlier, aged fifteen, for a spell in the army and some short-lived jobs in the BBC and record industry. He said that listening to a record of Jimmy Yancey during an air raid converted him to a life of playing the blues. He was also turning against his parents and a childhood of conventional piano lessons:

One day, my father came back to find me playing boogie-woogie, and he blew his top, totally and absolutely, and slammed down the lid of the piano, and locked it with a key which he carried in his pocket, and said, 'You don't play stuff like that on my piano.'[…] And then I decided to start playing the guitar, because it annoyed my father more than anything else I could do. He hated the guitar. He loathed it. He said it wasn't even a serious instrument; ladies played it and tied ribbons on it.[29]

The original Chris Barber's Jazz Band of 1954: Chris Barber, Lonnie Donegan, Jim Bray, Ron Bowden, Pat Halcox, and Monty Sunshine.
Photographer unknown.

The son of Cambridge academics, Barber was brought up on the classical violin, entered St Paul's as an eighth former and won a place to study violin and double bass at the Guildhall School of Music. Then, 'as a young man in a London club, he picked up a cheap and battered second-hand trombone'.[30]

They began to play together in 1949. At a time when jazz enthusiasts were thin on the ground, Barber's encounter with Korner was 'like meeting the only other Buddhist in Aberdeen'.[31] From 1952–54 they both performed in a skiffle group before the Chris Barber Jazz Band was formally launched and their careers separated.

Barber's band has expanded, broadened its repertoire and survived over an extraordinarily long period. It is now the eleven-piece all-instrumental Big Chris Barber Band — in earlier days it included Irish singer Ottilie Patterson. Korner went on to run the Roundhouse Blues Club and then co-found with harmonica player Cyril Davies the band Blues Incorporated. Korner's own attempts at the harmonica were short-lived: he called himself 'one of the first and one of the worst [...] players in the country'.[32] Later he worked as a solo guitar and singer and in partnership with bass player Colin Hodgkinson. There was an untypically lucrative spell when he too formed a big-band ensemble, CCS (The Collective Consciousness Society), and there was a 'pretty wild' band called SNAPE (Something Nasty 'Appens Practically Everyday) that fed the more bohemian side of his character. Korner also spent time writing and broadcasting.[33]

Making a record with Korner was for acoustic guitarist Davy Graham an odd experience: 'I couldn't help feeling Alexis and I were like the main characters in *Of Mice and Men* — me the big lummox and Alexis the little guy with the brains. All I could do was shut up and play some interesting chords. [...] I had the facility, he had the intensity — passion compensating for technique.'

Both men fought hard to overcome the prejudice that blues music was only for black musicians. Korner said, 'I'm part Turk, part Greek and part Austrian and as I don't know any part-Turk, part-Greek, part-Austrian music, I feel I'm perfectly entitled to play blues.'[34] Barber's response to the controversy was to take his blues band round the Dixieland clubs and become the first white band to play at Smitty's Corner in New Orleans. The legendary blues musician Muddy Waters proudly announced them as his 'guests from the State of England'.[35]

Barber's first contact with Waters was inviting him to England. He likes to tell the story:

It was John Lewis from Modern Jazz Quartet that put me on to Muddy [...] He suggested bringing Muddy over, but I

Alexis Korner.
© *Peter Ruthenberg.*

said, 'Well, how do I get hold of him? You can't write to him c/o third cotton bush on the left.' And he said, 'What do you mean? He's got an agent, a Cadillac. I'll get him for you.'

A less naïve Barber went on to invite other distinguished American performers, including Louis Jordan, Alex Bradford and the harmonica player James Cotton.

Christened the 'Bix Beiderbecke of British-style jazz', Barber now has no singers in his jazz band, but sees his trombone as a kind of voice: 'What jazz instrumental playing is, it's called *vocalized tone* — you make it sound like a voice does with an instrument. Trombone's perfect for that, much better than the old ones — you can bend the notes more, you see?'[36]

For these Old Pauline musicians, popular success has mattered less than the world of jazz and blues. A member of Korner's band said, 'If something looked like it had the remotest chance of becoming successful he stopped doing it.' Young players in Blues Incorporated would go on to bigger things — Mick Jagger, Brian Jones, Charlie Watts and Eric Clapton — and the Rolling Stones was first formed to stand in when Blues Incorporated had an outside engagement, but Korner did not become rich. His best-known success was a version of Led Zeppelin's 'Whole Lotta Love' which was adopted as the theme music for *Top of the Pops*. One of the tunes from Barber's early days, 'Rock Island Line', was a Top Ten hit when he accompanied Lonnie Donegan in 1956, but his major achievement has been 'introducing a whole nation to the idea you could make music as well as listen or dance to it'.[37]

There were other dimensions to Korner. He worked for children's television, 'demonstrating that you can get music from spoked wheels and hollowed-out logs as well as more conventional instruments such as the bouzouki'. A bizarre career move in 1977 found him playing Gessler in a Swiss musical on the life of William Tell: 'The whole point of this show was to send up William Tell — so you don't have to be Einstein to work out that it was unlikely to be a resounding success in Switzerland.' He had his own BBC Radio 1 programme, 'a model of erudition, wit and the well-turned phrase'.[38]

Barber now has 10,000 concerts to his credit. When asked recently about career ambitions he said, 'When you've done the Hollywood Bowl, played in New Orleans and […] to 12,000 people in Berlin one of only three times the hall was sold out for a jazz concert, what's left? Just good musicians playing the music they love.'[39]

In 1964 Korner was interviewed by *Beat Instrumental* for an article unkindly called 'The One They Left Behind.' His response was characteristically generous: 'This type of thing often happens; the person who starts a thing rarely carries it through. Anyway, I am still playing the music I love, am living comfortably, and frankly from this "boom" will emerge some really fine young musicians.'[40]

✢ *A legendary horn player*

DENNIS BRAIN (1921–57)

An alchemist, turning copper into gold.

(The *Scotsman's* comment on Dennis Brain's playing of the French horn)[41]

Dennis Brain playing the hosepipe at the Gerard Hoffnung 1956 music festival. © *The Hoffnung Partnership.*

The musical world of the nineteen fifties suffered within four years the deaths of three brilliant young performers, contralto Kathleen Ferrier, the pianist Noel Mewton-Wood, who often accompanied Dennis Brain, and Brain himself, killed in a car accident when driving back to London from the Edinburgh Festival on 1 September 1957. Recent growth of interest in classical music from long-playing records and radio broadcasts made the impact of these events all the stronger. James Morris had noticed Brain's popularity when travelling with the 1953 expedition to conquer Everest: 'It did not in the least surprise me, listening on the radio one day to Dennis Brain playing a Mozart horn concerto, to find a whole posse of film men bursting through the tent flap to hear him too.'[42]

Brain was born into a horn-playing dynasty and reputedly first produced a perfect note on this notoriously difficult instrument at the age of three. His first public appearance, with his father in Bach's First Brandenburg Concerto, was when he was seventeen and brought warm praise from the *Daily Telegraph*'s music critic: 'Son seconded father with a smoothness and certainty worthy of its [the family] name.' Despite the onset of war, his rise to fame was meteoric: broadcasts for the BBC, principal horn in the RAF band, twenty-six solo appearances in Myra Hess's National Gallery concerts, and a highly successful recording career, from 1943 on. Brain went on to play as principal horn in both the Philharmonia, founded in 1945, and the Royal Philharmonic Orchestra launched by Sir Thomas Beecham a year later. 'The horn quartet,' bragged Beecham, 'will be the finest in Europe. First horn, Dennis Brain, is a prodigy.'[43]

A mark of Brain's distinction was the number of works composed especially for him: concertos by Elisabeth Lutyens, Gordon Jacob, Malcolm Arnold, Paul Hindemith, and most significantly Benjamin Britten's *Serenade for Tenor, Horn, and Strings,* written in 1943, first recorded in 1944. This work is famous for its opening and closing horn passages where the soloist is instructed to use natural harmonics rather than valves to create his notes. When a new recording was launched in 1954, the *Tempo* music critic had the temerity to suggest that Brain was playing out of tune, provoking a gentlemanly response from Britten:

In the Prologue and Epilogue the horn is directed to play on the natural harmonics of the instrument; this causes the apparent 'out-of-tuneness' of which your reviewer complains, and which is, in fact, exactly the effect I intend. In the many brilliant performances of his part that Dennis Brain has given he has always, I am sure, played it as I have marked it in the score. Anyone, therefore, who plays it 'in tune' is going directly against my wishes! If the critics do not like this effect they should blame me and not Mr Brain.[44]

Brain had nerves of steel and extraordinary stamina. He would play two concerts in one night 'with the aid of a taxi'. There was a provincial concert where he appeared in the first and last items but was missing in between. Someone joked, 'He's probably giving a half-hour recital at the BBC,' and it turned out that he was. He revelled in his virtuosity, performing 'The Flight of the Bumble-Bee' at parties and rendering the presto from Leopold Mozart's Concerto for Alpenhorn on rubber hosepipe at the 1956 Gerard Hoffnung Music Festival, having trimmed the hose with garden secateurs to achieve the correct tuning.

Critics struggled to find the words to describe Brain's

Richard Timothy Watkins (1962–). Sir Peter Maxwell Davies wrote the solo horn piece 'Sea Eagle' for Richard Watkins in 1983 when he was twenty-one and studying at the Royal Academy of Music. Two years later he became principal horn of the Philharmonia, a position he held until leaving in 1996 to concentrate on his solo career. Dennis Brain professor of horn playing at the Royal Academy, Watkins has recorded a wide repertory and worked with many leading international conductors, but his special interest is new music for the horn, and he has premiered several works. *Courtesy Christa Phelps.*

playing. Neville Cardus (a prominent writer on music for the *Manchester Guardian*) said, 'He breathed a whole tradition of romance into his instrument.' For *The Times*, 'he played Mozart's Second Horn Concerto […] first as though he had just discovered it, and secondly as though his instrument was a supremely agile human voice, not a machine dependent on pistons and on harmonic series'.[45]

It was Brain's passion for fast cars that proved tragic. A copy of *Autocar* often lurked on his music stand. Perhaps Benjamin Britten best captured the shock of his sudden death, recalling the last time he heard Dennis Brain play, three months before the accident in his Triumph TR2:

What one remembers most clearly of that evening was […] the unfinished movement of Mozart's fragmentary Horn Concerto in E. The *tutti* started with its glorious richness […] all seemed set for the best of all the wonderful Mozart horn concertos. And then suddenly in the middle of an intricate florid passage, superbly played, it stopped: silence. Dennis shrugged his shoulders and walked off the Jubilee Hall platform. […] That was the last time I ever heard him play, the last time I saw him. That Mozart fragment sticks in my mind as a symbol of Dennis's own life. But it is not so easy for us to shrug our shoulders.[46]

❦ *Composer*

PETER RACINE FRICKER (1920–90)

Aren't you going to stay for the P. Racine Fricker?
  (Question asked of Jim Dixon as he tries to escape from Professor Welch's agonizingly pretentious musical soirée in
  Kingsley Amis's 1954 comic novel *Lucky Jim*)[47]

'they shall go twain and twain together soberly', manuscript. Page 39 of Peter Racine Fricker's *Colet Cantata*, a setting of St Paul's statutes composed for the school's 450th anniversary in 1959. The work was performed that year by the school orchestra and choir under the director of music, Ivor Davies. © *UC Santa Barbara.*

To be satirized by Kingsley Amis is surely a sign of success, and after the Second World War Peter Racine Fricker was for a time a prominent and highly regarded composer. His rigorously formal works appeared to release British music from the insularity of Holst and Vaughan Williams and make new links with the European intellectual tradition represented by Bartók, Berg and Schönberg. His fame was short-lived, and now he seems to belong with the tougher elements of fifties culture, but his defenders feel that a revival is long overdue. Fricker wrote an enormous range of music, including a horn sonata for his Pauline contemporary Dennis Brain and a setting of John Colet's statutes to mark the school's 450th anniversary in 1959.

Editor of Grove's Dictionary of Music

STANLEY JOHN SADIE (1930–2005)

[Sadie] confronted me one morning to say that our staff of ethnomusicologists would like to expand the number of non-Western instruments slightly. 'By how many?' I asked him, 'a hundred or two?' 'No,' he replied, calmly, 'by about 17,000.'

(Alyn Shipton of Macmillan, Grove's publisher 1981–87)[48]

Stanley Sadie. *By courtesy of Oxford University Press.*

Stanley Sadie began his writing career as a music reviewer for *The Times* and the *Gramophone*, where he had a formidable reputation for witty and caustic but scrupulously well-researched articles.[49] He was editor of the *Musical Times* for twenty years, but his enduring monument is the *Grove Dictionary of Music and Musicians*, which he expanded in its two latest editions from nine volumes to twenty-nine and liberalized, sometimes controversially, by including writing on jazz, rock and world music. He entered into this massive task with enormous enthusiasm, writing many new articles himself. Sadie liked to be in control. A colleague once slipped past him a fictional composer made up of two Danish villages linked with a hyphen — it got into the 1979 edition and he was not amused — but he was clearly held in great respect. One of his team wrote of:

His extraordinary productivity (he did so much besides, writing and reviewing into the night, often after a long day at Grove); his ability to coax or cajole copy from contributors; his own lucid, crisp and intensely musical prose ('Listen to the rhythm of the sentence,' he would say); his immense energy for life and work; his utter belief in, and defence of, what we were doing; his insistence on scholarly accuracy and pragmatism in equal measure; and his indefatigable urge to go the extra mile to make the dictionary that little bit better.[50]

Sadie and his wife, also a musicologist, led the campaign to create a museum in Handel's London house, a project that led them to visit three hundred other composers' homes in Europe. The result was a guidebook, *Calling on the Composer*, published after his death. They also ran a series of concerts in their local church at Cossington in Somerset. The day before he died, Sadie insisted on returning from hospital in London for the first concert. He was able to stay for the first half but then went home to his bed. When the performance ended the Chilingirian Quartet came over to his bedroom and played the slow movement of Beethoven's final String Quartet, no. 16 in F major, opus 135, as Sadie floated in and out of consciousness.[51]

Music and life

BENJAMIN DAVID ZANDER (1939–)

There was a shoe company that sent two people down to Africa many generations ago to check out what the likelihood of sales was of shoes. And one of them sent an old-fashioned telegram back saying, 'Situation hopeless, stop. They don't use shoes.' The other one wrote back, 'Situation glorious. They haven't got their shoes yet.'

(Ben Zander)[52]

Ben Zander is music director of Boston Philharmonic Orchestra and renowned for his recordings of Mahler's symphonies. He is also a popular lecturer on leadership and has on several occasions given the keynote speech at the World Economic Forum in Davos. It was teaching young performers at New England Conservatory that

Ben Zander giving a master-class. © *Sisi Burn.*

At Zander's corporate presentations a member of the audience stands on a chair while everyone else sings a heartfelt 'Happy Birthday' to him. He believes that business leaders and musicians alike should radiate possibility rather than surrender to the world's pessimism. When a student musician at one of his master classes makes a mistake, the reaction should be 'how fascinating' and not embarrassment. He rejects traditional models for leadership training which draw comparisons with military commanders and sports coaches and concentrate on winning, domination and control. Instead, he advocates a symphonic approach, where every voice is heard, and all are working together to discover new possibilities.

Zander's motivational talent is at its most impressive when he gives young musicians the confidence to go beyond technical issues and breathe emotional life into their performances, but he believes we should all step out beyond our comfort zones. His exuberant presentations often end with the whole audience singing the 'Ode to Joy' from Beethoven's Ninth Symphony.[53]

opened his eyes to the links between playing music and life skills, and led to *The Art of Possibility*, a book written jointly with his wife Rosamund.

❧ Religious thinker

WILLIAM HENRY ERNST [CORNELIUS ERNST OP] (1924–77)

This recollection of Cornelius Ernst comes from Father Timothy Radcliffe OP, former master of the Dominican Order.

I had the good fortune to study with a Dominican called Cornelius Ernst. His father was Anglo-Dutch and Anglican. His mother was Sri-Lankan and a Buddhist. In his young days in Sri Lanka he was a communist until he was expelled from the party for his deviant views. He came to Cambridge to study and was a pupil of the philosopher Wittgenstein. He was one of the 'young Cambridge poets'. Eventually he had found that only Catholicism was big enough to combine his father's Anglicanism, his mother's Buddhism, the communism of his youth and the philosophy he had learned to love with Wittgenstein. He found his home in the Church.

Cornelius played an extremely important part in my education. For almost six years we had a weekly tutorial — just the two of us. Once a month, I would buy a bottle of wine and we spent the evening together, talking about theology and listening to music. He was a man with an extraordinary breadth of vision and interest, symbolized by the opening words of one lecture, when he announced that he would consider the Prologue of St John's gospel in the light of later poetry of Rimbaud and recent mathematical theory! Not that I understood a word of it. He was not an easy man to understand; his writings are extremely dense. But he combined a deep sense of the Church and its tradition with a real sense of modernity and its questions. With him, I discovered that tradition and creativity need not be opposed.[54]

❧ Controversial Bible scholar

HUGH JOSEPH SCHONFIELD (1901–88)

If Jesus was convinced from the Scriptures that he was to suffer on the cross, but not to perish on it, there was no reason why he should not have been concerned to make what provision he could for his survival.

(Hugh Schonfield)[55]

With the publication of *The Passover Plot* in 1965, writer and broadcaster Hugh Schonfield threw himself headlong into religious controversy. The book was a great popular

success: it sold two million copies here and in the United States and was made into a film in 1986. It also shocked and offended, as doubtless was the author's intention. His main argument was that Jesus's life consciously followed 'a kind of blueprint of the Messiah's mission, with the prophetic requirements organized to show a progressive programme of events having their climax at Jerusalem, where he would suffer at the hands of the authorities'. In Schonfield's version Jesus's crucifixion was faked. The sponge of vinegar he was given while on the cross also contained a drugged liquid which had the effect of simulating death. The plan was that he would be taken down early and handed over to Joseph of Arimathea. The plot went wrong when the soldier pierced Jesus's side, and he did actually die.

The author described his approach as evidential and historical. It would provide people 'with a more correct understanding of Christ, which they can live with and from which they can draw courage and inspiration'. Instead, critics were bemused by its mixture of scholarship and hypothesis, and many Christians were outraged. 'A great publicist,' Schonfield revelled in his notoriety, and even put his ideas to antagonistic audiences of fundamentalist Americans.[56] In a radio debate Will Oursler of the *Christian Herald* said, 'A man who would fake his own execution to prove he was the son of God, didn't have any love for his fellow man. This is the kind of thing that Al Capone might do if he thought it up, as a way of getting out of jail.'[57]

Schonfield went on to write another subversive book, this time about plotting early Christians, *Those Incredible Christians* (1968) and a radically new translation, *The Original New Testament* (1985).

❧ Intellectual

SIR ISAIAH BERLIN (1909–97)

The most immediately striking thing about him was his unconventional appearance: his peculiar air of seeming to float in his clothing, a strange face that seemed almost a caricature of his two dominating characteristics: subtle intellect and Russian-Jewish ancestry […] Brilliant, original, witty and bold, truly erudite, he was unanimously admired as much for what he was as for what he did, and he was universally recognized as an exceptional, fascinating human being.

(Guy de Rothschild)[58]

The most important day in Isaiah Berlin's life was 14 November 1945. He was in a Leningrad (now St Petersburg) bookshop during an official Russian visit to explore post-war relations between Britain, America and the Soviet Union. Berlin himself came from a family of Latvian Jews and had seen the violence of the 1917 Revolution as a boy in Leningrad: the Berlins settled in England early in 1921. Now he was back looking for pre-revolutionary literature on sale to foreigners. In a back room of the shop he began talking to another writer, Vladimir Orlov, about the wartime siege, and asked about the fate of the pre-revolutionary poet Anna Akhmatova. To Berlin's delight, Orlov arranged a meeting with her that afternoon. They began talking at three o'clock and continued until well after dawn, despite a long interruption caused by Randolph Churchill (Winston Churchill's son), who had bought some caviar and called up from the courtyard for Berlin's assistance in instructing the staff at the Astoria to put it on ice. Any chance of the encounter with Akhmatova remaining secret was now lost, but they talked on, and her revelations of how Stalinism had stifled cultural and intellectual life were to shape all Berlin's subsequent writing on politics and freedom. Akhmatova's sequence of love poems, *Cinque*, was devoted to the meeting, but Berlin always denied any physical contact between them. The price of her conversation was high: close secret police surveillance, expulsion from the Writers' Union and her work censored.

The committee of the St Paul's School Union Society, 1927. Isaiah Berlin is in the centre and in front of him Arthur Calder-Marshall. Among the others is Cecil John Patterson (1908–92), later archbishop of West Africa. *Henry Hardy/St Paul's School.*

Sir Isaiah Berlin.
Courtesy Henry Hardy.

From his late schooldays, when he would lunch at The Dove on Hammersmith Mall with Pauline friends and discuss 'Eliot and Ezra, bitter and Burton, Cocteau and Cambridge', Berlin was a great talker.[59] A regular visitor to his rooms in the Albany in Berlin's old age said he seemed 'to bubble and rattle like a samovar on the boil'.[60] When he was awarded a knighthood in 1957, one friend suggested it should be for 'services to conversation'.[61] The conversation had to be good. After taking firsts at Oxford in classical Greats and the relatively new course of politics, philosophy and economics, he won a prize fellowship to All Souls in November 1932 and spent the happiest six years of his life dining there with City bankers, cabinet ministers and newspaper editors as well as Oxford intellectuals. He was the first Jewish fellow of All Souls in its five-hundred-year history, and his success brought congratulations from the chief rabbi and invitations from elevated and prosperous Anglo-Jewish families, the Rothschilds and the Sieffs (see later entry). Oxford dons accused Berlin of wasting his intelligence on high society, but his circle of friends, always a distinguished one, also reflected his enthusiasm for ideas, art and music.

His teaching at New College, both in the thirties and after the Second World War, was less satisfying. In 1932 Berlin found the dons there talked only about 'automobiles and by-passes', and by 1946 they were 'devoted grey nonentities and hacks' and his students 'dull and polite and spiritless'. Formal scholarship did not suit him: there were stories of his playing with clockwork toys during tutorials; having set an essay on human rights, he would advise, 'A lot of sawdust written on this topic — a lot of sawdust. Don't read any of it. Go away and think.'[62] He stopped teaching philosophy in 1950 to concentrate on the history of ideas and succeeded Old Pauline G. D. H. Cole as Chichele professor of social and political theory seven years later. His opening lecture, *Two Concepts of Liberty* and without doubt his most important work, explored how ideas of freedom could metamorphose into political tyranny.

The lecture was printed with three others, but until late in life publications were sparse. His friend from undergraduate days Maurice Bowra commented in 1971, 'Like Our Lord and Socrates he does not publish much.'[63] This was corrected soon afterwards. Berlin was president of a new Oxford graduate college, Wolfson, and Henry Hardy, a student there, approached him with a view to putting his writings in order. The result was a sequence of essay and letter collections, the last published in 2006, but he is still best known for what started as a party game. Introduced to the saying of Archilochus, 'The fox knows many things, but the hedgehog knows one big thing', Berlin began dividing great minds from history into hedgehogs and foxes, and then wrote an essay defining Tolstoy as a fox 'who believed passionately in being a hedgehog'.[64]

As for Berlin himself, 'I am like a taxi: I have to be hailed.'[65] A bizarre example of this was in 1940 when Guy Burgess persuaded him to travel to Moscow on an MI5 mission, except that he ended up in New York and spent the war years analysing American attitudes to the British war effort. Despite his only peacetime employment being as an Oxford academic, his outlook was liberal and international. A lifelong Zionist, he was disturbed by the existence of a maximum quota of non-Christian boys at St Paul's School (relations were restored after the quota was abolished).[66] He dictated a plea for reconciliation between Israelis and Palestinians on his deathbed: the papers in Israel printed it the day he was buried.

His final reputation remains to be seen, but people who met him or heard him lecture often speak of Berlin in superlatives:

He showed in more than one direction the unexpectedly large possibilities open to us at the top end of the range of human potential, and the power of the wisely directed intellect to illuminate, without undue solemnity or needless obscurity, the ultimate moral questions that face mankind.[67]

MAX BELOFF, BARON BELOFF (1913–99)

Oh, Max Beloff; most people think the better of anyone attacked by that great man.

(Quoted by Bernard Crick, *Guardian*, 25 March 1999)

In 1931, just before going up to read history at Corpus Christi College, Oxford, Max Beloff spent six months travelling in Germany. He described his experiences in an article for *The Pauline* the following year, writing already with an appetite for controversial ideas:

Most people travel with their eyes shut. For this reason, if one returns from Germany with the observation […] that it is the habit of the German people to eat sausages in the intervals of the opera, one is applauded as a brilliant observer of humanity; if one returned with the expressed conviction that it is the habit of the German people to dislike Poles, to bring political animosities into private life and the details of private life into political conflict, to a greater extent than is considered normal in this country — one would certainly be assailed as a scandalmonger.[68]

Beloff thought this article, which warned of 'the forces of destruction' gaining ground in Europe, the best piece he ever wrote. As an academic (becoming Gladstone professor of government and public administration at Oxford in 1957) he published a great deal, ranging from books for sixth form historians to a vast incomplete project on British imperial decline and theoretical work on democracy and foreign policy in the cold war. Beloff recognized himself as a historian in the Anglo-centric tradition without a genuinely international perspective, but he also came to see limits in all history:

Sometimes I think the novelist may be a better guide to what we need to know and understand. Trollope's political novels are worth innumerable academic theses about nineteenth-century politics; Paul Scott's *Raj Quartet* is more illuminating than anything else that has been written about the 'transfer of power' in India. Historians do a more mundane job and are perhaps rightly less well regarded and less well rewarded.[69]

He might have felt history to be limiting, but Beloff more than compensated for this in later life by a deluge of provocative letters and articles in the press. In Bernard Crick's words, 'He became a great character, vain but immensely able, an eccentric but formidably loose and cantankerous cannon.' He left Oxford in 1974 to run the privately financed University College of Buckingham, an enterprise strongly supported by Margaret Thatcher. She awarded Beloff a peerage in 1981, two years after his retirement. By this stage he had moved from schoolboy

Conservatism to student Socialism, adult Liberalism and back to the Conservative Party, although like the Vicar of Bray he was always himself. His anger with the MAs of Oxford was colossal when in 1985 they denied Thatcher an honorary degree; later he denounced her for insisting that universities 'should be more useful'.[70]

Beloff was an assiduous and vocal peer, with very strong views. He detested the European Union and spoke of the damage caused by Britain's abandoning its imperial past. He pronounced the Royal Shakespeare Company's productions so poor that its grant should be cut. In his final year he was strongly defending the hereditary principle in the House of Lords, and a month before he died he caught the headlines by comparing the rise of Tony Blair to the rise of Hitler.

Beloff 'firmly believed that intellectuals in public life […] have a duty to maintain integrity and independence of mind'.[71] Equally, he felt that universities must be left alone to think for themselves. He saw the University of Buckingham as an opportunity for business to fund a liberal arts college. Instead, he had to watch successive governments applying market principles to education. There is an excuse for his vitriolic old age.

Lord Beloff, oil by Irene Simpson.
Courtesy the University of Buckingham.

 ⚜ *Conservative cabinet minister, party chairman and writer*

KENNETH WILFRED BAKER, BARON BAKER OF DORKING (1934–)

Kenneth's strength was his presentational skill. As he braced himself, I reflected that if the prime minister had sent Beelzebub himself to the Foreign Office, Ken, with a straight face, would have presented his appointment to the media as that of a man with a wide experience of dealing with problems in a warm climate.

(John Major on Lord Baker's announcement of Douglas Hurd's appointment as foreign secretary in 1989 after Geoffrey Howe's dramatic resignation)[72]

Kenneth Baker's most enduring legacy is Gerbil, the great education reform bill, which received the royal assent in 1988, during his time as secretary of state for education, and remains 'the single most important piece of education legislation for England, Wales and Northern Ireland since the war'.[73] It saw the birth of the national curriculum, reformed management and budgeting of schools, abolished the Inner London Education Authority and expanded student numbers. Training days for teachers are still 'Baker days', and city academies are close relatives of his city technology colleges, if not the vocational institutions he hoped for. John Major recalls how he converted the prime minister, Margaret Thatcher, to his ideas:

As a former education minister herself, she enjoyed picking holes in his plans. […] It was a game they both enjoyed. 'That's absurd,' she would say. 'I know which official suggested that.' Ken would demur, deny that it was that official, make a joke of it, deflect her criticism, and gradually manoeuvre the prime minister into a position where he made tiny concessions to her, and she would appear graceless to seek more.[74]

Kenneth Baker under attack for the new national curriculum, cartoon, 1988. *Courtesy Lord Baker.*

Baker first entered the House of Commons in 1968. He found himself minister for information technology in 1981 after campaigning for such a position to be created and showing Margaret Thatcher round the IT company Logica — 'This was the first time that a minister had actually written out his own job specification before being appointed.'[75] His target of giving every secondary school a computer was ambitious then, however modest it may look now. Baker saw through the first major privatization of the Thatcher era, British Telecom. Privatization in his view ranks in importance with Henry VIII's redistribution of wealth when he dissolved the monasteries, an operation entrusted to another Old Pauline, Edward North (see chapter one).[76] Britain's space programme also fell within his remit, although the one European Space Agency launch he watched was a disaster. As minister for local government (1984–85) he set out proposals for a community charge but not 'the painful and voracious creature which emerged as the poll tax'.[77] Then, in his first cabinet post as environment secretary, he launched privatization of the water companies before taking the education portfolio.

In July 1989 Baker became party chairman during a difficult period for the Conservative administration. To boost morale at the annual conference, he conducted an audience poll on the outcome of the next election, saying, 'When it comes to political affiliations, I consider that you are as representative of a balanced cross-section as a typical BBC *Question Time* audience.' He was right about the election but got an indignant letter from the unamused editor of *Question Time*. As home secretary in John Major's administration, his final cabinet post, he found the pleasures of Dorneywood, his official residence, offset by the thorny problems of rising crime, an unreformed prison system and asylum abuse.

A member of the House of Lords since 1997, Baker continues to take an interest in educational issues and is pioneering a new type of school. University technical colleges for 14–19 year olds provide education and training in engineering, manufacturing production, design, construction and ICT. Half of the students will be apprentices and the other working eventually to foundation degrees. Each is sponsored by a university, and four are under way. 'Britain should have had these schools since the 1870s.'

He has edited several poetry anthologies. In his days as education secretary, Baker spoke out for 'the reading of good books […] a superior, richer and deeper experience than watching television'.[78] He is a keen collector of political caricatures, a subject on which he has published three works, and vice-chairman of the Cartoon Museum.

✢ *Labour cabinet minister*

FRANK SOSKICE, BARON STOW HILL (1902–79)

I have been […] watching the battle between Dennis Healey and poor old Frank Soskice, who was no match for this rough, rather ruthless young man.

(Richard Crossman, 16 December 1965)[79]

When Frank Soskice entered parliament as Labour MP for East Birkenhead in 1945, he had a high reputation for his work at the International Court of Justice at The Hague. Attlee made him solicitor-general. He held this position for six years, taking a special interest in revenue issues. As a parliamentarian he was courteous and unflappable, and Douglas Jay noted his 'utterly disarming' way of responding to opposition questions at the committee stage of the 1950 Finance Bill, when Labour had been returned with a tiny majority:

He gave the right answer — at some length. Almost nobody understood it except the Inland Revenue pundits trying to keep awake in the official box. I occasionally asked them quietly whether his erudite replies were really correct, or improvised mumbo-jumbo. 'Absolutely correct,' they always answered.[80]

Soskice was promoted to attorney-general a few months before the 1951 Labour election defeat and then joined the shadow cabinet. Hugh Gaitskell thought he was a possible future foreign secretary, but Soskice had to wait until 1964 for a Labour victory, and then Wilson made him home secretary.[81] It was too late — politics had moved on. Roy Jenkins called him a 'remarkably bad' home secretary: 'He had practically no political sense and an obsessive respect for legal precedent. In addition he was extremely indecisive.'[82] Richard Crossman in his diaries refers repeatedly to 'poor Frank Soskice'. He had to deal with immigration, 'the hottest potato in politics', and the unflappable courtesy of earlier years now appeared as 'liberal sloppiness'.[83] His most notable achievement was abolishing the death penalty.

Wilson, it seems, only saw him as a stopgap. In December 1965 he became lord privy seal and took a peerage.

✢ *Service to Jewish causes*

GREVILLE EWAN JANNER, BARON JANNER OF BRAUNSTONE (1928–)

People sometimes ask me why I am so involved in work for the Jewish people and I tell them that it is an hereditary disease. I would like to think that in some small way, the inheritance stretches back, beyond my father, to […] Moses.

(Lord Janner)[84]

In *One Hand Alone Cannot Clap* (1998) Greville Janner describes a week he spent with an Arab family on the borders of Israel in the hope of spreading goodwill. One day he visited Sheikh Abdullah bin Hussein Al Ahmar, ruler of the tribes of the north.

Around us were tribesmen, with white robes and curved daggers, and ministers and businessmen in smart Western suits. Suddenly, two young children walked into the room and smiled shyly. 'The Sheikh's grandchildren,' my neighbour whispered. I signalled to one of the lads to come over to me.

I produced a bouncy ball from behind his right ear and held out my right hand, inviting him to take the ball in his. When he found that my hand was empty, he screamed, *very* loudly. The room froze. Every tribesman's hand shot to his dagger. I stood, petrified — my end was nigh and magic was the cause of it. I pulled the errant ball from my pocket, held it up, bowed and presented it to the lad. He did not move.

Then one of the men realized what had happened. '*Hooa Sahhar*,' he said. 'The man is a magician!' They all laughed, sheathed their daggers and I breathed again.[85]

Lord Janner.

Janner must often have wished that his expertise as a member of the Magic Circle could have an effect on his

lifelong work for the Jewish community. He saw the horrors of Nazi anti-Semitism early, when at the age of eighteen he was the youngest war crimes investigator in the British Rhine Army and spent weekends working at the Bergen Belsen Jewish Children's Home. Trained as a lawyer, he was a Labour MP for twenty-seven years before receiving his life peerage in 1997. Among his other responsibilities were six years (1979–85) as president of the Board of Deputies of British Jews, the main body to represent Jewry in this country.

Janner is not afraid to speak his mind. As a QC and former president of the Cambridge Union he has a formidable debating style, which one journalist called 'aggressive and antagonistic'.[86] No one doubts his commitment to Jewish causes, be it defence of the Jewish state, preventing David Irving, convicted in Austria of holocaust denial, from returning to the United Kingdom, or the reclamation of Nazi gold from Swiss banks. In the debate on the War Crimes Bill, he described to the House of Commons how many of his family were herded by Lithuanian Nazi sympathizers into a synagogue and burned to death when it was set on fire.

✤ Diplomacy and defence

ROBIN WILLIAM RENWICK, BARON RENWICK OF CLIFTON (1937–)

I have known most British ambassadors, and Robin is simply the best.

(Richard Holbrooke)[87]

Lord Renwick.
© *Paul Leppard.*

When Robin Renwick became first secretary in the Paris Embassy in 1972, Christopher Soames, the ambassador, taught him the importance of giving good parties. This proved a vital skill during his tour as Britain's ambassador

to Washington, 1991–95: senators would ring up in advance to check the guest list for a function before accepting invitations. Appropriately enough, his departure from Washington was marked by a series of grand dinners.

Renwick's career also included four years as British ambassador to South Africa and key posts in the Cabinet and Foreign and Commonwealth Offices. He had to adapt to foreign secretaries with very different styles, Lord Carrington's respect for civil service methods being dramatically different from David Owen's preference for instant action ('the secret of dealing with David Owen was to dictate the telegram before he did') and Geoffrey Howe's legalistic pedantry which meant that speeches went through 'at least fourteen drafts before they ever saw the light of day'. Renwick is not a person for red tape and during a spell in the Cabinet Office found its 'hyperbureaucracy' frustrating.[88]

His diplomatic skills were also put to the test by Margaret Thatcher, with whom he worked closely over relations with Europe. It was acceptable, he found, to argue with her in private, but in public complete loyalty was demanded. She liked to feel in charge. When it came to negotiating the key Fontainebleau agreement in June 1984, reducing our net contributions to the European budget by two-thirds, Thatcher was allowed to believe that such a large reduction was the result of her own negotiating skills, although everyone else knew this would be the final figure.

He was head of the Rhodesia department at the FCO from 1978–80. The country's status had remained anomalous since Ian Smith's unilateral declaration of independence in 1965. He worked out with Sir Antony Duff a process whereby the country would temporarily return to British control before being de-colonized in the proper way. Renwick is certain that this gave Rhodesia the best start it could hope for as a properly independent country, but he also knew clearly at the time 'that Mugabe once in power was likely to turn out to be just as autocratic, just as tyrannical, just as dictatorial, as the White regime had been'.[89] During what has been called his 'triumphant ambassadorship' in South Africa (1987–91) Renwick helped to free Nelson Mandela from prison and end apartheid.

The move to Washington came when Britain and America were celebrating their victory in the First Gulf War, but the relationship soon came under strain. Renwick had to sort out the mess when it was inadvertently revealed that the Home Office had checked files to see whether the presidential candidate Bill Clinton had applied for a British passport in order to avoid the Vietnam draft. Then John Major became irritated with the Clinton administration's shifting attitudes to Northern Ireland. There were disagreements over Bosnia so serious that, in Renwick's view, NATO 'could have been in danger', and resolving them was almost his 'single most important task'. The Americans were criticizing the European forces for weakness but would not take any risks on the ground themselves. Renwick took the initiative by booking a meeting with Clinton, and eventually there was a change in policy.[90]

After four years as British ambassador when circumstances conspired to reduce the temperature of the so-called 'special relationship' to 'near freezing point' (Thatcher's phrase), the generous farewell dinners must have come as a relief. Colin Powell called him 'a remarkable ambassador'.

SIR MICHAEL O'DONEL BJARNE ALEXANDER (1936–2002)

A formidably intelligent and effective diplomat.
(*Daily Telegraph*)

The silver medal Michael Alexander won at the Rome Olympics in 1960 was for fencing, and his career in the Foreign Office was to be dominated by defence as well as East–West relations. His national service before going up to Cambridge was spent learning Russian and listening from Kiel to communications between Russian ships, and his first overseas posting was in Moscow. He was in Singapore from 1965–68, during the Vietnam War, and was soon convinced that the Americans were 'on a hiding to nothing'. In the course of one presentation, where he argued there was little danger of China's becoming involved in the war, an American colonel stood up and walked out, saying he would not listen to any more 'pink nonsense'.

Alexander's return to the Foreign Office in London required him to make as much sense as he could of allied nuclear policy and the 7,000 weapons spread around Europe. He played a key role in the complicated negotiations leading to the 1975 Helsinki agreement, a significant step towards the end of both the cold war and the Soviet Union. His final posting, as British permanent representative on the council of NATO in Brussels from 1986–92, turned out to be one of redirection for the alliance following the collapse of the communist threat. At Alexander's

last council meeting the Soviet ambassador, Afanasiev, was interrupted by a message. Upon reading it he removed the Soviet Union's nameplate from the table in front of him, explaining later it was 'because the Soviet Union has ceased to exist'. In Alexander's words, 'That was about as dramatic as it gets for a diplomat.'

Michael Alexander fencing. Unusually for this sport, he was left-handed and is therefore on the left of the photograph.
Courtesy Lady Alexander.

Michael Alexander with
Margaret Thatcher.
Courtesy Lady Alexander.

Between 1979 and 1982 he was diplomatic private secretary to the newly elected prime minister, Margaret Thatcher. At that time, he has observed, she was not expected to win a second term. What impressed him most was her unbelievable energy ('something all successful politicians seem to have') along with her 'excellent memory […] firm will and […] comprehensive set of prejudices'. Among the last, 'she was viscerally suspicious of the Germans'. At NATO he had to accept her lack of interest in building European cooperation and opposition to German reunification.

His most conventional diplomatic post was as ambassador in Vienna, 1982–86, although there too he was involved in negotiations between NATO and the Warsaw pact on mutual armed forces reduction, talks overtaken by subsequent events. Alexander spent three years planning a two-month-long 'Britain in Vienna' festival that took place just before he moved on to Brussels: a popular success, but politics again intervened, this time with the controversial election of Kurt Waldheim as president — suspicions about his war record led to a period of diplomatic isolation for Austria.[91]

SIR PAUL LEVER (1944–)

On 19 November 1990 Paul Lever was in Paris. As head of the Security Policy Department he had been involved in the final stages of preparing the Treaty on Conventional Armed Forces in Europe, signed that day by heads of state from NATO and Warsaw Pact members. It also happened to be the day the British prime minister, Margaret Thatcher, heard she had not won enough votes to be re-elected leader of the Conservative Party on the first ballot: three days later she announced her decision to stand down.

Much of Lever's distinguished civil service career was concerned with defence. He headed the United Kingdom delegation to the Vienna conventional arms control negotiations, 1990–92, and from 1994–96 he was head of the

Sir Paul Lever.

defence and overseas secretariat in the Cabinet Office and chairman of the Joint Intelligence Committee, responsible to the prime minister for co-ordinated intelligence assessment of issues affecting security, defence, foreign affairs and Northern Ireland. In this last role, one of his most interesting assignments was preparing a briefing paper for John Major, the prime minister who succeeded Thatcher, for a one-hour private meeting where he would educate President Clinton on the nature of the IRA. His final postings were as European Union and economic director in the Foreign Office and then six years as ambassador to Germany.

Lever is currently chairman of the Royal United Services Institute, a body founded by the Duke of Wellington for naval and military science which now studies all aspects of defence and security. His views are regularly sought on defence issues. In November 2007 he commented on detention centres such as Guantanamo Bay and their effect on the West's moral standing:

It has been very, very damaging. The best weapons we have in combating or at any rate mitigating and managing Islamist terrorism are our values, the values of liberalist democracy, of freedom, of tolerance, of the rule of law. That is how, to use the terminology, we will win the war. Military action plays an important part but it's a supporting role; it's by convincing young Muslims that the ideology with which they are sometimes tempted is fundamentally wrong and immoral. That's how we must hope to deal with the problem in our own society. And of course, if it seems that we or at any rate the United States, our closest ally, is failing to live up to those values, then it is very, very hard for us to promote them effectively.[92]

Co-author of 'Yes Minister'

SIR ANTONY RUPERT JAY (1930–)

'I am *fully* seized of your aims, minister, and of course I shall do my best to put them into practice.'

'If you would.'

'And to that end, I recommend that we set up an inter-departmental committee with fairly broad terms of reference. Then, at the end of the day, we will be in a position to think through all the implications and take a decision based on long-term considerations rather than rush headlong into precipitate and possibly ill-conceived action that might well have unforeseen repercussions.'

'You mean "no." '

(Yes Minister)

Between 1980 and 1988 Antony Jay and Jonathan Lynn wrote all thirty-eight episodes of *Yes Minister* and *Yes, Prime Minister*. In five series of satirical comedy the half-hour programmes traced the career of Jim Hacker MP (played by Paul Eddington), first as a cabinet minister and then as prime minister, as he struggled, and usually failed, to impose his will on his permanent secretary, Sir Humphrey Appleby (Nigel Hawthorne). Derek Fowlds played the third main character, Hacker's principal private secretary Bernard Woolley, who regularly hid behind verbal pedantry (a hallmark of the script, along with Appleby's elaborate syntax and Hacker's flights of pseudo-Churchillian rhetoric) as he tried to mediate between the other two. It was enormously popular with viewers and won several BAFTAs.

Video Arts Ltd was founded by Jay in 1972 to make comedy training films: its slogan today is 'humour with learning'. Some were devised with Lynn and featured John Cleese. With titles like 'How not to conduct a recruitment interview', and 'How not to appraise someone', they led naturally on to a series about how not to treat civil servants.

Yes Minister's novelty in Jay's view lay in the public's discovering a 'figure at the top of the civil service who was actually running the country, with the minister merely securing budget from the treasury and publicizing the department's activities'. He insists that fiction was never stranger than the truth:

We could never think up plots as funny as reality and one of the ones that looks a complete fantasy is about having a reception in an oil Kingdom in the desert and all having to be tee-total and Jim having the idea of setting up an emergency communications room where they could actually have lots of whisky to pour into the orange juice when they went in for urgent messages. That was based on an absolutely true incident.

In one episode they borrowed the Foreign Office's 'God Calls Me God' (GCMG) joke and paid it back with interest:

We had a phrase we invented for Bernard when Jim had a document that he thought was useless and Jim said, 'Well, what shall we do with it?' And Bernard said, 'Oh, er, let's CGSM it,' and Jim says, 'CGSM?' and Bernard says, 'Yes, Consignment of Geriatric Shoe-Manufacturers,' and Jim says, 'What?' and he says, 'Load of old cobblers, minister.' And CGSM is now appearing on civil service documents.

In *Doing the Honours* Hacker comments to Appleby, 'In private industry if you screw things up you get the boot; in the civil service if you screw things up I get the boot.' The series was undoubtedly cynical about the interaction of over-privileged civil servants and media-obsessed ministers, but politicians were among its keenest fans. It was apparently Margaret Thatcher's favourite programme: 'It's closely-observed portrayal of what goes on in the corridors of power has given me hours of pure joy.'[93]

Antony Jay in the prefects' photograph, 1947.
© *St Paul's School.*

Television reporters

(DAVID) JAMES MOSSMAN (1926–71)

To our left was a lagoon fringed with palm trees. Soldiers were swimming in the clear water, splashing one another and laughing like happy children. Some had climbed the trees and were hurling coconuts to their friends below. [...] It was a vivacious spectacle. It looked more like a school picnic than an armed invasion.

(James Mossman watching a beach-landing by government forces during the civil war in Indonesia)[94]

James Mossman committed suicide at the age of forty-four, leaving an enigmatic pencil note, 'I can't bear it any more, though I don't know what "it" is.' Round this note

Nicholas Wright wrote his play *The Reporter*, staged at the Cottesloe Theatre in 2007.

Mossman became a famous face working on *Panorama*

James Mossman, editor
and presenter of *Review*, a
new weekly television arts
programme, in 1969.
© *BBC*.

sion when Mossman condemned Prime Minister Harold Wilson in a studio interview for supporting American action in Vietnam. This was well before the age when confrontational interviews were not only acceptable but the normal pattern, and Mossman's behaviour was censured by the director-general. It did not stop him turning his fury later on the prime minister of Singapore for jailing his political opponents: 'Mossman's handling of the discussion last night was absolutely deplorable', read the director-general's memo. Since he was 'impervious to ordinary reprimands', he was moved away from the danger zone of front-line political interviews.[96] His final work for the BBC, curtailed by his sudden death, was a series of acclaimed discussions with figures in the arts.

Mossman worked in MI6 after graduating and he was always a secretive person. In researching his play Wright found that even close friends would say, 'You know, I'm not sure that I really knew him at all.' He was the funniest man the playwright Peter Shaffer ever knew,[97] but there was also a dark side, which Wright felt could go back to Vietnam, where he saw villages torched by US marines and a Buddhist monk set himself alight.[98] It seems that it was from him that Shaffer heard the story of a boy savagely blinding horses that led to *Equus* (see later entry). His Canadian lover Louis Hanssen died of an accidental overdose in 1968, and three years later Mossman took a fatal overdose of barbiturates himself. In his final television interview he had asked the philosopher Stuart Hampshire whether philosophy could help someone who was very unhappy.

in the 1960s, when the programme would regularly have ten million viewers. He reported for a time on the Vietnam War, an experience that gave new edge to his commentary: 'His account of life and death in a war-torn country was angrily humane.'[95] A key moment in *The Reporter* is Wright's reconstruction of the notorious occa-

JOHN CODY FIDLER SIMPSON (1944–)

I stepped forward into his path, microphone in the fixed-bayonet position, tape recorder running: 'Excuse me, prime minister.'

My entire world exploded. Wilson grabbed the shaft of the microphone with his left hand and tried to break it out of my grasp. With his right he punched me hard in the stomach. He was saying things to me, but I couldn't give them my undivided attention because I was too busy bending over and gasping. Wilson might not have much in the way of principle, but he certainly packed a punch. […] It was only five past eleven on my first working day, and I had been physically assaulted by the prime minister. My career was finished before it had begun.

(John Simpson)[99]

John Simpson, who is the BBC's world affairs editor, claims that hazardous moments are rare for television journalists, and there is always the temptation to use tricks to heighten the sense of menace: 'Whenever you are watching a television news report and there is a bang immediately followed by a television correspondent talking to camera, you know it's being done for effect. Especially if I'm the one doing it.'[100] Nevertheless, genuine danger has been a feature of his life. In Northern Iraq in 2003 a 1,000 pound

American bomb was dropped on the convoy of American special forces in which he was travelling, killing eighteen people including his translator and injuring both Simpson and his cameraman, Old Pauline Tom Giles. In 1979 he was flying to Tehran with Ayatollah Khomeini, who was about to launch a revolution and overthrow the Shah. It was announced in the plane that the Iranian air force were ordered to shoot it down. Simpson shrugged his shoulders and drank some coffee:

It wasn't that I didn't care whether I lived or died: I was thirty-four, and I had a wife and two daughters, and I wanted to live very badly indeed. But it wasn't going to be up to me. It would be up to a general with a lot of gold braid somewhere down below, and a pilot with his finger on the button of a missile.[101]

Simpson's journalistic experience is remarkable. He watched the Tiananmen Square massacre from a balcony and afterwards found he was woven into a videotape, distributed by the Chinese Embassy in London, as one of the sinister foreign elements who had manipulated the revolting students. In Baghdad a cruise missile passed the hotel window behind him as he was speaking. The hotel was directly over Saddam Hussein's underground bunker: 'So there we were, living and working a hundred feet or so above Saddam Hussein's head. We were his protection.' He evaded the Taliban's exclusion of journalists by wearing a blue burqa — 'it was just like putting on a cloak of invisibility'.[102] And of course, like James Mossman (see last entry) he incurred the wrath of Harold Wilson.

Apart from his unique knowledge and understanding, Simpson's reports are marked by their human interest, nowhere clearer than in the story of the end of the Berlin Wall:

And there was a strange echo, which turned out not to be an echo. When the men with the pick-axes paused, the hammering continued. There was a sudden upsurge of shouting and cheering, as we realized that someone was trying to break through from the other side. At last, by alternate strokes from East and West, another wound appeared in the Wall. In the candlelight a hand came through the little gap, and waved about; and the man with the pick-axe on our side grasped it and shook it. I had never thought anything of the kind was possible.[103]

Since joining the BBC in 1966, Simpson has interviewed more than 150 kings, presidents and prime ministers. Apart from his regular news reports, so often from trouble spots, he presents a current affairs programme, *Simpson's World*, seen in 200 countries. Among his many awards, he was twice named the Royal Television Society's Journalist of the Year. In 2002 he concluded an interview by saying:

I couldn't just sit in London — I think I'm now like the Flying Dutchman, condemned to travel for ever; my ghost will haunt BA flights. I think I'd be absolutely lost, actually, if I couldn't travel. My greatest fear is being one of those people who battens on to you at the Chelsea Arts Club or the Garrick and starts telling you what they used to do. I don't want to tell people what I used to — I want to die doing it. And, to be absolutely honest, if that meant a shorter life, I'd rather have a much shorter life.[104]

John Simpson fleeing the scene of a 'friendly fire' incident in Northern Iraq between Mosul and Kirkuk, where American special forces, Kurdish fighters and BBC film crew were killed and injured. *TX: BBC News 24, 6 April 2003.* ©*BBC screen grab.*

❧ *Gourmet, broadcaster and MP*

SIR CLEMENT RAPHAEL FREUD (1924–)

If you resolve to give up smoking, drinking and loving, you don't actually live longer; it just seems longer.

(Sir Clement Freud, 1964)[105]

Clement Freud was at St Paul's with Nicholas Parsons (see next article), appeared in the first episode of *Just a Minute* in 1967 and has taken part in every series since. He is the only surviving original panellist. Freud is renowned for his distinctive voice and deadpan delivery. He is a talented raconteur and appears to see his life as a sequence of entertaining anecdotes.

His grandfather was Sigmund Freud. At prep. school he recalls being sent to the headmaster to be beaten for talking in class: 'I [….] lay across the man's knees as he fondled my bum with his gnarled hand, whereafter he said, "I am not going to smack you because your grandfather would disapprove." '[106]

He served for a time as an aide to Montgomery, and was then posted to a war crimes investigation unit, where his taste for fine food got him into trouble. Posing as a general, he began requisitioning ducks from a local farm for the mess table. The mess quickly gained such a reputation for its cooking that detection and a court martial were inevitable.

It was soon after the Second World War that Freud became one of Britain's first celebrity chefs and opened a club in Sloane Square. Here he ran into the antiquated licensing laws that prohibited alcohol after midnight on Saturdays:

Very early one Sunday morning, after the midnight cabaret had finished and people were dancing, there was a panic phone call from the doorman to the receptionist announcing that half a dozen uniformed policemen were coming upstairs. She raced up to tell me. I dashed on to the floor, silenced the band and announced that tonight, to celebrate the fact that we had been open for two years and nine and a half months, we were, regardless of expense, presenting an additional floor show: please welcome the men from Gerald Road police station. As the assembled company began to applaud, half a dozen out-of-breath policemen [...] crashed into the restaurant. The applause increased in volume [...] The police asked members for their names and addresses; members told them not to overdo it. It was memorably chaotic. The Saturday drinking law was changed very soon after that.[107]

Freud was also becoming known for his journalism and for his television dog food advertisements, where he and a bloodhound with a similar hangdog expression shared the screen. He grew a beard in the hope of losing this image. Wanting 'something solid about which to be famous', he became a Liberal MP in 1973, serving for fourteen years. He was not expected to win the election and as a horse-racing enthusiast got Ladbrokes to give him odds of 33–1 against getting in: 'So Ladbrokes paid for me to have rather more secretarial and research staff than other MPs, which helped to keep me in for five parliaments.'[108] In 1978 he went with a more junior MP, Winston S. Churchill (Sir Winston Churchill's grandson), on a parliamentary delegation to China, but found that he was given a smaller suite at the Peking Palace Hotel. Asked to explain why, the Minister for Information said it was because Mr Churchill had a famous grandfather. In Freud's words, 'It is the only time that I have been out-grandfathered.'[109]

His other exploits have encompassed bobsleighing down the Cresta Run in St Moritz (copy for an article entitled 'The Ultimate Laxative') and sailing with Robin Knox-Johnston, where he discovered the culinary delight of new potatoes boiled in seawater: 'We drank our daily ration of wine, which I kept cool by trailing bottles behind the ship. Robin found me doing that, told me off for slowing us down. "Won't slow us down as much as drinking warm white wine," I said.'[110]

British Liberal Party MP Clement Freud, July 1978. *Photo by Evening Standard/Getty Images.*

🦎 *Actor and radio and television presenter*

(CHRISTOPHER) NICHOLAS PARSONS (1923–)

It's like going to a high-powered dinner party where you're in the company of very clever guests who are all trying to score points at the expense of each other but particularly at the expense of the host.

(Nicholas Parsons on *Just a Minute*)[111]

Nicholas Parsons has to his credit a long and remarkably versatile career as actor and presenter. He became a familiar figure on television in the 1960s as the straight man in a ten-year partnership with comedian Arthur Haynes:

If you analyse the sketches I am always the one who suffered the indignity or was put down. In most comedy partnerships, it is the comic who is always put down and the straight man provides the aggression. Somehow we had, without knowing it, reversed the roles. I played for sympathy and had laughs; the comic provided the aggression and had the big laughs.[112]

In the popular radio panel game *Just a Minute*, which Parsons has chaired ever since it began in December 1967, he has another and 'special kind of straight-man role, keeping the show moving and orchestrating all that takes place, as a good chairman should, while taking all the brickbats and insults that are thrown at me'.[113] His school

contemporary Clement Freud has appeared in every series.

From 1971–84 Parsons hosted from Norwich the Anglia Television quiz programme *Sale of the Century*. Despite some doubts from the critics, particularly about its unimaginative prizes, it too was a great popular success and on 22 December 1978 had 21.2 million viewers, the highest-ever audience for a television game show.

There is much more to Parsons than the television and radio presenter. He appeared in numerous comedy films in the fifties and sixties, including *Brothers in Law*, *Happy is the Bride*, *Doctor in Love* and *Carry on Regardless*. The West End stage has seen him in many roles: he starred for fifteen months in the farce *Boeing-Boeing* (1967–68) and was Narrator for the original London production of Sondheim's *Into the Woods* (1989–90). His aptitude for television drama was shown in the seventh *Doctor Who* series, *The Curse of Fenric*, where he played a Northumberland

Arthur Haynes and Nicholas Parsons (right) in a sketch from *The Arthur Haynes Show*, 1959.

vicar destroyed by vampires. At the age of seventy-one he discovered an unlikely new role in *The Rocky Horror Show*, reinventing the Narrator with an uninhibited cross-dressing routine. 'Some of the reactions I get from the young fans at the stage door when I come back after a performance of *Rocky* are, er, quite surprising,' was his enigmatic comment.[114]

Parsons is an enthusiastic and active supporter of children's charities. He has worked for the Lord's Taverners for forty-five years, serving as president in 1998 and 1999. The students of St Andrews University elected him as their rector in 1988: they went on to elect Sir Clement Freud in 2002. Versatile as ever in his mid-eighties, he continues to chair *Just a Minute*, appears at the Edinburgh Festival in 'The Nicholas Parsons Happy Hour', an interactive comedy show he has performed since 2000, and tours literary festivals with an evening on the life and work of Edward Lear.

❧ *Director and television presenter*

SIR JONATHAN WOLFE MILLER (1934–)

It's just that I think the world is very funny, and it's often funniest at the moments when it's most tragic and destructive and horrible [...] I see life as Samuel Johnson says Shakespeare did — as a world in which the reveller on the way to the bottle meets the mourner on the way to the grave, and the malice of one is undone by the frolic of another.

(Jonathan Miller)

'Few, if any, other directors have such a range of interests and breadth of experience,' wrote Jonathan Miller's biographer in 1992. 'Apart from being a theatre, opera, film and television director, he is also a doctor, neuro-psychologist, research fellow, lecturer, author, presenter and producer. [...] His productions embrace psychology, psycholinguistics, anthropology, sociology, [...] philosophy, [...] literature, photography, art and architecture.'[115]

Miller's father was a neurologist. Inspired by Sidney Pask's biology teaching at St Paul's (where study of evolution also made him a convinced atheist), he first trained as a doctor, but the stage quickly took over. It was 1961, and,

Jonathan Miller, bromide print by Geoffrey MacDomnic, 3 August 1954. *National Portrait Gallery, London.*

together with fellow Cambridge University Footlights star Peter Cook and two members of the Oxford University Revue, Dudley Moore and Alan Bennett, Miller brought *Beyond the Fringe* to London. It had opened at the Edinburgh Festival and toured the provinces without great acclaim, but now the show discovered a new metropolitan appetite for satire, running for a year in the West End before eighteen months on Broadway.

On Miller's return to England in 1964, there were new offers to distract him from a medical career. In his own words, he is 'pathetically susceptible to someone knocking on my door with a frisbee in their hand saying "Do you want to come out and play?"'[116] He became editor and presenter of the BBC's famous arts programme *Monitor*. Experience did not matter, he was told; he would pick it up as he went along. Two years later came his own innovative television adaptation of *Alice in Wonderland*, and in 1970 he was at the National Theatre, directing Sir Laurence Olivier as Shylock (reinterpreted as a Victorian businessman) in *The Merchant of Venice*. Many productions have followed, including twelve plays in the BBC Shakespeare cycle. Miller has turned his hand to directing opera. Not being able to read music does not stop him from shaking up opera house traditions.

The polymath and intellectual are ever-present in his productions. Miller likes to refresh a play or opera by casting it in a new, often controversial, light. He took *The Mikado*, set it between the wars in an English seaside hotel, and asked the *Monty Python* star Eric Idle to play Ko-Ko. 'I said to Jonathan, "What are you going to do with *The Mikado*?" He replied, "Well, I'm going to get rid of all that Japanese nonsense for a start." That just hooked me.'[117] One of his *Rigoletto* productions was set among the 1950s New York Mafia, and his *Tosca* in Mussolini's Rome as the allies advanced in 1944. Issues of race and imperialism prompted him to cast black actors as both Ariel and Caliban in *The Tempest* 'to see what would happen if I liberated Caliban from his fishy scales, and mythical monstrous identity, and made him monstrous simply in the eyes of those who arrive on the island'.[118] Charges of iconoclasm have only spurred Miller on. When attacked for cutting the first scene of *Hamlet*, he said, 'You can only vandalize an evening, you can't vandalize a play.'[119] In any case, he has little time for critics, dismissed as 'simply a chronic irritant', nor indeed for cultural shibboleths: he refused to work with Pavarotti — 'There's no point in trying to build a production around someone who's so massively inert.'[120]

Miller's medical knowledge has resurfaced in research fellowships and factual series for television, including *The Body in Question* (1978), which contained controversial footage of a body being dissected, and *States of Mind* (1983). It is not surprising to find Miller the atheist and scientist interviewing Richard Dawkins. His series, *Atheism, A Rough History of Disbelief*, was broadcast in 2004. He is president of the Rationalist Association.

Is he an optimist or a pessimist? He has identified with King Lear's 'atheistic pessimism' and yet finds life extremely amusing.[121] Perhaps he is primarily an observer. He recently described his 'preoccupation with the negligible, the things we do that are barely noticeable, but that make up our lives'.[122] According to John Cleese, cast by Miller in *The Taming of the Shrew*, 'He loves to watch what people do in those little private moments. What happens, for instance, if they trip over a paving-stone while they're walking along the street, and how they cover up this appalling damage that they've just done to their egos by then becoming angry with the paving-stone.'[123] The satirist and observer have also been observed and satirized, in *Private Eye* as a self-important reincarnation of Dr Johnson, 'Dr Jonathan', and on the television puppet show *Spitting Image* as an anteater.

❧ *Three playwrights*

ANTHONY JONATHAN SHAFFER (1926– 2001)
SIR PETER LEVIN SHAFFER (1926–)

Binky Beaumont, king of West End producers, rejected a new playscript from Anthony Shaffer in 1969: 'Everyone will know the trick within a week, dear, no one will keep quiet about that. It won't last a fortnight! Sorry.' The script was *Sleuth*, a highly ingenious reworking of the pre-war country house thriller, and it became one of only two straight plays to run for more than 2,000 performances, both in the West End and on Broadway — the other was *Arsenic and Old Lace*. Beaumont apologized by giving him a fine dinner a few years later. Shaffer recalled him saying you could never underestimate the British sense of fair play. *Sleuth* was twice made into a film. The 1972 version, directed by Joseph L. Mankiewicz and starring Michael Caine and Laurence Olivier, won four Oscars but missed the leading actor award as both actors were nominated and split the vote. The slimmed-down hi-tech 2007 version of *Sleuth*, with a new script by Harold Pinter, has disappointed.

Anthony Shaffer wrote several screen versions of Agatha Christie novels, but his main cinematic achievement was *The Wicker Man*, now a cult film, about strange supernatural activities on a Scottish island. It starred Edward Woodward and Christopher Lee. Shaffer was delighted when *Cinefantastique* called it 'The *Citizen Kane* of Horror Movies', and recently it was named by *Total Film* as the sixth greatest British film of all time.

Sleuth is set in the home of Andrew Wyke, a games-playing mystery writer. Anthony Shaffer loved puzzles and games. His addiction to practical jokes ('a legitimate extension of games-playing') was given a chapter in his autobiography, and the book's final pages, 'Death of a Blood Sport', lament the passing of the classic English detective story.[124]

As well as being a victim of his brother's practical jokes, Peter Shaffer co-authored with him two detective novels, *How Doth the Little Crocodile?* (1952) and *Withered Murder* (1955), under the pseudonym Peter Antony. Studying the structure of thrillers and detective stories, he said in 1992, was 'very, very valuable for a playwright',[125] and suspense and mystery are at the heart of *Equus*, first performed at the Old Vic in 1973 and revived at the Gielgud in 2007 with Daniel Radcliffe as Alan Strang, the disturbed boy who blinds a stable of horses. During the course of this play Dr Martin Dysart, a child psychiatrist, gradually uncovers the roots of the boy's behaviour by persuading him to re-enact what happened. Dysart, whose own life is

A scene from Sir Peter Shaffer's *The Royal Hunt of the Sun*, performed by the pupils of St Paul's School in 2005. The production was directed by Edward Williams. Design by Mamoru Iriguchi. *Photograph, M. Iriguchi.*

barren, finds in Strang a world of powerful religious and sexual awakening, focused on the god Equus, but fears that a cure will only 'return him to that rather neutered state of a lot of people in the modern world'. For all the play's theatrical brio, these ideas have not convinced critics. Reviewing the revival, Charles Spencer wrote of 'the play's absurd and dangerous psychobabble [...] in which we are asked to believe that the mentally ill are vouched an insight, and a passion, denied to the boringly sane'.[126]

Religion is also at the centre of *The Royal Hunt of the Sun* (1964), the conflict between Inca worshippers of the sun god in Peru and Spanish Catholics who invade in the name of religion and for their gold. An emblem of the sun dominated the first production, memorably so when the Indians were massacred at the end of act one:

It was all done as a huge mime of slaughter in which the Indians would die, and rise again, and again be slain, and finally, with this violent drumming and this terrifying noise of dying and slaughter, the entire cast of Indians raced to this gigantic sun at the back of the stage, and reached up and pulled out of the sun an enormous cloth of blood-red silk, so that the sun appeared to be vomiting blood all over the stage, and ululating and shrieking with these feathers on their heads and these wild gestures, they flung this across the stage, pegged it down, and then dashed out, and fled, up the aisles and away and disappeared. And all you saw was this — because of the air bubbling under the scarlet silk — you saw what appeared to be a lake of blood, bubbling. It was the most sinister and sickening and terrifying image.[127]

Peter Shaffer has also written several comedies, but his greatest success was *Amadeus*, a play depicting the co-existence in Mozart of God-given music and a boorish personality, and the jealousy of Salieri, an inferior composer who supposedly poisoned him. In its film version *Amadeus* won eight Academy awards.

PATRICK ALBERT CRISPIN MARBER (1964–)

Marber's is not a comedy of situation, but of wit and bleak irony.

(Peter Buse)

'My gravitational pull was towards solitude,' Patrick Marber said of his early years as a stand-up comedian, although it was also a way of conquering his own shyness.

He was fortunate to share the billing with Steve Coogan and Eddie Izzard and took the chance to enter the lucrative world of radio satire, co-writing and co-starring with

Coogan on the spoof chat show, *Knowing Me, Knowing You...with Alan Partridge,* a cleverly accurate caricature of an East Anglian radio host.

Solitude still beckoned, and one of Partridge's most avid fans, Richard Eyre of the National Theatre, provided the opportunity, supporting Marber as he wrote and directed *Dealer's Choice,* his first play, for the Cottesloe Theatre. This drama about a game of poker won the 1995 Evening Standard award for Best Comedy. For Marber it was also therapy. Before writing it he had been gambling away as much as £10,000 a night; he still played poker, but the losses were under control. Verbal economy is also a feature. Delete, he said, was his favourite key, and the dialogue is punctuated by 'ferocious and hilarious one-liners worthy of the finest stand-up'.

Dealer's Choice was an international success, as was *Closer* (1997), a tough comedy about the ugliness of sexual relations that won the Laurence Olivier award for best new play. Marber hinted that it too sprang from his own experience. A dark reworking of Noel Coward's *Private Lives*, it follows four characters whose business is bodies, an obituary writer, a stripper, a photographer and a dermatologist, as they change partners:

The idea was to create something that has a formal beauty into which you could shove all this anger and fury. I hoped the dramatic power of the play would rest on that tension between elegant structure — the underlying plan is that you see the first and last meeting of every couple in the play — and inelegant emotion.

A further study in self-destruction, *Howard Katz* (2001), featured a middle-aged show-business agent torn between deeper family values and the superficial world of television that provided his income. This play about judgment and redemption made less impact than his earlier successes. Other work includes *The Musicians* (a play written for young people in 2004), a modern reworking of Molière's *Don Juan* (2006) and the screenplay for *Notes on a Scandal* (2006), which earned Marber an Academy award.

His card-playing has continued. 'His is the definitive poker face,' writes another player, Anthony Holden, 'often hidden behind a plume of cigarette smoke.'[128]

Image from Patrick Marber's *Dealer's Choice,* performed by the pupils of St Paul's School in 2006. The production was directed by Tom Benyon. *Photograph, Lucy Barber.* © *St Paul's School.*

Michael Victor Codron (1930–), theatre producer. Photograph by Roy Jones, 16 June 1978. Codron has more than two hundred West End productions to his credit over a career of more than forty years. Orton's *Entertaining Mr Sloane,* Stoppard's *The Real Inspector Hound,* Mortimer's *A Voyage Round my Father,* Ayckbourne's *The Norman Conquests* and Frayn's *Donkey's Years* are among the many plays he introduced to London audiences. Several of his shows have run on Broadway, and he produced the film *Clockwise* (1986), starring John Cleese. *Evening Standard/Hulton Archive/Getty Images.*

🦂 *Grandmasters of chess*

JONATHAN SIMON SPEELMAN (1956–)
JULIAN MICHAEL HODGSON (1963–)

He's so good that if you can merely fail to lose against him you're doing well.

(Speelman on Kasparov)[129]

After an hour on the tube I felt as if I'd done a day's work. I'd come in sweating. It was disgusting. Then another hour going. No, it wasn't for me. So I've gone the other way, wearing track-suits, partly because I've put on so much weight that I can't get into any of my clothes. It's beer-drinking. It expands the gut.

(Hodgson on becoming a full-time chess player)[130]

Between the years 1978 and 2000 the British chess championship was won three times by Jon Speelman and four times by Julian Hodgson. Speelman's highest world ranking, fourth equal, came in 1989, the year he beat Kasparov on the way to winning a televised speed tournament. Hodgson played chess for St Paul's while still a Coletine and won the British Boys' U21 title at the age of fourteen. Once called 'the most charismatic of Britain's strong chess players', he has several open tournament victories to his name and in 2000, his best year, was half a point behind the leaders at the World Open.

Both players write about chess, but their styles are very different. Speelman has a doctorate in mathematics from Oxford, and his scholarly books include *Best Games 1970–1980* (1982), *Analysing the Endgame* and *Endgame Preparation* (both 1981). Hodgson's approach to writing is more exuberant, in keeping with someone who used to

bring his own executive chair to tournaments. His titles include *Attack with GM Julian Hodgson* (1996, 1997) and *Quick Chess Knockouts* (1996).

Speelman was called in as chess adviser on the film *The Luzhin Defence* (2000). He had to find games from about the year 1929 for use in the tournament, and junior games for Luzhin's simultaneous displays as a boy. More importantly, he needed to show actor John Turturro how to 'convey the emotions and body language of a chess-player under extreme pressure'.[131]

Asked whether he thought himself famous, Speelman replied, 'Not really no, happily not. If I were an Icelander I would be, if I were a Russian I would be, but in England certainly not.'[132] Hodgson is best known for his rediscovery of a forgotten way of opening chess games, the Trompowski Attack. He claims he adopted this out of laziness. He had a reputation for quick and destructive chess victories, and here he found an aggressive system that would obviate the need to learn a lot of conventional chess theory. It has been said that he put the 'romp' back into Trompowski.

Jon Speelman.
www.shropshirechess.org.

Julian Hodgson, captain of St Paul's chess team in 1981.
© *St Paul's School.*

Rowing blue

ALAN BURROUGH (1917–2002)

Burrough was a triple rowing blue at Cambridge. In 1937 and 1938 his boat was defeated by Oxford after thirteen consecutive victories. He attributed this to complacency and said that five-times Olympic medallist Jack Beresford's only contribution to the coaching was installing a beer barrel in the boathouse.[133] When he was elected president the following year, he persuaded his old school coach, Freddie Page, to return to Cambridge (he had trained the two victorious Oxford crews), and as a result Burrough's eight won by four lengths.

Burrough lost a leg in a tank battle after El Alamein but continued to row and remarkably came fifth in the 1947 European championship pairs at Lucerne. He became chairman of his family firm, James Burrough, makers of Beefeater gin, but never lost his passion for boats. His house faced the finishing line at Henley, and he purchased Temple Island, where the course began, in order to present it to the regatta. He was senior steward at Henley and organizer of the university boat race.

Burrough's horse Corbiere, registered in his son Bryan's name, won the 1983 Grand National. This made Bryan the youngest-ever owner of a Grand National winner, and Jenny Pitman the first woman trainer of a winner. Corbiere came third in both 1984 and 1985, a record surpassed in recent times only by Red Rum.[134]

Peter Kidner Stagg (1941–) playing in the Scottish lineout during a match against France. Stagg made twenty-eight appearances for Scotland. When first capped in 1965 he was said at 6 ft 10 in. to be the tallest man ever to play international rugby. Earlier in the century another Old Pauline, John Standish Cagney (1901–62), played for Ireland on thirteen occasions.

Wimbledon chairman

REGINALD EDWARD HAWKE (BUZZER) HADINGHAM (1915–2004)

You will be the first to admit that you do have, shall I say, a volatile temperament. My advice is that, whatever you may think of a linesman's or umpire's call, please keep your cool.

(Letter from Buzzer Hadingham to John McEnroe)[135]

Buzzer Hadingham retired as chairman of Slazenger, the sports equipment firm, in 1983 and spent the following six years as chairman of the All-England Lawn Tennis and Croquet Club, which hosts the Wimbledon championships. Tennis was in his blood. He was christened Reginald after Reggie Doherty, Wimbledon champion 1897–1900, and spent all his working life at Slazenger, joining straight from school when his father was managing director. His years running Wimbledon were ones of gentle modernization — introduction of yellow balls,

earlier starts to play, better facilities for television commentary — but it was also the John McEnroe era. The most celebrated event occurred in the pressroom in 1981, when Hadingham was on the Wimbledon committee but not yet chairman. Lady Diana Spencer was in the royal box (she would marry the Prince of Wales a few weeks later), and it was the year of 'you cannot be serious' from a highly temperamental McEnroe. The press box was swollen with Fleet Street news reporters, and McEnroe gave a conference after his bad-tempered semi-final

victory. When asked by a London reporter about relations with his current girlfriend, he launched a tirade against the press and stormed out, a move which triggered a press-room brawl between the British newsmongers and American serious tennis writers. The two ringleaders ended up on the floor and were sent separately to Hadingham for a reprimand. With supreme diplomacy he made both feel vindicated. Charlie Steiner of American RKO radio was offered a cup of tea and, in his view, thanked. Nigel Clarke, the *Mirror* tennis correspondent, remembers Hadingham saying 'he'd have done the same thing, but next time, old boy, do it in private'.[136]

John McEnroe during his match against Jimmy Connors at Wimbledon, 4 July 1980. Players' disputes came Buzzer Hadingham's way as member and then chairman of the Wimbledon committee. *Frank Tewkesbury/Evening Standard/Getty Images.*

❧ *Captains of industry*

MARCUS JOSEPH SIEFF, BARON SIEFF OF BRIMPTON (1913–2001)

Marcus Sieff began life in the family business of Marks & Spencer when he became a management trainee at the Hammersmith Broadway store in 1935, but the Second World War soon intervened. He served with the Royal Artillery, rising to the rank of colonel, and felt the experience taught him key management skills. It certainly proved his talent for organization. After the allies captured the port of Tripoli in January 1943, Sieff met Churchill:

He was complimentary about the speed with which the port was being put into working condition, despite the aerial bombardments. While I was flattered and delighted with what he said, I pointed out we had a lot to do to get the port working to anything like one hundred per cent and my people were weary. He said, 'Sieff, tell your men they are not unloading stores, they are unloading history.' I did so and the speed of unloading increased by twenty per cent.[137]

After the war he rose steadily through the managerial ranks, becoming chairman in 1972. One major achievement in his time was to make secret deals with manufacturers that bypassed the entrenched Wholesale Textile

Lord Sieff. *Kind permission of Marks & Spencer archive.*

Association. Sieff kept closely in touch with his suppliers and helped them to work more efficiently. It was boasted that ninety per cent of Marks & Spencer's goods were produced in Britain.

Sieff was also proud of his 'humans relations' policy: he wrote that 'the chief executive has a duty to treat his employees as he would like to be treated himself' and made sure that there were excellent facilities for his rapidly growing payroll, although some saw it as 'a system of enlightened paternalism that legitimized managerial authority'.[138]

The Sieff years saw the company become a blue chip investment and virtually a national institution. Margaret Thatcher shopped there when prime minister, and appropriately enough it was she who made Sieff a life peer in 1980.

LLOYD MARSHALL DORFMAN (1952–)

I guess there has to be something of the performer in you if you build a global business.

(Lloyd Dorfman)[139]

Under a scheme launched in 2003, tickets for the National Theatre and some of the best seats at the Royal Opera House have regularly been available for ten pounds each, thanks to sponsorship by Travelex Group, the company created by Lloyd Dorfman.

Travelex began life as a small currency exchange shop in central London in 1976: it is now the world's largest non-bank foreign-exchange business. Some of its most spectacular growth has come since the advent of the euro: while banks worried about the loss of business from individual European currencies, Dorfman concentrated on global expansion. In 2001 Travelex acquired Thomas Cook Global and Financial Services, a business three times its own in size. In 2005 he sold half his sixty-three per cent stake in the group to Apax, the private-equity company, for £348 million, although he remains chairman and chief executive.[140]

In 2007 Dorfman extended his involvement in the arts by becoming chairman of the Roundhouse Theatre, home of the BBC Electric Proms. He does not want this to become just another place for performance but to create a model that will be followed 'in other parts of the country and ultimately internationally too'.[141] He is on the board of the Prince's Trust and is a very even-handed sponsor of

Lloyd Dorfman.

cricket: he is a patron of Chance to Shine, a programme for promoting cricket in English state schools, and in 2007 he was given an 'Honorary Australian of the Year in the UK' award, partly for his support of the Australian cricket team and the Tsunami-aid world cricket match held in Melbourne.[142]

❧ *The chairman of Lloyd's in a crisis*

SIR (JOHN) DAVID ROWLAND (1933–)

Between 1988 and 1992 Lloyd's insurance market suffered unprecedented losses of £7.9 billion, much of it caused by high awards made in US courts on asbestos, pollution and health-hazard policies. David Rowland became its first full-time paid chairman (1993–97) and saw through a programme of 'reconstruction and renewal' that has enabled it to survive in a rapidly changing insurance world. Many members of Lloyd's or 'names' had to accept substantial individual losses, but a line was drawn separating claims on pre-1993 policies from subsequent business, and new members are now not permitted to assume unlimited liability for claims. Rowland went on to be chairman and chief executive of National Westminster Bank plc (1999–2000); from 1998–2003 he was president of Templeton College, now Green Templeton College, Oxford, a graduate institution for management studies.

Sir David Rowland.
© *Paul Leppard.*

❦ *A fraud case*

ERNEST WALTER SAUNDERS (1935–)

Repetition, as Goebbels taught, is one of the key elements of propaganda. You take emotive words like 'disgraced', 'theft' and 'steal' and pummel readers with them until they believe the message. It is insidious.

(Ernest Saunders)[143]

On 27 August 1990 Ernest Saunders, Jack Lyons, Anthony Parnes and Gerald Ronson, the so-called 'Guinness Four', were convicted on counts of fraudulent conspiracy, false accounting and theft, in connection with an illegal operation to boost the Guinness share price during its successful takeover bid for the Edinburgh company United Distillers four years earlier.

Before being appointed chief executive of Guinness plc in 1981, Saunders had managerial experience in Beecham and Great Universal Stores. He then became vice-president of Nestlé at a time when the company was under attack from the World Health Organization for marketing powdered milk in the third world, where it might easily be mixed with contaminated water and cause infant deaths. According to Kochan and Pym in *The Guinness Affair: Anatomy of a Scandal*,

For Nestlé, the powdered milk was an important new product, taking them into untried markets. A campaign was managed by Saunders, using public relations and media manipulation. Nestlé contributed $25,000 to a right-wing Washington research centre, which had commissioned *Fortune* magazine to write an article countering the WHO's campaign. The article was mailed to American churchmen who were seen as key 'opinion formers'.[144]

After a libel case Nestlé was awarded token damages and cleared of criminal responsibility for infant deaths, but advised by the judge to 'modify its publicity methods fundamentally'.[145]

One of his early moves at Guinness was another advertising campaign, featuring an empty glass and the slogan 'Guinnless isn't good for you'. It was not a success,[146] but overall Saunders's tough management (he was known as 'Deadly Ernest') and major strategic acquisitions 'revitalized Guinness, increasing its value on the stock market from £90 million to £3 billion' in five years.[147]

In its quest for control of Distillers, Guinness was aiming for a larger company than itself in the face of a hostile rival bid from Argyll Foods. It apparently boosted its share price illegally by paying other companies to buy Guinness stock and indemnifying them against loss should the price then fall.[148] The £2.6 billion buyout was at the time the biggest in British financial history.

From the start the Guinness affair was politicized. Saunders's failure to put Distillers directors on the new board angered the so-called 'Scottish mafia', and on 20 November 1986 an early day motion in the House of Commons accused him of breaking a promise to move the headquarters of Guinness-Distillers to Scotland, and called on the secretary of state for trade and industry 'to introduce measures to penalize severely companies and persons who pursue such blatantly dishonest practices to promote takeovers'. In Saunders's view he became a victim of the Thatcher government's wish to clean up the City's image after some scandals at the Lloyd's insurance market: 'I was not part of the Establishment, so an attack on me would not damage City credibility. I was considered to have achieved very big success too fast. I was very visible and totally identified with Guinness, making me the perfect fall-guy.'[149]

Saunders was dismissed, and arrested in 1987. His name became associated with City sleaze. *The Times* even ran an advertisement for the *Sunday Times* containing a picture of Boy George with the caption 'Coming Clean', and one of Saunders with the caption 'Playing Dirty'.[150] By September 1989, however, opinion was changing, and the *Mail on Sunday* felt that the forthcoming trial would 'add a quite unacceptable degree of suffering to a man already brought quite extraordinarily low by events which overwhelmed him'.[151]

Controversy did not end with the conviction. Saunders was sentenced to five years in prison but released on parole after ten months after the appeal court concluded that he was suffering from the incurable disease, Alzheimer's. The symptoms soon disappeared — Saunders said he 'was never diagnosed as having Alzheimer's'[152] and was suffering from a 'cocktail of tranquilizers and sleeping tablets'.[153] He has since worked as a consultant to Carphone Warehouse and for an American credit card company.

§ℓ *Three classical scholars*

SIR KENNETH JAMES DOVER (1920–)

I am told that as a baby I showed more interest in the columns of print on the front page of the newspaper than in the pictures. I certainly learned to read by the time I was three and vividly remember my horror, on my first day at school, when I was offered what I indignantly called 'a baby's' book to read. That is one thing which, if I could have my life over again, I would certainly not want to change.

(Sir Kenneth Dover)[154]

In 1985 Kenneth Dover was among those who successfully opposed Margaret Thatcher's receiving an honorary degree from Oxford University. There was great media interest in this decision, including a piece by Max Beloff (see earlier entry) in the *Daily Telegraph*, blaming Marxist agitators for leading unworldly dons astray and describing Dover as 'hitherto known to the public as the author of the standard work on Greek homosexuality'. This significant book, published in 1978, still carried with it a faintly disreputable air: it was not a subject to be lingered on by respectable classicists. However, it was and remains highly influential, affecting Michael Foucault's thinking in his *History of Sexuality* and many other books on related topics. It is no longer a risky subject of course; indeed, James Davidson in *The Greeks and Greek Love* (2008) attacks both Dover and Foucault for arguing from the limited perspective of a heterosexual culture.

Among Dover's other publications are learned commentaries and further books on Greek culture and history. The BBC television series *The Greeks* is said to have its origins in his classroom. In 1978 he succeeded Sir Isaiah Berlin (see earlier entry) for a three-year term as president of the British Academy, where he accepted Sir Anthony Blunt's resignation after his exposure as a spy. He was president of Corpus Christi College, Oxford, for ten years and chancellor of St Andrews University for twenty-five: his

Sir Kenneth Dover as chancellor of St Andrews University, *c.*2000.

successor is Sir Menzies Campbell, former leader of the Liberal Democratic Party. Dover still lives locally and is known as 'The Sage of St Andrews': in 2006 he was made honorary president of the university's student association.

MARTIN LITCHFIELD WEST (1937–)

At St Paul's School in London a legendary pair of teachers, W. W. Cruikshank and E. P. C. Cotter, concentrated on instilling in us a sense of Greek and Latin grammar and style. Week after week we translated passages of English prose and verse into Greek or Latin prose or verse, and our exercises were minutely and individually corrected and appraised. We also read authors, in class or by ourselves, but hardly saw beyond the meaning of the successive sentences and phrases.

(Martin West)

Martin West, now a fellow of All Souls' College, Oxford, has inherited a tradition of classical scholarship where, to quote his Oxford tutor Eduard Fraenkel, 'The text must come first'. He is cautious about secondary sources and has no time for the view 'fashionable in some quarters, that all interpretation of the past is necessarily subjective'. It is the classicist's task to discover the underlying facts as far as he can and build ideas from them. He is also wary of textual commentaries — it is easy for a particular point of view to be accepted out of inertia when what is needed is 'repeated independent evaluation'.[155]

Among West's fifteen major books are powerful

examples of how close investigation of original material has reshaped our view of the classical world. In *The East Face of Helicon*, 'an exciting vision of archaic Greece as an integral part of the wealthy, diverse and culturally rich contemporary Near Eastern world', he provides copious evidence to show the impossibility of studying Greek literature without knowledge of the West Asiatic.[156] True to his principles, he is cautious about speculating over how the cultural transmission took place: 'A corpse suffices to prove a death, even if the inquest is inconclusive' is his gnomic final sentence.[157] *Studies in the text and transmission of the Iliad* (2001) examines how entrenched views of

Greek epic have deceived scholars; in his controversial view the *Iliad* and the *Odyssey* are anonymous seventh-century works. *Ancient Greek Music* (1992) draws together an extraordinary mass of scattered evidence, but he is adamant that no scholar could ever reinvent lost melodies.

In 2002 the British Academy awarded West its Kenyon Medal for Classical Studies: 'In the field of classical scholarship, as traditionally understood, Martin West is to be judged, on any reckoning, the most brilliant and productive Greek scholar of his generation, not just in the United Kingdom, but worldwide.'[158]

PAUL ANTHONY CARTLEDGE (1947–)

Just by calling his lecture *What have the Spartans done for us?* Professor Cartledge showed how lightly he wears his impressive scholarship. It is not usual for an academic to borrow a title from the hilarious sketch in the film *Life of Brian* where a mock-serious, school-masterly John Cleese asks the assembled representatives of organizations of Judaean freedom fighters, "What have the Romans done for us?"

(Mark Dragoumis, *Athens News*, 28 March 2003, p. 40)

In 2001 Paul Cartledge, A. G. Leventis professor of Greek culture at Cambridge University, published an article on the inadequacies of the British general election as viewed from classical Athens. Not all his criticisms were to be taken solemnly, but he did observe in the final paragraph that Athenians 'live politics in a way you apathetic Britons simply could not begin to understand. Politics is not for us a separate sphere of activity, to be indulged in occasionally and for the most part reluctantly.'

Cartledge is a world expert on classical Athens and Sparta, about which he has published twenty-five books and eighty articles. Running through many of these is his belief that the classics belong in the modern world: 'The

Paul Cartledge.

contemporary historiography of war, placing less emphasis on battlefield manoeuvres than on the relationship between war and society, is especially appropriate for the history of ancient Greece.' But he also casts doubt in the same collection of essays (*Spartan Reflections*, 2001) on modern myths about liberated Spartan women: 'Readers [may] hesitate before seeking to enlist the women of ancient Sparta as allies in the just cause of feminism.'[159]

He has a talent for bringing scholarship to life. Cartledge's *Alexander the Great: The Hunt for a New Past* was called 'a book that combines the excitements of a soaring historical narrative with those of a subtle and deeply intriguing detective tale'.[160] It comes as no surprise that he was chief historical consultant for the BBC series *The Greeks* and the Channel 4 series *Spartans*. Regrettably, formal consultation over *300* (2006), a film of the battle of Thermopylae, was limited to advice on pronouncing Greek names, which was then ignored. Cartledge told an interviewer that he was entertained by the film despite its lack of veracity and, choosing his words carefully, labelled 'controversial' its portrayal of the Persians: 'They look a bit like the Teenage Mutant Ninja Turtles. The real emperor Xerxes was not a ten-foot-tall god-king with multiple piercings.'[161]

He is a member of the British Committee for the Reunification of the Parthenon Marbles but realizes that the problem will not be solved quickly: 'Reciprocal exchange is surely the only way forward.'[162] The president of Greece awarded Cartledge the Gold Cross of the Order of Honour of the Greek Republic in 2002, and two years later he was elected an honorary citizen of Sparta.

≈ *Neurologist and writer*

OLIVER WOLF SACKS (1933–)

There was a hint of a smile on his face. He appeared to have decided that the examination was over. He started to look around for his hat. He reached out his hand, and took hold of his wife's head, tried to lift it off, to put it on. He had apparently mistaken his wife for a hat! His wife looked as if she was used to such things.

(A case described by Oliver Sacks)[163]

Oliver Sacks.
© *Elena Seibert.*

Oliver Sacks was at school with Jonathan Miller (see earlier entry), where they both fell under the spell of biology teacher Sidney Pask. It's an intriguing coincidence that they have the similar middle names Wolf and Wolfe. For a time Sacks went by the name of Wolf. In 1960 he was a young doctor on holiday in Canada, decided to stay and hitchhiked down to California, where he worked first in San Francisco and then as a neurologist in Los Angeles. He met the motorcycle enthusiast and poet Thom Gunn, whose poem 'The Wolf Boy' haunted him. Sacks imagined for himself too a lycanthropic life where he took off for long, crazy rides into the moonlight.[164] This was the era of Jack Kerouac and the Beat Generation. Sacks also was a user of amphetamines. He would travel the continent on his bike or hitch lifts with truckers, and write 'through the day and night in fantastic bursts of energy'. He wanted to be another Freud or Darwin, bringing science and literature together. Hundreds of pages arrived on Gunn's doorstep — many of them chronicling the double lives of characters populating San Francisco's underground. He remains a compulsive writer; his autobiographical *Uncle Tungsten*, finally published in 2001, was originally more than two million words long.[165]

Sacks moved permanently to New York in 1965 and began a career of more than forty years as a neurologist at New York University School of Medicine and at Beth Abram, a hospital for the chronically ill, where he began work with patients still immobilized from the 1920s sleeping sickness. Sacks continues to link analysis to literature: 'My notes always have the quality of a narrative. […] to some extent I have to see someone as a story as well as a case, and a case as well as a story.'[166] His patients form the subject of popular books, to the extent that he was labelled 'the man who mistook his patients for a writing career'.[167] *Awakenings* (1973) inspired a play by Harold Pinter and a film starring Robert De Niro and Robin Williams; *The Man Who Mistook His Wife for a Hat* (1985) became an opera by Michael Nyman.

His stories are compelling. One essay describes how the impaired memories and recognition skills of a ward of aphasiacs and agnosiacs equipped them to see flaws in a speech by an unnamed actor-president normal observers

did not notice. Another describes his attempts to join in with twin autistic savants as they pass the time discovering very large prime numbers.[168]

Sacks is a skilled pianist and has successfully used music to help his patients. He received the Music Has Power Award for this work in 2000. In 2002 he was awarded the Lewis Thomas Prize, which recognizes the scientist as poet. He has received therapy himself twice a week for many years and has been prescribed anti-depressants, but finds writing the best cure: 'In fact my footnotes are my Prozac. I love writing them.'[169] Similarly, his success stories are the patients who have discovered new strengths within their disordered minds, such as the painter who could no longer see in colour but found working in black and white was even more satisfying.

Embryologist, writer and television presenter

ROBERT MAURICE LIPSON WINSTON, BARON WINSTON OF HAMMERSMITH (1940–)

Some people thought that when I dressed up as a pantomime dame to demonstrate the differences between the sexes, that was going too far. I didn't think so. And also, I've always wanted to play the part of a pantomime dame.

(Lord Winston, *Independent*, 17 October 2002)

Lord Winston.
Courtesy Imperial College, London.

Robert Winston describes himself as 'a medical scientist, who has spent his career fascinated with some of our most basic human instincts: the compulsion to reproduce'.[170] He has developed important new procedures in reproductive surgery, and during a long career at Hammersmith Hospital's infertility clinic he pioneered pre-implantation diagnosis, a method of screening embryos for genetic diseases. When he retired from Hammersmith as director of NHS research and development in 2005, Winston had been directly involved in the creation of several thousand lives that would not otherwise have existed. Even so, he thinks more of those couples he did not help:

No matter what people thought of me, and how they might have praised me or thanked me for what I was doing, what I was actually doing was trading in failure because two-thirds of the patients were not going to get pregnant.[171]

Winston has been honoured by many medical bodies, but he is no narrow clinician. He was brought up as a strictly orthodox Jew in a home that was otherwise refreshingly liberal and eccentric. His father, a diamond-cutter, would practise archery indoors, while his mother liked to go out tobogganing in the middle of the night. Conversation was uninhibited and intelligent: he was read Dante by his grandfather. Winston has taught his own grandson ancient Hebrew and Aramaic; he enjoys theatre, classical music, skiing and wine. He has even appeared on *The Archers* as a fertility consultant.

Reading in his twenties that most people are pigeon-holed as artists or scientists by the age of eighteen, he broke away from medicine for four years to produce plays professionally and win the Edinburgh Festival National Directors' Award in 1969 for Pirandello's *Each In His Own Way*. More recently, BBC television appearances and books have been the perfect media for Winston the scientist, doctor, theologian, performer and opponent of cultural divisions: 'The Sistine Chapel was painted by a man who was obsessed with that picture and was going to lie on his back for months on end getting exactly what he wanted. The scientist is quite similar.'[172] In *The Story of God* (2005) he has strong words for those scientists who attack faith:

Many people, including a considerable number of scientists, claim that a belief in God is harmful, citing in evidence the bitterness, damage, death and destruction that religion has caused throughout the ages. But this is rather like denigrating the pursuit of scientific investigation by reference to the amount of harm that has been done in developing terrible weapons and in damaging the earth's natural environment. We must not confuse religion with God, or technology with science. Religion stands in relationship to God as technology does in relation to science. Both the conduct of religion and the pursuit of technology are capable of leading humankind into evil; but both can promote great good.[173]

Running through his work is a fear of unthinking fundamentalists. As someone who respects religious principles, he was 'badly bruised' by the fierce reaction of some Christians to the 1984 legislation on embryo research. Winston received offensive letters and was attacked in the street: 'I have never forgotten the persistent lies that some religious people are prepared to make if they feel the means justifies the desired result.' He is equally opposed to scientific fundamentalists who accept no outside moral framework to their work, and to medicine founded on superstition: 'I have great difficulty, as do most responsible physicians, with medical practice which is based on magic, unsupported belief, pure ritual, or hare-brained theory.'[174]

Winston admits that IVF pioneers needed to be quite aggressive, arrogant and strong-minded to get their subject accepted, but shows his softer side in confessing nostalgia for the rabbits on which he experimented: 'People opposed to animal research don't understand the relationship between the animal and most researchers. It's very close. I had huge affection for the rabbits.' He used to assign his colleagues characters from *Winnie the Pooh*. Asked which character he was, he reflected, 'I suppose what I'm really saying is I'd like to be like Pooh.'[175]

❧ *The science of pain*

PATRICK DAVID WALL (1925–2001)

In the time-honoured tradition of physiologists, Wall often tested new procedures or therapies on himself before subjecting patients to them. It did not surprise his colleagues to see him arrive at work with two black eyes, following procedures to stimulate his own trigeminal sensory nerve electrically, in an attempt to block facial pain.

(The Times, 15 August 2001)

Pat Wall was at St Paul's when it evacuated to Crowthorne, where he found in Tony Barnett a remarkable biology teacher who 'knew nothing of teaching, deplored discipline, and decided to use his very considerable intelligence to reason with us'.[176] Wall was to spend his life as a medical scientist fascinated by ideas and firmly anti-authoritarian in outlook.

The key moment in his career came in 1960, when he was a professor at the Massachusetts Institute of Technology and met the Canadian psychologist Ronald Melzack, with whom he developed a radical new theory of pain. Wall was puzzled by the traditional view that pain was directly related to tissue damage. It did not explain how wounded soldiers continued fighting on the Anzio beaches and felt pain only when the action was over. Nor did it explain pain for which there was no detectable physical cause. Wall and Melzack argued that pain signals had to pass through what they called a gate in the spinal cord which controlled the size of the signal reaching the brain and could even block it off completely. Emotions and beliefs emanating from the brain could also affect the gate and influence pain signals. These ideas were at first treated with scepticism but are now fully accepted and have led to important new treatments, including spinal epidurals and changes in physiotherapy.

Wall was a gifted communicator who could readily hold a large audience at a scientific lecture without using slides. His books bring the subject to life with memorable examples, the woman with a phantom pain in the ring finger of her amputated hand who was cured by marriage counselling, the decorated soldier with a fear of pain:

I was assigned to take a blood sample from a massive sergeant-major in the Guards with the Military Medal ribbon on his tunic. Unwisely, I sat him upright in a chair and knelt in front of him to insert a needle in an arm vein. As the blood entered the syringe, he fainted and collapsed on top of me. I learnt two lessons: that one should stand to one side of a vertical patient, and that bravery depends on the situation.[177]

He was willing to use himself as an example, illustrating pain responses on television by plunging his forearm into a bucket of iced water, and movingly in his final book, *Pain, The Science of Suffering* (1999), written while he was treated for terminal cancer.

Wall liked those who were in his words 'witty, world-wise, opinionated, argumentative, iconoclastic, intolerant to fools, and original to the level of eccentricity', and he ran his research group with a stress on democracy and individuality.[178] He was a left-winger throughout his life and ready to speak his mind, condemning for example the use of rubber bullets in Northern Ireland. He even wrote a novel, *Trio, the Revolting Intellectuals' Organization* (1965).

❧ *Three retirements*

MAGNUS ALFRED PYKE (1908–92)

Whereas ordinary lecturers of my scientific standing, reluctantly agreeing to address a local branch of the British Association of Young Scientists, could after high tea in the canteen of the local polytechnic, expect to do their speaking in a half-empty lecture theatre, I could expect to find the canteen kitchen staff asking for my autograph and the lecture moved to the main hall to accommodate the crowd.

(Magnus Pyke on the effects of television fame)

The Pye Colour Television award for the most promising male newcomer to television in 1975 was presented to Magnus Pyke. He was sixty-six years old at the time and had recently retired from managing the Distillers Company's research station. With his spectacles, overex-cited speech and wild gestures, he fitted his viewers' image of the eccentric scientist and jumped at the opportunity of bringing scientific ideas to life for a mass audience. His demonstration of friction involved:

a row of four boys on a level platform, one standing on a buttered surface, one on an oiled surface, the third on banana skins and the fourth on dry wood. I would wind a handle which gradually tipped the platform at an ever-increasing angle. Crash goes boy on the banana skins, bump falls the boy on the lubricating oil, next, after a period of staggering, the feet of the boy on the butter fly from under him, leaving the boy on the bare boards steady to the last.

Behind the humour lay a longstanding belief in the importance of science in everyday life. Pyke had published several books on food technology and gave much of his time to the British Association for the Advancement of Science. He was never conventional. Science lessons at St Paul's 'seemed so remote from reality', but as a boy he enjoyed the challenge of making crystal radio sets. His first significant broadcast was a radio talk on insect-eating: 'To think of Queen Ranavolona II keeping a band of women whose sole function was to collect insects so that the royal table at Tananariva should never run short seemed to me so bizarre a sidelight on nutrition that the British public should be informed on the matter.' He even managed to weave a good measure of science into his frantic appearances on *Just a Minute*.

Pyke was undoubtedly surprised by his fame and how it was built on his gestures as much as his genius. He was probably wise to make his second career a brief one and retire from broadcasting in 1980.[179]

ADMIRAL SIR JOHN DEVEREUX TREACHER (1924–)

I had been in naval uniform for nearly thirty-five years. It was time for a change.

(Admiral Sir John Treacher)

John Treacher joined the navy in 1942. He was on HMS *Glasgow* during the landings on Omaha beach and after the war trained as a pilot in the Fleet Air Arm before flying in the Korean War. His subsequent flying, sea and staff appointments in the Royal Navy make impressive reading. From 1962–64 he was naval assistant to the near-legendary Admiral Le Fanu, third sea lord and controller of the navy. In 1968 he followed in Le Fanu's footsteps as captain of the *Eagle*, one of the two largest aircraft carriers to be built (the other was the *Ark Royal*). A series of high staff positions followed, culminating in his appointment in 1975 as commander-in-chief of the fleet and NATO commander-in-chief Channel and E. Atlantic. At the age of fifty-two he surprised many by retiring from the service, but his working life was certainly not over.

After a spell with National Car Parks, Treacher was summoned in 1981 by Hugh Hefner to his Beverley Hills headquarters, Playboy Mansion West, and took over responsibility for casinos in the UK and the Bahamas. His predecessor, Victor Lowndes, famous for his flamboyant lifestyle, had antagonized the Gaming Commission, and the organization was in danger of losing its licences for two large London casinos. There was also a very public feud with Ladbrokes to resolve. Treacher's appointment fascinated the press, who featured him in many cartoons. It was worlds away from the formality of the navy. Hall porters were able to introduce members to clubs virtually at whim, and players expected their cheques to be honoured without hesitation. In the event, the Gaming Commission refused to accept that matters had been

Admiral Sir John Treacher, cartoon by Mahood, *c.*10 July 1981. Treacher had just been recruited by Hugh Hefner to Playboy Enterprises.
© *Solo Syndication and Associated Newspapers Ltd.*

improved sufficiently by Treacher's reforms, and Hefner decided to abandon his UK business.

The excitements of retirement did not end there. As a former naval aviator Treacher had the experience to become executive director of Westland Helicopters, and in 1984 he was vice-chairman, just in time for the so-called Westland affair. This turned on whether the American company Sikorski or a European consortium would partner Westland in developing a new Lynx helicopter, and came to symbolize the Thatcher government's divided attitude to Europe and the USA. Public and acrimonious ministerial disagreements led to the resignation from the cabinet first of Michael Heseltine, defence minister, and then of the trade and industry secretary, Leon Brittan. The partnership with Sikorski went ahead.[180]

IAN McCOLL, BARON McCOLL OF DULWICH (1933–)

There is a high morale on the ships and the atmosphere in the theatre is hilarious. You get withdrawal symptoms when you leave.

(Lord McColl)[181]

Ian McColl is a former professor of surgery at Guy's Hospital. Since retirement in 1998 much of his time has been dedicated to Mercy Ships, an international Christian charity providing urgent surgical care in poor and developing communities. He is chairman of Mercy Ships UK and vice-president of the international board.

Most of the charity's work is in Africa, where its ships dock for months at a time. They are equipped with theatres and wards, and the volunteer staff, all of whom contribute to the costs, willingly work long hours every weekday. Among the commoner cases are eye surgery, huge goitres and enlarged thyroid glands. The charity performs life-changing operations common in developed countries but not available to the African poor more used to relying on local witch doctors: 'When people have cataracts they try to cure them by hitting the patient on the head repeatedly with a stick.' McColl speaks of the team's high morale ('It is like the NHS was forty years ago with a matron and things running smoothly') and adds, 'Over the years I have been involved in many charities, but there has never been one quite like Mercy Ships, which allows me to practise my profession of surgery under ideal circumstances for

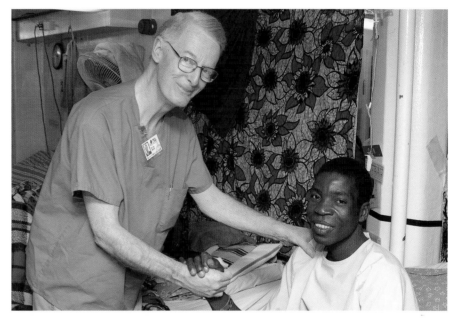

Lord McColl at work with the charity Mercy Ships.

people who are in desperate need and poverty.'[182]

McColl was made a life peer in 1989 for his work with disabled people. From 1994–97 he was parliamentary private secretary to the then prime minister, John Major. In opposition he became a shadow minister of health.

❧ A legal record

SIR NICHOLAS FELIX STADLEN (1950–)

In May 2005 Nicholas Stadlen QC sat down at the Royal Courts of Justice in London having completed the longest speech in legal history. He was opening the defence case for the Bank of England, which was being sued for £850 million by liquidators of the collapsed bank BCCI. His 119 day exposition beat an eighty-day speech record set by the prosecution's introduction in the same case. Twenty-two Bank of England officials, it was alleged, had made errors and omissions and knowingly endangered depositors' savings. The trial had been delayed for years while lengthy disputes over document disclosure went to the Court of Appeal and House of Lords. In the event the liquidators abandoned their action later in 2005, giving Stadlen his most memorable experience as a lawyer — 'being hugged by the governor of the Bank of England'.[183]

On 28 September 2007 Stadlen became the final high court judge to be announced under the existing appointment system.

SIR NIGEL COOPER THOMPSON (1939–)

Among the extraordinary range of projects in many countries involving Nigel Thompson during his forty-five year career with Ove Arup and Partners (consultant engineers, planners and project managers) are hospitals, theatres, offices, airports, arts buildings and universities. Several of his assignments in England in particular are strikingly innovative in their solution of unusual engineering problems.

In the 1960s and 1970s he worked on the Manchester Royal Exchange Theatre. This was built within the old corn exchange. Because the floor could not support the weight of a theatre and audience, it was constructed within the building as a seven-sided glass-walled module suspended from the original massive columns holding up the hall's central dome. With 700 seats it is Britain's largest theatre in the round and attracted much interest and critical praise when it opened in 1976.

Thompson was responsible for the design and construction of several major London office buildings. Two of these make bold use of air space. Embankment Place was built above Charing Cross Station. Eighteen columns rise through the station platforms to support the arch from which the office floors are suspended. This meant that work could proceed without interrupting services to the busy terminus station and isolated the offices from railway vibration. Alban Gate on London Wall is another air-rights structure, with a massive tower built over huge round arches spanning the street. The architects for both projects were Terry Farrell and Partners. At Britannic House the challenge was to rebuild the interior of BP's grand headquarters in Moorgate while retaining Edwin Lutyens's lavish façade.

In 1999 Thompson led a United Kingdom public and private sector task force for the reconstruction of Kosovo, and eighteen months later a similar force for Serbia and Montenegro. He received a knighthood for this work and his contribution to international trade. He retired from Ove Arup as non-executive deputy chairman in 2003, becoming chairman of the Campaign to Protect Rural England. He is currently chairman of the project steering group for redeveloping St Paul's School.[184]

The Royal Exchange Theatre, Manchester.
Courtesy Ove Arup Partnership.

Embankment Place.
Courtesy Ove Arup Partnership.

🐌 *Film costumes and sets*

ANTHONY MENDLESON (1915–96)

It had to look terribly old […] it had to look grand and imposing but theatrically gaudy, worn but not tatty. We had to make it from scratch, brand new. We ended up using real cobra skins and appliquéing them to the costume with very theatrical jewels […] His hat started with the snake idea. I got a skin and stuffed it and stuck it on this hat vaguely reminiscent of a bishop's mitre, gave the snake jewelled eyes and…*voilà!*

(Mendleson's conjuring costume for Sir Ralph Richardson in *Dragonslayer*)[185]

Anthony Mendleson was chief costume designer at Ealing Studios in its golden years. Among the films he worked on were *Whisky Galore* (1948), based on the story by Old Pauline Compton Mackenzie (see chapter five), *Passport to Pimlico* (1949), *Kind Hearts and Coronets* (1949), *The Lavender Hill Mob* (1951), *The Man in the White Suit* (1951) and *The Titfield Thunderbolt* (1952). When the studios closed in 1959 he moved to Pinewood, where he worked for Richard Attenborough and Roman Polanski. He showed Polanski the crown he had designed for his controversial film of *Macbeth* (1971), only to be told: 'I want the crown of a king, not a carnival crown.' Mendleson went to a sweet shop and decorated it with silver sweet papers. Polanski was delighted. 'This is wonderful, Tony, wonderful,' he said. Perhaps his biggest challenge was *Dragonslayer* (1981): the entire population of a sixth-century British kingdom had to be clothed, from the king right down to the poorest peasant.

SIR KENNETH (KLAUS HUGO GEORG FRITZ) ADAM (1921–)

Who is the real star of James Bond? Sean Connery? Roger Moore? The answer is Ken Adam.

(*Independent*, 21 November 1999)[186]

Ken Adam was production designer for seven James Bond films between 1962 and 1979. It was his imagination that conceived the films' command centres and villains' bases. He was influenced by the German expressionist art he saw as a child (the family emigrated to England in 1934), and Adam set out to make the villains' surroundings reflect their megalomania, at the same time adding a characteristic touch of humour. *Thunderball* (1965) features a chair which disappears beneath the floor, carrying a man who had betrayed Spectre, and then comes up empty. Looked at now, his futuristic interiors seem to epitomize the gloss and confidence of sixties modernism.

Adam's work for these films came before the age of computer graphics. In *You Only Live Twice* (1967) the villain plans a space launch from inside a volcano, requiring the construction of a sliding fibreglass lake 120ft above the ground on the back lot of Pinewood Studios. It had to cope with a helicopter flying inside and two hundred stuntmen sliding down ropes from the top, but that for Adam gave the film a realism no computer-generated images could ever achieve. In *Goldfinger* (1964) Adam discovered that a fantasy version of a vast gold repository was more acceptable and believable to the public than what Fort Knox probably looks like inside […] When the film came out United Artists received three hundred letters — mostly irate — asking how a British film unit and a British director were allowed to shoot in Fort Knox when even the American President is not allowed in. It was a great compliment.[187]

His other work includes the 1972 film version of Old Pauline Anthony Shaffer's sinister thriller *Sleuth* (see earlier entry) and Kubrick's *Dr Strangelove*: Adam thought its claustrophobic darkened war room was his most successful set because everybody became part of it. Ironically, his two Oscars were for untypical period films, *Barry Lyndon* and *The Madness of King George*.

SPECTRE's work crews inside the volcanic space station are alerted to the impending arrival of a helicopter. Set designed by Sir Ken Adam for *You Only Live Twice*, 1967.
Courtesy Eon Productions.

Film writers, directors and producers

CHRISTOPHER JOHN WEITZ (1969–)

Chris Weitz on the set of *The Golden Compass* (2007) with Nicole Kidman.

Chris Weitz is the younger son of Old Pauline John Weitz (see earlier entry). Chris Weitz and his brother Paul were two of the three scriptwriters for an unconventional animation film *Antz* (1998). Steering away from the Disney tradition, it is in effect a political allegory embedded in an anthill with a remarkable cast, including Woody Allen, Sharon Stone, Jennifer Lopez and Sylvester Stallone. The film is enlivened by some neat cinematic allusions and was successful both with the critics and viewers. A year later the brothers made their débuts as director and producer with the teen sex comedy *American Pie.* The film's humour was a telling mixture of Paul's all-American education and Chris's exposure to the more ironic worlds of St Paul's and Trinity College, Cambridge.

The Oscar-nominated film *About A Boy* (2002) was their next major venture. This recounts the sensitive story of a man who invents an imaginary son in order to have affairs with single mothers, but runs into trouble when a young misfit with a suicidal mother starts to regard him as a father figure. At first its star, Hugh Grant, thought the Weitz style would not suit the film, then he met them: 'They have a hugely juvenile humour streak, but they're also these scholarly, erudite guys. I've never worked with directors who read Trollope between setups.'[188]

Another turn in Chris Weitz's career came with *The Golden Compass* (2007). Working apart from his brother now, he directed the film and wrote the adaptation himself from the first part of Philip Pullman's trilogy, *His Dark Materials*, having rejected a previous screenplay by Tom Stoppard. He has called this the most important work in his life. Though very different from his previous films, it is one his English literature degree at Cambridge prepared him to undertake. He sees it as

> an enormously well-conceived parallel-world fable with bearing on the world in which we live and the issues that affect our lives as children, parents, and individuals in society. It is full of profound meanings, wisdom, and intellect. It requires an approach that is at every point cognizant of those strengths.[189]

The film received a mixed reception from the press, one critic accusing Weitz of taking 'the "supermarket sweep" approach to adapting the book', but by the end of February 2008 it had grossed more than $260m outside North America and won an Oscar for its special effects.[190]

Weitz's latest project was directing a screen version of investigative reporter Neil Strauss's first novel, *The Game: Penetrating the Secret Society of Pick-up Artists.*

OLIVER TOM PARKER (1960–)
BARNABY DAVID WATERHOUSE THOMPSON (1961–)

In 1995 Oliver Parker directed his own film adaptation of *Othello.* He already had varied experience as a stage, film and television actor (he played Mark Calder, one of the regular characters in the medical soap opera *Casualty,* from 1993–94). He did not fight shy of altering Shakespeare's text: 'To present the plays in their entirety would be a disservice to Shakespeare. I'm sure if he were alive today, he'd be radically reworking the text for a new medium, and would most likely want to direct it.'[191] Parker rewrote dialogue and rearranged scenes 'to make it youthful and passionate' and create 'an erotic thriller'.[192]

Barnaby Thompson worked on television documentaries before a spell in the United States co-producing comedy shows such as NBC's *Wayne's World.* Back in England he was on the production team of *Spice World* (1997).

The two joined forces in the late nineties for glossy films of Oscar Wilde's *An Ideal Husband* (1999) and *The*

A scene from the film *St
Trinian's*, co-directed by
Oliver Parker and Barnaby
Thompson, 2007.
Courtesy Ealing Studios.

Importance of Being Earnest (2002), both produced by
Thompson and adapted and directed by Parker. The
actress Cate Blanchett (Lady Chiltern) thought Parker's
version of *An Ideal Husband* preferable to the stage play:
'He's found the balance between the heightened wit of
Wilde and naturalism.'[193] *Earnest*, which had to compete
with Anthony Asquith's famous 1952 version starring
Dame Edith Evans as Lady Bracknell, was an adaptation
too far in the eyes of many critics, with tattoos on
Gwendolen, a hot-air balloon and flashbacks.

In 2000 Thompson led a consortium which acquired
Ealing Studios. After their heyday immediately after the
Second World War, the studios had been used by the BBC
for twenty-five years, and the new owners set out to revive
their film-making tradition. It was at Ealing that the
Parker and Thompson team co-directed *St Trinian's*
(2007), a film that combines the former's taste for traditional English settings with the latter's interest in girl
power. Peter Bradshaw of the *Guardian* dismissed it as
'dated, humourless and crass' but the *Daily Telegraph's* critic
commented, 'Anyone caught crying "Sacrilege" at the St
Trinian's remake has suffered a sense-of-humour failure',
and *The Times* thought it 'a spiky topical joy'.[194]

As this book goes to press, the two are directing and
producing *Dorian Gray*, a film based on the Oscar Wilde
novel.

A recent view of the fifth school and Hammersmith Bridge from the air. © *St Paul's School.*

Afterword

RISING STARS OF THE TWENTY-FIRST CENTURY

John Colet's Children concludes not with a full chapter but glimpses of old pupils whose achievements have come in the first few years of the new century. The youngest are still in their early twenties, the oldest is a remarkable centenarian.

James Kenneth Richard Clarke (1984–) rowing stroke for the St Paul's first eight in 2003. He rowed in the winning boat at the world championship fours in both Lucerne and Munich during 2007. © *St Paul's School.*

Simon John Dennis (1976–). In 2000 he won a gold medal for rowing in the victorious British eight at the Sydney Olympics.

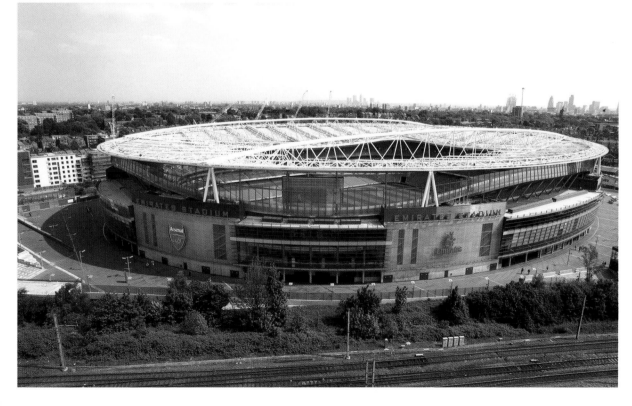

The Emirates Stadium. Daniel David Fiszman (1945–) began supporting Arsenal football club at the age of six. He made a fortune in diamond trading and was in the news in 2007 as the driving force behind the club's vast new stadium. *Arsenal Football Club.*

🪶 *Ministers in waiting*

GEORGE GIDEON OLIVER OSBORNE (1971–)
EDWARD HENRY BUTLER VAIZEY (1968–)

Chancellor and shadow chancellor: George Osborne (right) and Alistair Darling prepare for an interview with Andrew Marr.
Courtesy georgeosborne.co.uk.

Ed Vaizey playing cricket.

These two Old Paulines present unique problems as they may well have assumed high government office shortly after the book's publication, rendering out of date anything other than a brief account of their careers so far.

George Osborne joined the Conservative Research Department in 1994 and was speech writer and political secretary to William Hague during his four years as opposition leader (1997–2001). He was elected MP for Tatton constituency in 2001, succeeding Independent MP and broadcaster Martin Bell, who had unseated Neil Hamilton in 1997. He became shadow chancellor of the exchequer following the 2005 election.

Ed Vaizey has established himself as a freelance political commentator. Trained as a barrister, he directed a public relations company before working for the opposition leader, Michael Howard, as his chief speechwriter in 2004. He was returned as MP for Wantage in 2005 and made shadow culture minister in November 2006. Vaizey is president of Didcot Football Club.

🪶 *Editor of The Times*

JAMES PAUL HARDING (1969–)

One of the most outstanding British journalists of his generation.
(Robert Thomson, former editor of *The Times*)[1]

In December 2007 James Harding became the seventh editor of *The Times* since Rupert Murdoch bought the paper in 1981. His boss is Murdoch's son James, who assumed an expanded role as chairman and chief executive of News Corp Europe and Asia at the same time.

Harding, who speaks both Chinese and Japanese, began his career as speechwriter in the office of Japan's chief cabinet secretary, Koichi Kato. He spent twelve years working at the *Financial Times* — he opened its Shanghai bureau and saw through the paper's expansion in North America — before joining *The Times* as business editor in 2007. He is renowned for his energy and ambassadorial talent. One colleague at the *Financial Times* commented, 'He is very good at doing things well that he doesn't know anything about.'[2]

Harding is interested in widening opportunity. He has mentored schoolchildren in Southwark and while at the FT set up *justdosomething.net*, a charity 'encouraging people to take an active lead in public life'.

❧ *Novelist*

PATRICK WILLIAM THOMAS NEATE (1970–)

I am really obsessed with stories.[3]

In 2001 Patrick Neate's New Orleans' novel *Twelve Bar Blues* was a surprise winner of the Whitbread Novel Prize beating Ian McEwan's *Atonement*. Among many enthusiastic reviews, the *Guardian* summed it up as 'a genre-crossing peach of a fiction that neatly intertwines raucous tales of post-colonial Africa with lives of turn-of-the-century American prostitutes and jazz musicians.' His work includes three other novels. Neate sees *The London Pigeon Wars* (2004) as his 'most thematically and philosophically ambitious'.[4] This book interleaves a story of young Londoners ('twirtysomethings') with an outbreak of violence among the pigeon community: Geoffrey Wansell of the *Daily Mail* commented, 'Not since the publication of the late Anthony Burgess's *A Clockwork Orange* forty-one years ago have I come across a novel as adventurous and unexpected.' Neate believes in literary diversity and set up a 'storytelling salon' for writers and singers with Old Pauline Benjamin Brian Thomas Watt (1962–). Ben Watt is one half of the pop duo *Everything But the Girl*, which recorded nine albums between 1982 and 2000 and, with the refrain 'And I miss you, like the deserts miss the rain' from the single 'Missing', experienced worldwide stardom in 1994.

Patrick Neate. *Nick Cunard.*

❧ *Grand Theft Auto*

TERENCE JOHN DONOVAN (1971–)
DANIEL LOUIS HOUSER (1973–)
SAMUEL LEIGH HOUSER (1971–)

Grand Theft Auto IV is a violent, intelligent, profane, endearing, obnoxious, sly, richly textured and thoroughly compelling work of cultural satire disguised as fun.

(Seth Schiesel, *New York Times*)

On 29 April 2008 Rockstar Games launched the video game Grand Theft Auto IV. It was a phenomenal success, selling about six million copies in its first week, and HMV attributed a twenty-five per cent increase in profits, despite the economic difficulties of summer 2008, largely to its sales of the game.

Rockstar was founded by Sam Houser (now the company's president) with the help of his brother Dan and Terry Donovan. Dan Houser is creative director, and co-writer of the latest game. Terry Donovan looked after the marketing and business side of the company until 2006. Well over 100 million copies of its games have been sold altogether. Grand Theft Auto III, Vice City and San Andreas were each in turn the most successful

Niko Bellic in Liberty City,
screenshot from Grand
Theft Auto IV.
Courtesy Rockstar Games.

video games ever to be sold in the United Kingdom.

The Old Pauline founders set out to take video games to a more sophisticated audience, and a mark of their success is that this greater sophistication is now accepted as normal. The company's latest product has been praised for its 'pungent script', 'mastery of street patois' and 'richly, lusciously dystopian rendition of New York City in 2008'. The game echoes the world of mafia films and incorporates 'plot development, character depth and moral ambiguity'. *The Times* described it as a 'five-star interactive drama'.[5]

In its various incarnations Grand Theft Auto has many dimensions and has won plaudits from many quarters for its creative ingenuity. The company has received 'about ten' BAFTA awards, five of them from 2004, the first year they

were presented for games. Even so, there are some for whom the violent elements overshadow everything else. Hillary Clinton thought it was 'stealing the innocence' of American children, and criminals have claimed to be inspired by the game, including a gang of teenagers who went on a two-hour crime spree on Long Island in June 2008. Dan Houser's view is clear: the game contains nothing that cannot be found readily in films or television shows:

These are works of fiction. Playing a game that features violence is no different from choosing to see a violent movie. We're not trying to create a 'here's real life' sensation in a video game; it's 'you're the star of a movie. We want to re-create the sensations you have watching movies.' We're putting those in a video game.[6]

❧ *The Stage*

RORY MICHAEL KINNEAR (1978–)
NEIL ANTHONY AUSTIN (1972–)

He enters issuing a flurry of 'ciao' and 'tais-toi' into his mobile, waggling — 'woo, woo' — his fingers at his companions, mimicking the uncorking of a champagne bottle. Names — 'I knew a French count so like you' — drop from him like clouds of scent; he displays the tassels on his jeans, sleeves and shirt as if he were showing off prize pets.

(Susannah Clap, *Observer*, 11 February 2007)

Rory Kinnear's National Theatre début as Sir Fopling Flutter in *The Man of Mode* was called the comic performance of the year and won him the 2008 Olivier award for Best Performance in a Supporting Role. Son of the comedian Roy Kinnear, whose acting mannerisms older

members of audiences continue to discover within his own performances, he settled on a stage and screen career shortly after studying English at Oxford. He likes a varied diet. As a child Kinnear imagined he might become a decathlete, and he is attracted by the equivalent challenge

in different acting assignments. Recent roles include Dennis Thatcher in a BBC drama, a key part in the twenty-second James Bond film, *Quantum of Solace,* and starring in the National Theatre's *The Revenger's Tragedy.* The critics enthused about this last performance, Paul Tyler describing him in the *Independent* as 'our fastest-rising classical actor'. Kinnear is evasive about his ambitions. Actors, he says in a typically self-deprecating manner, are 'rather like a chef in a restaurant: you are only as good as your last meal'. He has confessed that another childhood dream was to become a butcher and claims, if we can believe him, to hold out a hope of playing Sweeney Todd: 'That could be the perfect marriage of my ambitions.'[7]

The Man of Mode was lit at the National Theatre by Neil Austin, whose lighting designs for plays, musicals, opera and dance have an international reputation. Among others, he has worked for the Donmar Warehouse, Royal Shakespeare Company and Royal Ballet. Austin's lighting of *Thérèse Raquin* at the National Theatre in 2007 was nominated for a Laurence Olivier award.

Rory Kinnear in *The Man of Mode*, Olivier Theatre, 2007. Lighting by Neil Austin. © *Johan Persson.*

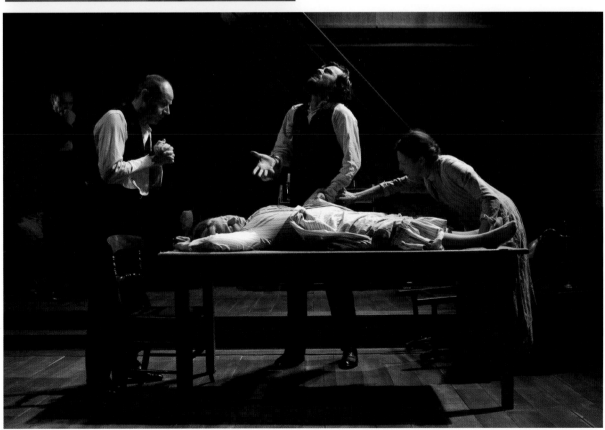

Final scene of Ibsen's *The Wild Duck*, Donmar Warehouse, 2005. Lighting by Neil Austin. © *Johan Persson.*

♫ *Two musicians*

ROBIN TICCIATI (1983–)
JOHN CLAUDE MYERSCOUGH (1982–)

Robin Ticciati. *Silvia Lelli, reproduced by kind permission of Askonas Holt.*

John Myerscough.
Simon Tottman.

Robin Ticciati began conducting under the guidance of Sir Colin Davis and Sir Simon Rattle when he was just fifteen years old and a member of the National Youth Orchestra. In 2005 he was the youngest-ever conductor at La Scala in Milan, and in 2006 the youngest début conductor in the history of the Salzburg festival. He became music director of Glyndebourne on Tour in 2007: his first appearance at the festival, performing *Così fan Tutte*, was called 'a demonstration of how to conduct Mozart'.[8] His London orchestral début in April 2008 at the Queen Elizabeth Hall with the Orchestra of the Age of Enlightenment was described by Neil Fisher of *The Times* as 'impressive' and 'galvanizing'. He is already in his third year as music director and artistic adviser to the Gävle Symphony Orchestra in Sweden, and the 2008–09 season sees his first appearance at the Royal Opera House, Covent Garden.

John Myerscough is cellist with the Doric String Quartet, which won first prize at the 2008 Osaka International Chamber music competition. He was awarded the gold medal and first prize at the Royal Overseas League competition in 2006. Of his Wigmore

Hall solo début in 2007 Hilary Finch wrote in *The Times*, 'It was only seconds before it was clear that here was a musician of quick, finely honed responses and firm, focused tone [who] artfully alternated song and virtuoso landscape.' The Doric Quartet regularly performs at Wigmore Hall and is much in demand for concerts both in the United Kingdom and abroad. Myerscough has also given solo recitals in Singapore, New Zealand and Australia. He is a fellow of the Guildhall School of Music and Drama.

Christopher Charles Surrey (1907–). The myth that James Solas Dodd (see chapter four) lived to 104 was believed by few, but Charles Surrey certainly achieved a unique record when he attended the Old Pauline annual dinner in 2008 at the age of 101. © *Paul Leppard.*

Appendix

THE HIGH MASTERS OF ST PAUL'S SCHOOL

(*left*) Arms of the Gill family featuring owls and a salamander. This was probably drawn in preparation for the armorial glass that decorated the great hall at Waterhouse's school in West Kensington. Alexander Gill (1596–1642?) was an Old Pauline. © *St Paul's School.*

(*centre*) Richard Roberts, bust by Joseph Nollekens. Roberts (*c.*1729–1823) 'went through all the classes' at St Paul's before going up to Jesus College, Oxford, in 1746. He was the school's longest-serving high master.

(*right*) Richard Stephen Baldock (1944–), oil by Stella Murray Whatley, 2004. The most recent Old Pauline high master.

William Lily   1509–1522
John Ritwise   1522–1532
Richard Jones   1532–1549
Thomas Freeman   1549–1559
John Cook   1559–1573
William Malym   1573–1581
John Harrison   1581–1596
Richard Mulcaster   1596–1608
Alexander Gill, Senior   1608–1635
Alexander Gill, Junior   1635–1640
John Langley   1640–1657
Samuel Cromleholme   1657–1672
Thomas Gale   1672–1697
John Postlethwayte   1697–1713
Philip Ayscough   1713–1721
Benjamin Morland   1721–1733
Timothy Crumpe   1733–1737

George Charles   1737–1748
George Thicknesse   1748–1769
Richard Roberts   1769–1814
John Sleath   1814–1837
Herbert Kynaston   1838–1876
Frederick William Walker   1877–1905
Albert Ernest Hillard   1905–1927
John Bell   1927–1938
Walter Fraser Oakeshott   1938–1946
Robert Leoline James   1946–1953
Anthony Newcombe Gilkes   1953–1962
Thomas Edward Brodie Howarth   1962–1973
James Warwick Hele   1973–1986
Peter Pilkington   1986–1992
Richard Stephen Baldock   1992–2004
George Martin Stephen   2004–

Notes

(These notes comprise a list of sources. For this reason there is no separate bibliography. Given the large range of material, multiple references to the same source within one entry have sometimes been gathered together as a single note.)

CHAPTER ONE

1 *Life and Works of Thomas Lupset*, ed. John Archer Gee, London: OUP, 1928, p. 282
2 Sir Michael McDonnell, *The Annals of St Paul's School*, Privately Printed, 1959, p. 55
3 ed. Gee, 1928, p. 197
4 Michael F. J. McDonnell, *A History of St Paul's School*, London: Chapman and Hall, 1909, p. 76
5 ed. Gee, 1928, p. 211
6 N. P. Sil, 'Sir Anthony Denny: a Tudor servant in office', *Renaissance and Reformation*, new ser., 8 (1984), p. 196
7 David Starkey, *The Reign of Henry VIII: Personalities and Politics,* London: Vintage, 2002, pp. 136, 141 (first published 1985)
8 J. Ponet, *A short treatise of politike power*, Amsterdam: Theatrum Orbis Terrarum, 1556 (New York: Da Capo Press, 1972)
9 P. R. N. Carter [http://www.oxforddnb.com/view/article/20300, accessed 14 July 2007]
10 Camden miscellany (BL Ac 8113/39) p. 22. Next quotation, p. 102
11 Sybil M. Jack [http://www.oxforddnb.com/view/article/21121, accessed 10 February 2008]
12 G. R. Elton, *Tudor Revolution in Government,* CUP, 1953, p. 312
13 James P. Carley[http://www.oxforddnb.com/view/article/16416, accessed 2 July 2007]
14 Leland, *The Itinerary of John Leland in or about the years 1535–43,* ed. Lucy Toulmin Smith, London: Bell, 1907–10, I, p. 142 (Bath), II, p. 53 (Wressel), III, p. 86 (dropping well), IV, p. 50 (Dover)
15 Translation by Simon May of original Latin ('duo continua Regna: Angliam, fertilio terri, urbibus frequentiorem, et magis morigerata: ac Scotiam, asperiorem et ob frigus infertiliorem.')
16 W. C. Richardson, *Stephen Vaughan Financial Agent of Henry VIII,* Louisiana State University Studies 3, Baton Rouge, 1953, p. 53
17 Ian Blanchard [http://www.oxforddnb.com/view/article/11505, accessed 1 February 2008]
18 Richardson, 1953, p. 21
19 Ann Saunders, *The Royal Exchange*, London: Guardian Royal Exchange, 1991, p. 12
20 Ian Blanchard [http://www.oxforddnb.com/view/article/28146, accessed 15 March 2008]
21 Rudyard Kipling, letter to E. V. Lucas, quoted in Thomas Tusser, *Five Hundred Points of Good Husbandry*, notes Daniel Hilman, London: James Tregaskis, 1931 edition
22 Quoted in Edward S. Creasy, *Memoirs of Eminent Etonians with Notices of the early History of Eton College*, London: Bentley, 1850
23 Tusser, 1931 edition, vv.112, 124; *A Hundred Points of Good Husbandry*, London: R. Tottel, 1557, vv. 97–99
24 Glyn Parry [http://www.oxforddnb.com/view/article/12453, accessed 28 June 2007]
25 Holinshed, *Chronicles,* London 1587, I, pp. 168 (diet), 172 (dress)
26 Wyman H. Herendeen [http://www.oxforddnb.com/view/article/4431, accessed 12 February 2008]
27 Camden, *Britannia*, London: Gibson, 1695 edition, pp. 707 (Halifax), 302 (Southwark)
28 *Laneham's letter describing the magnificent pageant presented before Queen Elizabeth at Kenilworth Castle in 1575*, London: J. H. Burn, 1821 edition, title page. Quotations from Laneham are to be found in this edition, pp. 42, 89, 29–31

29 H. R. Woudhuysen [http://www.oxforddnb.com/view/article/16002, accessed 10 February 2008]
30 Sir Michael McDonnell, *The Annals of St Paul's School*, Privately Printed, 1959, p. 81
31 Richard Bauckham [http://www.oxforddnb.com/view/article/10224, accessed 25 June 2007]
32 W. Fulke, *A Brief Confrontation of a Popish Discourse Lately set forth, and presumptuously dedicated to the Queen's most excellent Majesty: by John Howlet, or some other bird of the night, under that name*, London: T. Dawson for G. Bishop, 1581, p. 12
33 Edmund Campion, *Two Bokes of the Histories of Ireland*, p. 26, in Ware, *The Historie of Ireland, etc.*, pt. 2, 1633 (first published 1571)
34 Michael A. R. Graves [http://www.oxforddnb.com/view/article/4539, accessed 8 January 2008]
35 [http://www.catholic.com/thisrock/1994/9409clas.asp, accessed 25 September 2007]
36 Michael F. J. McDonnell, *A History of St Paul's School*, London: Chapman and Hall, 1909, p. 134
37 Susi Jeans, Watkins Shaw. 'Mudd, John; Mudd Thomas' [http://www.grovemusic.com, accessed 12 July 2007]
38 *Purchas His Pilgrimes*, Glasgow: James MacLehose, 1905, IX, p. 412
39 Michael F. J. McDonnell, *A History of St Paul's School*, London: Chapman and Hall, 1909, pp. 118–19
40 *Purchas His Pilgrimes*, 1905, IX, pp. 416, 437
41 John Westby-Gibson [http://www.oxforddnb.com/view/article/5041, accessed 9 July 2007]
42 Pliny, *Natural History*, Book XXXI, ch. 46
43 Lionel Charlton, *History of Whitby*, York: A. Ward, 1779
44 Charles Singer, *The Earliest Chemistry Industry*, London: Folio Society, 1948
45 Thomas Chaloner, *A Shorte Discourse of the most rare and excellent virtue of Nitre, wherein is declared the sundry and diverse cures by the same effected, and how it may be as well received in medicine inwardly as outwardly plasterwise applied: serving to the use and commodity as well of the meaner people as of the delicater sort*, London: Gerald Dewes, 1584
46 D. J. B. Trim [http://www.oxforddnb.com/view/article/28209, accessed 25 February 2008]
47 *The Commentaries of Sir Francis Vere, Being divers Pieces of Service, wherein he had command ; written by himself, in way of Commentary.* Cambridge 1657, in *An English Garner, Stuart Tracts 1603–1693*, Westminster, 1903, pp. 101 (Zutphen), 157 (Nieuwpoort)

CHAPTER TWO

1 M. E. Williams [http://www.oxforddnb.com/view/article/9391, accessed 10 August 2007]
2 Barten Holyday, *A Survey of the World in Ten Books*, Oxford: 1661, p. 141. Next quotation, p. 144
3 Sir Michael McDonnell, *The Annals of St Paul's School*, Privately Printed, 1959, p. 123
4 Barten Holyday, *Technogamia*, ed M. Jean Carmel Cavanagh, Washington: Catholic University of America Press, 1942, quoted in introduction
5 Linda Phyllis Austern, *Music in English Children's Drama of the Later Renaissance*, Philadelphia: Gordon and Breach, 1992, p. 212
6 Ravenscroft, *Pammelia*, London: William Barley, 1609, 'To the Reader'

7 Ravenscroft, *A Brief Discourse*, quoted in Austern, 1992, pp. 148, 217. Next quotation, p. 180

8 David Mateer/Ian Payne [http://www.grovemusic.com, accessed 11 September 2007]

9 Menna Prestwich, *Cranfield. Politics and Profits Under the Early Stuarts*, OUP, 1966, pp. 54, 56, 84

10 Prestwich, p. 230

11 Michael J. Braddick [http://www.oxforddnb.com/view/article/6609, accessed 28 October 2007]

12 Aubrey, quoted in Michael F. J. McDonnell, *A History of St Paul's School*, London: Chapman and Hall, 1909, p. 185

13 Gordon Campbell [http://www.oxforddnb.com/view/article/10730, accessed 28 October 2007]

14 Sir Michael McDonnell, *The Registers of St Paul's School, 1509–1748*, London: S.P.S. 1977, pp. 117–22

15 A. H. Mead, *A Miraculous Draught of Fishes*, London: James and James, 1990, p. 34

16 William Gouge, *Of Domestical Duties*, eight treatises, London: William Bladen, 1622, p. 389

17 T. Gouge, 'The life and death of Dr Gouge who dyed *anno Christi* 1653,' in *A collection of the lives of ten eminent divines*, ed. S. Clark (1662), London: Millere, 1662, p.105. Next quotation, p. 102

18 Henry Finch, *The World's Great Restoration or The Calling of the Jews*. See Brett Usher [http://www.oxforddnb.com/view/article/11133, accessed 28 October 2007]

19 Richard Cumberland, *de Legibus Naturae*, London, 1672, II, p. 20

20 Sarah Hutton [http://www.oxforddnb.com/view/article/6885, accessed 27 October 2008]

21 Nathaniel Culverwell, *An Elegant and Learned Discourse of the Light of Nature*, ed. Greene and MacCallum, University of Toronto Press, 1971, pp. 110–11

22 Nathaniel Culverwell, *An Elegant and Learned Discourse of the Light of Nature with several other Treatises*, London, 1661, p. 7. Next quotation, p. 74

23 Culverwell, ed. Green and MacCallum, p. 48

24 Culverwell, 1661, pp. 155, 175

25 Thomas Hobbes, *Leviathan*, London: A. Crooke, 1651, p. 84

26 John Parkin, *Science, Religion and Politics in Restoration England: Richard Cumberland's de Legibus Naturae*, Woodbridge: Royal Historical Society, 1999, p. 185

27 Richard Cumberland, 1672, V, p. 34; quoted Parkin, 1999, p. 201. Next quotation, I, p. 21, quoted Parkin, 1999, p. 100

28 *The Diary of Samuel Pepys*, 11 vols., ed. R. Latham and W. Matthews, London: Bell and Sons, 1970–83, II, p. 62 (29 March 1661)

29 A. H. Mead, *A Miraculous Draught of Fishes*, London: James and James, 1990, p. 39

30 Latham and Matthews, II, p. 109 (29 May 1661)

31 Latham and Matthews, IX, p.126 (22 March 1668)

32 Sir Michael McDonnell, *The Registers of St Paul's School, 1509–1748*, London: S.P.S. 1977, p. 196; Latham and Matthews, V, p. 356 (25 December 1664)

33 Latham and Matthews, VII, p. 235 (5 August 1666)

34 Latham and Matthews, VIII, p. 118 (18 March 1668), VIII, p. 56 (7 February 1668)

35 Latham and Matthews, I, p. 280 (1 November 1660)

36 Latham and Matthews, V, p. 37 (4 February 1664)

37 Latham and Matthews, III, p. 254 (10 November 1662), IV, p. 333 (13 October 1663), V, p. 221 (25 July 1664), VI, p. 145 (3 July 1665)

38 *Paradise Lost*, II, ll. 496–502

39 *Brief Lives by John Aubrey*, ed. Richard Barber, London: Folio, 1975, p. 208

40 *Paradise Lost*, VII, ll. 25–27

41 Anna Beer, *Milton, Poet, Pamphleteer and Patriot*, London: Bloomsbury, 2008, p. 25

42 R. B. McKerrow, 'A Publishing Agreement of the Late Seventeenth Century', *Library*, 4th ser., 1933, p. 186

43 *Brief Lives*, 1975, p. 210

44 *Paradise Lost*, I, ll. 25–6

45 [http://www.christs.cam.ac.uk/darknessvisible/critics.html, accessed 23 January 2008]

46 Blake, *The Marriage of Heaven and Hell*, 1793, ¶ 22

47 *Paradise Lost*, XI, ll. 743–45

48 F. R. Leavis, *Revaluation*, London: Chatto and Windus, 1936, p. 53

49 Stanley E. Fish, *Surprised by Sin, The Reader in Paradise Lost*, London: Macmillan, 1967

50 Robert Bell, *The Cabinet Cyclopaedia, Biography, Eminent Literary and Scientific Men, English Poets*, London: Longman, 1839, II

51 Quotations from Anthony à Wood, *Fasti Oxonienses*, A New Edition, London, 1820, IV, pp.377–80

52 Thomas Manley's translation, quoted in David Norbrook, *Writing the English Republic*, CUP, 1999, p. 234

53 *The Diary of Samuel Pepys*, 11 vols., ed. R. Latham and W. Matthews, London: Bell and Sons, 1970–83, I, pp. 200, 209 (July 14 and 28, 1660)

54 C. W. Upham, *Lectures on Witchcraft*, Boston: Carter, Hendee and Babcock, 1831, p. 213

55 John Wagstaffe, *The Question of Witchcraft Debated*, 2nd edition, 1671, p. 65 (first published 1669). Next quotation, p. 146

56 Upham, 1831, p. 214

57 Anthony à Wood, *Athenae Oxonienses*, A New Edition, London: 1817, III, p. 1114

58 *Brief Lives*, 1975, p. 129

59 Quoted in Colin A. Ronan: *Edmond Halley Genius in Eclipse*, London: MacDonald, 1970, p. 149

60 Alan Cook, *Edmond Halley, Charting the Heaven and the Seas*, Oxford: The Clarendon Press, 1998, p. 3

61 *Biographia Britannica*, quoted in Ronan, 1970, p. 8

62 Flamsteed in the *Philosophical Transactions*, quoted in Cook, 1998, p. 53

63 First Minute Book of the Royal Society, quoted in Cook, 1998, p. 183

64 Newton, *Philosophiae naturalis principia mathematica*, translated A. Motte, London, 1729, I, Prefatio

65 Ronan, 1970, p. 163

66 Sir Michael McDonnell, *The Registers of St Paul's School, 1509–1748*, London: S.P.S. 1977, p. 284

67 Letter to Sir Tancred Robinson, 8 July 1692, [http://www.coleopterist.org.uk/, accessed 5 March 2008]

68 Charles E. Raven, *John Ray, Naturalist*, CUP, 1942, p. 206

69 Philos. Trans. 1699, XX, p. 376

70 Miller Christy, 'Dr Benjamin Allen (1663–1738) of Braintree: A forgotten Essex naturalist' in *Essex Naturalist*, XVI, 1911

71 Gilbert Abbott A'Beckett, John Leech, *The Comic History of England*, London: Bradbury, Evans and Co., 1848, p. 236

72 Montgomery Hyde, *Judge Jeffreys*, London: Butterworth and Co., 2nd edition, 1948, p. 5

73 Edward Foss, *Biographica Juridica. A biographical dictionary of the Judges of England from the Conquest to the present time 1066–1870*, VII, London: 1870, p. 226

74 Charles Dickens, *A Child's History of England*, Oxford Illustrated Dickens, OUP, 1958, p. 522

75 State trials, VII, p. 138, quoted in Paul D. Halliday [http://www.oxforddnb.com/view/article/14702, accessed 27 October 2007]

76 *Bishop Burnet's history of his own time*, 2nd edition, OUP 1833, III, p. 61, quoted in Hyde, 1948, p. 228

77 Quoted in Hyde, 1948, p. 99

78 Quoted in G. W. Keeton, *Lord Chancellor Jeffreys and the Stuart Cause*, London: Macdonald, 1965, p. 478

79 Keeton, 1965, p. 479

80 [Samuel Johnson], *Julian the Apostate, being a short account of his Life*, London: Langley Curtis, 1682, p. 39

81 George Hickes, *Jovian, or an Answer to Julian the Apostate*, London: S. Roycroft for W. Kettilby, 1683, pp. 1–2

82 *Julian*, 1682, p. 47

83 Information from Melinda Zook [http://www.oxforddnb.com/view/article/14916, accessed 27 October 2007]

84 See Melinda S. Zook, *Radical Whigs and Conspiratorial Politics in Late Stuart England*, Pennsylvania University Press, 1999

85 Roger North's life of his relative the lord chief justice, quoted in James Alexander Manning, *The Lives of the Speakers of the House of Commons*, London: George Willis, 1851, p. 384

86 *Burnet's history*, IV, p. 76

87 BL, Lansdowne MS, 507, fol. 40

88 Thomas Babington Macaulay, *The History of England from the Accession of James II*, London: Harper and Brothers, 1856, p. 433

89 12 March 1695, Journal of the House of Commons: XI, 1693–1697 (1803), pp. 265–271. [http://www.british-history.ac.uk/ report.aspx?compid=39126, accessed 28 November 2007]

90 Journal of the House of Commons: XI, 16 March 1695

91 Sir Michael McDonnell, *The Registers of St Paul's School, 1509–1748*, London: S.P.S. 1977, p. 255

92 Thomas Babington Macaulay, 1856, p. 433

93 Eustace Budgell, *Memoirs of the Life and Character of the late Earl of Orrery and of the Family of the Boyles*, London: W. Mears, 1732, p. 247

94 Budgell, p. 158. Next quotation, p. 159

95 *The Works of Richard Bentley, D.D.*, ed. A. Dyce, London: Macpherson, 1836, I, pp. ix–x

96 Lawrence B. Smith [http://www.oxforddnb.com/view/article/ 3124, accessed 15 July 2008]

97 Budgell, 1732, p. 222

98 Will, PRO, PROB 11/646, fols. 241–2

99 'Judicial Puzzles – Spencer Compton's Case', reproduced in *Eclectic Magazine of Foreign Literature, Science and Art*, New York: Bidwell, September-December 1961, p. 70

100 Peter Burke, *Celebrated Trials Connected with the Aristocracy in the Relations of Private Life*, London: William Benning, 1849, p. 300

101 James Fitzjames Stephen, *A History of the Criminal Law of England*, London: Macmillan, 1883, pp. 421–422

102 Lorenzo Sabine, *Notes on Duels and Duelling alphabetically arranged with a Preliminary Historical Essay*, 3rd edition, Boston: Crosby, Nichols and Co. 1859, p. 4

103 David Lemmings [http://www.oxforddnb.com/view/article/ 6507, accessed 28 October 2007]

104 Timothy Harris, *The Pomp of Death. A Panegyrical Elegy on the Illustrious Duke of Marlborough, Prince of the Sacred Roman Empire, etc.*, London: printed for the author, 1722, ll. 150–4

105 Winston Churchill, *Marlborough, His Life and Times,* London: [s.n.] (1933–8)

106 J. R. Jones, *Marlborough*, CUP, 1993, p. 83

107 Anon, *The Royal Triumph: a Poem*, ll. 21–7, London, Tookey, 1704. Quoted in R D Horn, *Marlborough: A Survey. Panegyrics, Satires, and Biographical Writings, 1688–1788*, Folkestone: Dawson, 1974, p. 51

108 'Mr Paris of Trinity College Cambridge', *Ramillies, A Poem, humbly inscribed to his Grace the Duke of Marlborough*, ll. 339–51, quoted in Horn, 1974, p. 202

109 J Swift, *The Conduct of the Late Ministry in Beginning and Carrying on the Present War*, London: John Morphew, 1711, p. 60

110 Churchill, IV, p. 627

111 John B. Hattendorf [http://www.oxforddnb.com/view/ article/5401, accessed 15 July 2008]

CHAPTER THREE

1 Ronald Gowing, *Roger Cotes – natural philosopher*, CUP, 1983, p. 141

2 *Correspondence of Sir Isaac Newton, etc.*, compiled J. Edleston, Cambridge: John Deighton, 1850, p. 192, Letter XCVI (30 August 1701), John Smith to Cotes

3 *Philosophical Transactions of the Royal Society*, 29, 1714, p. 253

4 Edleston, p. 182, Letter XCI (13 May 1715), Cotes to Newton

5 Gowing, p. 16

6 Edleston, p. 167, Letter LXXXV (22 December 1713), Cotes to Newton

7 Domenico Bertoloni Meli [http://www.oxforddnb.com/view/article/6386, accessed 28 October 2007]

8 Edward Gibbon, *Autobiography*, OUP, 1907 edition, pp. 12–15 (first published 1796). Almost all our limited knowledge about Gibbon comes from this work.

9 Information about the South Sea Bubble from Richard Dale, *The First Crash, Lessons from the South Sea Bubble*, Princeton UP, 2004, and John Carswell, *The South Sea Bubble*, Stroud: Alan Sutton, 1960

10 J. Hervey, *Memoirs of the reign of George the Second*, London: John Murray, 1848, I, p. 24

11 J. Hatsell, *Precedents of proceedings in the House of Commons*, 4th edition, London: 1818, II, p. 108

12 Hervey, 1848, p. 31

13 A. A. Hanham [http://www.oxforddnb.com/view/article/6036, accessed 28 October 2007]

14 *The letters of Philip Dormer Stanhope, fourth earl of Chesterfield*, ed. B. Dobrée, London: Eyre and Spottiswoode, 1932. II, p. 281 (June 1734)

15 J. A. Manning, *The Lives of the Speakers of the House of Commons*, London: George Willis, 1851, p. 434

16 P. J. Grosley, *Tour of London*, 1772, II, p. 94, quoted in S. Jeffery, *The Mansion House*, Chichester: Phillimore, for the Corporation of London, 1993, pp. 41–42

17 Information from Roger Bowdler [http://www.oxforddnb.com/view/article/7096, accessed 23 September 2007] and S. Bradley and N. Pevsner, *The Buildings of England. London 1: The City of London*, London: Penguin, 1997, pp. 317–21

18 Descriptive note in *Vitruvius Britannicus*, cont. J. Woolfe and J. Gandon, plates 41–4, quoted in Jeffery, 1993, pp. 40–41

19 William Nicholson in Ralph's *Critical Review*, 1783 edition

20 Charles Burney, *A General History of Music*, London: published by the author, 1776–89, II, p. 489

21 Sir John Hawkins, A *General History of the Science and Practice of Music*, New edition, London: Novello, 1853, pp. 879, 884 (first published 1776)

22 Sir John Hawkins, 'Memoirs of Dr William Boyce', in W. Boyce, *Cathedral music*, 2nd edition, London: John Ashley, 1788, I, pp. x–xi

23 Mary Clapinson [http://www.oxforddnb.com/view/article/10294, accessed 28 October 2007]

24 John Nichols, *Literary Anecdotes of the Eighteenth Century*, London: privately printed, 1812,, VI, p. 402; Next quotations, V, p. 469; V, p. 434 (letter of 24 May 1750); V, p. 435 (letter of 18 August 1750); V, p .466; IX, p. 619

25 Edward Wedlake Brayley, *Londinia; or, Reminiscences of the British Metropolis*, London: Hurst, Chance and Co. 1829, II, p. 172

26 Michael F. J. McDonnell, *A History of St Paul's School*, London: Chapman and Hall, 1909, p. 353

27 A powerful case for Francis's authorship is in John Cannon [http://www.oxforddnb.com/view/article/10077, accessed 24 October 2007]

28 Junius, *Letters (stat nominis umbra)*, London: Gale, Curtis and Fenner, 1813 edition, pp. 113 (19 September 1769), 217 (14 November 1770), 50

29 *Memoirs of Sir Philip Francis, K.C.B.*, ed. Parkes and Merivale, London: Longmans, Green and Co., 1867, II, p. 275. Next quotation, I, pp. 309–10

30 Information from John Cannon [http://www.oxforddnb.com/view/article/24106, accessed 4 September 2007]

31 Nichols, 1812, VI, p. 436

32 J. Champion, *The Parallel, or comparative penmanship exemplified*, London: John Bowles, 1750, introduction

33 *New Craftsman*, 16 January 1731; *General Advertiser*, 4 September 1738

34 McDonnell, 1909, p. 336

35 C. Coote, *Sketches of the Lives and Characters of eminent English Civilians, with an historical introduction relative to the College of Advocates*, London, 1804, p. 133. Next quotation, p. 134

36 C. Coote, *Elements of the Grammar of the English Language*, London: privately printed, 1788, p. 45

37 W. Cobbett, *Cobbett's Easy Grammar*, reprint, London: Foulsham and Co. [n.d], p. 78

38 Coote, 1788, p. 157

39 F. D. A. Burns [http://www.oxforddnb.com/view/article/2035, accessed 7 September 2007]

40 Daniel Bellamy, *The Family Preacher consisting of Practical Discourses for Every Sunday throughout the Year*, London: Bellamy, 1754, p. 349

41 *Old Bailey Proceedings Online* [, 26 September 2007] November 1790, trial of Edward Lowe and William Jobbins (t17901027-17)

42 Quoted in *The Portfolio*, 1809, Philadelphia: Bradford and Inskeep, p. 509

43 Letter to his sister, March 1775, quoted in J. T. Flexner: *The Traitor and the Spy*, Boston: Little, Brown 1975, p 35. Next quotations, pp. 355, 357–8, 384, 392

44 William Hawes, *Transactions of the Royal Humane Society*, London: 1795, p. 478

45 Carolyn D. Williams [http://www.oxforddnb.com/view/article/12648, accessed 4 September 2007]

46 Hawes, 1795, p. 504

47 William Hawes, *An Account of the Late Dr Goldsmith's Illness*, London: 1774, quoted in Carolyn D. Williams

48 Unus Quorum, pseud. [i.e. William Wadd], *Nugae Canorae: or, Epitaphian Mementos (in stone-cutters verse) or The Medici Family of Modern Times*, London: Callow and Wilson, 1827, p. 27

49 W. Nisbet, 'Dr J. Clarke, licentiate of the Royal College of Physicians; and late senior physician to the Asylum for Female Orphans,' in *Authentic memoirs, biographical, critical, and literary, of the most eminent physicians and surgeons of Great Britain*, London: Shirley, Neely and Jones et al, 2nd edition, 1818, pp. 127–30

50 Kenneth R. Hunter, 'The FitzPatrick Lecture', 4 April 2001, [http://homepage.ntlworld.com/greenhall/tht/history/Wigginton.htm, accessed 10 November 2007]

51 Kenneth R. Hunter [http://www.oxforddnb.com/view/article/5512, accessed 11 November 2007]

52 J. Clarke, *Commentaries on some of the Most Important Diseases of Children*, London: Longman, Hurst, Rees, Orme and Brown, 1815, pp. 1–36

53 Unus Quorum, p. 27

54 Gordon Goodwin [http://www.oxforddnb.com/view/article/7737, accessed 7 September 2007]

55 James Solas Dodd, *A Satyrical Lecture on Hearts: to which is added A Critical Dissertation on Noses*, London: G. Kearsely etc., 1767, pp. 4, 9, 12

56 Quoted in Jim Davis [http://www.oxforddnb.com/view/article/21478, accessed 15 September 2007]

57 Bellamy, *Miscellanies in prose and verse*, London: published for the author, 1795, II, p. 54

58 H. Diack Johnstone [http://www.oxforddnb.com/view/article/16738, accessed 15 September 2007]

59 Alexander Dyce, Taylor's long-time friend, writing *c.*1868, quoted in G. E .Bentley Jr., *The Stranger from Paradise*, London: Yale University Press, 2001, pp. 83–4

60 'Mr Taylor, the Platonist' in *Thomas Taylor the Platonist*, ed. Raine and Harper, London: Routledge & Kegan Paul, 1969, pp. 105, 110, 113, 114

61 'Thomas Taylor in England', Raine and Harper, 1969

62 Raine and Harper, 1969, p. 34

63 Shelley, 'Adonais', l. iii

64 Raine and Harper, 1969, p. 18

65 'Thomas Taylor the Platonist,' Raine and Harper, 1969, p. 123

66 HoP, Commons, 1790–1820, V, p. 417

67 L. Kennedy, *Nelson's Band of Brothers*, London: Odhams Press, 1951, p. 80

68 *The dispatches and letters of Vice-Admiral Lord Viscount Nelson*, ed. N. H. Nicolas, London: Colburn, 1844–46, III, pp. 475–6

69 See Nicolas, 1844–46, III, pp. 357 ff., IV, pp. 166 ff.

70 Quoted in E. Vincent: *Nelson Love and Fame* Newhaven and London: Yale University Press 2003, p. 35

71 Nicolas, 1844–46, III, pp. 133–4

72 C. N. Parkinson, *Edward Pellew, Viscount Exmouth, admiral of the red*, London: [s.n.], 1934

73 Information also from P. K. Crimmin [http://www.oxforddnb.com/view/article/27765, accessed 6 September 2007]; T. Coleman, *Nelson: the man and the legend*, London: Bloomsbury, 2001; R. Knight, *The Pursuit of Victory – The Life and Achievement of Horatio Nelson*, London: Allen Lane, 2005

CHAPTER FOUR

1 T. Clarkson, *The History of the Abolition of The African Slave-Trade by the British Parliament*, London: Longman, 1808, I, p. 339. Next quotations, pp. 209, 210

2 Hugh Brogan [http://www.oxforddnb.com/view/article/5545, accessed 21 September 2007]

3 William Wordsworth, 'To Thomas Clarkson. On the Final Passing of the Bill for the Abolition of the Slave Trade.'

4 Clarkson, 1808, I, pp. 409–10

5 Quotations from John Owen, *The Fashionable World Displayed*, 8th edition, London: Seeley, 1817, pp. 115, 96–99

6 *Letters of Queen Victoria*, ed. Esher and Benson, London: John Murray, 1907, I, p. 14

7 Hester Lynch Piozzi, *Letters and Literary Remains*, ed. A. Hayward, London: Longmans, 1861

8 *John Constable's Correspondence*, ed. R. B. Beckett, Ipswich: Suffolk Records Society, 1962–78, VI, p. 9

9 Nigel Aston [http://www.oxforddnb.com/view/article/9500, accessed 13 September 2007]

10 Thomas Sadler, *Diary, Reminiscences, Correspondence of Henry Crabb Robinson*, ed. T. Sadler, 3 vols., London: Macmillan, 1869, II, p. 454

11 Quoted in E.Nitchie, *The Reverend Colonel Finch*, New York: Columbia University Press, 1940, p. 12

12 Quoted in Nitchie, 1940, p. 6

13 Quoted in Nitchie, 1940, pp. 9–10

14 Alan Bell [http://www.oxforddnb.com/view/article/9441, accessed 7 July 2007]

15 Robert Gittings, *Keats*, Harmondsworth: Penguin, 1971 edition, p. 141. Information also from W. Jackson Bate, *John Keats*, London: Chatto and Windus, 1979

16 J. H. Reynolds, *Poetry and Prose*, ed. Marsh, London: Humphrey Milford, 1928, p. 20

17 *Sonnet on a fly-leaf of the Volume of Shakespeare which Reynolds gave to Keats and in which Keats wrote his 'Bright Star' sonnet.*

18 Gittings, 1971, p. 142

19 *Life, Letters and Journals of Lord Byron*, by George Noël Gordon Byron, London: John Murray, 1835, p. 406

20 Quoted in *The Life, Letters and Opinions of William Roberts, Esq.* ed. Arthur Roberts, London: Seeley, 1850, pp. 47–8

21 Byron, *Don Juan*, ed. Steffan, Steffan and Pratt, London: Penguin, 1996, canto I, vv. 210–11

22 Quoted in Roberts, 1850, p. 50

23 Reprinted in *The Poetical Works of Lord Byron*, New York: Appleton, 1850, pp. 803–805

24 Edward Lytton Bulwer, *England and the English*, ed. Standish Meacham, The University of Chicago Press, 1970, p. 355

25 *The Age*, 11 June 1826, p. 455

26 *The News*, October 1830

27 *The Age*, 24 October 1830, p. 339

28 *English Spy*, London: Sherwood, Gilbert and Piper, 1826, II, pp. 42–44

29 Information from Ian McCalman, *Radical Underworld. Prophets, Revolutionaries and Pornographers in London 1795–1840*, Oxford: Clarendon press, 1988; David E. Latané Jr, 'Charles Molloy and the Spirit of *The Age*', *Victorian Periodicals Review* 40:1, Spring 2007, pp. 44–70

30 Joseph Knight [http://www.oxforddnb.com/view/article/9222, accessed 6 September 2007]

31 Thomas Gilliland, *The Dramatic Mirror*, London,1808, II, p.761

32 'Ellistonia', 'The Last Essays of Elia' in, *The works of Charles and Mary Lamb*, ed. E. V. Lucas, London: Methuen, 1903, p. 168

33 D. E. Baker, *Biographia Dramatica*, additions Stephen Jones, London: Longman, 1812, I, pt. 1, pp. 218–9

34 Gilliland, 1808, p. 749

35 Gilliland, 1808, pp. 752–53

36 Christopher Murray [http://www.oxforddnb.com/view/article/8724, accessed 6 September 2007]

37 Diary I, p. 46, quoted in William G Lane: *Richard Harris Barham*, University of Missouri, 1967, p. viii

38 *Bentley's Miscellany*, London: Richard Bentley, XVIII, 1845, p. 199

39 Michael F. J. McDonnell, *A History of St Paul's School*, London: Chapman and Hall, 1909, p. 357

40 *The life and letters of…Richard Harris Barham*, ed. R. H. D. Barham, 1870, I, p. 20

41 *Bentley's Miscellany*, 1845

42 ed. R H D Barham, 1870, I, p. 255

43 W. P. Lennox, *My Recollections from 1806–1873*, II, 1874, p. 162

44 *Telegraph*, 3 November 2007

45 [R. H. D. Barham] *The Ingoldsby Legends or Mirth and Marvels*, London: Richard Bentley, 1840, preface

46 *Lives of the Illustrious*, London: Partridge and Co., 1856, I, p. 67

47 Lane, 1967, p. 178

48 *English Review*, London: F. and J. Rivington, 1847, VII, p. 65

49 Julian Pooley and Robin Myers [http://www.oxforddnb.com/view/article/63494, accessed 20 August 2007]

50 *The letters of Charles Dickens*, ed. House and Storey, Oxford: Clarendon Press 1965, I, p. 250

51 Information from R. A. Gettmann, *A Victorian Publisher, A Study of the Bentley Papers*, Cambridge, 1960

52 *The Correspondence of William Hickling Prescott, 1833–47*, ed. Wolcott, Boston and NY: Mass. Hist. Soc., 1925, p. 173

53 R. L. Patten, *George Cruikshank's life, times, and art*, Cambridge: Lutterwort, 1996, II, p. 51

54 Letter of 16 December 1839, House and Storey, I, pp. 495, 617

55 Thomas Moore, *Journal*, V, p. 2023 (21 November 1838)

56 *Bookseller*, 3 October 1871

57 Felix Barker and Ralph Hyde, *London as it might have been*, London: John Murray, 1982, p. 131

58 Andrew Saint and Mike Chrimes [http://www.oxforddnb.com/view/article/23374, accessed 7 September 2007]

59 M. H. Port [http://www.oxforddnb.com/view/article/49437, accessed 11 November 2007]

60 'Romilly's Cambridge Diary, 1842–47', ed. M. E. Bury and J. D. Pickles, Cambridge RS., X, 1994, pp. 208–9

61 J. Mordaunt Crook, *The Architect's Secret, Victorian Critics and the Image of Gravity*, London: John Murray, 2003, p. 46

62 B. Webb and J. M . Neale, *The Symbolism of Churches and Church Ornaments, A Translation of the First Book of the Rationale Divinorum Officiorum* (William Durandus), Leeds: T. W. Green, 1843, p. xxiv

63 B. Cherry and N. Pevsner, *The Buildings of England, London 3: North West*, London: Penguin, 1991, p. 597

64 *Ecclesiologist* xx, N.S. xvii (1859), pp. 184–89. Webb confirmed he wrote this article in his diary, 25 May 1859

65 Webb and Neale, 1843, p. xxv

66 William Goode, *The Modern Claims to the Possession of the Extraordinary Gifts of the Spirit*, London: Hatchard, 1833, pp. 217–8

67 Goode, 1833, pp. iv–v

68 William Goode, *Aids for Determining Some Disputed Points in the Ceremonial of the Church*, London: Hatchard, 1851, pp. 27–28

69 Information from Gordon Goodwin [http://www.oxforddnb.com/view/article/10961, accessed 11 November 2007]; Stewart J. Brown [http://www.oxforddnb.com/view/article/14473, accessed 15 November 2007]

70 From A. C. Benson, *Life of E W Benson*, I. 39–40, quoted in David Newsome, *Godliness and Good Learning*, London: John Murray, 1961, p. 93

71 *Manchester Guardian*, 27 January 1912

72 ΣΑΛΠΙΣΕΙ. 'A Memorial Sermon preached after the death of the Rt Rev. James Prince Lee' 2nd Edition, ed. J.F Wickenden, London, 1870, p. 12

73 T. Gutteridge, *Report of the…Public Meeting held in the Town Hall, Birmingham, 19 May 1846*, Birmingham 1846, pp. 12–13

74 Quoted in Newsome, 1961, p. 134

75 Newsome, 1961, p. 140

76 *Manchester Guardian*, 27 January 1912

77 Information also from M. C. Curthoys [http://www.oxforddnb.com/view/article/16292, accessed 18 October 2007]

78 Reminiscence of Carver quoted in *Alleynian*, XXVI, 189 (October 1898), p. 247

79 R. J. Mackenzie, quoted in *Alleynian*, XXVII, 198 (October 1899), p. 301

80 W. R. M. Leake [http://www.oxforddnb.com/view/article/32317, accessed 15 July 2008]

81 J. R. de S. Honey, *Tom Brown's Universe*, London: Millington, 1977, p. 245

82 *The Times*, 31 July 1880

83 Jan Piggott, *Dulwich College A History, 1616–2008*, London: Dulwich College, 2008, p. 153

84 Quoted in S. Hodges, *God's Gift, A Living History of Dulwich College*, London: Heinemann, 1981, p. 49

85 Lord Hobhouse, quoted in *Life and letters of Benjamin Jowett, MA*, ed. E. Abbott and L. Campbell, London: John Murray, 1897, I, p. 55

86 Michael F. J. McDonnell, *A History of St Paul's School*, London: Chapman and Hall, 1909, p. 392

87 Abbott and Campbell, 1897. Next quotations, I, p. 217; II, p. 155; I, p. 199; II, p, 132

88 E. V. Quinn and J. M. Prest, *Dear Miss Nightingale, A Selection of Benjamin Jowett's Letters*, 1860–93, OUP, 1987, p. 74

89 To Earl Russell, 27 October 1867, Peter Hinchliff and John Prest [http://www.oxforddnb.com/view/article/15143, accessed 17 October 2007]

90 Quinn and Prest, 1860–93, p. 249. Next quotation, p. 111

91 Quoted in Abbott and Campbell, 1897, II, p. 224

92 Quotations from E. A. Knox, *Reminiscences of an Octogenarian, 1847–1934*, London: Hutchinson, 1935, pp. 92, 96, 96–7

93 *Kilvert's Diary*, ed. Plomer, London: Cape, 1960 edition, I, p. 223

94 Arthur Calder-Marshall, *The Enthusiast. An Enquiry into the Life Beliefs and Character of the Rev. Joseph Leycester Lyne alias Fr. Ignatius, O.S.B. Abbot of Elm Hill, Norwich and Llanthony Wales*, London: Faber and Faber, 1962, p. 34

95 Calder-Marshall, 1962, pp. 19, 73

96 Calder-Marshalll, 1962, p. 101

97 *Church Times*, 23 October 1908

98 Robert Bickers [http://www.oxforddnb.com/view/article/18494, accessed 7 September 2007]

99 W. Medhurst, *A Glance at the Interior of China*, Shanghai: Mission Press, 1849, pp. 11–13

100 *Atlas*, 28 October 1854, quoted in R. King, *The Franklin Expedition from First to Last*, London: John Churchill, 1855, p 138

101 Quoted in Hugh N. Wallace, *The Navy, The Company, and Richard King, British Exploration in the Canadian Arctic 1829–1860*, Montreal: Queen's University Press, 1980, p. 53

102 Letter from John Barrow to Sir Robert Peel, a junior lord of the Admiralty, quoted in Wallace, 1980, p. 148. Next quotation, p. 159

103 W. Ballantine, *Some Experiences of a Barrister's Life*, London: R. Bentley and Son, 1882, II, p. 96

104 D. M. Bennett, *Biographical Sketches*, New York: Bennett, 1876, pp. 98, 148

105 Michael F. J. McDonnell, *A History of St Paul's School*, London: Chapman and Hall, 1909, p. 374

106 *Gentleman's Magazine*, 2nd Series, 26, 1846

107 Information from *The Victorian Web*, Bloy, 'The Spa Fields Riots, 2 December 1816'; Mark Harrison, *Crowds and History, Mass Phenomena in English Towns, 1790–1835*, CUP, 1988

108 *State Trials*, XXXII, pp. 441–42

109 Lord Hanworth, *Lord Chief Baron Pollock, a memoir*, London: John Murray, 1929, p. 8

110 Lord Alverstone, *Recollections of Bar and Bench*, London: Arnold, 1914, p. 45

111 J. M. Rigg [http://www.oxforddnb.com/view/article/22479, accessed 6 September 2007]

112 Not in published admission registers, but described as a Pauline in his obituary notice, *Gentleman's Magazine*, 1847. See Michael F. J. McDonnell, *A History of St Paul's School*, London: Chapman and Hall, 1909, p. 468

113 Ballantine, 1882, I, p. 7. Next quotations, I, pp. 135, 139

114 Information from Thomas Seccombe, rev. H. C. G. Matthew [http://www.oxforddnb.com/view/article/1227, accessed 11 November 2008] and William Eleroy Curtis, *Modern India*, Chicago: Fleming H. Revill Co., 1905

115 J. Lester, *E Ray Lankester and the Making of Modern British Biology*, ed. P. J. Bowler, British Society for the History of Science, 1995, p. 61. Next quotation, p. 21

116 Huxley, *The Times*, 16 August 1929

117 *Nature*, 124, 1929, p. 345

118 Letter to Lankester's brother Owen, 16 April 1894, quoted in Lester, 1995, pp. 121–22

119 Lester, 1995, p. 135

120 *The Times*, 14 October 1895

121 G. T. Walker, 'On Boomerangs', *Philosophical Transactions of the Royal Society of London*, Series A, CXC, 1897, p. 41

122 *Enzyklopädie der mathematischen Wissenschaften*, 1900

123 Information from P. A. Sheppard [http://www.oxforddnb.com/view/article/36692, accessed 17 October 2007] and Geoffrey I Taylor, *Biographical Memoirs of Fellows of the Royal Society*, VIII, November 1962, pp. 166–174

124 G. K. Chesterton, *Autobiography*, London: Hamish Hamilton, 1986, p. 67 (first published 1936)

125 E. C. Bentley, *Those Days*, London: Constable, 1940, p. 149

126 *Res Paulinæ*, ed. R. B. Gardiner and John Lupton, St Paul's School, 1911, p. 242

127 Bentley, 1940, p. 150

128 *Dictionary of Biography*, m.s., p.18

129 Published as *The First Clerihews*, OUP, 1982

130 Bentley, 1940, p.25. Next quotations, pp. 254, 249

131 Sydney C. Roberts, rev. Michael J. Tolley [http://www.oxforddnb.com/view/article/30720, accessed 17 October 2007]

132 E C Bentley, *Trent's Last Case*, London: Nelson, 1913, dedication

CHAPTER FIVE

1 A. G. Gardiner, *Prophets, Priests, and Kings*, London: Dent, 1914, p. 340

2 Leonard Woolf, *Sowing, An Autobiography of the Years 1880–1904*, London: The Hogarth Press, 1961, p. 91

3 *World*, 2 June 1903, quoted in *G K Chesterton: The Critical Judgments, Part I, 1900–37*, ed. D. J. Conlon, Antwerp Studies in English Literature, 1976, p. 65

4 G. K. Chesterton, *Shaw*, London: Lane, 1909, p. 141

5 *The Times*, 25 March 1904

6 *Vanity Fair*, 7 April 1904

7 *Academy*, 2 May 1908

8 G. K. Chesterton, *Autobiography*, London: Hamish Hamilton, 1986, p. 102 (first published 1936)

9 League of National Life: G. K. Chesterton, *Social Reform versus Birth Control*, London, 1927, p. 11

10 *Autobiography*, p. 54

11 Joseph Pearce, *Wisdom and Innocence, A Life of G K Chesterton*, London: Hodder and Stoughton, 1996, p. 301

12 *English Review*, July 1911, p. 666

13 *Spectator*, 10 June 1911, p. 875

14 *Spectator*, 17 June 1911, p. 923

15 *Spectator*, 8 July 1911, p. 68

16 C. G. Johnson, *The Early History of Motoring*, London and Cheltenham: Burrow and Co., 1927, p. 56

17 W. J. Oldham, *The Hyphen in Rolls-Royce*, London: Whitefriars, 1967, p. 28. Next quotation, p. 63

18 *Autocar* 89, 14 January 1944, p. 21

19 Oldham, 1967, p. 58

20 *Motor*, August 1907

21 Oldham, 1967, p. 58. Next quotations, pp. 105, 150, 174

22 A. Verdon-Roe, *The World of Wings and Things*, London: Hurst and Blackett, [n.d.], p. 62 (first published 1939). Next quotation, p. 19

23 *The Times*, 24 January 1906

24 Verdon-Roe, [n.d.], pp. 41, 67–68

25 J. L. Pritchard [http://www.oxforddnb.com/view/article/36641, accessed 8 December 2007]

26 Verdon-Roe, [n.d.], preface, pp. 6, 226

27 Verdon-Roe, [n.d.], p. 225

28 *Daily Chronicle*, 29 May 1914

29 Quotations from Ursula Bloom, *He Lit the Lamp, a biography of Professor A.M. Low*, London: Burke, 1958, pp. 117, 149, author's note

30 Katherine Lambert, *Hell with a Capital H*, London: Pimlico, 2002, p. 182

31 Lambert, 2002, p. 12

32 Lambert, 2002, p. 94

33 Lambert, 2002, p. 131

34 Raymond Priestley [http://www.oxforddnb.com/view/article/34508, accessed 28 July 2008]

35 *Eugenics Review*, XVI, no. 4, January 1925, p. 267

36 V. Cornish, *A Family of Devon: their homes, travels and occupations*, St Leonards: King Bros and Potts, 1942, p. 54

37 V. Cornish, *The Poetic Impression of Natural Scenery*, London: Sifton, Praed & Co., 1931, p. 12

38 Quotations from,: Charles Lyte, *Frank Kingdon-Ward: The Last of the Great Plant Hunters*, London: John Murray, 1989, pp. 72, 84, 97, 72, 137, 179. Information also from : D. E. Allen [http://www.oxforddnb.com/view/article/34327, accessed 17 October 2007]

39 Quoted in Wilfred Blunt, *Cockerell, The Life of Sydney Carlyle Cockerell, friend of Ruskin and Morris and Director of the Fitzwilliam Museum*, London: Hamish Hamilton, 1964, p. 135. Next quotations, pp. 239, 56, 135, 142, 142, 273, 262

40 Siegfried Sassoon, in *Siegfried's Journey, 1916–1920*, London: Faber, 1945

41 Some information from Alan Bell [http://www.oxforddnb.com/view/article/32475, accessed 17 October 2007]

42 *Littlewood's miscellany*, ed. Bollobás, CUP, 1986. Quotations from foreword, pp. 148, 25, 100, 259

43 Francis Watson, 'The Death of George V', *History Today* 36, December 1986, p. 28. Next quotation, same source

44 Quoted in Stephen Lock [http://www.oxforddnb.com/view/article/32751, accessed 17 October 2007]

45 Edward Roux, *S. P. Bunting: A Political Biography*, South Africa: Mayibuye Books, 1993, foreword

46 Edward Roux, *Sidney Percival Bunting*, [http://www.sacp.org.za/docs/history/spbunting.html#Chapter%201, accessed 8 May 2008] The article quotes from ch. 3, 7, 12, 13, 17

47 Quotations from Nicholas Mosley, *The Life of Raymond Raynes*, London: The Faith Press, 1961, pp. 92, 71, 104. See also Trevor Huddleston, *Naught for your Comfort*, London: Collins, 1956

48 Philip Curtis, *A Hawk among Sparrows, A Biography of Austin Farrer*, London: SPCK, 1985, p. 27. Next quotations, pp. 9, 13, 129

49 Loades and MacSwain, *The Truth-Seeking Heart, Austin Farrer and His Writings*, Norwich: Canterbury Press, 2006, p. 172

50 P. Heehs, *Sri Aurobindo: A Brief Biography*, OUP, 1989, p. 46

51 Talk of June 28, 1926, quoted in Heehs, 1989, p. 11

52 Heehs, 1989, pp. 28, 29

53 Sri Aurobindo, *On Himself*, Sri Aurobindo Ashram, Pondicherry, 1972, p. 375

54 Heehs, 1989, p. 87

55 Sri Aurobindo, *On Himself*, p. 406

56 Sri Aurobindo, *The Supramental Manifestation*, Pondicherry, 1972, p. 326

57 Compton Mackenzie, *Sinister Street*, London: Secker, 1923 edition, pp.151, 157

58 Gavin Wallace [http://www.oxforddnb.com/view/article/31392, accessed 25 November 2007]

59 Quotations not separately noted from A. Linklater, *Compton Mackenzie, A Life*, London: Chatto and Windus, 1987, pp. 189, 111, 155, 151, 171, 248–9, 190, 216

60 R. D. Edwards, *Victor Gollancz: A Biography*, London: Collins, 1987, p. 194

61 Frederic Warburg, rival publisher at Secker and Warburg, quoted in Edwards, 1987, p. 169

62 Edwards, 1987, p. 255

63 Letter to Leonard Woolf, 19 October 1938, quoted in Edwards, 1987, p. 283

64 Edwards, 1987, p. 376

65 Norman Bentwich, *My 77 Years: An Account of my Life and Times, 1883–1960*, London: Routledge, 1962, p. 225

66 Edwards, 1987, p. 209

67 Edwards, 1987, pp. 535, 175, 169

68 Edwards, 1987, p. 205

69 The Marquess of Winchester, *Statesmen, Financiers and Felons*, London [self-published] 1934, p. 268. Next quotation, p. 265

70 *New York Times*, 17 December 1929, p. 12

71 *Time*, 25 February 1946

72 Winchester, 1934, p. 272

73 *The Times*, 25 January 1930

74 Richard F. Kahn, *The Making of Keynes' General Theory*, CUP, 1984, p. 175

75 *The Times*, 8 June 1989

76 Margaret Cole, *The Life of G. D. H. Cole*, London: Macmillan, 1971, p. 92. Next quotation, p. 36

77 Raymond Postgate, quoted in Margaret Cole, 1971, p. 85

78 Margaret Cole, 1971, p. 87

79 Maurice Reckitt, quoted in Margaret Cole, 1971, p. 84

80 Marc Stears [http://www.oxforddnb.com/view/article/32486, accessed 11 November 2007]

81 *The Times*, 15 January 1959

82 Harold Wilson, Memoirs, *The Making of a Prime Minister*, London: Weidenfeld and Nicolson, 1985

83 Quoted in *Letters of Leonard Woolf*, ed. Frederic Spotts, London: Weidenfeld and Nicolson, 1989, p. 165

84 Quoted in Hermione Lee, *Virginia Woolf*, London: Vintage, 1997, p. 760 (first published 1996)

85 Leonard Woolf, *The Journey not the Arrival Matters, an autobiography of the years 1939–1969*, London: The Hogarth Press, 1970, p. 172

86 *The Flight of the Mind, The Letters of Virginia Woolf*, I, 1888–1912, ed. Nigel Nicolson, London: The Hogarth Press, 1975, letter no. 628, p. 503

87 *Letters of Leonard Woolf*, p. 173 (letter of 29 April 1912)

88 Leonard Woolf, *Beginning Again, an autobiography of the years 1911–1918*, London: The Hogarth Press, 1964, p. 157

89 Leonard Woolf, 1970, pp. 91–2. Next quotation, pp. 95–6

90 *The Letters of D. H. Lawrence*, ed. George J. Zytarck and James T. Boulton, II, June 1913–October 1916, CUP, 1981, p. 263

91 F. Spalding, *Duncan Grant*, London: Chatto & Windus, 1997, p. 168. Next quotation, p. 13

92 *Cambridge Magazine*, 31 November 1912

93 *Sunday Times*, 20 May 1934

94 *Listener*, 8 April 1936

95 See Shone (ed.) *The Art of Bloomsbury*, London: Tate, 1999

96 Spalding, 1997, p. 84

97 Hermione Lee, *Virginia Woolf*, London: Vintage, 1997 edition, pp. 282–84

98 Information from Nicholas Usherwood [http://www.oxforddnb.com/view/article/64221, accessed 6 February 2008]

99 R. Streeton, *P. G. H. Fender*, London: Faber and Faber, 1981, p.19. Next quotation, p. 25

100 E. W. Swanton [http://www.oxforddnb.com/view/article/31101, accessed 5 December 2007]

101 Streeton, 1981, p. 30

102 Streeton, 1981, pp. 28, 29. Next quotation, p. 21

103 Martin Williamson, 21 October 2006 [www.cricinfo.com, accessed 3 February 2008]

104 Streeton, 1981, p. 147. Next quotation, p. 25

105 J. Olliff, *The Groundwork of Lawn Tennis*, London: Methuen, 1934, p. 55

106 J. Olliff, *Olliff on Tennis*, London: Eyre and Spottiswoode, 1958, p. 141

107 Information from M. Hardy, *The Encyclopaedia of Lawn Tennis*, London: Robert Hale, 1958, p. 95

108 *The Times*, reprinted in *Pauline*, LXXIX, 466 (December 1961) p.246

109 Letter to the Editor, 7 March 1920, *Pauline*, XXXVIII, 252 (March 1920) pp. 47–8

110 Arthur Calder-Marshall, 'More Frank than Buchman', *The Old School*, ed. G. Greene, London: Jonathan Cape 1934, p. 61

111 Greene, 1934, preface

112 Article in *New Statesman*, see Phil Baker [http://www.oxforddnb.com/view/article/50937, accessed 29 December 2007]

113 Arthur Calder-Marshall, *More Frank than Buchman*, p. 72. Next quotation, pp. 64–5. By kind permission of Anna Calder-Marshall

114 Laura Whetter, *Picturegoer*, 3 August 1940, p. 8

115 Whetter, p. 8

116 Unknown source listed in BFI library as 21 December 1933 [not consistent with film's date of 1935]

117 Harold Truscott, *Silent Picture*, July 1, 1973, p. 13. Next quotation, also p. 13

CHAPTER SIX

1 Quoted in Bernard Terry, 'Randolph Nesbitt, Mashonaland Rebellion VC', *Journal of the Victoria Cross Society* 6 March 2005, p. 21

2 R. E. Vernède, *Letters to his Wife*, ed. C. Vernède, London: Collins, 1917, p. 219

3 A. H. Mead, *A Miraculous Draught of Fishes*, London: James and James, 1990, p. 101

4 Vernède, *Letters*, p. 167

5 Garnett, *Kenneth Gordon Garnett: A Memoir* (written by his mother) London: Chiswick Press, 1917, p. 167

6 Denis Oliver Barnett, *His Letters from France and Flanders, October 1914–August 1915*, privately printed, 1915, p. 196

7 Stephen Snelling, *Gallipoli*, Stroud: Alan Sutton, 1995, p. 21

8 *Pauline*, XXXV, 232 (April 1917) pp. 59, 14

9 Myfanwy Piper, rev. Andrew Causey [http://www.oxforddnb.com/view/article/35186,accessed 10 January 2008]

10 P. Nash and H. Read, *Outline, an autobiography and other writings,* London: Columbus, 1988, p. 88. Next quotation, p. 105

11 Letter of 16 July 1918

12 Nash, 1988, p. 218

13 Letter from Nash to Kenneth Clark, 11 March 1941

14 M. & S. Harries, *The War Artists,* London: Michael Joseph, 1983, p. 46. Next quotation, p. 51

15 C. Dodgson and C. E. Montague, *British artists at the front, Eric Kennington,* 1918, p. 4

16 Quoted with kind permission from The Society of Authors as the Literary Representative of the Estate of Laurence Binyon

17 Eleanor Farjeon, *Edward Thomas: The Last Four Years,* OUP, 1958, p. 218

18 E. C. Bentley, *Those Days,* London: Constable, 1940, p. 58

19 Helen Thomas, *Under Storm's Wing,* Manchester: Carcanet, 1997 edition, p. 48 (first published 1988)

20 Edward Thomas, *Letters to Gordon Bottomley,* OUP, 1968

21 Quoted in Jan Marsh, *Edward Thomas, A Poet for his Country,* London: Paul Elek, 1978, p. 113

22 Eleanor Farjeon, 1958, pp. 41, 81

23 *English Review,* August 1914

24 Robert Frost, 'Into My Own', *A Boy's Will,* London: David Nutt, 1913

25 Edward Thomas, *The Childhood of Edward Thomas, A Fragment of Autobiography,* London: Faber, 1938, p. 152. Next quotation, p. 143

26 Helen Thomas, 1997, p. 113. Next quotations, pp. 157–8

27 Helen Thomas, 1997, p. 307

28 Quoted in Tresham Lever, *Clayton of Toc H,* London: John Murray, 1971, pp. 27–8

29 Clayton to Mrs Clayton, 27 November 1915, *Letters from Flanders,* London: Centenary Press, 1932, p. 21

30 Quoted in Melville Harcourt, *Tubby Clayton, A Personal Saga,* London: Hodder and Stoughton, 1953, p. 63

31 F. G. Finch to Clayton, 17 November, 1960, quoted in Lever, 1971, p. 12. Next quotation, p. 68

32 Harcourt, 1953, p. 13. Next quotations, pp. 59, 172

33 Alex Danchev, *Alchemist of War, The Life of Basil Liddell Hart,* London: Weidenfeld and Nicholson, 1998, p. 88

34 Bernard Newman, *Spy,* London: Gollancz, 1935, p. 113

35 *The Memoirs of Captain Liddell Hart,* London: Cassell, 1965, I, pp. 9–10

36 Liddell Hart, 'Some Personal Impressions' 1920, 7/1920/32. Quoted in Danchev, 1998, p. 70

37 Brian Holden Reid [http://www.oxforddnb.com/view/article/33737, accessed 29 January 2008]

38 Danchev, 1998, p. 151. Next quotation, p. 146

39 Liddell Hart, *Paris,* London: Kegan Paul & Co.,1925, pp. 88–9

40 Danchev, 1998, p. 156

41 C Barnett, *The Collapse of British Power,* Gloucester: Sutton, 1984, p. 502

42 Danchev, 1998, pp. 82–92; N Hamilton, *The Full Monty, Montgomery of Alamein 1887–1942,* London: Penguin 2001, pp. 180–1

43 Frank Longford, 'The CIGS', in *Monty at Close Quarters,* ed. T. E. B. Howarth, London: Leo Cooper, 1985, p. 71

44 Nigel Hamilton, *Monty, The Battles of Field Marshal Bernard Montgomery,* London: Hodder and Stoughton, 1994, p. 241. Next quotation, pp. 239–40

45 Nigel Hamilton, *Monty,* London: Hamilton, 1981/6, I, p. 129

46 *The Memoirs of Field-Marshal the Viscount Montgomery of Alamein, K.G.,* London: Collins, 1958, p. 20

47 N. Hamilton, 1981–6, I, p. 4

48 *Memoirs,* p. 112. Next quotation, p. 137

49 N. Hamilton, 1981–6, II, p. 791. Next quotation, p. 178

50 *Memoirs,* p. 314

51 Charles Whiting, *Monty's Greatest Victory,* Crowood, 1989

52 T. E. B. Howarth, 'Education and Leadership' in *Monty at Close Quarters,* p. 62. Next quotation, p. 66

53 Lucien F. Trueb, 'Monty's Little Swiss Friend', in *Monty at Close Quarters,* p. 134

54 *Memoirs,* p. 44

55 Quoted in Hamilton, *Battles,* 1994, p. 78

56 Information from *Telegraph,* 30 January 1995 and *The Times,* 17 January 1995

57 *London Gazette,* 25 May 1943

58 Information from *The Times,* 8 January 2007; *Independent,* 6 January 2007; *Telegraph,* 5 January 2007

59 *Pauline,* LXI, 412–413 (July 1943) p. 63. Next quotations, LX, 404–05 (June 1942) pp. 30, 30, 6, 13

60 *Pauline,* LX, 404–405 (June 1942) p. 30

61 Quoted in John Baynes, *Urquhart of Arnhem, The Life of Major General R E Urquhart CB, DSO,* London: Brassey's, 1993, p. 246

62 *The Times,* 15 December 1900

63 R. E. Urquhart, *Arnhem,* Barnsley: Pen and Sword, 1997, p. 15 (first published 1958); John Frost, *A Drop too Many,* Barnsley: Pen and Sword, 1994, p. 195 (first published 1980)

64 [http://www.pegasusarchive.org/arnhem/roy_urquhart.htm, accessed 22 May 2008]

65 Baynes, 1993, p. 155

66 Sefton Delmer, *Black Boomerang,* London: Secker and Warburg, 1962, pp. 47–8. Next quotations, pp. 65, 252 (Cripps)

67 Derek Hill, *Tribune,* quoted in Michael Powell, *Million-Dollar Movie,* London: Heinemann, 1992, p. 400

68 *Telegraph,* 23 January 2001

69 Leopold Marks, *Between Silk and Cyanide,* London: Harper Collins, 2000, p. 11

70 Leo Marks, *Peeping Tom,* London: Faber and Faber, 1998, interview with Chris Rodley, p. xii

71 Marks, 2000. Leo Marks, *The Life That I Have,* London: Souvenir Press, 1999. Quoted by kind permission of Elena Gaussen.

72 Marks, 2000, pp.210–211

73 Marks, 1998, p. xiii

74 Marks, 2000, p. 273

75 Marks, 1998, p. xii. Next quotations, pp. xx, xiv, xix

76 T. Bower, *Blind Eye to Murder: Britain, America and the purging of Nazi Germany,* St Albans: Granada, 1983, p. 144

77 G. R. Rubin [http://www.oxforddnb.com/view/article/75607, accessed 12 February 2008]

78 Quotations from Bower, 1983, pp.144, 147, 148, 235, 241, 265 (letter to Attlee)

79 Edward Behr, *Anyone Here Been Raped and Speaks English?,* London: Hamish Hamilton, 1981, pp. xvi-xvii. Next quotation, pp. 31–32

80 Quoted in *Telegraph,* 29 May 2007

81 Edward Behr, *Hirohito: Behind the Myth,* London: Penguin, 1990 edition, quoted in *Telegraph,* 29 May 2007

82 Edward Behr, *Kiss the Hand You Cannot Bite: The Rise and Fall of the Ceaucescus,* London: Hamish Hamilton, 1991

83 Edward Behr, 1981, pp. xii-xiii

CHAPTER SEVEN

1 H. Conway, *Ernest Race,* London: Design Council, 1982, p. 45

2 Letter, Jordan to Race, August 14 1945, in Conway, 1982, p. 13

3 Penny Sparke [http://www.oxforddnb.com/view/article/38554, accessed 25 September 2007]

4 Information from Oliver Chapple, Race Furniture Ltd

5 Conway, 1982, p. 72. Next quotation, p. 73

6 *Forbes* magazine, 5 May 1997

7 Andrew Dannat, *Independent,* 11 October 2002

8 *Telegraph,* 21 October 2002

9 Veronica Horwell, *Guardian,* 12 October 2002

10 Dannat, *Independent*

11 Private information

12 Information from *The Times,* 3 April 2003

13 Eric Newby, *A Traveller's Life*, London: Collins, 1982, p. 87

14 *Independent*, 23 October 2006

15 Eric Newby, *A Short Walk in the Hindu Kush*, London: Collins, 1989 edition, p. 247 (First published 1958) Next quotation, p. 193

16 Information from [http://www.ianallangroup.com/group.html, accessed 21 March 2008]

17 *Architectural Review*, March 2002

18 Quoted in *Independent*, 29 January 2002

19 J. M. Richards, *The Functional Tradition in Early Industrial Buildings*, London: Architect Press, 1958

20 Richard Davenport-Hines, *Gothic, 400 Years of Excess, Horror, Evil and Ruin*, London: Fourth Estate, 1998, p. 11

21 Richard Davenport-Hines, *A Night at the Majestic*, London: Faber, 2006, p. 3

22 Richard Davenport-Hines, 1998, p. 381

23 Richard Davenport-Hines, *The Pursuit of Oblivion, A Social History of Drugs*, London: Phoenix, 2002 edition, pp. 215, 367 (first published 2001)

24 *The Times*, 18 October 1983

25 Murray, *One Day I'll Forget My Trousers*, London: Everest, 1975, p. 195

26 Peter Gammond [http://www.oxforddnb.com/view/article/68150, accessed 15 February 2008]

27 Harold Shapiro, *Blues in Britain* 72, December 2007

28 *British Blues Review*, December 1988

29 *Woke up this morning and get this I've never been on Desert Island Discs, Star Choice or My Top 12 Bar Blues*, transcript of radio broadcast, [http://www.geocities.com/Paris/Metro/5556/akbio.html, accessed 15 January 2008]

30 *Saga Magazine*, July/August 1994

31 *British Blues Review*, December 1988

32 Radio broadcast, [http://www.geocities.com/Paris/Metro/5556/akbio.html, accessed 15 January 2008]

33 Harold Shapiro, *Alexis Korner, The Biography,* London: Bloomsbury, 1996, p. 190. Next quotation, pp. 87–8

34 Foreword, [http://www.geocities.com/Paris/Metro/5556/akbio.html, accessed 15 January 2008]

35 Shapiro, 2007. Next quotation, ibid.

36 *Blue print Magazine*, November 1994

37 Shapiro, 1996, p. 193, Shapiro, 2007

38 Shapiro, 1996, pp. 139, quoted 207–8; Peter Gammond [http://www.oxforddnb.com/view/article/68150, accessed 15 February 2008]

39 Shapiro, 2007

40 Shapiro, 1996, p. 137

41 Quoted in Stephen J Pettit, *Dennis Brain: A Biography*, London: St Edmundsbury, 1989, p. 114

42 [http://www.telegraph.co.uk/arts/main.jhtml?xml=/arts/2007/11/01/bmbrain101.xml accessed 1 November 2007]

43 Quoted in Pettit, 1989, pp. 60, 88

44 Letter of December 13, 1954, *Tempo*, new ser., No 34 (Winter, 1954–1955), p. 39

45 Quoted in Pettit, 1989, pp. 122, 134

46 *Tempo*, new ser., Winter 1958, p. 6

47 Kingley Amis, *Lucky Jim*, London: Victor Gollancz 1984 edition, p. 53 (first published 1954)

48 Quoted in *The Times*, 24 March 2005

49 *Telegraph*, 25 March 2005

50 Christina Bashford, [http://www.grovemusic.com/grove-owned/music/Stanley-Sadie.html, accessed 4 February 2008]

51 *New York Times*, 23 March 2005

52 [http://www.ibm.com/developerworks/podcast/dwi/cm-int121906txt.html, accessed 18 January 2008]

53 Information from presentation at St Paul's School

54 Quotation by kind permission of Timothy Radcliffe, from Radcliffe, *I Call You Friends*, London: Continuum, 2004

55 H. Schonfield, *The Passover Plot*, 1993 edition, London: Element, p. 186 (first published 1965). Next quotations, pp. 52–3

56 *The Times*, 26 January 1988

57 The Long John Nebel Show, 1987 [www.bringyou.to/MartinSchonfieldDebate.mp3, accessed 10 February 2008]

58 Roy Foster, *Financial Times*, 13 March 2004

59 A. Calder-Marshall, 'More Frank than Buchman', *The Old School*, ed. G. Greene, London: Jonathan Cape, 1934, p. 71

60 M. Ignatieff, *Isaiah Berlin, A Life*, London: Chatto & Windus, 1998, p.3

61 Foster, *Financial Times*

62 Ignatieff, 1998, pp. 59, 172

63 Letter in Noel Annan, quoted in Hugh-Lloyd Jones (ed.), *Maurice Bowra, A Celebration*, London, 1974, p. 53

64 R. Jahanbegloo, *Conversations with Isaiah Berlin*, London: Phoenix, 2000, p.189

65 Henry Hardy, 'A Personal Impression of Isaiah Berlin', in Isaiah Berlin, *Flourishing: letters 1928–46*, ed. Henry Hardy, London: Chatto and Windus, 2004, p. xli

66 A. H. Mead, *A Miraculous Draught of Fishes*, London: James and James, 1990, p. 115

67 Berlin ed. Hardy, 2004, p. xliv

68 *Pauline*, L, 336 (June 1932) p.72

69 M. Beloff, *An Historian in the Twentieth Century*, Yale University Press, 1992, pp. 3, 24

70 Bernard Crick, *Guardian*, 25 March 1999

71 Nevil Johnson, *Independent*, 26 March 1999

72 John Major, *The Autobiography*, London: Harper Collins, 1999, p. 135

73 Will Woodward, *Guardian*, 25 March 2008

74 John Major, 1999, p. 103

75 Kenneth Baker, *The Turbulent Years, My Life in Politics*, London: Faber, 1993, p. 57

76 [http://www.pbs.org/wgbh/commandingheights/shared/minitextlo/int_kennethbaker.html, accessed 3 May 2008]

77 Baker, 1993, p. 138. Next quotation, p. 298

78 *Sunday Times*, 28 February 1988

79 Richard Crossman, *The Diaries of a Cabinet Minister*, London: Hamish Hamilton and Jonathan Cape, 1975, I, pp. 414–15

80 Douglas Jay, *Change and Fortune, a political record*, London: Hutchinson, 1980, p. 207

81 *Diary of Hugh Gaitskell*, London: Jonathan Cape, 1983, p. 334

82 Roy Jenkins, *A Life at the Centre*, London: Macmillan, 1991, p. 175

83 Crossman, 1983, pp. 270, 292, 366

84 G. Janner, *One Hand Alone Cannot Clap*, London: Robson, 1998, p. 16

85 G. Janner, 1998, p. 45

86 Paul Routledge, *Independent*, 26 March 1995

87 Quoted in Martin Fletcher, *The Times*, 14 July 1995

88 British Diplomatic Oral History Project, interview with Malcolm McBain, 6 August 1998 [http://www.chu.cam.ac.uk/archives/collections/BDOHP/Renwick, accessed 12 December 2007] by kind permission of the master and fellows of Churchill College, Cambridge

89 Interview with McBain

90 Quotations from Martin Fletcher, *The Times*, 14 July 1995

91 Quotations and information from *Telegraph*, 17 June 2002 and British Diplomatic Oral History Project, interview 25 November 1998 [http://www.chu.cam.ac.uk/archives/collections/BDOHP/Alexander, accessed 24 February 2008] by kind permission of Lady Alexander

92 World Security Network, 2 November, 2007

93 *International Herald Tribune*, 2 May 1988. All other quotations by kind permission of Antony Jay from [http://www.bbc.co.uk/bbc7/comedy/progpages/yesminister.shtml, accessed 3 March 2008]

94 J. Mossman, *Rebels in Paradise: Indonesia's Civil War*, London: Jonathan Cape, 1961, p. 157

95 *The Times*, 6 April 1971

96 Nicholas Wright, *The Reporter*, London: Nick Hern, 2007, introduction

97 [http://www.ingecenter.org/interviews/PeterShaffertext.htm#Playwriting_as_a_living, accessed 21 January 2008]

98 *Financial Times*, 16 February 2007

99 John Simpson, *Strange Places, Questionable People*, London: Pan Macmillan, 1998, p. 88

100 John Simpson, *News from No-Man's Land: Reporting the World*, London: Macmillan, 2002, p. 350

101 John Simpson, 1998, p. 227. Next quotations, pp. 321, 409, 392

102 John Simpson, 2002, pp.177–78

103 John Simpson, 1998, p. 334

104 Lynn Barber, *Observer*, 24 February 2002

105 *Observer*, 27 December 1964

106 Clement Freud, interview with Jed Rubenfeld, *The Times*, 14 April 2007

107 C. Freud, *Freud Ego*, London: BBC Worldwide Limited, 2001, pp. 120–21

108 *Racing Post*, 23 August 2006

109 Rubenfeld, *The Times*, 14 April 2007

110 Freud, 2001, p. 185

111 Quoted in James Rampton, *Independent*, 18 August 2000. (James Rampton is an Old Pauline.)

112 Nicholas Parsons, *The Straight Man*, London: Weidenfeld and Nicolson, 1994, p. 147, rev. orally 2008

113 Parsons, 1994, p. 214

114 *Independent*, 18 August 2000

115 M. Romain, *A Profile of Jonathan Miller*, CUP, 1992, pp. 89, 1

116 [www.bbc.co.uk/news/1/hi/entertainment/arts/2045941.stm, accessed 12 December 2007]

117 Romain, 1992, pp.156–57

118 J. Miller, *Subsequent Performances*, London: Faber, 1986, p. 160

119 Romain, 1992, p.2

120 [www.bbc.co.uk/news/1/hi/entertainment/arts/2045941.stm, accessed 12 December 2007]

121 Romain, 1992, p. 89

122 *Spectator*, 17 November 2007

123 Romain, 1992, p. 138

124 Anthony Shaffer, *So What Did You Expect?: a Memoir*, London: Picador, 2001

125 [http://www.ingecenter.org/interviews/PeterShaffertext. htm#Playwriting_as_a_living_, accessed 17 November 2007]. Next quotation, ibid.

126 *Telegraph*, 28 February 2007

127 [http://www.ingecenter.org/interviews/PeterShaffertext. htm#Playwriting_as_a_living_, accessed 17 November 2007]

128 [http://www.thegoodgamblingguide.co.uk/thisweek/2001/ profileofpatrickmarber.htm, accessed 29 October 2007] All other quotations from [http://www/contemporarywriters.com/authors/?p=auth255, accessed 29 October 2007]

129 [http://www.turowski.com/chess/speelman.html, accessed 13 March 2008]

130 Fay Ainscow, *Financial Times*, 14 November 1987. Next quotation, ibid.

131 *Independent*, 15 November 1999

132 [http://www.turowski.com/chess/speelman.html, accessed 13 March 2008]

133 *Guardian*, 13 August 2002

134 *Telegraph*, 5 August 2002

135 Quoted in *Guardian*, 4 January 2005

136 Simon O'Hagan, *Independent*, 3 July 2006

137 M. Sieff, *Don't ask the price: the memoirs of the president of Marks & Spencer*, London: Weidenfeld and Nicolson, 1986, p. 68

138 S. D. Chapman [http://www.oxforddnb.com/view/article/75438, accessed 15 July 2008]

139 [http://www.independent.co.uk/news/people/lloyd-dorfman-roundhouse-ringmaster-seeking-starstruck-corporate-sponsors-399828.html, accessed 4 May 2008]

140 [http://www.coutts.com/approach/entrepreneurs/speakers/ lloyd-dorfman.asp, accessed 5 May 2008]

141 *Independent*, 15 November 1999

142 [http://www.australiaday.co.uk/2007australiad-ayawardsintheuk, accessed 6 May 2008]

143 J. Saunders, *Nightmare: Ernest Saunders and the Guinness Affair*, London: Arrow Books, 1990, p. 235

144 N. Kochan and H. Pym, *The Guinness Affair: Anatomy of a Scandal*, London: Christopher Helm, 1987, p. 13

145 S. Prakash Sethi, 'Multinational Corporations and the Impact of Public Advocacy on Corporate Strategy: Nestlé and the Infant Formula Controversy,' *Journal of International Business Studies* 25 (3), 1994, pp. 658–60

146 Trade Marks Rectification Decision, 0/323/99

147 Saunders, 1990, p. 268

148 D. Levine and W. Hoffer, *Inside Out*, New York: Putnam, 1991

149 Saunders, 1990, pp. 190, 196, 199

150 Saunders, 1990, p. 235

151 *Mail on Sunday*, 10 September 1989

152 John Shepherd, *Independent*, 30 December 1994

153 *The Times*, 18 January 1992

154 Kenneth Dover, *Marginal Comment, a memoir*, London: Duckworth, 1994, p. 3. Next quotation, p. 255

155 Quotations from: M. L. West, *Forward into the Past*, Balzan prize for Classical Antiquity, 2000 [http://www.balzan.it/ premiati.aspx?lang=en&Codice=169&from=162&show=1, accessed 14 January 2008]

156 *Times Literary Supplement*, 29 May 1998

157 M. L. West, *The East Face of Helicon*, West Asiatic Elements in Greek Poetry and Myth, Oxford: Clarendon Press, 1997, p. 630

158 [http://www.britac.ac.uk/misc/medals/kenyon.html, accessed 15 January 2008]

159 Paul Cartledge, *Spartan Reflections*, University of California Press, 2001, pp. 154, 126

160 Tom Holland, *Sunday Times*, 12 December 2004

161 *Guardian*, 2 April 2007

162 Sarah Lozo, Lecture at Hamilton College, 2005, [http://www.elginism.com/20051008/208/, accessed 12 March 2008]

163 O. Sacks, *The Man Who Mistook His Wife for a Hat*, London: Pan, 1986, p. 7 (first published 1985)

164 Andrew Brown, *Guardian*, 5 March 2005

165 Steve Silberman, 'The Fully Immersive Mind of Oliver Sacks', *Wired*, April, 2002

166 Hugh Herbert, *Guardian*, 10 March 1983

167 Tom Shakespeare, quoted in Silberman, 2002

168 'The President's Speech' and 'The Twins', in Sacks, 1986, pp. 76, 185

169 Andrew Duncan, [http://www.fortunecity.com/emachines/ell/86/duncan3 /html, accessed 5 February 2008]

170 R. Winston, *The Story of God*, London: Bantam, 2005, p. 3

171 Peter Ross, *Sunday Herald*, 12 November 2006

172 Peter Ross, 12 November 2006

173 R. Winston, 2005, p. 7. Next quotation, p. 329

174 R. Winston, *Superhuman*, London: BBC Worldwide, 2000, p. 13

175 Peter Ross, 12 November 2006

176 *Telegraph*, 23 August 2001

177 P. Wall, *Pain, the science of suffering*, London: Phoenix, 2000, p. 73

178 *Guardian*, 16 August 2001

179 Quotations from Magnus Pyke, *The Six Lives of Pyke*, London: Dent, 1981, pp. 163, 158, 148, 159

180 Information from, Admiral Sir John Treacher, *Life at Full Throttle, From Wardroom to Boardroom*, Barnsley: Pen and Sword, 2004

181 Jane Elliott, BBC News 24, 1 April 2005, [http://news.bbc.co. uk/1/hi/health/4214629.stm, accessed 12 October 2007]

182 [http://www.mercyships.org.uk/en/pers_mccoll_e.php, accessed 14 March 2008]

183 *The Times*, 15 November 2005

184 Information from [http://www.royalexchange.co.uk], S. Bradley and N. Pevsner, *The Buildings of England, London 1: The City of London*, London: Penguin, 1997,

[http://www.terryfarrell.co.uk/projects/working/
work_embankmentPl.html, accessed 17 May 2008]

185 *Screen International*, 16 January [no year given in BFI library],
p. 68
186 *Independent*, 21 November 1999
187 C. Frayling, *Ken Adam and the Art of Production Design*,
London: Faber and Faber, 2005, p. 139
188 Quoted in *Christian Science Monitor*, 17 May 2002
189 [http://www.bridgetothestars.net/?p=weitzinterview, accessed
10 January 2008]
190 Nicholas Barber, *Independent on Sunday*, 9 December 2007
191 *Cineaste*, v. 24 no.1, 1 December 1998
192 *The Times*, 29 May 1995
193 Press release, July 1999
194 Peter Bradshaw, *Guardian*, 21 December 2007; Tim Robey,
Telegraph, 21 December 2007; James Christopher, *The Times*,
20 December 2007

AFTERWORD

1 Ciar Byrne, *Independent*, 8 December 2007
2 Quoted in Stephen Brook, *Guardian*, 7 December 2007
3 [http://news.bbc.co.uk/1/hi/entertainment/arts/1741108.stm,
accessed 3 June 2008]
4 [http://www.patrickneate.com/]
5 Seth Schiessel, *New York Times*, 28 April 2008; Peter Travers,
Rolling Stone, 12 June 2008; *The Times*, 26 April 2008
6 *Playboy*, June 2008
7 Ben Sloan, *Metro*, 19 July 2005
8 Andrew Clark, *Financial Times*, 24 May 2007

Index of Old Paulines

(This index gives page references to Old Paulines appearing in the book; the main entry is in bold. Years at the school are given as far as they are known for boys who entered St Paul's after admission registers were established in 1748. Systematic records of when boys left the school were not kept until after Kynaston became high master in 1838.)